Beginning Red Hat● Linux● 9

Sandip Bhattacharya, Pancrazio De Mauro,
Shishir Gundavaram, Mark Mamone, Kalip Sharma,
Deepak Thomas, Simon Whiting

wrox

Programmer to Programmer

Beginning Red Hat® Linux® 9

Published by
Wiley Publishing, Inc.
10475 Crosspoint Boulevard
Indianapolis, IN 46256
www.wiley.com

Library of Congress Control Number: 2003107085

ISBN: 0-7645-4378-4

Manufactured in the United States of America

10 9 8 7 6 5 4 3 2 1

1B/RV/QX/QT/IN

For general information on our other products and services or to obtain technical support, please contact our Customer Care Department within the U.S. at (800) 762-2974, outside the U.S. at (317) 572-3993 or fax (317) 572-4002.

Wiley also publishes its books in a variety of electronic formats. Some content that appears in print may not be available in electronic books.

About the Authors

Sandip Bhattacharya is an independent technology consultant specializing in Open Source technologies. He is a Red Hat Certified Engineer (RHCE) and besides holding degrees in engineering and management is the author of a number of books and articles on Open Source software. He currently runs Puroga Technologies, a small startup with a focus on helping businesses use the Open Source revolution to their advantage. He can be contacted at sandip@puroga.com. Sandip is an active participant in various Open Source communities in India, especially his local LUG, the Indian Linux Users Group, Delhi (ILUGD).

Pancrazio 'Ezio' de Mauro has been using Red Hat Linux since 1996. He is a Linux consultant specializing in system integration, mobile technologies, and training. He actively supports and advocates the use of free software. Ezio spends most of his free time traveling and backpacking. He welcomes comments and questions at his e-mail address, pdm@demauro.net.

Shishir Gundavaram is the Chief Technology Officer for MechanicNet Group, a company that specializes in providing CRM services for the automotive repair and maintenance industry. When he is not dealing with auto mechanics and broken-down cars, Shishir consults for a number of companies, designing architecture and providing technical expertise. He has more than a decade of experience in various aspects of software development and is considered a foremost expert in wireless applications, distributed systems, electronic commerce, and web backend architecture. He is also the author of various articles and books, including *Professional Perl Development*, *CGI Programming on the World Wide Web*, and *Scripting Languages: Automating the Web*, and he is regularly invited to speak at technical conferences around the world.

Mark Mamone, a Solutions Specialist working for Syntegra Ltd in the UK, has 16 years of experience in the IT industry ranging from Assembler and MS-DOS and now specializing in the development of enterprise and mobile systems using a variety of technologies, including Microsoft .NET, Java, and Linux. *I would like to thank my parents for the Commodore Vic-20, without which my life would have never taken this path. I would like to thank my children – Tanya, James, and Cameron – whose love is my foundation and, most important, my girlfriend, Rachel, whose support, love, and never-ending drive enabled me to complete this book!*

Kapil Sharma, an Internet security and Unix consultant, has been working on various Unix systems and Internet security technologies for more than five years. He has deployed many Unix, high availability, clustering, and Internet security projects. Kapil is also a Sun Certified System Administrator (SCSA) and Sun Certified Network Administrator (SCNA). He enjoys working on new challenges in Internet security, Internet architecture design, and various Unix flavors. He also fancies technical writing and sharing his knowledge with the community. He is actively involved in the open source community and has written many technical articles on system and network security. Apart from his hectic technical life, Kapil also enjoys clubbing, music, and touring the world. Kapil currently lives with his wife, Usha Sharma, in London, U.K. and can be contacted via e-mail at kapil@linux4biz.net. He maintains a consultancy company and a web site with loads of security resources at www.linux4biz.net. *This book is dedicated to my beloved wife Usha Sharma for her continuous support, love and cups of coffee at night, without which this book would have been a dream. I thank my parents, Girdhari Lal Sharma and Bimla*

Devi Sharma, for providing continuous support and motivation in my life.

Deepak Thomas lives and works in the San Francisco Bay area. His interests include PHP, Linux, and J2EE technologies. He has co-authored and reviewed several books for Wrox in these areas. In their spare time Deepak and Ansu go bike riding along the many beautiful trails in their part of the country.

Simon Whiting, a graduate of Clare College, University of Cambridge, is a Principal Consultant for AnIX Group Ltd and has been a Unix system administrator. He is an expert in Linux, storage area networks, and C, Perl, and Korn Shell programming.

Contents

Introduction

Linux is quickly becoming a major player on the world's operating system scene – it's fast, it's stable, and above all it's freely available. Within the Linux market, Red Hat Linux holds the distinction of being the most popular distribution, and with Red Hat Linux 9 it's now even easier to install and use than ever!

This book teaches you everything you need to know in order to install, configure, use, and maintain your Red Hat Linux system. It's been specially written for Red Hat Linux 9, though you will also find it a very useful guide if you're planning to use its slightly older brother, Red Hat Linux 8.0, and any subsequent Red Hat Linux releases.

Who Is This Book For?

This book is targeted primarily at readers who are using (or planning to use) the Red Hat Linux operating system for the first time. It offers the simple, plain-speaking guidance you need as you begin to explore the vast potential of open source software.

We assume that the reader is familiar with using an operating system before such as Apple's Macintosh, Unix, or one of the many versions of the Microsoft Windows operating system. An awareness of concepts like file systems, applications, and users and permissions would be an advantage, but is not essential; the book will provide insight for those readers who have not considered these concepts before.

No previous knowledge of Linux is assumed.

What You Need to Use This Book

All you need for this book is a **machine** and a copy of the Red Hat Linux 9 **distribution**. The easiest option (and the one we'll use in this book) requires:

❑ A single machine that you can dedicate to your Red Hat Linux 9 installation. Red Hat advises at minimum a Pentium class CPU with 650MB hard disk space and 128MB memory, but recommends a 200MHz Pentium with 2.5GB hard disk space and 192MB memory for better performance. It also says that most factory-built machines made in the last two years will be compatible with Red Hat Linux 9, and many older machines too. (See Chapter 1, and http://hardware.redhat.com, for more on hardware compatibility.)

❑ A copy of Red Hat Linux 9 included with this book.

Other Alternatives

There are other ways to obtain the Red Hat Linux 9 distribution. You could:

❑ Download the Red Hat Linux 9 distribution images for free via FTP, and burn them onto CDs. However, this is quite complex – for example, you'd need an ISO burner (this is a piece of software that unpacks the ISO files as you burn them onto your chosen media). If you're feeling ambitious, follow the guidelines at http://www.redhat.com/download/howto_download.html); the distribution is available at a number of mirror sites around the world.

❑ Buy installation disks cheaply from a third-party vendor. However, these disks tend to come with no technical support and no documentation.

It's also possible to install Red Hat Linux 9 as part of a dual boot setup on your machine. This gives you an option if you just have one machine and you don't want to give up your Windows or other operating system.

While you're welcome to explore these alternatives, and while they are totally compatible with the material you'll find in this book, we don't discuss them in any detail.

What Is Linux?

When you ask this question of a Linux aficionado, their answer will almost invariably make some reference to Linus Torvalds and the open source community. As you'll see from our potted history, Linus is a pivotal character in the creation and development of Linux, and the open source roots of Linux are central to its popularity.

Linus Torvalds and the Birth of Linux

Linus Benedict Torvalds was studying at the University of Helsinki, Finland, when his interest in computing led him to become curious about operating systems and how he could improve upon the existing systems of the day – and specifically the various Unix derivatives. With this small step, the development of the Linux kernel (its core) was begun; and in October 1991 version 0.02 was released onto the Internet with this now famous posting:

From: torvalds@klaava.Helsinki.FI (Linus Benedict Torvalds)
Newsgroups: comp.os.minix
Subject: Free minix-like kernel sources for 386-AT
Message-ID: <1991Oct5.054106.4647@klaava.Helsinki.FI>
Date: 5 Oct 91 05:41:06 GMT
Organization: University of Helsinki

Do you pine for the nice days of minix-1.1, when men were men and wrote their own device drivers? Are you without a nice project and just dying to cut your teeth on a OS you can try to modify for your needs? Are you finding it frustrating when everything works on minix? No more all-nighters to get a nifty program working? Then this post might be just for you :-)

As I mentioned a month(?) ago, I'm working on a free version of a minix-lookalike for AT-386 computers. It has finally reached the stage where it's even usable (though may not be depending on what you want), and I am willing to put out the sources for wider distribution. It is just version 0.02 (+1 (very small) patch already), but I've successfully run bash/gcc/gnu-make/gnu-sed/compress etc under it.

Sources for this pet project of mine can be found at nic.funet.fi (128.214.6.100) in the directory /pub/OS/Linux.

The directory also contains some README-file and a couple of binaries to work under linux (bash, update and gcc, what more can you ask for :-). Full kernel source is provided, as no minix code has been used. Library sources are only partially free, so that cannot be distributed currently. The system is able to compile "as-is" and has been known to work. Heh. Sources to the binaries (bash and gcc) can be found at the same place in /pub/gnu.

It doesn't exactly sound like the kind of system you use for your home accounts, does it? However, there is one *very* significant thing about the release of this software: it was released under the **GNU General Public License**, which allowed the source code to be distributed freely to anyone who wanted it, and also allowed these people to extend it at will.

Very quickly, communities of interested programmers and testers took Linus's original code, and extended it in all manner of ways. They expanded the range of hardware configurations on which Linux could run, they swelled the range of software written for Linux, and they improved the stability of the whole Linux system. This support and development has continued right up to the present day, spreading worldwide and encompassing whole communities of developers.

Of course, this phenomenon, and its potential, has been noticed in the commercial sector, and now Linux has a healthy complement of commercial vendors achieving the seemingly impossible – doing business by selling a product that is essentially free! Of course, in order to do this, these organizations (which include SuSe, Debian, Mandrake, Red Hat, and so on) have been required to innovate and add value to the basic Linux package. The various distributions, packages, and add-ons created by these organizations have matured alongside the basic Linux operating system itself.

The latest Red Hat Linux release – version 9 – is a perfect example of this innovation. While it's available for free download, Red Hat also sells the package in a variety of forms. For home users there's a boxed set of CDs containing the Linux operating system, a huge assortment of open source productivity software, Red Hat's patented Bluecurve interface, and a Demo subscription to Red Hat Network – the vendor's support, updating, and information network. For corporate users the deal is much the same, but with the emphasis placed more firmly upon support.

Finally, through the combined efforts of both individual developer communities and distribution vendors, there are now Linux versions available that can compete on a level playing field with proprietary software such as Microsoft Windows. This means that Linux is a serious contender both on your home PC and in large-scale production situations.

Why Choose Linux?

Why might you choose Linux for your operating system, rather than one of its competitors? Here are a few points you might like to consider:

❑   **Size and speed:** A basic Linux installation can consume as little as 475MB of hard disk space and will run quite happily on as little as 6432MB of RAM. Compare this to Unix (which often requires more than 500MB) or Microsoft Windows 2000 (which recommends a minimum 2GB hard disk and 128MB RAM). The difference is due to the efficiency of the Linux operating system and (most of) the applications that run on it.

❑   **Security:** One significant reason for Linux's excellent reputation as a secure environment is that its source code is completely accessible, and continues to be viewed by many pairs of eyes. Linux's open source standpoint means that people *other than the vendor* can check for incomplete or tampered source code. The more people that study Linux's source code, the more bugs (and security flaws) can be spotted.

Of course, that's only half the story – the other half is that the infrastructure is in place for easy bug-reporting, discussion, and bug-fixing. The result of all this is that *more* of the bugs get spotted *more* quickly, and they're fixed faster.

In addition to the numerous security applications (such as firewalls) available, many Linux distributions are *specifically* created with a view to providing a highly secure environment. Examples include the Immunix OS (http://www.immunix.com – a commercially available hardened Linux) and Bastille Linux (http://www.bastille-linux.org – a hardening script that can be run on your Linux machine after installation).

❏ **Standards and support:** Linux's compliance with both Unix standards allows it to interoperate with a number of different operating systems and file systems. Linux can talk to Netware, Macintosh, and Windows networks with ease.

❏ **GNU software support:** There is a wide variety of software freely available through the GNU project – including development software, office applications, system administration tools, and so on. The OpenOffice suite of applications is one such example and is covered in more detail in Chapter 5. You'll come across others over the course of this book, and we survey a selection of open source applications in Chapter 13.

❏ **GUI support:** If you like to communicate with your operating system through a nice graphical user interface (GUI) with windows, panels, and menus, then Linux will satisfy you. Whether you're using the GUI to increase productivity or just for fun, you can choose from a number of GUIs, including Bluecurve, KDE, and GNOME.

Moreover, Linux does not *force* you to use the operating system GUI, and for those who are prepared to explore the command line interface (CLI) the benefits include greater flexibility and lower overheads. It's for this reason that many server administrators in serious production environments eschew the GUI in favor of better flexibility and performance.

❏ **Cost:** Linux is freely available – what more can you say?! And if you're a business customer, the healthy vendor competition makes for very reasonable support contract prices.

What Is Red Hat Linux 9?

As we've already mentioned, a number of organizations have created distributions of Linux. Typically, a Linux distribution includes a specific version of the Linux kernel, a collection of components and applications, an installation program (the type of thing more commonly associated with the Windows platform), and often some kind of support arrangement.

One of the most popular distributions comes from Red Hat Inc. – indeed, depending on which of the independent studies market reports you read, Red Hat currently holds more than 50% of the Linux vendor market.

Red Hat Linux comes in a variety of different versions, including:

❏ Personal Edition (currently at version 9)

❏ Professional Edition (currently at version 9)

❏ Advanced Server (currently at version 2.1)

❏ Itanium (64-bit processor – currently at version 7.2)

Each version contains features appropriate to certain scenarios; these are:

❑ Small office or home

❑ Small or medium business

❑ Enterprise or corporate applications

The following matrix demonstrates which versions are suited to which scenarios:

	Home	Small Business	Medium Business	Large Business	Enterprise	Other
Personal	✓	✓				
Professional	✓	✓	✓			
Advanced Server			✓	✓	✓	
Itanium						✓

NOTE: For simplicity, the Enterprise entry in the table is a consolidation of different versions available from Red Hat; these are branded as AS, ES, & WS. For more information on these, take a look at http://www.redhat.com/software/rhel/.

You'll notice that we've used ticks to indicate where a version is suitable for a particular scenario, but we haven't placed any crosses in the table. This is quite deliberate: if you're the kind of power user who has a home network and wishes to use some of the advanced features offered only by the Advanced Server edition, then why not? The beauty of Linux is that it's open and doesn't demand anywhere near the hardware requirements expected of other operating systems.

So that old machine you had hidden under your desk, destined for the rubbish heap, may be of use after all – dig it out, install Red Hat Linux 9, and use it as a web server or printer server!

What Is Covered in This Book?

Each chapter in this book builds upon the knowledge developed in earlier chapters, so that there's a natural path through the book from beginning to end. As you gain confidence and begin to explore Linux further, you'll also find that this arrangement of topics should help you use the book as a reference.

Here's a brief description of the chapters in this book:

❑ **Chapter 1** takes you through the process of **installing** the operating system. It explains how to prepare for the installation, so that you don't get any nasty surprises halfway through. It also explains each step of the installation process, so you know what it's doing, and helps you to get exactly what you want from the installation.

❑ **Chapter 2** introduces the **basics** of Linux. This chapter takes a tour of the desktop interface, so you can see exactly how to start using Linux. It also explains some **fundamental topics** that will help you to get the most out of your Linux machine – user accounts, the Linux file system, hardware configuration, and managing your machine's resources.

❑ **Chapter 3** discusses how to configure your Linux machine to **connect to the Internet**, or to a local area network, so that you can start to send and receive e-mails and use the Internet.

❑ **Chapter 4** introduces the concept of **packages**. In order to use the components and applications that are supported by Red Hat Linux, we must first install the packages that contain them. This chapter will explain how to go about installing new packages, upgrading packages, and removing any packages that you don't need. There are also many applications out there that are not available in package form, so we'll also have a look at another common format – tarballs.

❑ In **Chapter 5** we'll start to explore the many **applications** that we can use on Linux to perform our everyday tasks – things like web browsers, office applications, and MP3 players. This chapter introduces just a small proportion of the bewildering array of applications that come with Red Hat Linux 9, and explains where you can find more!

❑ **Chapter 6** tackles the notion of the **shell**. In fact, you will have been using the shell already in the first five chapters of the book, to type commands and execute them, so that Linux can run them and respond accordingly. Now we examine the shell more closely, and look at combining commands into a script, defining the input to (and output from) a script, and how to build logical structures into scripts, get them to run in specific circumstances, and manage multiple tasks at the same time.

❑ **Chapter 7** presents a detailed explanation of the Linux **file system**. We'll talk about how to manage your files and directories, and how to use the shell to generate and manipulate the output from predefined or custom scripts. We'll also talk about how Linux allows you to access the file systems of remote and detachable devices such as networked file systems, floppy disks, CD drives, and handheld devices, using a process known as mounting.

❑ **Chapter 8** takes a closer look at **user accounts** and **user groups**, and how to manage them. This includes a discussion of permissions and privileges, and provides just enough on the basics of security to prepare us for Chapter 9.

❑ **Chapter 9** describes how you might configure your Linux machine to provide **services** to other machines on a network. In particular, we'll examine how to set your machine up as an FTP server, a web server, a file server, a printer server, a mail server, or a DHCP server.

❑ **Chapter 10** covers some advanced **administration** topics. We'll see how to analyze system log files, and use them to track down problems with the system. We'll talk about backups and archives. We'll expand on the discussion of tarballs in Chapter 4, to see how to install new applications from source code. We'll also explore how to customize and recompile the Linux kernel – the heart of the operating system.

❑ **Chapter 11** demonstrates how we can use scripting (and specifically, the **Perl** programming language) to automate the common task of managing the log files. The chapter presents a good handful of simple but useful Perl applications, with just enough explanation of the code to give you an idea of how each one works. If you've never used Perl before, then this chapter will help you to appreciate its power, flexibility, and potential – and it will also provide the inspiration to get you using Perl to work with your Linux operating system.

❑ **Chapter 12** is all about **security**. Security is a complex topic; this chapter provides an introduction to a number of security-based topics as they relate to Red Hat Linux. Its purpose is to raise your awareness of the various issues you need to consider, problems you might encounter, and solutions and preventative measures to can employ to combat them. It describes how to secure your machine using a firewall, and how to get all the latest information about critical software updates by registering with the Red Hat Network Alert service.

❑ **Chapter 13** presents a survey of some of the many other **applications** supported by Red Hat Linux 9, focusing in particular on system administration software and application development software. We'll also take a closer look at some of the different open source licenses out there.

❑ At http://www.wrox.com, you'll find a bonus chapter that explores in more detail the inner workings of the **SysAdmin** system administration program mentioned in Chapter 13. The SysAdmin application is written in Perl, and the complete source code for this application is available at http://www.wrox.com – allowing you both to install and use it to manage your own Linux machine, and to explore and experiment with the code for yourself.

Conventions in This Book

We have used certain layout and font styles in this book that are designed to help you to differentiate between the different kinds of information. Here are examples of the styles that are used, with an explanation of what they mean.

As you'd expect, we present code in two different ways: in-line code and displayed code. When we need to mention keywords and other coding specifics within the text (for example, in discussion relating to an `if...else` construct or the GDI+ `Graphics` class) we use the single-width font as shown in this sentence. If we want to show a more substantial block of code (such as a script, or part of a script), then we display it like this:

```
echo -n Deleting temporary files...
```

```
rm -f *.tmp
```

Sometimes, you will see code in a mixture of gray and white backgrounds, like this:

```
echo -n Deleting temporary files...
rm -f *.tmp
echo Done.
```

In cases like this, we use the gray shading to draw attention to a particular section of the code – perhaps because it is new code, or it is particularly important to this part of the discussion. We also use this style to show output that is displayed in the console window.

We show commands typed at the command line, and their output, like this:

```
$ cat bookdetail.txt
Title: Beginning Red Hat Linux
ISBN: 1861-00847-3
Authors: Bhattacharya, Gundavaram, Mamone, de Mauro, Sharma, Thomas, Whiting
```

Commands that must be executed as root are shown with a # prompt, like this:

```
# make install
```

Advice, hints, and background information comes in an indented, italicized font like this.

> **Important pieces of information (that you really shouldn't ignore) come in boxes like this!**

Bulleted lists appear indented, with each new bullet marked as follows:

- ❑ **Important words** are in a bold type font.
- ❑ Words that appear on the screen, or in menus like the File or Window, are in a similar font to the one you would see in a Linux or Windows graphical user interface.
- ❑ Keys that you press on the keyboard, like *Ctrl+C* and *Enter*, are in italics.

Customer Support

We offer source code for download, errata, and technical support from our web site, http://www.wrox.com. In addition you can join mailing lists for author and peer discussion at p2p.wrox.com.

Source Code and Updates

As you work through the examples in this book, you may choose either to type in all the code by hand, or to use the source code that accompanies the book. Many readers prefer the former, because it's a good way to get familiar with the coding techniques that are being used.

Whether you want to type the code in or not, it's useful to have a copy of the source code handy. If you like to type in the code, you can use our source code to check the results you should be getting – they should be your first stop if you think you might have typed in an error. By contrast, if you don't like typing, then you'll definitely need to download the source code from our web site! Either way, the source code will help you with updates and debugging.

Therefore all the source code used in this book is available for download at http://www.wrox.com. Once you've logged on to the web site, simply locate the title (either through our **Search** facility or by using one of the title lists). Then click on the **Download Code** link on the book's detail page and you can obtain all the source code.

The files that are available for download from our site have been archived using both Linux's File Roller archiving software and WinZip. When you have saved the attachments to a folder on your hard drive, you need to extract the files using a decompression program such as File Roller, WinZip, or PKUnzip. When you extract the files, the code is usually extracted into chapter folders. When you start the extraction process, ensure that you've selected the **Use folder names** under **Extract to** options (or their equivalents).

Errata

We have made every effort to make sure that there are no errors in the text or in the code. However, no one is perfect and mistakes do occur. If you find an error in this book, like a spelling mistake or a faulty piece of code, we would be very grateful to hear about it. By sending in errata, you may save another reader hours of frustration, and of course, you will be helping us provide even higher quality information. Simply e-mail the information to techsupwrox@wrox.com; we'll check the information, and (if appropriate) we'll post a message to the errata pages, and use it in subsequent editions of the book.

To find the errata page for this book, go to http://www.wrox.com/, and locate the title through our **Search** facility or title list. Then, on the book details page, click on the **Book Errata** link. On this page you will be able to view all the errata that has been submitted and checked through by editorial. You can also click the **Submit Errata** link on this page, to notify us of any errata that you have found.

Technical Support

If you would like to make a direct query about a problem in the book, you need to e-mail techsupwrox@wrox.com. A typical e-mail should include the following things:

❑   In the Subject field, tell us the **book name**, the **last four digits of the ISBN** (3784 for this book), and the number of the **page** on which the problem occurs.

❑   In the body of the message, tell us your **name**, **contact information**, and the **problem**.

We *won't* send you junk mail. We need these details to save your time and ours.

> **Note that the Wrox support process can only offer support to issues that are directly pertinent to the content of our published title. Support for questions that fall outside the scope of normal book support is provided via the community lists of our http://p2p.wrox.com/ forum.**

p2p.wrox.com

For author and peer discussion, join the **P2P mailing lists**. Our unique system provides **programmer to programmer**™ contact on mailing lists, forums, and newsgroups, all *in addition* to our one-to-one e-mail support system. Wrox authors and editors and other industry experts are present on our mailing lists.

At p2p.wrox.com you will find a number of different lists that will help you, not only while you read this book, but also as you develop your own applications. To subscribe to a mailing list just follow this these steps:

1.   Go to http://p2p.wrox.com/ and choose the appropriate category from the left menu bar.

2.   Click on the mailing list you wish to join.

3.   Follow the instructions to subscribe and fill in your e-mail address and password.

4.   Reply to the confirmation e-mail you receive.

5.   Use the subscription manager to join more lists and set your mail preferences.

Installing Red Hat Linux 9

Installing an operating system is often a long, drawn-out process that requires a lot of upfront planning. Installation of traditional Unix-based operating systems seems to have been particularly painful in the past, requiring even experienced administrators to fret about partitions and drivers. Early versions of Linux were no different in this respect. The first version of Linux, back in 1993, could be booted up only using Minix (another Unix-like operating system). That version of Linux could support only the Finnish keyboard because the author of Linux didn't have access to a US keyboard!

However, since then Linux has grown by leaps and bounds. Each of the major distributions has put a lot of thought and effort into the Linux installation process, and today installing Linux for desktop use is, in common talk, a no-brainer.

Red Hat, in particular, has caught the attention of the public, breaking away from the standard tradition of distributing disk images and pioneering the concept of distributing software in the form of packages. (Right now, the Red Hat Package Manager – RPM – is a standard in distribution of pre-compiled software packages in the Linux world, and we'll learn more about the RPM in Chapter 4.)

Red Hat has also been improving Linux usability and features in that most daunting area of any operating system – installation. The latest version of Red Hat Linux, version 9, is truly the most user-friendly ever, with extensive inputs from professional usability experts and a ravishing new look to attract even the most hardened of technophobes.

The Red Hat Linux distribution offers four different configurations, and your choice will depend on how you plan to use the operating system:

❑ **Personal desktop:** This configuration is targeted at users who are new to Linux, or those who like to use Linux for day-to-day applications like office productivity tools and Internet browsing. This is the option we'll install in this chapter.

- ❑ **Workstation:** This configuration is targeted at developers or system administrators. It provides various tools for software development and system management.

- ❑ **Server:** This configuration is mainly intended for systems that will not be used directly, but are primarily for offering network-based services like e-mail, file sharing, network connectivity, and web resources.

- ❑ **Custom:** This configuration is for experienced users who want more control over exactly what is installed onto their systems. The user can select which packages are to be installed and how the hard disks are to be used, and has control over various other configuration options that are pre-selected in the other three configurations.

In this chapter, we are going to take a look at getting a Personal Desktop installation in place on a new computer. We are going to look at each step of the installation and the decisions that you would have to take at various stages of the installation to get a working Red Hat desktop in place. By the end of the chapter, you will have a desktop up and running that you will be able to use right away for your daily needs like Internet browsing, e-mail, and office productivity tools.

Preparing for the Installation

While the installation process is quite straightforward, it is important that you do a little bit of preparation to ensure that the installation process goes as intended. Of course, you'll need the necessary installation disks to install the system; but it's also worth looking over your hardware too. In this section, we'll examine both software and hardware aspects of preparation.

The Software

Of course, to begin you need to have the necessary **software** for the job. The Red Hat Linux 9 distribution can be obtained from a number of sources. Here are a couple of options:

- ❑ **The Publisher's Edition CD set included with this book.** This includes all the CDs that you need for the installation process itself. In this chapter, we'll look at installation using the CDs that are included in this pack.

- ❑ **The official retail box set.** This includes all the CDs that you need for the installation process itself. It also includes other CDs that contain the source code for all the packaged software, and a CD that contains Red Hat–supplied documentation. Much of the software on these disks can be freely copied and distributed, but only the customer who bought the CD is entitled to official technical support from Red Hat. The box set also includes an array of bonus software packaged by Red Hat, as well as some proprietary software that may not be freely distributed.

❑   **The downloadable CD images.** In the true spirit of Open Source (http://www.opensource.org), Red Hat also makes all the installation CDs downloadable for free public use. While the contents of the downloadable CD images are identical to those in the official box set, users of these CD images are not entitled to official technical support from Red Hat.

These CD images can be obtained from any of Red Hat's various mirror web sites. You can find a list of mirror FTP and HTTP sites at http://www.redhat.com/ download/mirror.html. Alternatively, you can obtain the CD images from VA Linux's extensive Sourceforge download mirror servers, at http://download .sourceforge.net/pub/mirrors/redhat.

When you have the CD images, you can write them onto CD recordable disks (be sure to tell your CD-burning software that you're burning *CD images*), and then you can use the CDs for installation.

The Personal Desktop configuration of Red Hat Linux that is downloaded or in the boxed set requires all three binary installation CD disks during the installation. Moreover, as you begin to explore some of the many applications supplied with the Red Hat Linux 9 distribution, you'll need these disks for installing the applications themselves. Therefore, it's worth keeping all the three binary CD disks in your possession.

The Hardware

Before you start the installation, it's a good idea to make a note of the hardware details of the machine you plan to use for your Linux installation. These details can help you to get the most out of the installation process, and even in detecting problems in the hardware configuration itself – problems that can prevent Red Hat Linux from installing correctly.

Determining Your Hardware

During the process of installation, Red Hat Linux may need some extra help to determine the exact hardware composition of your computer. To help it out, it is a good idea to make a note of the details on the following checklist, before you begin the installation:

❑   **Keyboard type:** The Red Hat Linux installation defaults to a standard US English 105-key keyboard. Unless you are using a language-specific keyboard like those used in many European and East Asian countries, you don't have to worry about this detail.

❑   **Mouse type:** Red Hat Linux supports two-button and three-button mice, as well as wheel-mice and the cordless variety. It's worth noting the exact make and nature of your mouse. Red Hat Linux also supports tablets; to verify that your make of tablet is compatible with Red Hat Linux, check the Hardware Compatibility List.

❑   **Hard disk size:** Make a note of the size of the hard disk that you'll be installing Red Hat Linux onto. If the installation process fails to detect the hard disk size correctly, it might point to an underlying hardware problem. Also note that a Personal Desktop installation will require around 1.8GB of hard disk space to cater for the programs loaded during installation. If you plan to install other applications, then you will need more.

❑   **Video (graphics) card:** Note the chipset of the video card and the amount of RAM. While the Red Hat X-server configuration program can usually probe and detect the video card, it sometimes fails. If it does fail, you'll need to tell Red Hat Linux the name of your video card chipset. Note that the video RAM is sometimes also displayed on the computer screen during boot up of the machine.

If you can't find the name of your video card chipset in the Hardware Compatability List (see below), don't worry. Note that this means only that the GUI of Red Hat Linux is affected. Generally, if you intend to use the computer only as a server system, you're recommended not to install any GUI – this is for reasons of resource load and security. If you do want a GUI, you'll still be able to configure your machine to use the VESA interface for running the X-server. The VESA interface standard is supported by most of the commonly available video cards.

❑   **Monitor:** If you have an unusual monitor model, then the configuration of the GUI X Server software (during the installation process) might not detect it. Therefore, it's worth noting information regarding your monitor. You'll need the horizontal and vertical sync rates, which can generally be found either in the monitor manual or at the monitor manufacturer's web site.

❑   **Sound card:** While the installation tries to detect the sound card, it sometimes doesn't succeed. Therefore, it's good to note the name of the sound card chipset in advance.

❑   **Network card:** During installation, Red Hat Linux tries to detect the network interface card (NIC) and load the appropriate software driver automatically. You should note the name of the chipset of the NIC in advance of installation, just in case the installation process fails to determine it.

How do you get hold of this information? Well, if you have the technical specification documents that were supplied with your computer, then you'll find the information in there. If not, then the machine's existing operating system will probably offer some way of browsing the hardware being used. For example:

❑   In Windows 2000, you can find out about existing hardware via Start | Settings | Control Panel | System (select the Hardware tab, and click the Device Manager button).

❑   In other Linux systems, you can find out about existing hardware through via various menu options of the GUI. For example, try the options in Programs | Settings or Main Menu | System Tools, depending on which version of Linux you're using.

The Hardware Compatibility List

Red Hat maintains a list of **officially supported hardware**, called the Hardware Compatibility List (HCL). The HCL lists all the hardware components against which the operating system has been checked extensively for proper functioning. The list is available at http://hardware .redhat.com/hcl/.

It's worth checking for your own hardware components in this list before buying new hardware for your Red Hat desktop; if you find them, it can give you some peace of mind. You shouldn't panic, however, if your hardware *doesn't* appear in the HCL; there's still a good chance that it will work with the Red Hat Linux 9 installation. Many hardware components behave using standardized interfaces that can be persuaded to work with Linux (although sometimes in a less efficient way). For example, most modern video cards support the VESA mode of graphic display, which can be used by Red Hat Linux to present a GUI front-end to the user. While the VESA mode is not suitable for performance-intensive graphic displays, it is a quick and easy way to persuade an incompatible video card to work with the GUI software in the Linux operating system.

It is well worth using the HCL to check out the compatibility of hardware with Red Hat Linux (or, indeed, any distribution of Linux) before investing your money into it. A significant proportion of all queries submitted by new users of Red Hat Linux relate to hardware for which Red Hat has not confirmed official support.

While any new motherboard or processor should safely work with a Linux basic console mode, the most common problems lie with compatibility of sound and display hardware. Due to the nature of the Open Source movement, the compatibility of Linux with specific hardware configurations can take some time to develop. Not all hardware manufacturers are quick to offer Linux versions of their driver software.

The Boot Disk

The installation process will also offer you the opportunity to create a **boot disk**. The boot disk can help you to recover gracefully if you have boot problems. While creation of the boot disk is optional, it is recommended – you never know when you might need it.

For this, it's a good idea to have a floppy disk ready during the installation process. Make sure there's nothing important on the disk, because the boot disk creation process will overwrite it!

Network Details

We've already talked about compiling a hardware checklist before installation. If you intend to use your new Red Hat Linux desktop within an existing network, you should also compile a checklist of network-related information for use during the installation process. You may need to ask your network administrator some of these details:

❑   **DHCP or Fixed IP:** An IP address is essential for any computer to participate in any networking activity. So, you must ask: Is your desktop assigned an IP address dynamically (by a DHCP server), or should it be configured with a static IP address? By default, Red Hat Linux will configure your machine to request an IP address from a DHCP server, but if you need to, you can change this either during the installation process itself or after the installation is complete. If your computer is to be configured to get its IP address dynamically from a DHCP server, you can skip the rest of these questions:

❑ **IP Address:** If your machine is to have a fixed IP address, you need to know what IP address to use. An IP address is always mentioned along with its **network mask**, so make a note of both the IP address and network mask.

❑ **DNS Host and Domain Names:** You also need to note some DNS (domain name service) details – specifically the machine's host name and domain name. For example, if your network administrator assigns your machine the DNS name arwen.acme.com, then your machine host name is arwen and your domain name is acme.com. The combination of host name and domain name (here arwen.acme.com) is called the **fully qualified domain name (FQDN)**.

If your office is running an internal DNS server, this host and domain name combination should refer to the IP address that we've already mentioned. Many network applications perform optimally when a local DNS server is present in the network.

❑ **DNS Servers:** DNS servers are responsible for resolving Internet names to the corresponding IP addresses. You should note the IP address(es) of your network's DNS server(s). If there is no local DNS server, then it's possible that an external DNS server is used for Internet name resolution. Red Hat Linux allows you to specify up to three DNS servers.

❑ **Internet Gateway:** Finally, you should note the IP address of your machine's Internet gateway. While any network traffic for your local LAN will be sent directly to those local machines, any traffic to other networks (like those of the Internet) will be sent out through this gateway. Failure to set this value will prevent you from accessing the Internet after installation.

Getting Help

If you find problems, there are plenty of ways to get answers. In fact, the Open Source community boasts of a huge number of avenues that can help you to resolve your technical difficulties.

For example, Red Hat itself has an extensive bug reporting and resolution database, freely available for public access at http://bugzilla.redhat.com. In addition, there are many Linux users' communities world-wide, hungry to share experiences and thriving on a diet of mutual support (see http://www.linux.org/groups). In fact, the extent of third-party support in Red Hat Linux is unparalleled among the various Linux distributions.

The Installation

Having collected all the information in our hardware and network checklists, you're ready to begin the installation itself. This section will walk you through the graphical installation tool, explaining the steps as we go. Although this section is quite long, it includes quite a number of screenshots, so you'll soon see how simple it is to install Red Hat Linux 9 using the graphical installation tool.

Booting off the CD

We normally begin the installation process by booting off the first CD of the distribution. To do this, you need to have the machine switched on, so that you can open your CD-ROM drive. Insert Disk 1 of your Red Hat Linux distribution into your CD-ROM drive, and then restart the machine. The installation process should start automatically, as soon as the computer's power-on self test is complete:

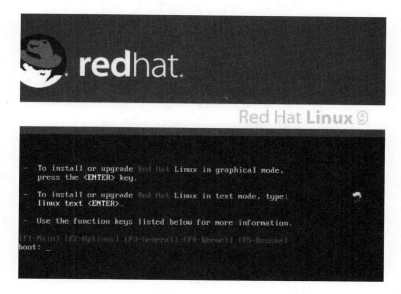

If you don't get this screen, then it may be because your computer is not configured to boot off the CD-ROM drive by default. In this case, you may need to adjust the configuration of your machine by changing the boot sequence of your computer, so that it begins with the CD-ROM drive.

The best way to do this is to reboot your computer, and take it into the BIOS setup menu immediately after boot up. The exact way to access the BIOS setup menu varies from machine to machine, but it usually involves hitting a button such as F2 or F10 or Escape. Check your motherboard's manual if you have it, or follow the instructions on screen immediately after the reboot.

The dialog asks you to select whether to install in graphical or text mode. Text mode is suitable in situations where a minimal configuration is required, or where there is a problem with the display. We will conduct our installation in graphical mode, so just press the *Enter* key.

When you've selected the mode of installation, the boot program proceeds by displaying a flurry of messages on the screen. Don't be alarmed by this – this is perfectly normal in a Linux operating system boot up. When Linux boots up, it stays in text mode briefly to perform a few routine checks and processes, and then launches the installation in graphical mode after that. So, let's deal with these initial questions of the installation.

Testing the Media

In version 9, Red Hat has introduced a **media test module** into the installation process. The purpose of the media test module is to eliminate one of the most frequent sources of installation problems – defects in the CDs themselves. As shown below, the module asks you whether you would like to test the CD media before proceeding with the installation:

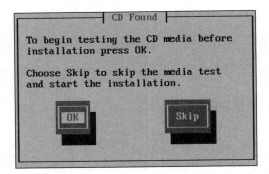

This module will check your installation CDs and tell you if it finds any problems reading their contents. If you're installing from CDs included as part of Red Hat's retailed box set, then your CDs are likely to be fine. But if you've downloaded CD images and burned your own disks, then it's definitely a good idea to use this module, to check the validity of your disks.

If you want to *skip* this test (for example, if you're in a hurry or you already know that the disks are OK), use your cursor keys and *Enter* key to select Skip; and you yourself can skip to the next section.

Alternatively, to *run* the media check module (which we recommend if the disks have never been used before), press OK. This will take you to the CD media check screen:

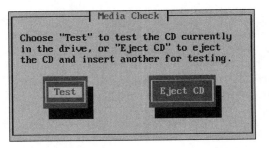

Since the first disk is already in the drive, you can simply press Test to start the media test of the disk right away. The progress of the test is shown like this:

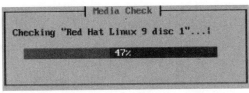

If the test completes and doesn't find any errors, you'll see confirmation that the disk passed the test:

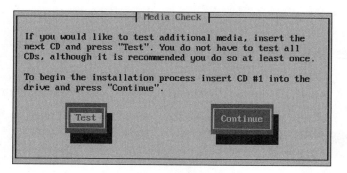

If you see an error message instead, it indicates that your CD is defective. This means that you'll need to arrange to replace it and restart the installation.

When Disk 1 has been tested, you will be prompted as shown below, which asks you whether you want to insert any other disks for checking:

You should check all the remaining CDs, by pressing the Test button each time. When all of the CDs have passed, you can press the Continue button to continue with the remainder of the installation.

The Graphical Installation Launch

Having tested all the CDs (or skipped the test altogether), the Red Hat Linux installer program – called **Anaconda** – begins, launching the graphical installer. It tries to detect the video card, monitor, and mouse, as shown below:

```
Running anaconda, the Red Hat Linux system installer - please wait...
Probing for video card:    Unsupported VGA compatible
Probing for monitor type:   Unknown monitor
Probing for mouse type:    Generic - Wheel Mouse (PS/2)
```

*Note that Anaconda has failed to detect the exact make and model of video card and
monitor here, and so has opted for a configuration that it thinks should work. Its choice
will probably not give the best performance, but it should at least see you through the
installation process to the point at which you can use your checklist to adjust the
hardware configuration details more precisely.*

Then it launches into the GUI install
screen, as shown here. Press **Next** (in
the bottom right corner) to continue to
the next screen.

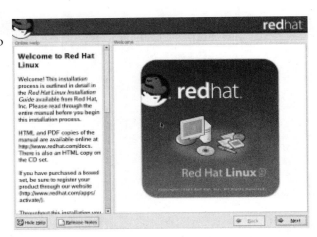

Selecting the Default Language

Red Hat supports many languages other than English during the installation process. Those
more comfortable with their native language can use this screen to select the language
appropriate for their use:

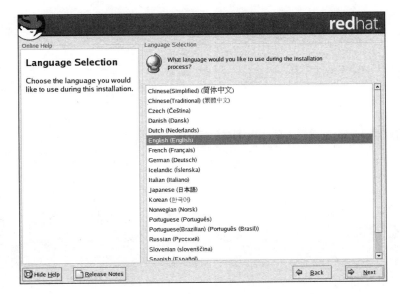

Note that many languages, notably those using various Asian Indic scripts, are missing from this list. This is because the version of the GUI toolkit used for developing the installation, GTK+, doesn't support the display of these languages. Red Hat is continually adding local language support for the installation process and the desktop itself for various localities. If your language of choice is not listed here, you will probably see it added to this list in future versions of the distribution.

Selecting the Keyboard

For many non–English speaking countries, language-specific keyboards are available for the computer. These keyboards make it easier to type in the native language. In the next screen, Red Hat Linux allows you to specify the keyboard layout of your choice:

Choose your preferred keyboard option (the screenshot shows a user selecting the default keyboard layout, US English), and click Next to proceed to the next screen.

Selecting the Mouse

In the next screen, Red Hat shows the list of mouse types that it supports:

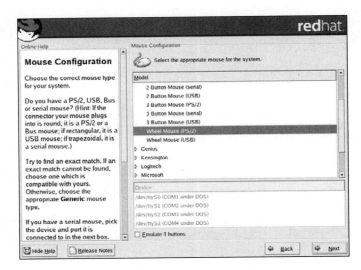

It tries to detect and select the correct mouse type automatically for you. If everything goes well, you can just click Next to go on to the next screen.

Selecting an Installation Type

At this stage, the installation will look for an existing version of Red Hat Linux on your machine. If it finds one, it will invite you to choose between **upgrading** the existing version and **replacing** it. An upgrade will take less time, and allow you to preserve any existing data on your drives while bringing the software packages up to date with the latest distribution. By contrast, a replacement may overwrite your existing data but will provide a completely up-to-date installation. Here, we'll opt for a completely new installation:

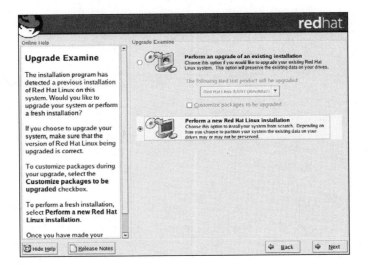

Then we come to the screen that asks us to specify the installation type desired:

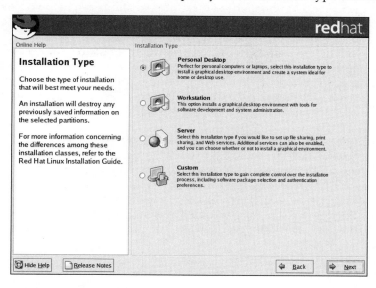

As we mentioned at the beginning of this chapter, we will use a **Personal Desktop** installation for our machine. We therefore select the **Personal Desktop** option, and click **Next** to proceed to the next screen.

Setting up the Disk Partitions

The next screen allows you to organize the storage space on your machine's hard disk:

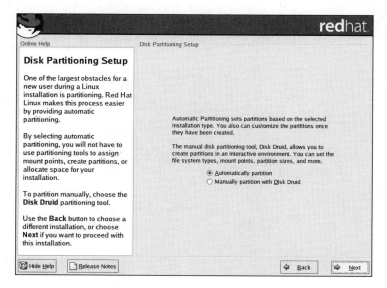

The space on your hard disk is normally divided into sections, called **partitions**, for better management of the space. Dividing a hard disk into partitions can help you segregate the available disk space according to its usage.

For example, you might choose to dedicate one partition solely to your executable programs, and to set aside another partition just to hold your work-related data files. This type of organization has the advantage that when you are upgrading your system, you can ask Red Hat Linux to leave the *data* partition of your disk alone, and upgrade only the software packages installed in the *other* partitions.

The optimum number and size of partitions on your disk depends on many factors – the overall disk size, the purpose of each partition, and so on. Such decisions are usually made on anticipated future requirements and data organization structure, and often rely heavily on previous experience. However, Red Hat Linux makes this decision simpler by offering an **automatic partitioning** option, which creates an arrangement of partitions based on your install type preferences. So, if you chose the **Personal Desktop** installation type in the previous screen, your hard disk can be automatically reorganized into partitions that are likely to be used for day-to-day personal work.

Red Hat Linux also offers an option for creating partitions manually, and if you feel comfortable and confident with creating your own partitions, then feel free to do so. However, it is normally safe enough to accept the default **automatic partition** option, and that's what we'll do here.

Dealing with Existing Partitions

If you already have partitions on your disk, then you can use the next screen to remove the older partitions:

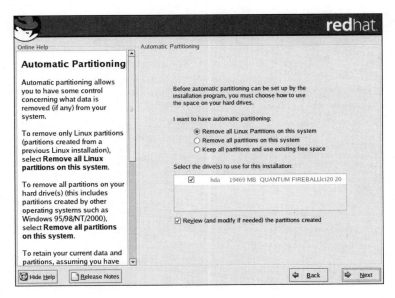

Unless you have data left on the disk, it is normally safe to accept the removal of existing partitions on the disk, by clicking on the **Next** button.

> *If your machine has an existing Windows partition that you want to keep, then you should note that it's not sufficient to choose the* **Remove all Linux Partitions** *option here. Rather, you will need to go* **Back** *to the* **Disk Partitioning** *screen, and configure your partitions manually using the Disk Druid tool. You may even need to resize your Windows partition using a partitioning utility like PartitionMagic, to create some free space onto which you can install Red Hat Linux*

If you have existing partitions, and you have asked Red Hat Linux to remove them for you, you will be asked to confirm your desire to remove the partitions:

Before accepting the removal of the partitions, be aware that removal of partitions leads to complete loss of any existing data on the disk. If you are sure about your decision, confirm the deletion (by clicking **Yes**) and move on to the next screen.

Setting the Boot Loader

In the next screen, Red Hat Linux allows you to set various boot loader options. A **boot loader** is normally required when you have multiple operating systems on the hard disk, and an option (at boot time) for choosing the operating system to boot from. Red Hat provides the **GRUB** boot loader for this purpose.

The screen provides you with an option to specify the *default* operating system to boot from:

In this example we are dealing with a new installation, and for this reason the screenshot above displays just a single option in this list.

You can also set a **boot loader password** in this screen. A boot loader password prevents others from modifying the boot time parameters of the Linux kernel. Any user can, for example, boot the computer into a maintenance mode and then change the root password, thereby taking control of the whole computer. If your computer is unlikely to be handled by others, or if you implicitly trust others who will be using this computer, you can safely ignore this option. If you set a boot loader password, you should keep the password safely in your personal records.

So, in most situations, you will not need to change anything in this screen. You can just click Next to move on.

Setting the Network Parameters

The installation process now takes you into the network configuration section. Your network configuration checklist will come in handy in this section:

Note that if Red Hat Linux does not detect your network card automatically, your Network Devices table (at the top of the screen) might be empty. This will prevent you from setting the network parameters for your computer. If that happens, don't panic; all the network parameters on the screen can be configured after the installation process is complete, via the Network Configuration dialog (Main Menu | System Settings | Network).

By default, Red Hat Linux selects automatic network configuration of your computer using the **DHCP protocol**. Therefore, if you have a single desktop at a home or office environment, or if your machine exists in a LAN environment whose IP addresses are provided by a DHCP server, then you can skip this screen and proceed to the Firewall screen that comes next.

However, if your machine exists in a LAN environment that requires static IP addresses, then you have an opportunity now to set your network configuration.

Again, you don't have to do this now; if you prefer, you can skip the network configuration at this stage and configure your network settings after the installation is complete, via the Network Configuration dialog.

Manually Configuring the Network Devices

If you choose to do it now, you can use your network configuration checklist to fill up the entries on the screen. First, click on the Edit button at the top section of the screen to bring up the network device configuration dialog box:

Here, deselect the Configure using DHCP option, and enter the IP Address and Netmask details as per your network configuration checklist. For example, in the screenshot we have set the IP address and the network mask to 192.168.1.1 and 255.255.255.0 respectively.

When you've set the network parameters, click OK; the Network Devices section will now reflect your new settings.

Configuring DNS Hostname and Servers

While you're on this screen, you can also set the DNS hostname and the DNS servers (which you should have noted in your network configuration checklist). You can specify these values in the appropriate entry boxes near the bottom of the screen. At the end of your configuration, your screen should look something like this:

Setting up the Firewall

The next screen of the installation relates to the setup of a **network firewall** for your machine. A network firewall protects your computer from attacks or intrusions from malicious crackers in the network, and we'll learn more about configuring firewalls in Chapter 12. For now, Red Hat Linux provides you with three levels of network firewall security:

❏ **Highly secure firewall:** This level of security is suitable for those who are quite concerned about their security. Here, all incoming network connections are disallowed unless specifically listed in the services list on the screen. To facilitate normal working, only two exceptions are made – incoming DHCP connections are allowed so that the machine can configure itself, and incoming DNS replies are allowed so that Internet applications can work normally.

❏ **Medium grade secure firewall:** This is the default level of security, and is generally adequate while using the Internet. This level disallows incoming network connections to privileged ports like web, SMTP mail, etc. However, you can customize this level to allow certain incoming connections to services that your desktop is providing. For example, if you set up a web server on your machine and want others to access it, you can check the **WWW** option in the services list on the screen.

❏ **No firewall:** If you are unlikely to connect to the Internet, or if you are not concerned with cracking activities that can be directed by troublesome individuals on the Internet or your LAN, then you can select this option. This option doesn't set up any firewall on your machine. In other words, it allows any outside individuals to access network resources on your computer.

*Selecting the **No firewall** option doesn't necessarily mean that all users on the network have direct and unchecked access to your computer's network resources. A firewall is just the first line of defense against intruders. Most network applications have some form of access control that decides who finally gets to use these resources.*

You can also customize the firewall rules within these different levels of security. Red Hat Linux allows you to select the trusted devices – network interfaces that are expected to carry traffic from sources that you can trust blindly. In a home network this would generally be the interface card connected to the rest of your home network. You should definitely not mark your Internet interfaces as trusted, unless you are absolutely sure about your security needs.

Apart from these devices, this screen also allows you to specify network services that external network identities will be able to access from your computer. To be on the safe side, select only the services that you actually expect to be used, and that do not have insecure software behind them. For example:

❑ SSH (Secure Shell) allows you to work on a remote machine while ensuring that the data exchanged in the process is kept encrypted and secure. It is generally safe for SSH servers to be open; indeed, this is recommended if you want to be able to access your computer from other machines.

❑ If you want to use this machine to receive mails from others, you may choose to have an SMTP server on your machine receive these mails. In this case you should allow incoming connections to the SMTP server.

❑ Many FTP servers have had a long history of insecurities. It is advisable to leave incoming connections to such FTP services closed, and open them up in the firewall only when you need them. When you've finished, you should immediately cut off their access using the firewall.

Setting Additional Language Support

If you're expecting to use multiple languages, you can select them in the next screen:

Normally, it is safe to continue to the next screen after accepting the defaults that are offered by Red Hat Linux.

Setting the Time Zone

In the next screen, you can set the time zone of your location:

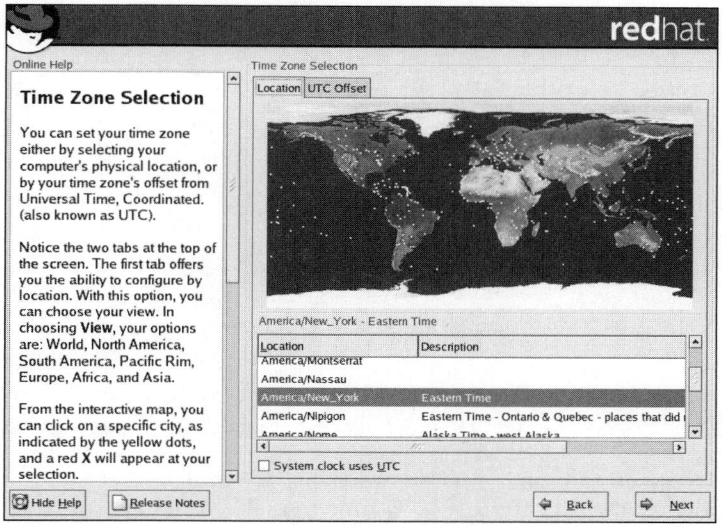

Red Hat provides a very usable graphical method for intuitively selecting your time zone. To use it, bring your cursor to any point of the displayed world map – this allows you to set the time zone of your computer to that of the selected region. A green sticky arrow in the mouse cursor makes the job easier by selecting the city time zone nearest to the cursor. In the screenshot above, we have set the time zone to that of New York.

Note the option at the bottom of the screen to enable UTC time in the computer clock. This allows the system to run with correct timezone and daylight saving changes. (Note that you shouldn't use this if you have a dual-boot machine that also boots Windows.)

Root Account Configuration

By default, the installation process creates a single administrative user account for your machine, called **root**. We'll learn more about the system's users in subsequent chapters of the book – particularly Chapter 8. For now all you need to know is that whenever you use the system, you do so through the context of a **user account**, and that to do so you log in by specifying the user account's name and a password.

Every user account on the system has its own password, and the root user (or superuser) is no different in this respect. In this screen, you are asked to supply the root user's password:

Of course, you are asked to type the password twice, to confirm that you didn't mistype the first time. Type the password carefully each time to make sure you type it correctly.

You might encounter a message that tells you that the password is too short or too simple. This is a security feature, designed to remind you of the importance of choosing an unguessable password. If you consider your chosen password to be adequate for your needs, you can ignore these messages. However, for the sake of security you should make an effort to set an uncommon password for the superuser account. We'll talk more about password security (and the techniques that people use for breaking passwords) in Chapters 8 and 12.

Selecting Packages for Installation

Now, you have an opportunity to choose the software packages that you want installed along with the system. Red Hat Linux has already chosen a combination of software packages for the installation type that you selected at the beginning of the installation process. If you want to fine-tune the package selection, you can do so here by selecting the Customize... option:

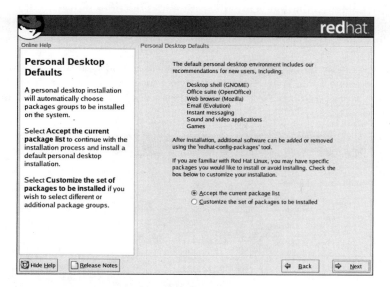

You don't have to fiddle with the choice of installed packages here – it's easy to add and remove packages after the installation is complete, as we'll see in Chapter 4. So, to keep things simple, we'll select the Accept the current packages list option here, and proceed to the next screen.

The Automatic Installation Process

The Red Hat Linux graphical installation tool has now collected all the information that it needs to begin the installation. The next screen prompts you to begin the software installation:

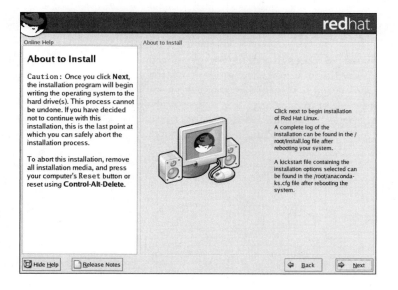

The software package installation is mostly automatic; the only thing you'll need to do at this stage is change the CD a couple of times (when prompted to do so) and admire the photographs that are displayed while the necessary packages are installed.

Before the software is installed, the installation process formats all the partitions that are supposed to hold these data. Then, the installation process continues by installing the software packages. Progress bars display the total time taken so far, and the estimated time of the software installation:

Creating a Boot Disk

With all the software packages installed, we go on to the screen shown opposite. Here, you are asked whether you would like to create a boot disk for your computer. A **boot disk** is a safety measure against problems that might occur in the boot loader. For example, installation of another operating system in the computer might overwrite the Red Hat Linux boot loader, GRUB – if that happened, it would be impossible to boot back into Linux. The boot disk helps us tackle such situations by providing an alternative way to boot into Linux.

You don't have to create a boot disk, but we recommend that you do (unless you already have a boot disk from a previous installation of this particular operating system):

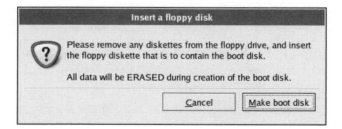

The installer asks you to insert a suitable floppy disk for the boot disk creation process. Remember that the installation process overwrites all the contents of the disk, so you should provide a blank floppy disk or one that doesn't contain any important files:

When you insert the disk and confirm the creation, the installer starts the boot disk creation process. When the boot disk has been created, you should take it out of the floppy drive, label it, and put it in a safe place.

Setting up the GUI

The final step of the installation process is to set up the graphical interface (X) for your computer:

Red Hat Linux should normally be able to detect the type of your video card and select it for you, and it is quite safe to accept the default values. If you want to be *sure* that it's got the right configuration, check the setting here against the make, model, and RAM you noted in your hardware checklist, and adjust as necessary.

> Note that if you try experimenting with graphics modes during the X server configuration, you run the risk of crashing the computer, leaving the installation process unfinished. If you have any element of doubt regarding the compatibility of your video card with Red Hat Linux, you should probably skip the X-server installation process by checking the **Skip X configuration** checkbox at the bottom of the screen. You can always configure the X server after the installation.

> If you can't find your video card in the list, you should skip the X server configuration. It's possible to configure your graphics card after the installation. Alternatively, you can try using the generic VESA card from the given list, which is likely to work with most of the unsupported video cards.

Red Hat Linux then proceeds to detect the type of monitor being used. The monitor detected during installation will be highlighted on the screen as shown:

If you don't find your monitor in the list, you can enter the horizontal and vertical sync information in the textbox entries at the bottom of the screen instead.

The video card and the monitor type allow Red Hat to formulate a list of video modes that can be supported on your computer. The video mode is determined by the screen resolution and the color depth (number of colors) in which objects can be shown on screen. The available color depth and resolution choices are displayed by Red Hat Linux in the next screen:

While you can test the chosen setting using the **Test Setting** button, be aware that for graphic cards with partial support by the X-server, improper modes can crash the system and leave the installation process unfinished. If you're not sure about the compatibility of the chosen video card with the X server, you can skip the X configuration and configure it after the installation is finished.

Red Hat Linux also offers you a choice between booting into a text-based interface and a graphical interface. If you haven't had any issues with your graphics card in the installation process until now, you should accept the pre-selected setting of a graphical login.

Finishing

This completes the installation of the Red Hat Linux operating system. Now, you need to remove any CDs and floppy disks from their respective drives, and click on the **Exit** button to reboot the machine:

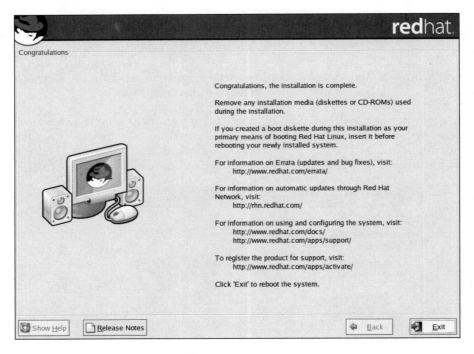

Booting Up

When the computer has restarted, the boot loader takes over initially, as shown in the following screenshot:

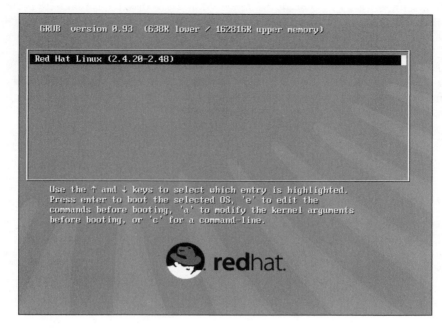

The boot loader shows the available operating systems to boot from. For this chapter we used a new installation, and so there is just a single entry in the list shown above. The selected option will be booted automatically within a few seconds, and you can hasten the process by pressing the *Enter* key. This screen should be followed by a long list of rapidly moving text messages, as Linux boots into its new installation.

First Boot

Before the new installation is fully usable, Red Hat configures the last few parameters:

- ❑   Setting up new user accounts
- ❑   Setting the date and time
- ❑   Configuring the system for the Red Hat Network
- ❑   Selecting additional distribution software or documentation to be installed

The welcome screen (which we won't show here) shows the list of parameters to be configured. Click Forward to move on to the first of these screens.

Creating New User Accounts

We've already talked a little about the root user account – this is an administrative (or "superuser") account that is created by default, and has privileges for performing just about any task that you need on the computer.

The problem with working as root all the time is that these privileges make it very easy to accidentally delete important files that you don't mean to delete. For this reason, it's recommended that you create a "normal" (non-administrative) account for your personal use, and use that most of the time.

The following screen allows you to do that – you just need to choose a username and password, and (if you like) type your full name too:

When you've done that, click Forward to continue.

Setting the Date and Time

Next, check (and if necessary set) the date and time for the computer:

As you can see, this page has a fairly intuitive calendar interface, and you can set the time using the entry fields toward the right of the screen.

Over a period of time, the clock in the computer tends to drift away from the actual time of the computer. To keep the clock in sync, you can use the **Network Time Protocol** (**NTP**) option in the same screen – this allows you to specify an NTP server, and the machine will keep in sync with it.

You can find a public NTP server on the Internet from www.ntp.org.

Registering for the Red Hat Network

The next step is the Red Hat Network configuration. This is a service provided by Red Hat, and is designed to help you keep the computer updated with whatever new packages, improvements, or bug fixes have happened since the Red Hat 9 distribution. For this service to start working, you need to create an account on the Red Hat Network (RHN, http://rhn.redhat.com) and register the computer:

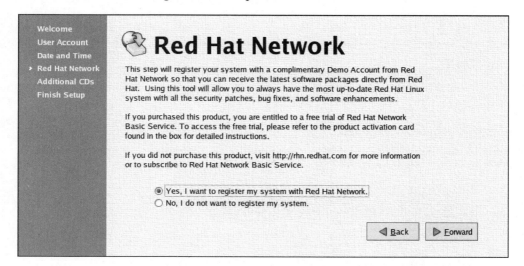

While registering your system in the Red Hat Network is highly recommended, you might decide to defer the registration process (by selecting No...) until the installation process is complete. The Red Hat Network registration process can be invoked again from the desktop menu (Main Menu | System Tools | Red Hat Network) at any time.

Installing Additional Software

We've already had one opportunity to install additional software and documentation from the range of material available on the Red Hat Linux distribution CDs, and now we get another chance. The process now presents us with another opportunity:

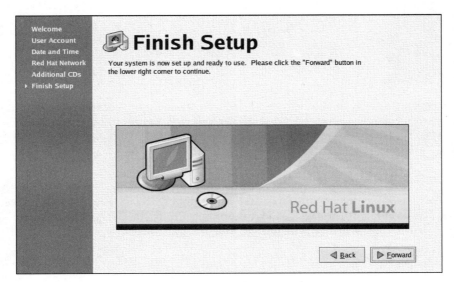

If you have a documentation CD (for example, the one that is included in the box set distribution), it's a good idea at this stage to install the documentation contained within it (that's the top Install button). The subsequent dialogs will talk you through the process, telling you when to insert the CD and so on.

If you like, you can also click the other Install buttons here to install further applications. However, you don't need to do that now; you can install and uninstall applications anytime, via the package manager, as we'll see in Chapter 4.

Completing the Installation Process

Finally, the installation process is over. You can now start to use your brand new desktop – just click Forward one last time:

Logging In

In the login screen, you'll be prompted for a username. Type the username you created earlier on. Here, I'll use the sandipb account I created a few pages back:

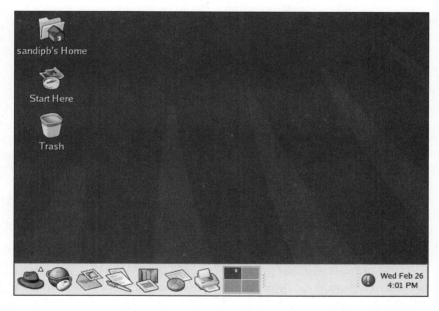

Then you'll be prompted for the password for your user account – enter that too. This will start up the desktop. The default desktop in Red Hat Linux 9 is the **GNOME** desktop. You'll see a user interface like the one shown below, with icons in the top-left corner, and a panel at the bottom:

That's it! The installation is complete, and you're ready to start using the graphical user interface to start making the most out of your Red Hat Linux 9 operating system. We'll begin to explore it in the next chapter.

Summary

In this chapter, we looked at the various steps of the installation of the Red Hat Linux 9 operating system.

We started by noting that the installation process requires various pieces of background information about the hardware and network configuration of the computer, and compiled two checklists of information. The Red Hat Linux installation is easier if you prepare these checklists before you start the installation.

After choosing the native language of the installation, the first important choice you make in the installation itself is the installation type. We chose the Personal Desktop installation type for this chapter, though there are four installation types offered by the installation process.

The installation continues with configuration of the keyboard and mouse, and searches for existing installations – offering you the opportunity to upgrade an existing installation if it finds one. The next choice relates to disk partitioning – the organization of your hard disk into logical partitions. If you feel comfortable with this, you can configure your own partitions; otherwise, you can allow the installation process to do it for you (as we did in this chapter).

After choosing the default boot loader – the software that is used to boot the operating system – we moved on to network configuration options. In single machine situations it's enough to use the default network configuration, but in situations where you plan to connect to a local area network (LAN) it helps to know whether to choose the default setup (which configures the machine to use a DHCP server), or insert specific static details of the IP address, subnet mask, and so on. Of course, you don't have to get these right the first time – if you're not sure or if you get them wrong then you can reconfigure them using the dialogs, any time after the installation is complete.

The next decision relates to the firewall options available for the desktop – again, we decided to go ahead with the default standard firewall for this installation. After setting the time zone, a password for the root user, and adding any additional software we choose to add at this stage, the process of collecting information is complete and the installation can proceed.

After the software installation, we did the sensible thing by creating a boot disk (just in case we have problems with the boot loader). Finally we set up the X-server to give us the GUI of the desktop, and reboot the machine, and this completes the initial installation of the Red Hat operating system.

On the first boot of the new installation, Red Hat asks us to create a non-administrative user account, check the date and the time on the computer, and register with the Red Hat Update agent (if we like); and it gives us yet another chance to install software and documentation. When this is complete, we can log on to the machine and begin our work!

In the next chapter, we will look at how to use the freshly installed desktop. We will begin to explain important concepts like the file hierarchy and devices, which will help you to work effectively in Linux. We'll look at various components of the desktop and how to customize them, and we'll take a look at how to check the hardware configuration of the machine and how to manage and control processes in the system.

Red Hat Linux 9 Basics

Now that you have installed Red Hat Linux on your machine, you can start to familiarize yourself with your new operating system. Red Hat Linux 9 sports a new interface that is not only aesthetically pleasing but also extremely usable. This is all due to the initiative taken by Red Hat to hide the different modes of operation of the open source software that are part of the distribution.

The result is an operating system in which applications are neatly organized according to their function, configuration can be handled centrally, and a uniform interface exists among all the applications that are part of the distribution.

Nevertheless, in spite of the intuitive nature of the desktop, there are several concepts to be aware of before you can use the desktop effortlessly and customize it to your needs. This chapter will attempt to familiarize you quickly with the various components of the desktop that you're likely to use frequently. Many of the concepts that we cover briefly in this chapter will subsequently be explained in greater depth in later chapters of the book.

By the end of this chapter, you will have a good idea of how to:

- ❑ Navigate throughout the desktop and access the various applications that you will require for your work
- ❑ Navigate through the files in your desktop using either a graphical user interface (GUI) or a command line interface (CLI)
- ❑ Examine and adjust the hardware configuration of your installation
- ❑ Manage the various processes running on your system
- ❑ Manage the users on your system

Moving Around the Desktop

The first view of the desktop after you log in is the typical interface of the GNOME desktop. GNOME is the default desktop interface for Red Hat Linux 9, and the one that we'll use throughout this book. This is what it looks like when you see it for the first time:

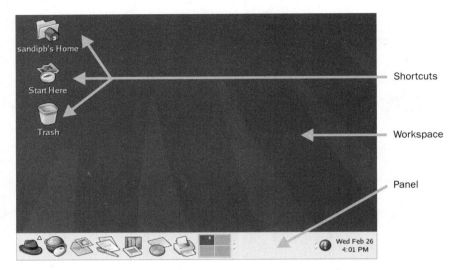

There are other desktop interfaces. One such is the KDE desktop, which is included in the Red Hat Linux 9 distribution but not installed by default. To install it, you'll need to install the necessary KDE packages. We'll talk about package installation that is discussed in Chapter 4, although we'll prefer GNOME to KDE in this book.

Before we begin discussing the desktop, let us quickly familiarize ourselves with the two main components of this desktop interface:

❑ **The panel:** This is the complete gray rectangular box at the bottom of the screen. It contains various shortcut buttons (which launch applications when clicked), a menu that provides access to more applications, a workspace switcher, an application tab bar, a status notification bar, and the date-time applet. As we'll soon see, it's quite easy to modify the panel, by adding more options to the menu, more applets, and other application shortcut buttons.

❑ **The workspace:** This is the large area that makes up most of the screen. When you run (or **launch**) a GUI application, it becomes visible in the workspace. By default, Red Hat Linux places a few application shortcuts (or launchers) on the workspace – the screenshot above shows three such shortcuts in the top left of the workspace. As you'll see later, it's easy to add your own shortcuts too.

Let us look at the panel more closely in the next figure. If you click on the red hat icon at the left-most end of the panel (the **Main menu** button), you bring up the main desktop menu. This menu offers an organized set of applications that can be launched from the desktop, as you can see here:

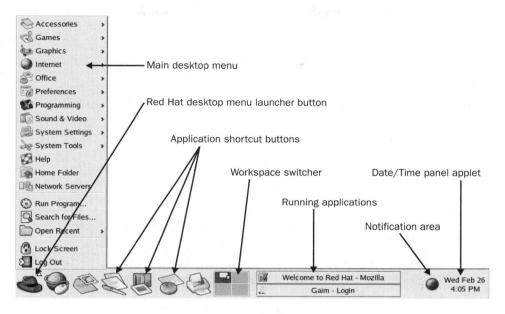

Going from left to right along the remainder of the panel:

❑   The next six items of the panel are shortcut buttons for various frequently used applications – browsers, mail applications, word processors, spreadsheets, and a printer manager. We'll return to these shortly, and see how to add our own shortcuts here.

❑   The curious-looking square (with four equal divisions in it) is the **workspace switcher**, which we shall explain shortly.

❑   Next we have the application task bars, which provide a convenient way of switching between whatever GUI applications are currently running in the workspace. The image above shows two applications running – the Mozilla web browser, and the Gaim instant messenger application.

❑   At the right-most end of the panel we have the **notification area**, where various applications can indicate their status using icons:

❑   The red round icon with an exclamation sign is the Red Hat Network Agent icon, which is indicating critical updates pending for your desktop.

❑   Finally, we have the **date and time applet**, which displays the current date and time in the desktop.

As you can probably tell from what you've seen so far, the look and feel of this interface should be familiar to users of other GUI-based operating systems. However, Red Hat Linux boasts several additional features in this interface. For example:

❑ The main menu can be accessed not only from the panel, but from *anywhere* on the workspace. You can bring up the main menu near the mouse pointer at any time, by typing the keys *Alt-F1*.

❑ All GUI applications that you execute run in the workspace of the screen, and to switch between GUI applications, you can click on the corresponding bar on the panel. Of course, it's easy to fill up the workspace with various executing GUI applications, so to avoid overcrowding, Red Hat Linux offers you a number of workspaces. By default, you have four such workspaces to work with. The **workspace switcher** (on the panel) allows you to switch from one workspace to another.

So this allows you to have, say, a web browser and an instant messenger open in one workspace, and a spreadsheet open in a different workspace. In such a case, your workspace switcher would give you a tiny preview of the applications running on the various desktops, as shown in the figure given below:

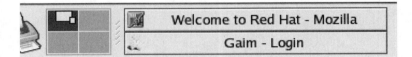

The workspace switcher shows the current active workspace by shading it blue, while the others are shaded gray. Only the GUI applications and their respective task bars in the active workspace are visible at any time. You can switch to a different workspace by clicking on the corresponding workspace in the switcher.

Also note that the workspace switcher itself is configurable. If you right-click on the workspace switcher and select Preferences, you'll get a dialog that allows you to control the number of workspaces and the way they're displayed in the panel.

❑ The panel allows you to add small applications (called **applets**) in the panel itself. In fact the workspace switcher and the date/time sections of the panels are both small applets that are designed to reside in the panel.

Using Applications

Of course, a desktop is meant as a place for launching applications for your various needs. Red Hat Linux offers you several ways to launch applications, and in this section we'll discuss four techniques.

Using the Main Menu

Major applications and configuration programs for your desktop have been neatly organized into various categories in the main menu as shown below:

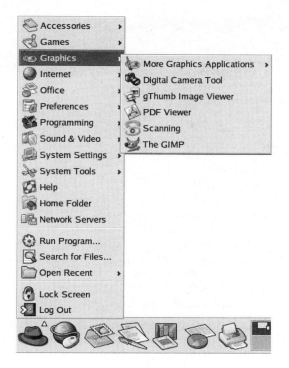

The applications that you find here are the applications that Red Hat recommends as the first choice for users. There are many other applications in the distribution, some of which duplicate the functionality of the applications found here. Some of them are installed by default and can be invoked using the other techniques given in this list; others must be installed (perhaps using the RPM utility that we'll use extensively in Chapter 4). For example, there are various mail clients included in the distribution (Evolution, balsa, sylpheed, and others); but only Evolution has been installed and placed in the menu as the mail client to use.

> *It was the habit of earlier versions of Red Hat Linux to list many similar applications together in the menus. This used to confuse new users because they had no idea which application was the right one to use for a job. To remove such confusion, Red Hat Linux 9 lists only one application of each function in the menu.*

So, you really are spoilt for choice for applications in Red Hat Linux. More than one choice of application exists for every function. In Chapters 4 and 5 you'll learn more about discovering the different applications available in the distribution, and how to install them if necessary.

Using the Run Program... Menu Item

You may have noticed the Run Program ... menu option near the bottom of the main menu that we saw in the screenshot above. When you select this option, you get a dialog box like the one shown below, within which you type in the name of the application you want to launch:

Run Program

xterm

☐ Run in **t**erminal   Append File...

▷ Known Applications

🔘 **H**elp   ✖ **C**ancel   🔗 **R**un

This option is particularly useful when the application you want is installed on your machine but not present in the menu. It's also handy if you know the name of the program you want to invoke but you don't know where it is in the desktop menu. The Run Program... dialog can also be invoked by using the shortcut key combination *Alt-F2*.

Sometimes, it's not sufficient to specify only the name of the application, and you must specify its location as well. This distinction is related to the value of an environment variable called $PATH, which we'll discuss later in this chapter.

Using a Panel Shortcut to an Application

You can also create shortcuts to your most frequently used programs, and place them on the panel for single-click invocation. As we've seen already, the default Red Hat Linux 9 installation comes pre-configured with six such shortcut buttons as shown below:

The first icon on the panel shown here is that of the Main Menu launcher. The next six icons are shortcuts to six commonly used applications. From left to right these are:

- ❑ GUI web browser: This is pre-configured to launch the Mozilla web browser for browsing the Internet

- ❑ Mail client: The Evolution mail client for accessing your mail

- ❑ Word processor: The Open Office Writer word processing program for writing documents

- ❑ Presentation software: The Open Office Impress presentation software

- ❑ Spread sheet software: The Open Office Calc spreadsheet application

- ❑ Print manager: This enables you to manage your printer connections and print jobs

We'll discuss the browser, mail client, and office applications in more detail in Chapter 5.

Adding New Shortcuts to the Panel

You can add new shortcuts into the panel too. The easiest way is to right-click with your mouse somewhere on the panel (but not on top of any existing shortcuts or applets), and select Add to Panel | Launcher from menu. This will open up the desktop menu, allowing you to select the application that you wish to add to the panel. The following image shows how to add a launcher for the Gaim instant messaging client to the panel:

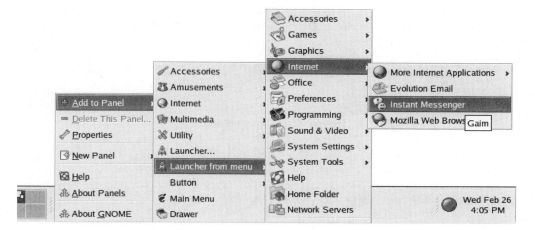

This will add the launcher to the panel, as shown below:

Changing the Size of the Shortcut Icons

If you're not happy with the size of the shortcut icons in the panel, you can adjust them by right clicking on the panel and selecting Properties. Then, in the Edge tab of the resulting dialog, select the appropriate value in the Size field (the default value is Medium).

Using a Terminal Emulator

Perhaps one of the most common methods employed by seasoned Linux users is the **terminal emulator** interface. This is an interface in which we can invoke GUI and non-GUI applications by typing out the complete command. The interface in a terminal emulator is completely character-based and non-graphical. When you invoke a GUI program from the terminal, the operation system opens up a separate GUI window for the program you've invoked.

> *Since all the work done in a terminal emulator requires character based command input, the terminal emulator is also known as the **command line interface** (or **CLI**). It's also often referred to simply as the **terminal**.*

There are many terminal emulators in existence, such as the gnome-terminal and xterm. In this book we'll make significant use of the gnome-terminal emulator that comes with Red Hat Linux. To invoke this particular terminal emulator, you can open up a Run program... window (by pressing *Alt-F2*) and type in the name gnome-terminal; or select Main Menu | System Tools | Terminal.

When you invoke gnome-terminal in this way, you get a terminal-like window that looks like the one shown here. You can now start typing away the name of the programs that you want to execute. In this screenshot you can see that we've executed the program ls with the options -al to show all the files in the current directory:

```
sandipb@localhost:~                                                    _ □ ✕

 File   Edit   View   Terminal   Go   Help

[sandipb@localhost sandipb]$ ls -al
total 132
drwx------   12 sandipb   sandipb      4096 Feb 12 13:50 .
drwxr-xr-x    7 root      root         4096 Feb 12 13:47 ..
drwxr-xr-x    3 sandipb   sandipb      4096 Feb 12 13:50 8473
-rw-r--r--    1 sandipb   sandipb        24 Aug 23 21:01 .bash_logout
-rw-r--r--    1 sandipb   sandipb       191 Aug 23 21:01 .bash_profile
-rw-r--r--    1 sandipb   sandipb       124 Aug 23 21:01 .bashrc
-rw-r--r--    1 sandipb   sandipb       854 Aug 29 00:57 .emacs
-rw-------    1 sandipb   sandipb        16 Feb 12 13:48 .esd_auth
-rw-rw-r--    1 sandipb   sandipb     38800 Feb 12 13:48 .fonts.cache-1
drwx------    5 sandipb   sandipb      4096 Feb 12 13:48 .gconf
drwx------    3 sandipb   sandipb      4096 Feb 12 13:54 .gconfd
drwxrwxr-x   17 sandipb   sandipb      4096 Feb 12 13:49 .gimp-1.2
drwx------    5 sandipb   sandipb      4096 Feb 12 13:48 .gnome
drwxr-xr-x    5 sandipb   sandipb      4096 Feb 12 13:49 .gnome2
drwx------    2 sandipb   sandipb      4096 Feb 12 13:48 .gnome2_private
drwxr-xr-x    2 sandipb   sandipb      4096 Feb 12 13:48 .gnome-desktop
-rw-r--r--    1 sandipb   sandipb       120 Sep 10 20:00 .gtkrc
-rw-rw-r--    1 sandipb   sandipb       138 Feb 12 13:48 .gtkrc-1.2-gnome2
-rw-------    1 sandipb   sandipb       189 Feb 12 13:48 .ICEauthority
drwx------    3 sandipb   sandipb      4096 Feb 12 13:49 .metacity
drwxr-xr-x    3 sandipb   sandipb      4096 Feb 12 13:48 .nautilus
-rw-------    1 sandipb   sandipb       497 Feb 12 13:49 .rhn-applet.conf
-rw-------    1 sandipb   sandipb       213 Feb 12 13:48 .Xauthority
-rw-------    1 sandipb   sandipb        93 Feb 12 13:48 .xsession-errors
[sandipb@localhost sandipb]$
```

Pros and Cons of the CLI

Using a CLI has advantages over the GUI, but it has disadvantages too:

❑   To execute programs in this interface, you need to know their names. Unlike a GUI menu interface where the available options are visible, the CLI doesn't offer such ready convenience.

❑ However, a GUI is generally limited by the amount of space available in the display screen. Even after proper organization using menus, it is difficult to put each and every program of the operating system at your reach, and too many levels of menu makes accessing a given program more long winded. In contrast, using a CLI you can reach at all the programs that are available.

Ultimately, the CLI offers the strength and the flexibility to give you more complete control over the computer, and if you're performing a lot of similar tasks then it has the potential to improve your productivity over using the GUI. There is a learning curve – mainly related to learning the names of the programs and the appropriate parameters – but this effort generally pays off. To point you in the right direction, here are a couple of handy tools that will help you get started with CLI applications.

Finding the Right Program

Knowing the right program to use for a particular job is the kind of thing you tend to learn from experience. Of course, to begin with you need help, and there are a number of ways to find out the names of the programs you need.

One handy utility is the `apropos` program, which can be used to list system commands whose descriptions contain the keywords you specify. For example, the screenshot below shows the `apropos` program being used to find a text editor application:

```
sandipb@localhost:~                                                    _ ☐ ✕
 File  Edit  View  Terminal  Go  Help
[sandipb@localhost sandipb]$ apropos editor
atobm [bitmap]      (1x)  - bitmap editor and converter utilities for the X Window System
bitmap              (1x)  - bitmap editor and converter utilities for the X Window System
bmtoa [bitmap]      (1x)  - bitmap editor and converter utilities for the X Window System
ed                  (1)   - text editor
ed [red]            (1)   - text editor
editres             (1x)  - a dynamic resource editor for X Toolkit applications
gedit               (1)   - small and lightweight text editor for Gnome
psed                (1)   - a stream editor
psed [s2p]          (1)   - a stream editor
red                 (1)   - text editor
red [ed]            (1)   - text editor
sed                 (1)   - a Stream EDitor
vim                 (1)   - Vi IMproved, a programmers text editor
vim [ex]            (1)   - Vi IMproved, a programmers text editor
vim [rvi]           (1)   - Vi IMproved, a programmers text editor
vim [rview]         (1)   - Vi IMproved, a programmers text editor
vim [rvim]          (1)   - Vi IMproved, a programmers text editor
vim [vi]            (1)   - Vi IMproved, a programmers text editor
vim [view]          (1)   - Vi IMproved, a programmers text editor
xedit               (1x)  - simple text editor for X
xpeek               (8)   - shell-type JFS file system editor
[sandipb@localhost sandipb]$
```

As you can see, there are a number of different types of editors here! For example, the text editor program called vim, shown in the list above, is an extremely powerful and popular editor (in fact, there are a number of incarnations of vim, which is why there are so many entries for it in the list above). In later chapters of this book, we'll make use of the gedit text editor.

Learning How to Use a Program

To find out more about a command, you can use the man command, which gives you a **program manual** for that command. For example, if you want to know more about the vim editor, you can type the following at the command line:

```
$ man vim
```

This will show the following output:

```
sandipb@localhost:~

File  Edit  View  Terminal  Go  Help
VIM(1)                                                           VIM(1)


NAME
        vim - Vi IMproved, a programmers text editor

SYNOPSIS
        vim [options] [file ..]
        vim [options] -
        vim [options] -t tag
        vim [options] -q [errorfile]


        ex
        view
        gvim gview
        rvim rview rgvim rgview

DESCRIPTION
        Vim  is a text editor that is upwards compatible to Vi.  It can be used
        to edit all kinds of plain text.  It is especially useful  for  editing
        programs.

        There  are a lot of enhancements above Vi: multi level undo, multi win-
        dows and buffers, syntax highlighting, command line  editing,  filename
```

To see the next page of this document, you press the space bar; in fact you can navigate up and down the document using the arrow keys. To exit the manual (and return to the command line prompt), press *q*.

In fact, the manual comes in a number of sections; some keywords have more than one entry, and in that case you may need to specify the correct section. For example, Section 1 covers user commands, and so the following will give you the manual page that describes the passwd command:

```
$ man 1 passwd
```

By contrast, Section 5 covers file formats, so this next command will give you the manual page that describes the /etc/passwd file:

```
$ man 5 passwd
```

For a quick overview of all the sections in the manual, try the following command, where *N* is the section number you are interested in:

```
$ man N intro
```

Using a Program

Once you have understood how to use a program, you can execute it from the terminal. In time, you might find it more convenient to use the terminal rather than the Main Menu. In that case, you might need to know the program names that correspond to the menu items – so here's a trick that allows you to do that easily:

1. Find the menu item by clicking the Main Menu button and then navigate to the item in question.

2. Don't select the item, but right-click on it instead. In the resulting submenu, select the Put in run dialog option. This opens up a Run program... dialog with the corresponding command name in it:

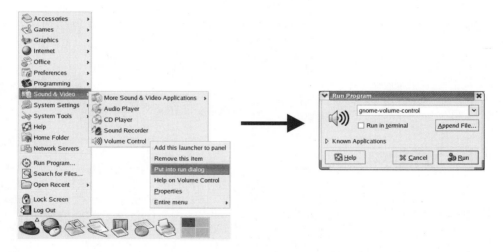

The screenshot above shows how this happens when we use this technique on the Volume Control menu option. The corresponding Run Program dialog shows that the CLI command to invoke this program is actually gnome-volume-control.

Once you've learned the command name for a particular program, you use it to execute the program from the terminal.

Shutting Down the Computer

One of your more immediate needs will be to find out the way in which you can shut down the machine when you are done, or to restart it for some reason. Moreover, it might be necessary to log out of your desktop when you are finished, so that some other user can use the computer to log in and do their work.

The options for logging out and shutting down are all controlled by the Main Menu | Log out option.

If you select Log Out, your current desktop session will terminate, and the login screen will appear – allowing you or another user of the machine to log in and use the desktop. The options Shut Down and Restart the computer are self-explanatory – they allow you to shut down the machine or to restart it.

> These are the recommended options for shutting down and restarting the machine, to ensure safety of data and to keep the operating system running reliably into the future.

Note the Save current setup checkbox at the top of the dialog. For each of these options, if you select this checkbox then Linux will save the desktop settings before logging you out. The main advantage of this option is that the desktop will make a note of the running applications, and the next time you log in it will try to restart those applications.

The File System

For users migrating from a non-Unix-based operating system (such as any Microsoft Windows OS), Linux's organization of files, directory, disk drivers, and other devices takes a little getting used to. Red Hat Linux, being a flavor of Unix, organizes files the Unix way – using one grand **hierarchy of directories**. In this section, we will look at the file system hierarchy and how to use the file system in our work; and we will study the file system in further detail in Chapter 7.

The File System Hierarchy

In the Linux operating system, every file, directory, and device is one part of a grand hierarchy. The topmost member of this hierarchy is the **root directory**, and it is denoted by the symbol /. A subdirectory of a given directory is denoted by the concatenation of the names of the parent directory and the child directory. For example:

❑ There is a subdirectory called usr under the root directory, and we denote the full path to that subdirectory by the expression /usr

❑ A subdirectory of the usr directory named local can be denoted by the expression /usr/local

This simple hierarchy of directories can be represented by the following tree diagram:

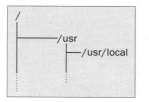

Files within a directory are named similar to subdirectories. In fact, behind the scenes a directory is just a special kind of file, which contains the names of the files inside it and their respective locations on the disk.

Note that the directory separator character in Red Hat Linux is /, while in Windows it is \.

Listing the Contents of a Directory

You can find out the contents of a directory by using the ls command. The following screenshot shows the output when invoking the ls command with the root directory (/) as its argument:

```
sandipb@localhost:~
File  Edit  View  Terminal  Go  Help
[sandipb@localhost sandipb]$ ls /
bin   dev  home    lib          misc  opt   root  tmp  var
boot  etc  initrd  lost+found   mnt   proc  sbin  usr
[sandipb@localhost sandipb]$
```

In general, the ls command takes an argument, which we can use to specify the file or directory to be displayed. If we specify a directory (as we did in the screenshot above), then the ls command will display the files contained in that directory.

For a detailed description of the different ways in which you can customize the output of the ls command, take a look at the program manual by typing man ls at the command line.

The Red Hat Linux file system consists of thousands of directories and files arranged in the hierarchy described above. Within this hierarchy, all the various programs and data files on the system are carefully organized into directories. The directories have generally been organized with the purpose of keeping related programs and files together. For example, the directory /bin contains the essential binary (or executable) programs available to all users, while the directory /sbin contains the binary programs essential to the super user (or root user – the user who has complete administrative control of the system).

> *Of late, Red Hat and all major Linux distributions are trying to conform to the Filesystem Hierarchy Standard (FHS). This standard tries to bring a uniform file organization to the Linux world (which, until some years back, was plagued by different file organizations in the various distributions). You can learn more about FHS at* **http://www.pathname .com/fhs/.**
>
> *The current specification, available at* **http://www.pathname.com/fhs/2.2/,** *explains the various standard directories to expect in a Linux system and the type of files that they are supposed to contain. That said, Red Hat still has some distribution-specific directories that you won't find in other Linux distributions.*

You can see some of the regular directories in the system in the directory tree given below:

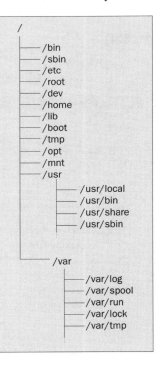

The Top-level Directories

A moment ago, we used the `ls` command to list the contents of the root (/) directory, and we found 17 subdirectories. Each of these top-level directories has a very specific purpose, and you will encounter at least some of them very frequently. Let's take a look at some of these directories now, and find out what they're for:

Directory	Description
/bin /usr/bin	Contain programs available to all users.
/sbin /usr/sbin	Contain programs meant to be used by system administrators.
/var/log	Contains the log files made by various applications. The log files are invaluable in keeping track of applications' activities and errors.
/home	Contains all the personal directories of the users of the system.
/boot	Contains the files needed by the operating system to load itself into memory.
/etc	Contains the system configuration files used by various applications.
/mnt	Contains the mount points for any removable devices in the system (such as CD-ROMs, floppy disks, and network drives).
/proc	Contains the system state information. The information in the files of this directory is maintained directly by the operating system kernel.

Invoking a Program by Using Its Path

When you launch a terminal, the terminal in turn executes a command interpreter program called the **shell**. In fact, the command prompt that you see in the terminal is generated by this shell program – the shell outputs this command prompt, and then waits for you to type in a command. When you launch a program from the prompt, the shell searches for it within the file system, and then executes it.

You can execute programs by typing out their **full path name** at the terminal prompt, like this:

```
$ /bin/ls
```

Alternatively, you can simply use the program's name like this:

```
$ ls
```

The second of these two commands does not specify the exact location of the ls program, and so the shell searches for the program among a specific set of locations. These locations are specified by a special environment variable, known as the **search path**. An environment variable consists of a name and a value, and is maintained by the shell for use by programs executed with it. The name of the search path environment variable is $PATH, and you can find out its value by executing the following command:

```
$ echo $PATH
/usr/local/bin:/usr/bin:/bin:home/sandipb/bin
```

As you can see, the value of $PATH consists of a number of directories, separated by : characters. If you launch a program by typing only its file name (rather than its full path name) then the shell will try to find the program among the directories names in your path.

The value of your $PATH variable will depend on what account you're using. By default, Linux discourages normal users from executing certain programs, such as the various administrative programs located in the directories /sbin and /usr/sbin that are intended for execution only by the superuser (the root account). The way Linux does this is to omit these directories from any normal user's $PATH (as in the example above) – so that they cannot invoke these programs without specifying the full path name.

Even if you do try to invoke an administrative program from a non-root account, you will still be challenged to authenticate yourself as a root user before the program will run. This has the added effect of reminding you that you're accessing an administrative program, and to take the appropriate care when doing so.

Finding a Program's Location

The which command allows you to find the location of programs contained within any of the directories listed in the $PATH variable. In the following example, we use which to find the location of the vim text editor:

```
$ which vim
/usr/bin/vim
```

The whereis command is also useful for locating programs. This command also allows you to find the location of programs that are not contained in directories listed in $PATH. In the example below, you can see how which and whereis behave differently:

```
$ which ifconfig
/usr/sbin/which: no ifconfig in /usr/local/bin:/usr/bin:/bin:home/sandipb/bin
$ whereis ifconfig
ifconfig: /sbin/ifconfig /usr/share/man/man8/ifconfig.8.gz
```

Here, which is unable to locate the ifconfig program because ifconfig is not located within any of the locations specified by the $PATH. However, whereis locates two files by the name of ifconfig: one (/sbin/ifconfig) is the program we're looking for, and the other is the file that contains the pages of the manual that cover ifconfig.

Adding Devices to the Filesystem

In Linux, almost every device is treated as a file. This concept might be a bit unusual to you if you're more familiar with other non-Unix operating systems like the Windows family, but you'll quickly get used to it.

The idea behind this is to provide a uniform interface to all resources – whether that resource is a hard disk, a serial device, a floppy disk, the sound card, or even the TV tuner! The notable exceptions in this concept are the network devices, which are handled differently by the operating system.

Mounting a Device

For users coming from a Windows background, there are some notable differences here. In Linux, the different hard disks and their partitions are not considered as different "drives." Instead, when we need to use such a device, it is **mounted** to a directory within the file system hierarchy (which is called its **mount point**). Mounting a disk drive causes its own filesystem to appear as a child of the directory on which the device is mounted. Then, the content of the disk drive can be accessed by navigating the directory hierarchy, just like any other file in the file system.

For example, suppose we have a floppy disk that contains a single directory, /doc, and that this directory contains a single file called readme.txt. We can make the contents of this floppy disk accessible by *mounting* the floppy disk (say, to the computer directory /mnt/floppy). Then, the file readme.txt will be accessible using the path /mnt/floppy/doc/readme.txt:

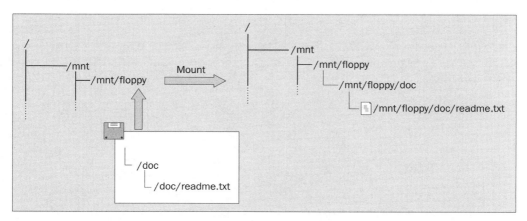

Thus, when the floppy is mounted, it appears to be joined seamlessly to the file system – even though it is an entirely different type of media than the hard disk on which the main file system is situated. By convention, we create mount points in the /mnt directory – for example, we might mount a floppy disk onto /mnt/floppy or a CD-ROM onto /mnt/cdrom.

Representation of Devices on the System

Every device on the system is represented by a file in the /dev directory. For example:

❑ The first floppy drive in the computer is represented by the **device special** file, /dev/fd0

❑ The first master IDE hard disk or CD-ROM is represented by the file /dev/hda

❑ The first audio DSP device of the computer is represented by the file /dev/dsp

❑ The first video capture device is represented by the file /dev/video

❑ Similarly, the first serial port of the computer is /dev/ttyS0

Not all devices are mountable. Only devices that can contain a recognized file system are mountable. For example, floppy, CD-ROM, IDE, and SCSI hard disks generally contain file systems to store their data, and can hence be mounted onto the file system of the computer.

Mounting a Device Automatically

The Red Hat Linux desktop has an application called magicdev, which detects media in the disk drives and mounts them automatically. Whenever you insert a data CD into the CD-ROM drive of your Red Hat desktop, magicdev will:

❑ Detect it and mount it on the directory /mnt/cdrom

❑ Open a GUI filesystem explorer (called Nautilus), with the contents of this directory displayed in it

❑ Create a desktop shortcut button for quick access to the contents of the CD

For example, if you put your Red Hat Linux 9 Documentation CD into your CD-ROM drive, magicdev auto-detects it and displays a Nautilus file system explorer window and desktop shortcut like this:

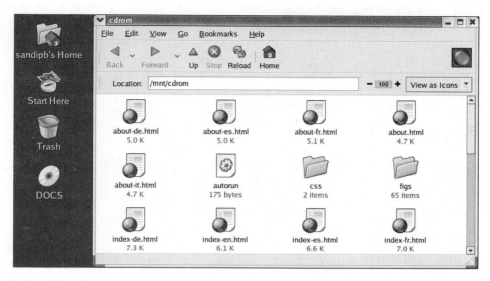

Ejecting a Mounted CD

Once the CD-ROM is mounted, the CD-ROM driver **locks** it into the drive. This means that you won't be able to eject the disc by pressing the *Eject* button on the CD-ROM drive! To eject a mounted CD, you can right-click with your mouse on the desktop shortcut of the CD and click the Eject option in the resulting menu:

This will unmount the CD from the mount point and eject the disk.

Mounting and Unmounting from the Command Line

You can also perform the tasks of mounting and unmounting from the command line. To mount a CD-ROM onto the file system, you can use the mount program. The mount program needs to be told the device that has to be mounted, the file system that is present on it, and the mount point (the point in the existing file system where the device needs to be mounted). For example, the following command takes the CD contained in the CD-ROM drive /dev/cdrom, and mounts it at the mount point /mnt/cdrom:

```
$ mount -t iso9660 /dev/cdrom /mnt/cdrom
```

Some of the parameters for mounting a CD in a Red Hat Linux desktop are pre-configured and stored in the system configuration file /etc/fstab. Therefore, you will need to execute only the following command to mount the CD-ROM on the mount point /mnt/cdrom:

```
# mount /mnt/cdrom
```

To mount the CD-ROM on a mount point other than /mnt/cdrom, you can no longer rely on the pre-configured information and have to give all the information to the mount program. For example, to mount the CD-ROM on the mount point /mnt/cdrom1, you need to execute the following command:

```
$ mount -t iso9660 /dev/cdrom /mnt/cdrom1
```

This instructs the mount program to mount the CD-ROM device /dev/cdrom onto the mount point /mnt/cdrom1. It also specifies the filesystem to be iso9660, which is present on most standard CD-ROM media.

You can find all the parameters that can be passed to the mount program in the corresponding manual page by executing the command man mount at the terminal.

To unmount devices from the file system, you need to execute the umount program. The umount program takes only one parameter – the mount point of the device. For example, the following command unmounts the CD-ROM disc from its mount point:

```
$ umount /mnt/cdrom
```

For unmounting a device from the filesystem, it is absolutely necessary that no application is currently using the device filesystem data. If the device is being used at the time of the unmount process, the process will be unable to unmount the device you specified.

Navigating in the File System

This section will help you navigate the file system and all the files in your computer. The file system can be navigated using either a GUI file explorer (such as **Nautilus**) or the terminal.

Navigating Using the GUI

To start the GUI file explorer, you will have to execute the Nautilus file manager. A quick way to start Nautilus is to select it from the menu, by choosing **Main Menu | Home Folder**. This will open up the Nautilus file manager, which (as we've already seen) resembles Microsoft's Windows Explorer. When you open the Nautilus file manager in this way, the directory shown in the location bar is your home directory:

*A user's **home directory** is the location in the computer where that user can store their personal data. Many applications store their user-specific configuration and customization data in the home directory. The home directory of the user is by default named after the user login ID and is located under the directory /home. For example, my own personal user account on my machine has the login ID sandipb; the home directory of this account is named sandipb and placed under the directory /home. Thus the complete path to my home directory is /home/sandipb.*

Once it's open, you can type any location into the location bar, and Nautilus will display the contents at that location. Alternatively you can click on the button marked **Up** to make Nautilus display the contents of the parent directory instead. In this way, you can navigate all the way up to the root directory (/), where you will find all the top-level directories of the computer that we met earlier in the chapter. You can then double-click on the directories here to navigate inside them.

Overall, the navigation of the file system using the file manager is very intuitive, and if you have any experience with a GUI-based operating system like Windows then you'll find yourself right at home with Nautilus.

Navigating using the Terminal Emulator

Opening up a terminal emulator window places you at the shell prompt, and in your home directory. As we've already noted, the **shell** is the program that interprets each of the commands that you type at the terminal.

The directory that you are located in at any particular time is called the **current directory** (or **present working directory**). When you first open up the terminal, your current directory is set to be your home directory. At any time, you can find out which directory that is by executing the command pwd:

```
$ pwd
/home/sandipb
```

This example shows the pwd program being used to confirm that the current directory just after opening the terminal application is the user's home directory.

Displaying the Contents of a Directory

To display the contents of a given directory, we can use the ls program that we met earlier in the chapter. If the ls program is executed without any arguments, it displays the files in the present working directory.

If you try this in your home directory, just after installation (before you've created any new files in your home directory), the output of the ls program will give no output (to reflect the lack of content in the directory). However, you should note that the default behavior of the ls program is to *not* display the **hidden files** in a directory. Hidden files are generally used to store user-specific configuration data, and you can usually spot a hidden file because its name begins with the '.' (dot) character.

To display these files you need to use the -a parameter with the ls command. The following example shows how the -a parameter affects the output of the ls command:

```
$ ls
$ ls -a
.     ..     .bash_logout    .bash_profile    .bashrc    .emacs    .gtkrc
.xauthkIUlWu
```

The lack of output from the first command suggests that the directory is empty. However, the output from the second command reveals the existence of a number of hidden files.

Changing the Current Directory

To change the present working directory to a different directory, you need to use the cd command. Executing this command without any parameters changes the working directory to be the user's home directory. Adding a directory name as the parameter causes the working directory to be the one specified. These can be understood from the terminal session shown below:

```
$ cd /usr/bin
$ pwd
/usr/bin
$ cd
$ pwd
/home/sandipb
```

Here, the first cd command changes the current directory to be /usr/bin (as confirmed by the subsequent pwd command). The second cd command changes the current directory to be this user's home directory (which happens to be /home/sandipb).

Searching for Files

There are two different CLI programs that enable us to search for files – locate and find:

❑ The locate program works by building a daily database of files and their respective locations. When a search is conducted, it simply looks up this database and reports the file locations. (However, this database is updated once a day and may not therefore reflect the actual contents of the file system if changes have happened in the last 24 hours.)

❑ The find program, by contrast, doesn't use any database and actually looks inside directories and their subdirectories for files matching the given criterion.

The find program is more powerful because of the wealth of search criteria that it allows in searches. You can see both these commands being used to find a file named pam.ps in the example given below:

```
$ locate pam.ps
/usr/share/doc/pam-0.75/ps/pam.ps
$ find /usr/share/doc -name pam.ps
/usr/share/doc/pam-0.75/ps/pam.ps
```

The find and the locate commands are explained in more detail in Chapter 7.

Red Hat Linux has a separate GUI program for finding files. This program can be executed by selecting the Main Menu | Search for Files option. This opens up the dialog box as shown below:

In this dialog we can specify the name of the file that we want to search for, and the path in which the search should be performed. By clicking Find, the Search Tool will perform a file search based on these criteria and return the name and location of any files found in the directory mentioned in this box and in any of its subdirectories. For example, the figure above shows an attempt to search for a file named readme.txt in any directory under /mnt.

The **Search Tool** also offers more advanced options, which allow us to specify more fine-tuned parameters for the search. This mode is selected by clicking on the **Additional Options** caption. You select the options you want from the drop-down list (shown below), add it to the list, and then specify the parameter of the restriction:

In the screenshot above, we've already added one restriction, stating that we want the search to return only files exceeding 10Kb in size.

Managing the Hardware

The Red Hat Linux installation process automatically tries to detect the available hardware and configure it for use in the desktop. However, sometimes this hardware configuration needs to be fine-tuned, or the auto-detection of hardware during the installation process doesn't work as planned. In such cases it is necessary to know how to adjust the hardware configuration of the desktop manually.

Many of the programs shown in this section are executable only by users with administrative privileges. Therefore, you will be able to perform the various operations shown in this section only if you have access to the root account of your system.

In fact, this is a security feature of the Linux platform – and we will see it often over the course of this book. If you are using the terminal emulator for executing the command, you can switch to a root shell by using the following command:

```
$ su -
```

When prompted, you'll need to enter the root password. For safety and security reasons, it is advisable to avoid using the root account except when you need to perform administrative tasks. We'll discuss this further when we talk about user accounts in Chapter 8.

Finding the Existing Hardware

You can find out the current major hardware configuration of the system by using the **hardware browser**. To launch the hardware browser, select Main Menu | System Tools | Hardware Browser, or type hwbrowser at a command line. The hardware browser searches for the hardware on the system and displays results as shown below:

While the depth of information in this program is not great, it is a good indication of whether a particular device has been detected correctly.

You can gather more information about the hardware by working from the terminal itself. The remainder of this section explains how you can gather information about your system using the CLI. The major areas that we'll consider for investigation in this section are:

Area	Description
CPU	The type of CPU and the amount of processing load
Memory	The amount of memory installed on the system and its usage pattern
Hard disk, CD-ROM, and floppy drives	The disk capacities and their usage status
Network cards	The network devices which are operational and their usage statistics
Mouse	The kind of mouse being used by the system
Keyboard	The kind of keyboard being used by the system
Display	The display card detected by the system and its current usage status.
Various PCI and USB devices	The various devices detected by the system
Sound	The sound card detected and used by the system

Much of the information can be found using special files that are maintained dynamically by the operating system. These files can be found by looking in the /proc directory. The files are special because they are generated "on demand" by the operating system, and do not actually exist on the file system except when requested (for example, by the ls /proc command).

You can view the contents of these files by using the cat command (which prints to the screen the contents of any file whose name is passed as a parameter to it, as we'll see in the next few examples). Alternatively, you could use a text editor such as gedit.

CPU-related Information

The CPU information detected by the operating system can be found by displaying the contents of the file /proc/cpuinfo. This is shown below:

```
sandipb@localhost:~
File  Edit  View  Terminal  Go  Help
[sandipb@localhost sandipb]$ cat /proc/cpuinfo
processor       : 0
vendor_id       : GenuineIntel
cpu family      : 6
model           : 8
model name      : Pentium III (Coppermine)
stepping        : 6
cpu MHz         : 930.355
cache size      : 256 KB
fdiv_bug        : no
hlt_bug         : no
f00f_bug        : no
coma_bug        : no
fpu             : yes
fpu_exception   : yes
cpuid level     : 2
wp              : yes
flags           : fpu vme de pse tsc msr pae mce cx8 sep mtrr pge mca cmov pat pse36 mmx fxsr sse
bogomips        : 1850.04

[sandipb@localhost sandipb]$
```

The `bogomips` value given at the bottom of the display is a rough calculation of the processor's speed, made by the operating system. This figure can be used to get a rough comparison of the relative speeds of two different computers running different processors.

The CPU usage can be found in a number of ways. There is a graphical tool called the **System Monitor** (you can launch it by selecting **Main Menu | System Tools | System Monitor**). The **System Monitor** tab in this application displays the CPU usage over time in a nice graphical format, as shown below:

```
System Monitor
File  Edit  View  Help
Process Listing | System Monitor
% CPU Usage History

CPU Used : 1.00 %

% Memory / Swap Usage History

Memory  Used : 119 MB  Total : 123 MB
Swap    Used : 69.2 MB  Total : 251 MB

Devices
Name          Directory    Used Space   Total Space
//dec3/wrox   /mnt/wrox    36.3 GB      39.4 GB
/dev/hda1     /boot        9.2 MB       98.7 MB
/dev/hda2     /            1.7 GB       18.4 GB
```

Aside from the CPU usage information, the **System Monitor** tab also provides information on usage of memory (RAM and swap) and mounted file systems.

Swap memory isn't actually memory in the conventional sense. It's disk space that the operating system uses to store information temporarily – the operating system swaps data from RAM to the swap memory as necessary. Hence, it functions as if it were extra RAM, and hence allows the operating system to handle programs and data that require more actual RAM than is installed on the machine. The amount of swap memory available is determined by the size of the **swap** *partition created when installing the operating system.*

Using Load Average to Measure CPU Usage

In Linux and other Unix-based operating systems, the CPU usage is often measured in terms of **load average**. Load average is displayed using three numerical values. Put simply, the load average is the average number of processes waiting to be executed by the operating system over a given time interval. Over a period of time, these readings give a good indication of the processing load of the computer at the present instant and in the recent past. You can examine the load average in various ways:

❑ You can examine the contents of the file `/proc/loadavg`. The following screenshot shows the display of such a case:

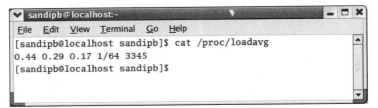

In this example, the first three figures (0.44, 0.29, 0.17) show the load average of the system taken over the last one, five, and fifteen minutes.

❑ You can execute the `uptime` program, as shown below:

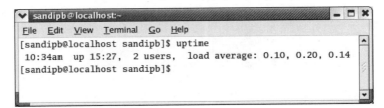

The screenshot above shows output from a machine whose load average is currently very low, and has actually been decreasing over the last fifteen minutes.

The output from this program also shows the amount of time the computer has been running – the screenshot above shows that the machine has been up for nearly fifteen and a half hours. It also shows that there are two terminals with users logged into this machine, and the current time on the system.

❑ You can execute the `top` program. This program shows a wealth of information, as shown in the following screenshot. The display also updates itself every few seconds:

```
sandipb@localhost:~                                                      _ □ ✕
File   Edit   View   Terminal   Go   Help
 10:36am  up 15:29,   2 users,   load average: 0.30, 0.29, 0.18
 65 processes: 63 sleeping, 2 running, 0 zombie, 0 stopped
 CPU states:  3.1% user,  1.1% system,  0.0% nice, 95.6% idle
 Mem:    125924K av,  119736K used,    6188K free,       OK shrd,     840K buff
 Swap:   257032K av,   21244K used,  235788K free                  27800K cached

   PID USER     PRI  NI  SIZE   RSS SHARE STAT %CPU %MEM   TIME COMMAND
   864 root       5 -10 44488   12M  5316 S <   1.7 10.5  32:39 X
  3206 sandipb   15   0 12304   11M  8740 S     0.5  9.4   0:05 gnome-panel
  3351 sandipb   15   0  1032  1032   840 R     0.5  0.8   0:00 top
  3190 sandipb   15   0  6784  6568  5456 S     0.3  5.2   0:07 metacity
  3318 sandipb   15   0  9120  9116  6796 R     0.3  7.2   0:01 gnome-terminal
  3203 sandipb   15   0  1456  1388  1172 S     0.1  1.1   0:00 xscreensaver
  3208 sandipb   15   0 19764   19M 10636 S     0.1 15.4   0:15 nautilus
  3282 sandipb   15   0  3216  3216  2648 S     0.1  2.5   0:00 screenshot
     1 root      15   0   460   424   412 S     0.0  0.3   0:04 init
     2 root      15   0     0     0     0 SW    0.0  0.0   0:00 keventd
     3 root      15   0     0     0     0 SW    0.0  0.0   0:00 kapmd
     4 root      34  19     0     0     0 SWN   0.0  0.0   0:00 ksoftirqd_CPU0
```

The first part of the display shows the load average of the system, and the memory usage in the system. The rest of the display shows the processes running on the system, along with a wealth of information on each process – such as the user privilege under which the process is running, and the process identifier.

This output is also interactive, allowing you to change various properties of the display and even to kill processes. For more on this, take a look at the *Interactive Commands* section of the manual (type `man top` at the command line and space down until you find it).

When you want to exit the `top` display, press *q* on your keyboard.

Memory-related Information

To find information about the total amount of RAM in the system, the amount of swap memory, and their respective uses, you can look at the **System Monitor** dialog (as we saw in the section on CPU usage above). A quick alternative for finding out the status of RAM and swap is to display the contents of the file `/proc/meminfo` as shown below:

```
sandipb@localhost:~                                          _ □ ✖

File   Edit   View   Terminal   Go   Help
[sandipb@localhost sandipb]$ cat /proc/meminfo
          total:      used:     free:  shared: buffers:   cached:
Mem:   128946176 121614336  7331840        0  1773568 37392384
Swap: 263200768 21753856 241446912
MemTotal:        125924 kB
MemFree:           7160 kB
MemShared:            0 kB
Buffers:           1732 kB
Cached:           29020 kB
SwapCached:        7496 kB
Active:           62420 kB
Inact_dirty:      32572 kB
Inact_clean:       2432 kB
Inact_target:     19484 kB
HighTotal:            0 kB
HighFree:             0 kB
LowTotal:        125924 kB
LowFree:           7160 kB
SwapTotal:       257032 kB
SwapFree:        235788 kB
Committed_AS:    100244 kB
[sandipb@localhost sandipb]$
```

The memory usage can also be examined via the **System Monitor** or the top program, as we saw earlier in the section on CPU usage.

Information about the File System Devices

To find information on the mounted file system in the computer, you can use the graphical interface offered by the **System Monitor** (as we saw in the previous section on gathering CPU usage). However, there is also a quick CLI-based way to find similar information, and this involves the df program. A typical usage of the df program is shown below:

```
sandipb@localhost:~                                          _ □ ✖

File   Edit   View   Terminal   Go   Help
[sandipb@localhost sandipb]$ df -h
Filesystem            Size  Used Avail Use% Mounted on
/dev/hda2              18G  1.7G   15G  10% /
/dev/hda1             99M  9.2M   84M  10% /boot
none                  61M     0   61M   0% /dev/shm
/dev/cdrom           271M  272M     0 100% /mnt/cdrom
[sandipb@localhost sandipb]$
```

Here, the -h option displays the output in a more readable format (indicating size in megabytes and gigabytes, rather than bytes).

On the subject of file systems, another useful nugget of information is the list of devices that are mounted and their mount points and filesystem types. This information can be found out by invoking the `mount` command itself, without any arguments:

```
[sandipb@localhost sandipb]$ mount
/dev/hda2 on / type ext3 (rw)
none on /proc type proc (rw)
usbdevfs on /proc/bus/usb type usbdevfs (rw)
/dev/hda1 on /boot type ext3 (rw)
none on /dev/pts type devpts (rw,gid=5,mode=620)
none on /dev/shm type tmpfs (rw)
/dev/cdrom on /mnt/cdrom type iso9660 (ro,nosuid,nodev,user=sandipb)
[sandipb@localhost sandipb]$
```

If you are using a hard disk with multiple partitions and multiple operating systems, it's handy to be able to check the partition structure of your hard disk and the various partition types existing on it. This can be shown using the `fdisk` program, with the `-l` option. The following screenshot shows how to use this program:

```
[sandipb@localhost sandipb]$ su -
Password:
[root@localhost root]# fdisk -l

Disk /dev/hda: 255 heads, 63 sectors, 2481 cylinders
Units = cylinders of 16065 * 512 bytes

   Device Boot    Start      End    Blocks   Id  System
/dev/hda1   *         1     1275  10241406    7  HPFS/NTFS
/dev/hda2          1276     2480   9679162+   f  Win95 Ext'd (LBA)
/dev/hda5          1276     1288    104391   83  Linux
/dev/hda6          1289     1353    552081   82  Linux swap
/dev/hda7          1354     2480   9052596   83  Linux
[root@localhost root]#
```

Note that you need root permissions to access some of this information, so we log in as root using this command:

```
$ su -
```

As you'll recall, the superuser mode is indicated by the change in the prompt – the last character of the prompt changing from a $ sign to a # sign.

Note that the `-l` option shown in the screen above is used to query the hard disk structure, and is quite safe. However, other `fdisk` options are designed for manipulating your hard disk partitions, and incorrect usage of these options can destroy your hard disk data. Therefore:

> **Use the `fdisk` program only with caution.**

Information about the Network Devices

To display information about the network devices configured and running in the system, you can use the `ifconfig` utility as shown below.

```
sandipb@localhost:~                                          _ □ ✕
File  Edit  View  Terminal  Go  Help
[sandipb@localhost sandipb]$ /sbin/ifconfig -a
eth0      Link encap:Ethernet  HWaddr 00:04:76:36:0D:3D
          inet addr:172.16.11.40  Bcast:172.16.11.255  Mask:255.255.255.0
          UP BROADCAST RUNNING MULTICAST  MTU:1500  Metric:1
          RX packets:2478533 errors:0 dropped:0 overruns:1 frame:0
          TX packets:4133 errors:0 dropped:0 overruns:0 carrier:0
          collisions:0 txqueuelen:100
          RX bytes:3167264385 (3020.5 Mb)  TX bytes:490561 (479.0 Kb)
          Interrupt:3 Base address:0xdc00

lo        Link encap:Local Loopback
          inet addr:127.0.0.1  Mask:255.0.0.0
          UP LOOPBACK RUNNING  MTU:16436  Metric:1
          RX packets:349 errors:0 dropped:0 overruns:0 frame:0
          TX packets:349 errors:0 dropped:0 overruns:0 carrier:0
          collisions:0 txqueuelen:0
          RX bytes:33186 (32.4 Kb)  TX bytes:33186 (32.4 Kb)

[sandipb@localhost sandipb]$
```

The `ifconfig` utility is contained in the `/sbin` directory. This directory is listed as part of the root user's `$PATH`, but is not listed (by default) in the `$PATH` of normal user accounts. Therefore, to run `ifconfig` you need either to specify the full path, `/sbin/ifconfig` (as we've done here), or switch to the root user's account and launch it from there (as we did with the `fdisk` utility above).

As you can see, this command displays a lot of network configuration information about the network devices on the computer. Using the `ifconfig` program without any arguments shows the status of only the network devices that are up and running. Adding the `-a` argument (as above) shows all the devices, whether they are running or not.

You can use the output of this command to find out the exact status of these devices. In the example above, we see two network devices – `eth0` and `lo`. The first is an Ethernet device and the second is the local loopback network device. (The loopback device is always present, even when no real network devices exist in the system. This device is necessary for many network applications to work properly.)

So, you can check the *network configuration* of the devices via the `ifconfig` command. However, if you want to find out the *nature* of your networking devices, there are several other utilities at your disposal. One such utility is the **Hardware Browser** program described earlier in this chapter. Another is the `lspci` program, which we run in the CLI, as shown below. The `lspci` program lists all the devices that it finds on the PCI bus of the computer:

```
sandipb@localhost:~                                                      _ □ ✕
File  Edit  View  Terminal  Go  Help
[sandipb@localhost sandipb]$ /sbin/lspci
00:00.0 Host bridge: VIA Technologies, Inc. VT8363/8365 [KT133/KM133] (rev 81)
00:01.0 PCI bridge: VIA Technologies, Inc. VT8363/8365 [KT133/KM133 AGP]
00:07.0 ISA bridge: VIA Technologies, Inc. VT82C686 [Apollo Super South] (rev 40)
00:07.1 IDE interface: VIA Technologies, Inc. VT82C586B PIPC Bus Master IDE (rev 06)
00:07.2 USB Controller: VIA Technologies, Inc. USB (rev 16)
00:07.3 USB Controller: VIA Technologies, Inc. USB (rev 16)
00:07.4 Bridge: VIA Technologies, Inc. VT82C686 [Apollo Super ACPI] (rev 40)
00:07.5 Multimedia audio controller: VIA Technologies, Inc. VT82C686 AC97 Audio Controller (rev 50)
00:0e.0 Ethernet controller: Realtek Semicontudctor Co., Ltd. RTL-8139/8139C/8139C+ (rev 10)
00:0f.0 Multimedia video controller: Brooktree Corporation Bt878 Video Capture (rev 11)
00:0f.1 Multimedia controller: Brooktree Corporation Bt878 Audio Capture (rev 11)
01:00.0 VGA compatible controller: S3 Inc. ProSavage KM133

[sandipb@localhost sandipb]$
```

We can see from the figure above that the only Ethernet controller in this list is a Realtek 8139/8139C/8139C+ model. Note that this output also confirms the other devices on the system – like the audio card, the TV tuner, and the video card of the system. We'll make use of this when we cover these devices later in the chapter.

We can confirm whether this Ethernet controller is the one configured as the eth0 device by checking the network driver loaded for this device. To do this, take a look at the contents of the file /etc/modules.conf. This file specifies the drivers to be loaded for various devices and their corresponding loading parameters:

```
sandipb@localhost:~                                                      _ □ ✕
File  Edit  View  Terminal  Go  Help
[sandipb@localhost sandipb]$ cat /etc/modules.conf
alias parport_lowlevel parport_pc
alias eth0 8139too
alias sound-slot-0 via82cxxx_audio
post-install sound-slot-0 /bin/aumix-minimal -f /etc/.aumixrc -L >/dev/null 2>&1 || :
pre-remove sound-slot-0 /bin/aumix-minimal -f /etc/.aumixrc -S >/dev/null 2>&1 || :
alias char-major-81 bttv
alias usb-controller usb-uhci
[sandipb@localhost sandipb]$
```

In the second line of the file in the figure above we find an instruction for loading the 8139too driver for the eth0 device. This confirms that the eth0 network device is actually a Realtek network card. Incidentally, the third line of this file reveals that the audio card on the machine is a VIA82xxx family audio controller.

Details of the network can be found out by using the netstat and the route programs. The route program displays the network routes active in the system including the gateway through which this desktop sends and receives network traffic from the Internet. The netstat program shows the currently active network connections and networking services that are available on the machine. We'll take a look at netstat in Chapter 12, and you can learn more about route by typing man route at the terminal.

Information about the Mouse and the Keyboard

Red Hat Linux's tool for configuring the mouse is the program `redhat-config-mouse` – you can run this from the command line or by selecting Main Menu | System Settings | Mouse. You will have encountered this program already, because it was run during the installation process. Here's a reminder of what that dialog looks like:

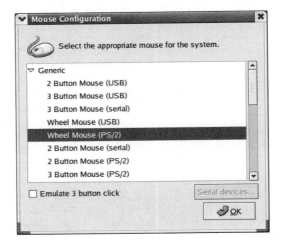

The dialog box shows the present mouse configuration in the system. In the screenshot above, the mouse is a PS/2 based wheelmouse. The program stores the configuration of mouse at `/etc/sysconfig/mouse`, which it uses while starting the mouse driver (called `gpm`) at system startup.

For configuring the keyboard layout, the GUI tool to use is the `redhat-config-keyboard` program. Executing this program brings up the following dialog, which shows your current keyboard layout:

You can also change the keyboard layout from this dialog. The program stores the configuration of the keyboard in the file `/etc/sysconfig/keyboard`. The option that you choose here will ensure that the appropriate keyboard map is loaded at boot time.

Information about the Display

The information about the display card on the system can be found using the `lspci` command (which we mentioned earlier). This generally reveals the actual video hardware on the system. In the `lspci` output (which we also saw earlier), the video hardware was revealed to be a S3 ProSavage card.

The X-Server software is responsible for the basic graphical display of the desktop. This server loads appropriate display drivers according to the video hardware. While recognized good video cards like S3 have hardware-accelerated drivers, unrecognized video cards are put to use by loading generic display drivers which are low on performance. So if you see choppiness in the display, it's possible that your video card has been detected incorrectly, and that a generic display driver like Vesa is loaded.

To check or modify the video card and monitor settings of the display, you can use the Red Hat configuration tool `redhat-config-xfree86` (either by typing this command at the command line or by selecting Main Menu | System Settings | Display). Here is the dialog that you get when this tool is executed:

These dialogs show that the card has been detected correctly and the resolution and the color depth are as expected. You can change these values if you wish. The changes will take effect only when the X server is restarted.

However, they also show that the monitor doesn't seem to be detected correctly. The model name of the monitor is set to a generic Monitor Model, indicating that manual configuration details given during installation are in effect. If you are happy with the display that is generated using these settings, then you can just click OK and exit the program. If you want to adjust the settings to try to get something better, click on the Configure button to select the precise configuration of the monitor and the video card (as you did to configure X server, during installation).

Information about the Sound Card

The sound card configuration tool is redhat-config-soundcard (again, you can run this from the command line, or from the menu shortcut Main Menu | System Settings | Soundcard Detection). This program displays a simple dialog box showing the sound card detected on the system and the kernel sound driver loaded:

You can test the sound configuration by using the Play test sound button.

Information about Various PCI and USB Devices

Information about various other PCI and USB devices can be viewed using the lspci and the lsusb programs. We looked at the lspci program output in an earlier section. As a reminder, here's the output we saw earlier:

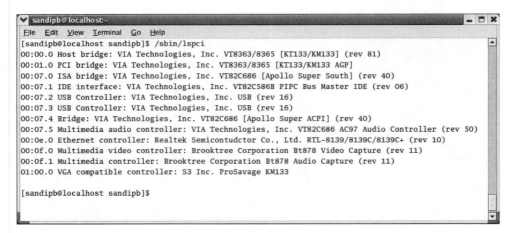

This output allows us to confirm the PCI based hardware in our machine. As an example, we can find out the audio controller card (VT82C686), the Ethernet network controller card (RTL-8139), the video capture card (Bt878), and the graphics card (S3 ProSavage). These details are extremely useful when hardware auto-detection hasn't happened as planned, and you need to tell the configuration program explicitly about the hardware that you want to configure.

The `lsusb` program output lists the characteristics of all the USB devices plugged into the computer. Its output is very verbose and might be too technical for the average user. However, when you hot-plug a USB device, the device characteristics can be verified from the `lspci` output.

Configuring the Desktop

The workspace and the panel all are part of the desktop environment. The default desktop environment that you have used so far is the **GNOME** desktop environment. This environment controls the behavior of the panel and the application GUI windows, session management, and various other behavioral GUI functions. In Red Hat Linux 9, the default GNOME desktop has a new look called the **Bluecurve theme**.

This theme covers all the color design in the menus, the panels, the desktop background, and the window decorations. Of course, this is not the only theme available for use on the desktop, but it is certainly the one on which the Red Hat design team has spent most of their effort. The result is a desktop whose look and feel is far more superior to and aesthetically pleasing than that of its predecessors.

Using the Desktop Control Center

You can control a lot of the features of your desktop using the **GNOME desktop control center**. The control center program displays a number of options to configure the desktop (and if you're familiar with the Windows operating systems, then you'll find that the control center is quite similar to Windows' Control Panel).

You can reach the control center by selecting Main Menu | Preferences | Control Center:

Let's look at the options in this configuration program in more detail.

- ❏ **About Myself:** This allows you to put additional information about yourself into the system – like your name, office, and phone numbers. It also allows you to select a **command shell**. The command shell interpreter that is used by default in Red Hat Linux is bash. We'll look more closely at the bash shell in Chapter 6.

  The information entered in this dialog is stored in the user account database in `/etc/passwd`. You can also enter this information at the terminal by using the `chfn` command. We'll see more about `/etc/passwd` and the `chfn` command in Chapter 8.

- ❏ **Accessibility:** This allows you to enter various accessibility options for users with disabilities. If you select the **Enable keyboard accessibility** checkbox in this dialog, you reveal various options designed to ease the usability of the GUI. For example:

- ❏ The **Enable Mouse Keys** option allows you to use the numeric keypad on the keyboard to control mouse movements. This is useful for users who have difficulty handling the mouse.

- ❏ The **Enable Bounce Keys** option allows you to set the optimum key repeat rate. This is handy for users who have a tendency to hit a key repeatedly when they intend to hit it only once.

- ❏ The **Enable Slow Keys** option allows one to set the keyboard key acceptance period (the time between the keystroke and its acceptance), for users who type successive keys after unusually long intervals.

- ❏ The **Enable Sticky Keys** option allows us to configure the keyboard for users who have difficulties in making the simultaneous keystrokes (such as *Alt-F1*) that are required in many applications.

- ❏ The **Toggle keys** option allows an audible indication to be made whenever a toggle key like *Num Lock* or *Caps Lock* is toggled.

- ❏ **Background:** This allows us to set the background of the desktop. We can set the background to an image file present in the system. Alternatively we can specify the background to be a simple color or a gradient of two colors.

- ❏ **CD Properties:** This allows us to configure the automatic CD detection program `magicdev`. We can ask `magicdev` to mount CD media automatically when the CD is inserted into the drive. We can also specify whether we want to have the file manager open with the CD contents in this case or whether we want the `autorun` program in the CD to be executed automatically.

  This dialog also allows us play audio CDs or DVDs automatically on insertion.

- ❏ **Control Center:** this is just a link to the **Preferences** folder.

- ❏ **File Management:** this allows you to control the appearance of file icons, and their behavior when you click or double-click on them.

❑ **File Types and Programs:** This allows you to set program associations for different file types. You can categorize each file type according to its extension (the portion of the filename after the last period), and tell the operating system what application it should use to open files of each type when the user clicks a file of that type in the Nautilus file manager.

Unlike the Windows operating system, file name extensions don't matter as such in the Linux operating system. A program is considered executable according to the permissions set on the program file, and not according to its file name extension. However, in GUI applications like Nautilus, file name extensions are used not for executing programs but rather for opening data files in appropriate applications.

❑ **Font:** This allows you to set the different fonts for the desktop widgets. It also allows you to specify the rendering of fonts on the desktop.

❑ **Handheld PDA:** For users with Palm or other handheld PDAs, this option allows you to setup synchronization of your local data with that of the PDA. The configuration is done by using an easy wizard-like interface.

❑ **Keyboard:** This allows you to set the behavior of a keyboard key when it's depressed for an extended period (in particular, the length of time that a key must be depressed before it generates repeat signals, and the rate at which a key will repeat). You can also control cursor blinks here.

❑ **Keyboard Shortcuts:** This allows you to set the various keyboard shortcuts that you can use in the desktop (such as the *Alt-F2* shortcut, which invokes the **Run Program** dialog).

❑ **Login Photo:** This allows you to select an image to be used instead of your name at the initial desktop GUI login screen. To see the effect of this, you also have to make changes in the configuration of the Gnome Desktop Manager (GDM) using the program `gdmconfig`. (In the **General** tab, you need to change the local greeter to be the **Standard Greeter** rather than the default **Graphical Greeter**, and in the **Standard Greeter** tab you need to check the **Show choosable user images** checkbox.) The effect of these changes is visible the next time you start GDM. GDM is started at the beginning of each boot.

*To be more accurate, GDM is started each time the **run level 5** is entered – we'll talk more about run levels later on in this chapter. You can change run levels to make GDM restart and show you the changes without rebooting. The standard greeting is however not as attractive as the graphical login which is endowed with the Bluecurve interface.*

❑ **Menus & Toolbars:** This allows you to specify the look of the menus and the button icons.

❑ **More Preferences:** This icon opens up a dialog with three sub-options:

❑ **CD Database:** This sub-option allows us to specify a CD database server for retrieving CD and track information when we play an audio CD in the computer.

❑ **Panel:** This sub-option configures the behavior of the panel in the desktop. You can opt to disable the animation of panels in the desktop or to change their animation speed.

❑ **Sessions:** This sub-option allows you to configure the behavior of the GNOME desktop for maintaining states between successive log-in sessions. The GNOME desktop can save the open applications and their current settings when you log out. When you log back in later, these applications are restarted with their saved settings. Note that the feature of saving settings works only with applications that are compatible with the GNOME desktop environment.

❑ **Mouse:** This allows you to control the mouse behavior in the desktop. You can change the mouse pointer, control its speed and double-click delay, and even set it for use for left handed individuals in which case the right and the left button functionalities are exchanged.

❑ **Network Proxy:** For HTTP clients, this allows you to specify the HTTP proxy details and (optionally) the authentication information to use this proxy server.

❑ **Password:** This allows the current user to change their login password. Note that you can also perform this action at the terminal using the `passwd` program.

❑ **Preferred applications:** This sub-option allows you to select preferred applications for opening web pages and text documents. It also allows you to specify your default terminal emulator application (by default, you can set it to be `gnome-terminal` or `xterm`).

The `gnome-terminal` is more feature-rich than `xterm`, but it's also heavy on memory requirements. When your system is low on RAM, it can make sense to use the `xterm` — which has less memory overhead and also loads quickly. However, it can be beneficial to use `gnome-terminal` when you need multiple terminals. You can get multiple GNOME terminals with just a single launch of the `gnome-terminal` application, but for multiple xterm terminals you need to run `xterm` once for each terminal.

❑ **Screensaver:** This allows you to configure a screen saver for your desktop. You can set a single screen saver, set multiple screen savers, or disable the screen saver completely.

❑ **Sound:** This allows you to associate sound events with desktop events like opening or closing of applications. By default, sound events are disabled. But if you enable them, you can set individual sound files to be played for each desktop event.

❑ **Theme:** The GNOME desktop ships with the Red Hat Bluecurve theme. This dialog allows you to change the theme of the desktop to others available in the menu. Many of these alternative themes are also very attractive and well worth a close look.

❑ **Window Focus:** This option allows you to define the behavior for working with different windows in the desktop. You can opt to either click on a window to work in it, or merely point the mouse pointer inside it to start working in the window.

Managing Processes

To manage a desktop and control its resources, it is very important to grasp the concepts behind **processes** running in the computer. You can think of a process simply as an independent program entity, executing and using computer resources such as CPU time and memory. Any application that is executed is started as an independent process. An application may start its own child processes – and indeed many applications like web servers and database servers have multiple processes to tend to the needs of different clients at the same time.

Understanding Processes

Normally, a process is started by a **parent process**. The newly launched process can in turn launch **child processes** if it wants to. When you are working at the desktop, any new program is executed as a child process of the program that is receiving and interpreting your commands. For example, when you are at the terminal prompt, you are interacting with the shell interpreter program (by default, this is bash). The shell itself is running as a process in the computer. Any program that you execute at the bash prompt is launched as a child process of the bash program.

In fact, every executing program on the computer is a process that has been launched by some other parent process – and hence, all the running processes in the computer can be represented in the form of a hierarchical tree. There is only one exception – the first process of the computer. This is the init program, which is launched by the operating system itself just after booting. Thereafter init **forks** off child processes which in turn may fork off other child processes of their own.

> *Because of the underlying manner in which new processes are launched, the process of launching a child process in the Unix environment is also frequently referred to as forking. When launching a child process, the parent process makes a copy of itself by forking, and then executes the child program in the memory space of the new copy.*

Viewing Running Processes

The System Monitor program that we came across earlier in the chapter also allows us to see the processes running in the machine. You can see this list of processes in the following screenshot:

You can view the processes sorted by any of the columns on display – to do this you just click the respective column header. Here, you can see that we've sorted the processes according to their memory usage.

At the terminal, you can use the ps program to view the processes running in the machine in a non-dynamic way. This program can be invoked in a variety of ways, which you can learn from its man page. However, we will mention some commonly used arguments of this program.

To view all the processes running within your current logging session, you can use the ps program without any arguments. To view all the processes running in the machine, you can use the command ps ax:

```
 ▼  sandipb@localhost:~                                                    _ □ ✕
 File  Edit  View  Terminal  Go  Help
[sandipb@localhost sandipb]$ ps ax
  PID TTY      STAT    TIME COMMAND
    1 ?        S       0:04 init
    2 ?        SW      0:00 [keventd]
    3 ?        SW      0:00 [kapmd]
    4 ?        SWN     0:00 [ksoftirqd_CPU0]
    5 ?        SW      0:01 [kswapd]
    6 ?        SW      0:00 [bdflush]
    7 ?        SW      0:00 [kupdated]
    8 ?        SW      0:00 [mdrecoveryd]
   12 ?        SW      0:00 [kjournald]
   68 ?        SW      0:00 [khubd]
  160 ?        SW      0:00 [kjournald]
  474 ?        S       0:00 /sbin/dhclient -1 -q -lf /var/lib/dhcp/dhclient-eth0.leases -pf /var/ru
  529 ?        S       0:00 syslogd -m 0
  533 ?        S       0:00 klogd -x
  550 ?        S       0:00 portmap
  569 ?        S       0:00 rpc.statd
  650 ?        S       0:00 /usr/sbin/apmd -p 10 -w 5 -W -P /etc/sysconfig/apm-scripts/apmscript
  688 ?        S       0:00 /usr/sbin/sshd
  702 ?        S       0:00 xinetd -stayalive -reuse -pidfile /var/run/xinetd.pid
  725 ?        S       0:00 sendmail: accepting connections
  735 ?        S       0:00 sendmail: Queue runner@01:00:00 for /var/spool/clientmqueue
  745 ?        S       0:00 gpm -t imps2 -m /dev/mouse
  754 ?        S       0:00 crond
  785 ?        S       0:01 xfs -droppriv -daemon
  803 ?        S       0:00 /usr/sbin/atd
  812 tty1     S       0:00 /sbin/mingetty tty1
  813 tty2     S       0:00 /sbin/mingetty tty2
  814 tty3     S       0:00 /sbin/mingetty tty3
```

The `pstree` program is an interesting program to try out – it allows us to view all the processes in the system in a tree format, and hence gives a good idea of the hierarchical nature of processes in the computer. The following shows just a small part of the output of this program, beginning with the `init` process:

```
 ▼  sandipb@localhost:~                                         _ □ ✕
 File  Edit  View  Terminal  Go  Help
[sandipb@localhost sandipb]$ pstree
init-+-apmd
     |-atd
     |-bdflush
     |-bonobo-activati
     |-crond
     |-dhclient
     |-esd
     |-gconfd-2
     |-gdm-binary---gdm-binary-+-X
     |                         `-gnome-session---ssh-agent
     |-gimp---script-fu
     |-gnome-panel
     |-gnome-settings-
     |-gnome-system-mo
     |-gnome-terminal-+-bash
     |                `-bash---pstree
     |-gpm
     |-kapmd
     |-keventd
```

As we saw earlier in the chapter, the terminal also provides the `top` program, which allows us to view the process list in an interactive manner. It shows the process list in a similar way to the GUI system monitor, and allows us to sort the results by pressing various keystrokes. To get more help on the keys to use for sorting the display, you can press the help (?) key.

Taking Control of Running Processes

Sometimes we need to exercise some control on a process to keep our memory or CPU resources in check. A process might take up all the available memory in the system and make the system virtually unusable. In such a case, it might be appropriate to terminate the offending process to regain control of the system. The act of terminating a process is also referred to as **killing** it.

We can use the System Monitor to kill runaway processes. You can select the target process in the list and select the End Process button at the bottom right of the dialog box. Of course, killing a process can result in loss of unsaved data (depending on how you kill it, as we explain below). For this reason, there is a confirmation dialog that allows you to confirm your decision to kill the process:

Note that you can kill a process only if you have permission to – that is, if it's running under your user account or if you have permission to take control of another user's processes. This is a security feature that ensures that a user's processes are safe from being terminated by other users of the machine. The only exception is the root (super user). In the screenshot above, the user called sandipb has complete access and control over all the processes you can see in the process list.

The root user can kill any process of the machine, and therefore it is necessary to take precautions to ensure that (as the root user) you don't kill a process by mistake. To prevent this, it's a good idea not to log in as the root user to the machine and instead to login using a normal user account. Then, whenever you need to perform a task as the root user, you can assume superuser permissions using the following command, as explained earlier in the chapter:

```
$ su -
```

After finishing your immediate job as the root user, you should log out and return to the login shell of the previous user.

We can also use the `top` program to kill processes. We can sort the display of the `top` utility by resource usage (in just the same way as we can sort the processes using the **System Monitor**) – which is useful when a process is taking up too much CPU or memory resource. Sorting the processes in this way brings the offending program to the top of the list and makes it easy to identify. We can then use the process ID of the process to kill it using the `k` command of the `top` program.

Notice that the `top` program asks for a signal number to send to the process. A kill signal is a special message sent to the process by the current process. If you just accept the default option of 15, a signal called `SIGTERM` is sent to the target process asking it to shut down on its own. This allows the target process to shut down cleanly after saving all its unsaved information. However, if the program seems to be ignoring this signal, you can repeat the process sending the signal number of 9 instead – this simply terminates the process without giving it a chance of shutting down on its own.

Understanding Run Levels

When the computer is started up, the operating system loads and starts off the first process – the `init` process. The `init` process then starts off any required sub-processes before the computer is ready to be used by the user. The processes that the operating system needs to start off after the booting process are specified using **run levels**. A run level is a state of the machine, which determines the processes to be run.

There are seven run levels – numbered from 0 to 6 – and they are described below:

❑ **Run level 0** signifies the halted state of a machine. While changing run levels, if you set the new run level to be 0, it effectively halts the machine.

❏ **Run level 1** stands for the **single user mode**. This brings the machine to a super user mode and disallows external users from using the machine. All networking functions are disabled at this level. This level is also called the **system maintenance mode** because it is generally used to recover from serious system problems. An important thing to note is that at this level, the root prompt is displayed without any attempt to check the corresponding password. This is necessary to allow for the various maintenance functions that need to be done without the hindrance of an authentication system; however, it also leaves the system open to any malicious users physically present at the computer. Therefore, this run level should be used only when absolutely necessary.

❏ **Run level 2** allows multiple users to log in to the machine through **virtual terminals** and other login devices, but still doesn't activate any networking functions.

❏ **Run level 3** finally allows networking processes to be started, and allows the complete resources of the system to be used effectively. However, until this level the interface to the desktop is through a CLI interface. Since the GUI interface uses the computer resources (such as CPU, memory, and hard disk) intensively, this run level is mainly used by server class workstations where precious computer resources are used to deliver networking and other application services more effectively.

❏ **Run level 4** is unused. It can be used to define your own custom run level.

❏ **Run level 5** finally allows the X-server process to be started and the accompanying desktop to be loaded to allow users to use the system with a GUI. The desktop that you have been using until now has been working at run level 5.

❏ **Run level 6** signifies the rebooting state of a machine and is used to restart the machine.

When a machine is booted, the `init` program examines the contents of the configuration file `/etc/inittab` to determine the run level to boot the computer to, and executes all the processes for that run level. The processes to execute for a particular runlevel are specified as special program scripts in the directory `/etc/rcx.d/` where x is the run level to boot to.

The present run level of the computer can be found out by using the program `runlevel`. This outputs two numbers, which represent the previous and current run levels.

The current run level can be changed using the program `telinit`. This program needs to be executed as root, and takes a single argument – the run level to boot to. For example, to reboot the system you can execute the command `telinit 6`.

Managing Users

At the end of the day, a desktop is intended to be used by people. Users coming from operating systems like Windows 9x and Windows Me will find in Red Hat Linux a more strict arrangement of permissions that describe what each user can and cannot do. One user's processes and data can't be accessed or modified by other users of the system, unless they are specifically permitted to do so. This concept of user security runs through the heart of the Linux system.

We'll talk about user management in depth in Chapter 8. However, it will be useful to summarize the key points, and so we'll do that now.

Understanding User Management

As we discussed earlier in the chapter, the root (or super user) of the computer has complete access over all the resources of the computer. For this reason, various security restrictions are put in place in the system to ensure that this user privilege is not compromised. Even as the administrator of the system, you should attempt to do most of your work as a less privileged user, and assume super user privileges only when they're needed.

Many new users will also find it unusual that the Linux desktop allows many users to work on the system simultaneously. While only one user can work *physically* at the desktop, other users can log in through network services like `telnet` and its more secure equivalent, `ssh`.

Linux has a simple way of organizing users. Every user can be the part of one or more **groups**. Therefore, as well as securing a resource by applying permissions to individual users, you can also place users into a group and apply permissions to the group instead.

Understanding Permissions

We have already talked about how privileges are required to control *processes* of other users; the same applies to *files* and *directories*. Every file and directory is associated with a single user (its owner) and also with a group. Then, specific permissions to access a file are given to the three classes of users:

- ❏ The owner
- ❏ The group members
- ❏ Everybody else

Each of the above classes is allowed a combination of three kinds of access permissions:

Permission	Meaning when applied to files	Meaning when applied to directories
Read	Enables the user to read the contents of the file	Enables the user to list the contents of the directory
Write	Enables the user to change the contents of the file	Enables the user to create or remove files within the directory
Execute	Enables the user to execute the file	Enables the user to access files and subdirectories

The permissions of a given file can be found out using the `ls` program. In the example given below, we use the command `ls -l` to display a "long" version of the file information:

```
$ ls -l /usr/bin/top
-r-xr-xr-x    1  root      root       56406  Aug 12 15:50 /usr/bin/top
```

The read, write, and executable permissions are represented using the characters `r`, `w`, and `x` respectively. The first part of the file information (in the above example, the expression `-r-xr-xr-x`) indicates the permission of the file. The first character indicates the file type (directory, character device, and so on), but it is the remaining characters that we're interested in right now. This sequence consists of three sets of three characters – one set each to describe permissions of the owner, the group, and the others. For example, the sequence `r-x` indicates that only the read and execution permissions are set, and no write permission is available. Therefore the permission of this file specifies that all possible users can only read and execute the content of the file but not modify the file contents.

You can use the CLI tools `chown`, `chmod`, and `chgrp` to modify the permissions of files and directories in the system. You will learn more about these tools in Chapter 8.

Managing Users

The task of adding, removing, and modifying user accounts on the system can be accomplished in a GUI by using the Red Hat user configuration tool – `redhat-config-users` – which you can launch using Main Menu | System Settings | Users & Groups. The primary interface of this tool is shown in the figure below:

You'll need to provide the root password to use this utility. Using this interface you can add, edit, or modify users and groups.

The same operations can be carried out in the CLI too. The various tools for the job are described below:

Program	Purpose
useradd	Adding a user
userdel	Removing a user
chfn, chsh	Modifying user details

Again, we'll see more about the use of these programs in Chapter 8. For now, the following screenshot demonstrates these programs being used to create, configure, and then delete a user called markm at the terminal:

```
root@localhost:~

File  Edit  View  Terminal  Go  Help

[sandipb@localhost sandipb]$ su -
Password:
[root@localhost root]# useradd markm
[root@localhost root]# passwd markm
Changing password for user markm.
New password:
Retype new password:
passwd: all authentication tokens updated successfully.
[root@localhost root]# chsh markm
Changing shell for markm.
New shell [/bin/bash]: /bin/csh
Shell changed.
[root@localhost root]# chfn markm
Changing finger information for markm.
Name []: Mark Mamone
Office []: Wrox Press
Office Phone []: +1-234-5678
Home Phone []: +1-235-4678

Finger information changed.
[root@localhost root]# userdel markm
[root@localhost root]#
```

Summary

In this chapter, we took a quick look at how to use the desktop for our everyday needs. Many of the topics that we covered lightly in this chapter will be explained in more detail later in the book.

We started our overview with a look at the basic components of the desktop – the workspace, the panel, and the desktop menu. We saw that there are various methods of launching GUI applications – through the desktop menu, the run dialog, the shortcuts on the panel, and the terminal emulator.

Moreover, while there is a good deal of functionality available through Red Hat Linux's GUI-based utilities, we can achieve more *complete* control over the desktop at the terminal – there are many command line interface (CLI) utilities, and each one offers a plethora of options. We looked at how to launch programs via the terminal, and saw that the apropos and man commands help us to find out the right program for the job, and how to use that program.

We've seen the hierarchical nature of Red Hat Linux's file system. There's a single directory (known as the root directory, and denoted /) at the top of the hierarchy, and a subdirectory structure beneath it. To examine the file structure of any external device (such as a CD-ROM, a floppy, or a network drive), we *mount* the device to a directory in this hierarchy – and then treat the device's file system as a part of the overall file system. We also looked at how to navigate the computer's file system – using both the CLI and the Nautilus GUI.

It's useful to be able to check the hardware configuration of the machine – CPU, memory, storage and network devices, the display and peripherals like the mouse, keyboard, and the sound card. As we saw in Chapter 1, there's an attempt to detect hardware automatically during the installation process, and in this chapter we saw the utilities that allow us to check and adjust this configuration manually at any time after installation – including the GUI-based **Hardware Browser**, and CLI-based utilities like lspci. We also met the GUI-based **System Monitor**, and files like /proc/cpuinfo and /proc/loadavg, and CLI programs like top that allow us to monitor performance.

We've also seen how the desktop control center allows us to customize the Red Hat Linux desktop in many ways, to suit our convenience and taste.

One important area of desktop usage is process management – and we examined the various methods for observing processes and controlling them when necessary. We also looked at run levels – the various states of the machine that determine which processes and services are available in the machine at any given time.

Finally, we took a quick look at user management. We took a quick look at how Red Hat Linux allows us to organize a system's users into groups (which is handy for allowing or denying access to system resources), and we met the special administrative user (called root). We took a quick look at the GUI-based User Manager, and command line utilities like useradd and passwd, that allow us to begin managing our accounts; we'll see more of that in Chapter 8.

3

Connecting to the Internet

One of the first things most of us want to do after installing an operating system is to take it for a ride on the Internet. Connecting to a network in general and to the Internet in particular has come a long way from the days of manually setting up network cards and hacking modem dialup scripts. Red Hat Linux 9 offers a vastly improved configuration interface while retaining the flexibility of allowing the users to roll up their sleeves and dive into the configuration files should the need arise (rarely if ever). In this chapter we shall be looking at the following aspects of connecting to the Internet:

- ❑ Connecting to the Internet through an ISP
- ❑ Dealing with network devices, connections, and profiles
- ❑ Configuring and using the various software we need to access the Internet
- ❑ Considering the safety of our machine while connected to the Internet
- ❑ Contending with common problems related to connecting to the Internet

Connecting to the Internet

Regardless of whether we plan to connect to the Internet using an analog modem, an *x*DSL 'broadband' connection, Ethernet card, or any of a variety of other methods, we need to configure our system before that connection can take place. Enter the **Internet Configuration Wizard** (Main Menu | System Tools | Internet Configuration Wizard):

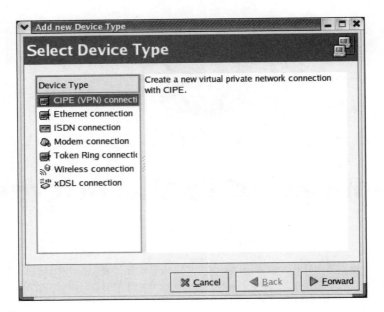

From here you simply choose the type of connection that you'd like to make, and walk through the easy-to-follow steps until your connection is configured! It really is that simple, so we won't cover it here – press Forward and see for yourself.

Of course, it's not always quite as simple as that, is it? Sometimes your connection doesn't quite work the first time you set it up, or you need to change something after you've configured it once (perhaps your ISP has changed the dial-up number, or perhaps you've just upgraded to 'broadband'). In this event you'll need to use the Network Configuration tool to edit the settings you've already entered.

Network Configuration Tool

In fact, once you've become reasonably confident setting up connections you'll probably bypass the connection wizard and come directly to this tool, as your first port of call. It can be accessed from the Main Menu by selecting System Settings | Network:

> Please note that the Network Configuration tool is also known as the Network Administration Tool.

Before we look at setting up the different types of connection in detail, let's take a quick tour around this tool so that we know where everything is (if not necessarily what it does) before we start.

The first thing to notice here is that the panel we're presented with contains a number of tabs. The **Devices** tab is the first of these, and lists the device connections that we have available on our machine. This provides us with very versatile control over the way that our machine behaves – we'll be leaving it alone for the moment, and coming back to it in a later section of this chapter, where we can deal with it more thoroughly. Next is the **Hardware** tab that allows us to manage the various network devices on the system, such as Ethernet cards, internal modems, and wireless cards. Third is the **DNS** tab that allows us to specify DNS server information (if this doesn't mean anything to you, don't worry; it applies to only certain types of connection, and we'll be explaining it in detail a little later on). Users of DHCP (more on this later, too) can usually leave this alone safely since DHCP automatically sets up the DNS information. Finally, there is the **Hosts** tab that allows us to modify the hostname of the machine and add aliases to the same host (so the same machine may be called foo.widgets.com or bar.widgets.com).

In the sections that follow, we'll discuss the most common methods of connecting to the Internet. Obviously you're not going to want to read about connecting analog modems if you're got a high bandwidth connection, so just skip ahead, using the headings, to find the section that applies to you.

Analog Modem Connections

Despite the advent of easily available and quite affordable high-speed Internet connectivity, using an analog modem attached to a phone line is still the most popular way of connecting to the Internet. Most personal computers available today come with an internal modem, usually as a modem card although some of the cheaper models have them built into the motherboards, or operated through software (so called 'soft-modems').

In the case of soft-modems there's a chance that they may not operate correctly under Linux, as they rely upon device driver software to operate correctly. If you believe this problem affects you, you should consult the manufacturer of your modem to see if there is a Linux driver available.

Technical Operation

Before we deal with connection details, here's a quick overview of what's actually going on when you use your analog modem to connect to the Internet.

Typically your modem connects to a phone line and dials out to a phone number provided by your ISP. Most commonly, the underlying protocol used on the wire is PPP (point to point protocol). The TCP/IP protocol is then layered on top of this PPP protocol layer. Once your machine has successfully connected to the gateway interface at your ISP, it is then connected to the Internet, and you can send and receive information:

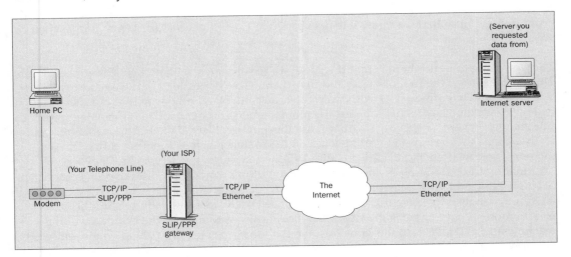

If this seems a little complicated to you, don't worry; like most other modern operating systems, Red Hat Linux 9 hides all the details from you (unless you want to look at them) and makes connection a breeze. Simply follow these simple steps:

Connecting an Analog Modem to the Internet

1. Move to the Devices tab, and select New in the Network Configuration tool:

2. Choose the Modem connection option, then press Forward to reach the following screen:

3. In this screen, we can either choose from the expandable list of ISPs on the left, or enter our own dial-up information into the boxes provided on the right. You should do whichever is appropriate for you.

*If you wish to connect to the T-Online network, you'll need to press the **T-Online Account Setup** button, and provide the additional information that you're asked for.*

4. To turn on your Internet connection, select your newly created device, and then click the Activate button at the top of the panel. To turn it off, simply click the Deactivate button that's next to it:

5. Finally, when you come to close the window, click on the Yes option in the dialog that asks you if you want to save your changes.

High-bandwidth Connections

While connecting to the Internet using a dial-up modem is sufficient for activities such as checking e-mail or browsing the web, this technology is not exactly keeping pace with the content offered online. Web sites are offering richer content by the day – and file downloads are getting bigger and bigger. This is where high-bandwidth Internet connections come in. Even though ISDN (Integrated Services Digital Network), the predecessor of today's high-bandwidth solutions, enjoyed only a lukewarm response, Cable and DSL (Digital Subscriber Line) modem–based solutions are becoming very popular in many countries. Their large bandwidth also means that several machines can now be connected to the Internet simultaneously. What this means is that we connect our single machine to either a Cable or DSL modem using an Ethernet cable. In the case of multiple machines, we connect these machines to a network router, which in turn is connected to the Cable or DSL modem.

Technical Operation

High-bandwidth connections typically layer the TCP/IP protocol over one of the two hardware protocols: Ethernet or PPPoE (PPP over Ethernet). In fact most of the Cable modem providers use Ethernet as the hardware protocol while DSL providers use PPPoE :

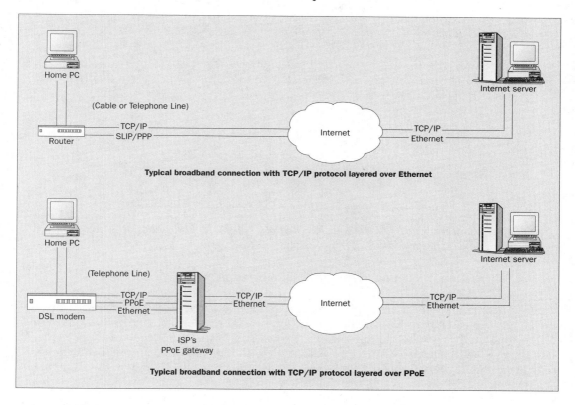

Connecting a High Bandwidth Connection to the Internet

1. Choose xDSL connection from the Internet Configuration Wizard.

2. Enter your account details such as the **Provider Name** (which is just an arbitrary name that you can identify the connection by) together with your **Login name** and **Password**:

*If you're connecting to T-Online you'll need to press the **T-Online Account Setup** button, and supply the additional information that it asks for.*

3. Select **Forward**, then **Apply**, to finalize your configuration.

You can turn your connection on or off using the **Activate** and **Deactivate** buttons at the top of the panel. Typically, high-bandwidth connections are 'always on', that is, unlike a dial-up connection, there is no need to initialize the device every time a connection is to be made. In order that a device and the connection associated with it be activated automatically at boot time, from the **Network Configuration** screen we need to click on **Edit** and on the **General** tab enable the checkbox that says **Activate device when computer starts**. Now that you've done this your connection will come online as soon as you turn your computer on.

Cable Modem Providers tend to use the Ethernet protocol. As such connections to their service can be configured in the same manner as for a LAN. We'll discuss this in the next section.

Connecting to a LAN

This section considers how to connect a Linux machine to a LAN, such as might be found in a home or business office. In these circumstances your machine takes on the role of being a **networked device**. A network device connected to a TCP/IP network (such as the Internet or an Intranet LAN) has an IP address associated with it, such as 192.168.100.20. Using the IP address of a machine, other machines on the network can address it uniquely. An IP address may be **static** or **dynamic**:

❑   Static addresses are allotted to machines indefinitely and do not change. Typically
     static addresses are allocated to servers.

❑   Dynamic addresses are allotted to machines for a specific period with no guarantee that
     the same address will be available next time the machine connects to the network.

Dynamic IP addresses are distributed and managed via dynamic address allocation protocols.
In the case of a machine connected to a LAN using a dynamic IP address (or in the case of an
ISP providing TCP/IP over Ethernet), the address is allocated either using the **Dynamic Host
Configuration Protocol (DHCP)** or the **Bootstrap Protocol (BOOTP)**. In these cases we choose
either dhcp or bootp from the drop-down list on our Configure Settings menu. For ISPs that use
PPPoE, the address is allotted by the PPPoE protocol, in which case we need to choose dialup.

For a machine connected to a LAN or ISP using a static IP address, we need to obtain the
network details such as the IP Address, the Subnet Mask for the network, and the Default
Gateway Address which is the IP address of a router for the network. The local network
administrator (or the ISP) should be able to provide these details.

Choose Ethernet connection from the Internet Configuration Wizard. Pick the Ethernet card you
wish to configure, press Forward, and provide your addressing information in the next screen:

If you've performed a LAN-based network configuration during the installation, as detailed in
Chapter 1, then you can skip the rest of this section, because your LAN should already be up
and running.

DNS

Rather than remember the IP address of the Wrox web site, it is easier for us to remember www.wrox.com. **Domain Name System (DNS)** servers provide the mapping between human-readable addresses (such as www.wrox.com) and the IP addresses of the machines acting as the web servers for the corresponding web service. Applications such as web browsers and e-mail clients require the IP address to connect to a web site or a mail server respectively. In order to get this from the human-readable input that we provide them with, they query a DNS server for the corresponding IP address information. Obviously, this also means that the browser and other clients on the machine need to know the IP address of the DNS server. For machines that use DHCP, the information about the DNS server is automatically available when the machine is configured.

Other Connection Types

The Internet Connection Wizard also allows us to configure some of the less common types of connection devices, such as ISDN and Token Ring adapters:

External ISDN terminal adapters (the ones that are connected to the serial port on a machine) can be configured **just like ordinary analog modems**. This discussion deals with ISDN adapters that are **internal ISDN cards**. In this case, we need to know the name of the adapter, its IRQ, the IO address and the D-Channel protocol used, so as to configure it properly. This information should be available as part of the vendor's documentation for your adapter (if you've not got it you could try calling them, or using Google if you've a second machine). Similarly, for configuring a Token Ring adapter, we need to know the name of the adapter we intend to use before we can configure it.

Wireless Connections

The Internet Configuration Wizard allows us to configure a couple of emerging device and connection types: **Wireless cards** and **VPN connections**. Most of the popular wireless cards provide connectivity using the 802.11b protocol and are known as Wireless Ethernet devices.

Even though the wizard has a separate option for configuring a Wireless card, it is essentially the same as configuring an Ethernet device (dealt with under LAN) with the added ability to specify some wireless-specific parameters. These parameters are best left as set to Auto unless you're sure of what you're doing and wish to alter them to address a performance issue, or similar.

> *These parameters may be specific to the vendor of the card and need to be set based on vendor recommendation.*

VPN (Virtual Private Network) connections allow us to securely connect to a corporate network via the public Internet. In other words, typical VPN users connect to work over the Internet either from home or while on the road by using a VPN connection which provides an encrypted channel of communication.

CIPE (Crypto IP Encapsulation) is a Linux implementation of VPN access software. However we need to have connection information for the particular VPN network that we intend to connect to, before we can configure a CIPE connection. **As a reality check, we need to note that most corporations require that users connect using company-supplied VPN clients that may not necessarily be available for Linux**. In such a situation, using the CIPE-based VPN solution may not work.

Managing Multiple ISPs and Connections

Often we may have a single machine with different characteristics when connecting to different networks. We may use the machine to browse the Internet while connected to an ISP or use it to connect to work and even perhaps take it to work to use on an Intranet. The thing to note is that even though it is the same machine, it tends to have different connectivity requirements at different times since different service providers and possibly different devices are involved.

Connection Profiles

Connection profiles help us manage not just multiple ISPs, but also devices that need to behave differently at different times. For the latter, that is, physical devices that require different settings at different times, it is possible to associate multiple logical devices with a single physical device. The logical devices can have a variety of settings, the only restriction being that only one logical device associated with a physical device can be used at a time. A **connection profile** is a collection of logical devices and their configurations representing certain connection characteristics. Typical connection profiles could be Work, Home, On the road, etc.

We touched upon connection profiles when looking at the Internet Configuration Wizard at the start of this chapter. Open the Network Configuration tool up again, and, at the bottom on the screen, on the Devices tab you'll see Active Profile followed by details on the profile that's currently active. By default, we are provided with a Common profile, which works well for machines that have fixed connection characteristics.

Before we get started with profiles, we need to configure all the **physical network device** types on the machine. Available network device types are – Ethernet, ISDN, Modem, xDSL, Token Ring, CIPE, and Wireless.

The steps below describe creating and managing profiles. These might seem a little unclear on first reading, but hopefully the *Try It Out* example that comes afterward will serve to clarify things:

❑　Create a new profile, by clicking New. A profile is typically associated with a location. Locations have their distinct network configuration requirements. The new profile represents these configuration settings.

❑　Once the profile is created, we create all the logical devices necessary for the profile. The general rule is that if a particular physical device will be used in the context of the new profile, it needs a logical device for that profile.

❑　Once the logical devices for the new profile are created, we need to associate the logical devices with the profile.

❑　We may choose to create more profiles by following Steps 1 to 3, again.

Try It Out   Creating Multiple Profiles and Logical Devices

Let's try to configure connection profiles for a hypothetical Red Hat Linux 9 laptop that we use at work to write articles, at home to browse the web, and while on the road to read e-mail. At work, the laptop is connected to the company's Intranet via an Ethernet card. While on the road we use the laptop's internal modem to dial an ISP and check our e-mail. At home, we use a Wireless Ethernet card so we can web browse from the living-room couch. On occasions when pets monopolize the couch, we're forced to browse over a Cable modem connection from the study, thereby using the same Ethernet card we used at work. To manage all these connections, we'll create four profiles, namely Work, Home, Road, and Couch.

Before we begin, let's get our machine's hardware profile fresh in our minds. It looks like this (with what you've learned so far, you should be able to create this with fictional information if you want to follow along – you can always delete it when we're done):

Create the required profiles using the following steps:

1. Choose Profile from the drop-down menu, and select New.

2. Enter Work in the pop-up box that appears:

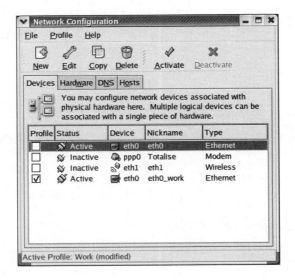

3. Now that we have our profile created (look at the bottom of the Network Configuration Tool, and you'll see that it's changed from **Common** to **Work**), we need to create a logical device for it based on the physical device eth0 – the Ethernet card.

4. Highlight the physical device eth0 and click **Copy**.

> We might be tempted to click the **Add** button to create a logical device, but this is incorrect. We should use the **Copy** button after highlighting the physical device in question.

5. Select the copy, and click the Edit button and specify the nickname **eth0_work** along with other properties such as the DNS server to be used and the IP address (you can make these up for the purposes of the demonstration). Finally click **OK**.

6. Finally, add the newly created logical device to the **Work** profile by marking the **Profile** checkbox on the left-hand side for those logical devices that belong to the profile.

7. To save our changes we need to click the **Apply** button. A logical device may belong to only one profile. Here's the result:

8. We can use the same routine to create profiles for our Home, Road, and Couch accounts:

A particular profile can be activated at any time from the Network Configuration tool by choosing the profile from the drop-down list.

Starting Connections

So how do we actually connect to a network using each of these devices? Some of them, such as the Ethernet device, remain connected (or activated) as long as they are physically connected to the network. Others such as a modem need to be activated on an as-needed basis.

Therefore, to connect using a configured connection, at any time, we could go to the Main Menu and choose System Settings | Network, highlight the appropriate connection, and click on Activate.

In order to activate a connection as soon as the machine starts up, highlight the connection and click on Edit and enable the radio button that says Activate device when computer starts.

It's also possible to configure Red Hat Linux 9 to automatically establish a modem connection when needed, using a daemon called `diald`. However, using such a process can make your system considerably less secure than it is at the moment (currently you have to manually 'OK' any modem network connections). We'd advise that you read on a little further through the book and familiarize yourself with the command shell and security issues before deciding if `diald` is right for you. If you decide to proceed, all the configuration information you need can be found at:

http://www.linux.org/docs/ldp/howto/Diald-HOWTO.html

111

Software and Configuration

So, now we've got our Internet connection set up, we're ready to fire up our browser and go places! Let's look at the tools that Red Hat Linux 9 makes available for you to do this.

Web Browsers

Obviously, the most common and popular way of accessing the Internet is by using a web browser. Red Hat Linux 9 comes with the highly functional Mozilla browser installed by default. You can start it from the Panel at the bottom of your screen, by clicking on the 'globe and mouse' icon. Alternatively, you can type `mozilla` at the command prompt. For those of us who connect directly to the Internet, that's it. Up pops Mozilla, helpfully set to a **Welcome to Red Hat** page, and you're ready to go:

> *Notice it's actually browsing HTML pages on your local file system at the moment, rather than the web – just type **file:///** to explore your machine.*

Mozilla Proxies

Those of us who connect through an HTTP Proxy, however, have a little bit more work to do. First, we need to get hold of the following information from whoever supervises our network:

❏   The DNS name of the proxy and the port number it listens at for HTTP connections.

❏   Most of the time the same proxy server handles other protocols such as SSL, FTP, Gopher, and SOCKS. If we intend to use any of these protocols, we need to get the address of the proxy server for each of these protocols and the port at which they listen for incoming requests.

❏   Some intranets publish a URL that has JavaScript in it that can configure the proxy settings automatically for the user. In this case, we need to provide that URL .

Once you've got your information, fire up Mozilla, and open Edit | Preferences | Advanced | Proxies:

Configuring Mozilla

The best thing about Mozilla is that it comes with a horde of functionality to make browsing much more fun. Here's a list of a few of the settings that you might find useful.

Privacy and Security Settings

Mozilla comes with a host of privacy and security settings that allow us to browse the web without being bothered by security concerns or prying eyes.

Pop-up ads: Most, if not all of us are annoyed by the often-distracting pop-up advertisements that appear when we attempt to load a page. These pop-up windows can be blocked by choosing the menu item Edit | Preferences | Advanced | Scripts & Plugins and unchecking Open unrequested windows.

Blocking ad images: Besides pop-up ads, the other annoying mode of online advertisement is banner advertisements that are served up by online ad-banner companies that embed links to images in web pages. These ads can be blocked by right-clicking the ad image and selecting Block images from this server. We could reinstate permissions to allow a blocked server to display its images from the Tools | Image Manager | Manage Image Permissions menu by highlighting the site in question and clicking on Remove.

Browsing and Appearance

Mozilla allows us to customize our browsing experience by providing a tabbed browsing interface and also the ability to change the appearance of the browser itself. Further, several other convenient features exist that make browsing as fast as it is fun.

Tabs rather than Windows: Using tabs to browse is faster and results in less clutter than using new windows every time we needed to have multiple pages open at the same time (look at the top of the page, just below the Bookmarks line):

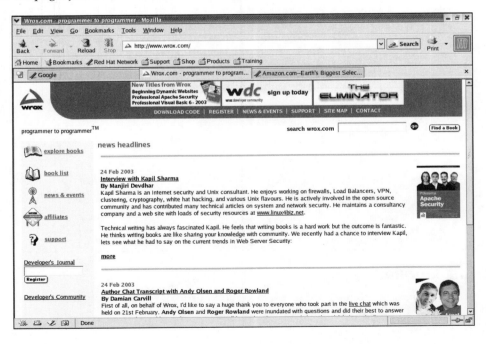

We can open a new tab with the *Ctrl+T* key combination, or open a link in a new tab by right-clicking the link and choosing **Open Link in New Tab**. Further, if we enable the **Middle-click or Control-click of links in a web** page option, we can open links in new tabs by clicking links using the middle mouse button or a *Ctrl + left-click* of the mouse. These options are available from the **Edit | Preferences | Navigator | Tabbed Browsing** menu. From the same menu, by enabling *Ctrl+Enter* **in the location bar** option, we can open a location in a new tab by typing in the URL followed by *Ctrl+Enter*.

Themes: The appearance of the Mozilla browser can be changed by applying themes that change the look and feel of the user interface. Mozilla has the classic theme and a modern theme available by default, and new themes can be downloaded from http://www.mozdev.org.

We can have several themes available and switch between them by choosing the menu option **View | Apply Themes** and selecting the name of the theme to be applied. Newly selected themes take effect only after restarting Mozilla.

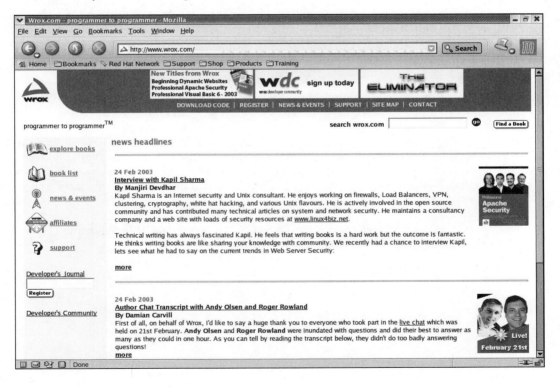

Auto-completion: Some users may prefer to have Mozilla automatically complete a URL that they are typing in. This behavior can be enabled by ensuring that the **Automatically complete text typed into Location bar** option from the **Edit | Preferences | Navigator | Smart Browsing** menu is checked.

Installing Plug-ins

Plug-ins, from a generic standpoint, allow the browser to process non-HTML data. Mozilla by default does not have plug-ins installed. Details about plug-ins for various software, some of them commercial, are available at the Plugindoc page, http://plugindoc.mozdev.org/linux.html. Some of the more interesting plug-ins worth considering include Java, Real Audio, and Macromedia Flash plug-ins.

E-mail and News Clients

Now that we have configured our web browser, it is time to look at the options Red Hat Linux 9 presents us with for accessing e-mail and newsgroups. The default e-mail client is Ximian Evolution, but your Mozilla installation also has excellent mail client facilities built in, and also functions as an Internet News client.

The Ximian Evolution Client

The Ximian Evolution client is similar in both look-and-feel and functionality to Microsoft Outlook minus the virus issues commonly associated with Microsoft's e-mail clients. The similarity makes it a viable alternative for users moving to Red Hat from a Microsoft environment. The Evolution client also integrates a calendar and contacts management software. In fact, it is possible to access calendar information hosted on a Microsoft Exchange server from your Evolution client (using a commercially licensed connector available from www.ximian.com). On starting Evolution for the first time from the panel, a wizard will prompt us to enter account information for our e-mail. Once this is done, the program starts, and we're able to start using it.

> *Additional accounts can be added from the **Tools | Settings** menu while in the Inbox screen by choosing the Mail **Accounts** tab and clicking on **Add**.*

As mentioned earlier, Ximian Evolution also comes with an integrated calendar, task manager, and address book that makes mail and schedule management on Red Hat Linux 9 simple and intuitive.

Accessing Microsoft Exchange Mail from Ximian

Several corporations use Microsoft Exchange as a groupware server, that is, a server that allows users to manage and share calendar events, contacts, e-mail, and even files. Unfortunately, the Exchange server is designed to work primarily with Microsoft Outlook and quite often it is not configured to allow clients to access e-mail using the POP or IMAP protocols. However, Ximian provides a commercially licensed connector to access e-mail from an Exchange server. It should be noted that if POP access is enabled, the connector is not required if we use the Microsoft Exchange server only for e-mail. We definitely need the connector if we rely on a Microsoft Exchange server for calendar and file-sharing features.

The Ximian connector can be downloaded from http://www.ximian.com. To install the connector, we need to also download Red Carpet, the Ximian installer, from the same web site.

117

To configure Ximian to retrieve and send mail using an Exchange server, from the **Tools Mail Settings** menu we set the Server Type as **Microsoft Exchange** and supply the following information:

1. The mail user's full name.

2. The login name for the Exchange server. This is usually the part of the e-mail ID preceding the @ symbol, also known as the mail user ID. It may also be a different name altogether, depending upon how this is configured locally. Some installations have multiple NT domains, in which case the login name is of the format `domainname\login name`.

3. If the mail user ID is different from the login name, we need to provide that id as the mailbox name. In any case, there is no need to prefix the domain name.

4. The DNS name of the Exchange server, for example `exchange.foobar.com`.

5. If an LDAP-based corporate directory server such as the Netscape Directory Server is deployed locally, the DNS name of the server can be entered to look up contacts using LDAP. LDAP stands for Lightweight Directory Access Protocol.

If you're unsure about any of this information, you should speak to whoever is responsible for the running of your Exchange Server.

The Mozilla Mail Client

The Mozilla mail client is fast gaining popularity as a fully featured mail client. It has several features for managing multiple e-mail accounts and most importantly news accounts. For users who subscribe to news groups besides accessing e-mail, the Mozilla client is an excellent choice. The Mozilla client can be started from **Main Menu | Internet | More Internet Applications | Mozilla mail** or by clicking the mail icon (bottom, left) of the Mozilla browser:

When the Mozilla mail client is started for the first time, it prompts us to set up an account for sending and receiving e-mail. Also, a new account can be set up from the Edit | Mail & Newsgroups settings menu by clicking on the Add account button. In either case, the settings are similar to the settings for the Ximian Evolution client that we saw in the previous section. The news reader client can be set up from the same menu by specifying the new account as a Newsgroup account and entering the DNS name of the news server:

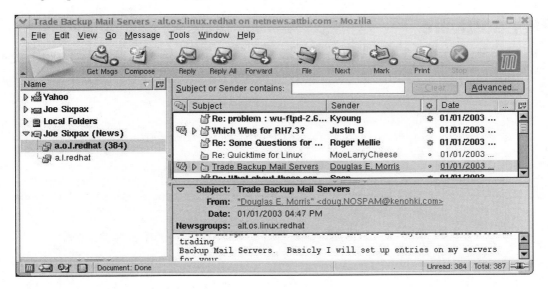

Switching Mail Transfer Agents

Mail transfer agents (MTAs) relay outgoing mail to its destination using the SMTP protocol. If you're using either of the mail clients that we've mentioned in this chapter, then you don't need to worry about them too much, as they're not involved in sending your mail. However, for completeness, you should know that they're there, and what they do.

Red Hat Linux 9 comes with a choice of two mail transfer agents, Sendmail and Postfix. The Mail Transfer Agent Switcher tool can be accessed from the Main Menu | System Settings | Mail Transfer Agent Switcher. We can switch the MTA to be used, by clicking the appropriate radio button and then selecting Apply.

Sendmail (official site http://www.sendmail.org) is the oldest and therefore the most time-tested of the MTAs. It is easily the most popular mail transfer agent, delivering more than half of all the e-mail on the Internet. However, Sendmail has numerous security and performance issues owing to its age. Several new MTAs have emerged to take its place, improving upon the security aspects, performance, and ease of configuration. Postfix (official site http://ww.postfix.com) is an MTA focused on better security and easier configuration. Exim (offical site http://www.exim.org) and qmail (official site http://www.qmail.org) are other popular MTAs. Most of the time Sendmail will work very well as the default MTA, but if we intend to do some serious re-configuration, Postfix might make the task much easier.

The important thing to note is that if we are using using a mail client like Mozilla or Evolution, then the outgoing mail is sent directly to a mail server using SMTP. In this case, an MTA is not involved and it can be left alone with little impact. However, some older mail clients such as UNIX mail and some programs that send notification e-mail may require the MTA to be configured and enabled.

Other Software

In this section we shall look at the other software beside browsers and mail clients that we can use to access the Internet.

FTP Clients

We often need to download software over the Internet or transfer files between machines. The most popular protocol for this function is FTP or the File Transfer Protocol.

The gFTP tool (Graphical FTP) available with Red Hat Linux 9 installations is a graphical FTP tool that has several power features lacking in the other clients. The gFTP client can be started from the Main Menu | Internet | More Internet Applications | gFTP, or by typing gftp at the command line:

The gFTP client is multi-threaded, allowing transfer of multiple files simultaneously, and supports transferring files between two remote servers over FTP (that is, not onto the machine you're working on). It also supports downloading entire directories and subdirectories, as well as being able to bookmark FTP sites allowing you to quickly reconnect to remote sites. gFTP also supports resuming interrupted file transfers.

Traditionally the most popular FTP client has been the command-line FTP tool, simply called `ftp`. The command-line tool is interactive and suitable for quickly fetching a file or two.

Xchat

IRC or Internet Relay Chat is the predecessor of peer-to-peer and instant messaging systems of today. Owing to its huge user base, it is still one of the major reasons people connect to the Internet. Red Hat Linux 9 comes with an IRC client called Xchat that can be accessed from the Main Menu | Internet | More Internet Applications | Xchat menu:

IRC consists of *channels* that are essentially topics of discussion, similar to the *chat room* of today's messaging clients. To join a channel we need to connect to a server that hosts the channel. We can choose a server from the list of servers available by default from the X-Chat | Server list menu or add some of our own to the list from the same menu.

Most IRC servers expect that we identify ourselves to the server. This is achieved by running the `identd` server on our machine. The `identd` server listens on port `113` for connections using the `identd` protocol and processes requests from remote machines asking for the identity of the user attempting to connect to the remote machine. `identd` is available as an RPM that should be installed separately as it is not part of the default installation. Chapter 4 has information on using the package manager for installing RPMs.

Note that Xchat cannot connect to an IRC server through a firewall, at the current time.

Instant Messaging

Instant messaging is fast emerging as the latest Internet application to connect people together. Most of today's instant messaging applications allow users to chat one-on-one or in a group in real time as well as allow them to share files. Unfortunately, all of the instant messaging applications are not based on a common protocol, but on proprietary protocols that do not interact with each other. What this means is that a user on AIM (AOL's instant messaging solution) cannot seamlessly connect with a user on a different messaging network, say Yahoo! Messenger.

This is where Gaim comes in. Gaim is an instant messaging client that supports multiple protocols and also allows a user to be logged on to different networks with different account names simultaneously. In fact Gaim can even connect to IRC servers. Pretty clever, eh? Gaim can be invoked from Main Menu | Internet | Instant Messenger:

Before we can use Gaim, we need to set up a couple of things. For Gaim to work with a certain instant messaging network, it needs to have a plug-in for that network loaded. This is a one-time task that can be accomplished by clicking on the Plugins button followed by the Load button and choosing the appropriate plug-in, say libyahoo.so for Yahoo! Messenger or libicq.so for ICQ. Once the plug-ins are set up, we need to fill in account information for each of the networks that we intend to connect to. Account information can be entered by clicking the Accounts button followed by the Add button. The official Gaim web site is http://gaim.sourceforge.net. Chapter 5 discusses Gaim configuration in detail, so we'll leave it at that for the time being.

Summary

In this chapter we explored the issues associated with connecting our Red Hat Linux 9 installation to the Internet. Hopefully you should now have a working Internet connection, and be able to surf web pages, check your mail, transfer files by FTP, and use IRC with confidence.

In brief, we have:

- ❑ Investigated the use of various wizards such as the Internet Configuration Wizard, and Network Configuration Tool to configure devices and connections in the context of different connection requirements.

- ❑ Learned how to create logical devices and profiles in order to better manage our resources.

- ❑ Explored some of the important Internet access software available with the Red Hat Linux installation.

4

Installing Software

As you would expect from a Linux distribution, Red Hat Linux 9 comes bundled with a vast array of software applications for your use. Major applications such as the Open Office productivity suite and Ximian Evolution e-mail client are installed as part of the installation, but there are a great number of other applications that are not. This software maybe stored on a CD, on the Internet, or somewhere else entirely. In this chapter we'll be looking at how you can get hold of it, and install it on your system.

During the course of the chapter, we'll be looking at the following areas:

❑ The RPM and its advantages

❑ The RPM Package Management Tool

❑ RPM console commands

❑ RPM security features

❑ A few examples of RPM package installation

In the course of this chapter, we will be using the terms RPM Package Management Tool, Package Management Tool, and Red Hat Package Manager interchangeably to refer to Package Management GUI provided by Red Hat Linux 9 (based on which variant scans best in natural language). We will also use the term rpm to refer to the RPM command line interface.

What Is RPM?

The RPM package manager is an open source packaging system distributed under the GNU GPL. It runs on most Linux distributions and makes it easy for you to install, uninstall, and upgrade the software on your machine. RPM files can be easily recognized by their .rpm file extension and the 'package' icon that appears in your navigation window:

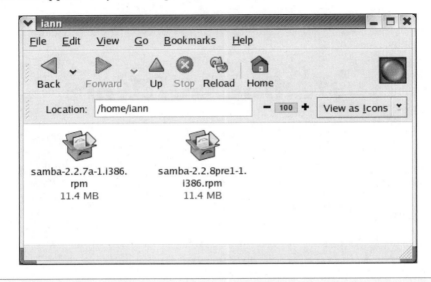

More information about the background of RPM can be found at:
http://www.redhat.com and **http://www.rpm.org/max-rpm/**

The benefits of using RPM can be summarized as follows:

❑ **Simplicity**: RPM simplifies the task of installing software. RPM packages can be managed using the RPM GUI interface, or via the command line.

❑ **Upgradeability**: RPM gives us the flexibility to upgrade existing packages without having to reinstall them. You can freshen and upgrade parts, or all, of your system automatically, with the minimum of fuss.

❑ **Manageability**: RPM makes it easy to manage software packages. It maintains a database of all the packages installed on the system, so you know exactly what you've got installed, what version it is, and when it was added.

❑ **Package queries**: RPM provides options to query packages for more details in different ways. You can search the package installed on the system. You can also find out what package a file belongs to. It helps in keeping track of all packages installed on your system.

❏ **Uninstalling**: RPM makes it easy to uninstall packages. This helps us to keep the system clean.

❏ **System verification**: RPM also provides a feature to verify packages. In case of any doubt about file deletion, packages can be verified against the original package information using RPM. This checks all the files on the system with the package information and verifies that the files on the system are the same as those installed from the package originally.

❏ **Security**: RPM provides commands for the user to check the integrity of packages. Packages can be checked using md5sum to verify that they have not been corrupted or tampered with since they were created. RPM also provides functionality to verify a package provider's identity and package integrity using gnupg (very handy if you're downloading sensitive material from the Internet, as you want to be sure that you're installing what you think you're installing).

Now that we've an understanding of what RPM is, and what it can be used for, let's move on to consider how it works. In point of fact, RPM can be used in two different, yet complementary ways – from the desktop, using the GUI interface, and from the command line. We'll look at the GUI first, because it's simpler, and will give us a good grounding from which to proceed.

The RPM Package Management (GUI) Tool

Red Hat has added a lot of new features to its latest operating systems to make them easier to manage. One of these new features is the **Package Management Tool**. This tool is a graphical user interface (GUI) designed for the management of package installation and removal. The GUI allows us to add and remove packages at the click of a mouse.

> *The package management tool, as accessed from the Main Menu, is able to manage only packages provided as part of a Red Hat Linux 9 installation. To install other RPMs from disk, or download, you need to navigate to the RPM in question and double-click on the file. This will load the package management tool, and skip you straight to the 'Install' screen, bypassing the system-specific install options.*

Starting the RPM Package Management Tool

There are two ways to start RPM. To do it from the Main Menu, select Main Menu | System Settings | Add/Remove Applications. Alternatively, from the command line you can type the following command:

```
$ redhat-config-packages
```

Either way, if you're logged in with privileges other than root privileges, you'll be prompted to enter the root password.

127

Once you've identified yourself as an administrator, you'll see the following window:

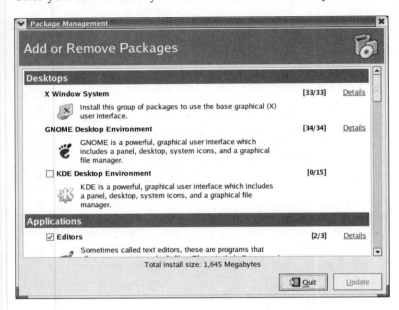

Package Management Tool Functions

Let's take a closer look at the GUI:

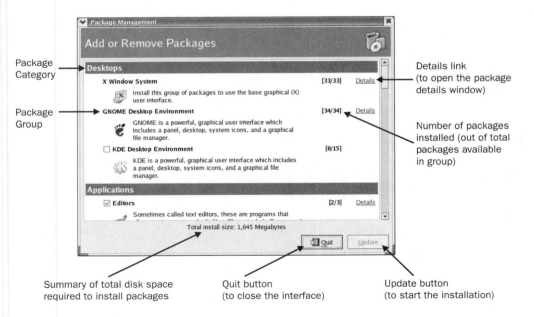

As you can see from the figure, the package manager presents packages divided up into different categories, each containing different groups. The following table lists of all the available package categories and package groups on a typical system. If you look through the entries on your machine you'll find an explanatory note next to each one explaining what it does on your machine.

Package Category	Package Groups
Desktops	X Window System
	GNOME Desktop Environment
	KDE Desktop Environment
Applications	Editors
	Engineering and Scientific
	Graphical Internet
	Text-based Internet
	Office/Productivity
	Sound and Video
	Authoring and Publishing
	Graphics
	Games and Entertainment
Servers	Server Configuration Tools
	Web Server
	Mail Server
	Windows File Server
	DNS Name Server
	FTP Server
	SQL Database Server
	News Server
	Network Servers

Package Category	Package Groups
Development	Development Tools
	Kernel Development
	X Software Development
	GNOME Software Development
	KDE Software Development
System	Administration Tools
	System Tools
	Printing Support

You can view the details of any group of packages by clicking on the Details link. Details of each group look like the following:

Each group may have **standard packages** and **extra packages**, or just extra packages. Standard packages are always available when a package group is installed – so you can't add or remove them explicitly unless the entire group is removed. However, the extra packages are optional so they can be individually selected for installation or removal at any time.

Adding and Removing Packages

The package management tool makes adding and removing packages very simple. In fact, it's just as easy as using the Add/Remove Programs menu under Microsoft Windows.

Installing Packages

Installing new software from the package management tool is very simple. When we select any group using the RPM package management tool interface, it automatically selects the standard packages (if any) that are needed for the category as well as any dependent packages that it may have.

> Dependent packages are packages needed in order for the main package to run properly. RPM checks for these before installing any new package. If they're not present it adds them to the list of files to be installed. There's nothing unusual in this – Windows software also depends on other files (like DLLs), but it packages them all together for simplicity, while Linux leaves them separate for ease of updating, and bug-fixing.

We can customize the packages to be installed by clicking on the Details button. Once you've made your selections, click on the Update button on the main window. The package management tool will then calculate the disk space required for installing packages, as well as any dependencies, before displaying the following dialog:

If you click on the Show Details button in the above dialog, you'll see a list of all the packages to be installed – with the disk space needed for each individual package. If you click on the Continue button, the installation procedure will start. When the installation is finished, an Update Complete dialog will appear.

Removing Packages

It's also very simple to remove a package. To remove *all* the packages installed within a package group, uncheck the checkbox beside the package group. To remove *individual* packages, click the Details button beside the package group and then uncheck the individual packages. After selecting all the required packages to uninstall, it's just a case of clicking the Update button in the main window.

The package management tool will take care of finding and removing any dependent packages that might also be installed, just as it did in the install routine. However, if the package you're trying to remove is required by other installed packages, removal will stop, and you'll be shown the following warning:

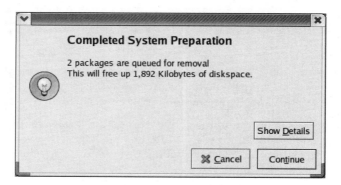

If this happens, you'll have to leave the package where it is – unless you want to go and delete the program that's using it first (in which case it will probably be removed anyway, as a dependent package).

However, if the package isn't dependent on the package management tool will calculate the disk space that will be freed from removing selected packages (and any dependencies), and display a summary window. Once again, more details of the packages to be removed can be seen by clicking on the Show Details button:

It just remains to say that you can combine installation and removal, at the same time, by respectively checking or un-checking package install options. If you do this you'll receive a combined summary window like this:

Completed System Preparation

4 packages are queued for installation
2 packages are queued for removal
This will take 9,408 Kilobytes of diskspace.

Hide Details

Packages to be Installed

amanda-2.4.3-4	180 Kilobytes
amanda-client-2.4.3-4	424 Kilobytes
ethereal-0.9.8-6	8,712 Kilobytes
libpcap-0.7.2-1	356 Kilobytes

Packages to be Removed

finger-server-0.17-16	20 Kilobytes
vsftpd-1.1.3-8	244 Kilobytes

✖ Cancel   Continue

Package Installation and Configuration Files

Before we leave the subject of package installation and removal, it's important that we consider the topic of configuration files for a moment. What follows can seem a little daunting, so it's important to realize that this happens only rarely. If you're installing a new version of older software, or upgrading your existing version, there's a small chance that the installation will encounter pre-existing configuration files as it installs. This presents a dilemma, as those files may have been specially customized by you, so it doesn't want to just overwrite them and lose your settings.

It therefore deals with the problem in the following ways:

❑   If you're **installing** a package, a new configuration file with an `.rpmnew` extension is created. The old file is left in place, and you'll need to swap them manually if you want to take advantage of the new files settings – a warning message will be displayed telling you where the file is.

133

❑   If you're **upgrading** a package, the old configuration file will be renamed with an
.rpmsave extension, and the new file will take its place. Again you will be shown a
warning message telling you this has taken place.

❑   If you're **removing** a package, and the tool detects that a configuration file has been
modified, it will warn you of this, and leave a version of the file behind with an
.rpmsave extension – so it's still available if you should need it.

This situation isn't likely to occur very often, but you're aware of the issues now, should you
encounter it. Try to bear in mind the differences between how installs and upgrade handle
configuration files. This will stand you in good stead as we move on to look at the command line
package installer (RPM), next.

The RPM Command Line Tool

Up to now, we've talked about how to install and remove packages using Red Hat's graphical
package management tool. While this tool is simple to use, it's lacking in functionality. For
example:

❑   It cannot install packages using network, FTP, or HTTP connections.

❑   It does not show the location the files in a package are installed to.

❑   It lacks the capability to query for specific packages installed on the system.

❑   It does not provide full details of the RPM package – such as the vendor, build date,
signature, description, and so on.

❑   It does not have a function to verify a package. That means it cannot compare
information about files like size, MD5 sum, permissions, type, owner, and group
installed from a package with the same information from the original package.

❑   It does not show all the packages available in a product. So you won't always know if
you've got the whole thing.

The **RPM Command Line Interface tool (RPM)** provides a solution to the Package Manager's
limitations. RPM is very versatile and can be used to manipulate packages in a great number of
ways. In the remainder of this section we'll look at some of the most common tasks you're likely to
want to perform, and consider how best to do them.

> *Complete details of all RPM's options can be found by typing* man rpm *at the command
> prompt; because there are so many, we'll be covering only the most common here.*

Querying Packages

Let's begin by discussing **querying** packages. RPM keeps a record of all the packages installed on
your system in a database. By querying the database you obtain a complete list of all the packages
that you've installed on your system. Should you want to, you can then go further and query each
individual package for more details about itself.

The syntax for a basic query is as follows:

```
rpm -q [options] <filename>
```

1. Open a terminal window (by selecting **Main Menu | System Tools | Terminal**).

2. RPM package operation can be performed only by a user with root privileges. So, if you're not logged in as root, do so now, by using the su command:

```
$ su -
Password:
#
```

3. Change to the packages directory of CD 2 in your Red Hat by inserting the CD and typing the following, once it has mounted:

```
# cd /mnt/cdrom/RedHat/RPMS/
```

4. Now, let's find the information for the lynx package (Lynx is a text-based browser). To do this, type the following at the command line:

```
# rpm -qip lynx-2.8.5-11.i386.rpm
```

Here, -qip represents the command options (which we'll discuss in more detail shortly), and lynx-2.8.5-7.i386.rpm is the RPM package file we're interested in. After a short while, you should see the following response:

```
Warning: lynx-2.8.5-11.i386.rpm: V3 DSA signature: NOKEY, key ID db42a60e
Name        : lynx                    Relocations: (not relocateable)
Version     : 2.8.5                        Vendor: Red Hat, Inc.
Release     : 11                      Build Date: Sat 25 Jan 2003 05:10:43 GMT
Install Date: Thu 15 May 2003 11:41:58 BST    Build Host: porky.devel.redhat.com
Group       : Applications/Internet   Source RPM: lynx-2.8.5-11.src.rpm
Size        : 4021040                    License: GPL
Signature   : DSA/SHA1, Mon 24 Feb 2003 06:34:45 GMT, Key ID 219180cddb42a60e
Packager    : Red Hat, Inc. <http://bugzilla.redhat.com/bugzilla>
URL         : http://lynx.isc.org/
Summary     : A text-based Web browser.
Description :
Lynx is a text-based Web browser. Lynx does not display any images,
but it does support frames, tables, and most other HTML tags. One
advantage Lynx has over graphical browsers is speed; Lynx starts and
exits quickly and swiftly displays webpages.
```

*Notice the **warning** in the first line? We'll explain it later in the chapter, when we cover verification.*

Useful, isn't it? You can use this information to make sure you're installing what you think you're installing and to check that you've got the right version of software.

5. RPM can also be used to query a specific package installed on the system. Issue the following command as root:

```
rpm -qi lynx
```

Here, -qi represents the command options, and lynx is the RPM package file name we're interested in. After a short while, you should see the following response:

```
Name        : lynx                        Relocations: (not relocateable)
Version     : 2.8.5                            Vendor: Red Hat, Inc.
Release     : 11                           Build Date: Sat 25 Jan 2003
05:10:43 GMT
Install Date: Mon 26 May 2003 14:50:02 BST     Build Host:
porky.devel.redhat.com
Group       : Applications/Internet        Source RPM: lynx-2.8.5-11.src.rpm
Size        : 4021040                         License: GPL
Signature   : DSA/SHA1, Mon 24 Feb 2003 06:34:45 GMT, Key ID 219180cddb42a60e
Packager    : Red Hat, Inc. <http://bugzilla.redhat.com/bugzilla>
URL         : http://lynx.isc.org/
Summary     : A text-based Web browser.
Description :
Lynx is a text-based Web browser. Lynx does not display any images,
but it does support frames, tables, and most other HTML tags. One
advantage Lynx has over graphical browsers is speed; Lynx starts and
exits quickly and swiftly displays webpages.
```

6. Now let's try something a little different, but no less useful. Issue the following command (still as root):

```
# rpm -qa
```

This command makes a query for all the packages that are installed on your system; you should get something like this in response:

```
rpm404-python-4.0.4-8x.27
ksymoops-2.4.5-1
libgal19-0.19.2-4
setup-2.5.25-1
....gnome-media-2.2.1.1-4
redhat-switch-printer-0.5.16-1
```

136

```
sharutils-4.2.1-14
vnc-server-3.3.3r2-47
```

7. Here's another example. You are likely to encounter situations in which you need to know about the package that owns a particular command on the system. For example, let's find out which package owns the command /usr/bin/lynx. To do this, type the following ad the command line:

```
# rpm -qf /usr/bin/lynx
```

You should get the following response:

lynx-2.8.5-11

Thus, it is the lynx-2.8.5-11 package that is used by the system, whenever a user calls the command /usr/bin/lynx

8. Finally, RPM also provides a command that allows us to find out list of all files contained in an RPM package. Let's find out what files are contained in a samba-client package... To do this, type the following:

```
# rpm -ql lynx
```

Here's the response you should get:

```
/etc/lynx-site.cfg
/etc/lynx.cfg
/etc/lynx.cfg.cs
/etc/lynx.cfg.ja
/etc/lynx.cfg.sk
/usr/bin/lynx
. . . . . .
```
/usr/share/locale/sl/LC_MESSAGES/lynx.mo
/usr/share/locale/sv/LC_MESSAGES/lynx.mo
/usr/share/man/man1/lynx.1.gz

How It Works

When we query an RPM package file using RPM command line options, it displays the information like name, version, release, group, summary and description of the package. The exact type of the query and the format of the resulting output depend on the command options that we specify:

❑ In all five of the queries in the example above, we used -q. The q is to indicate that we're making a query.

❑ In the step 4 and 5, we used -qip. The p indicates that we are querying a package, and the i indicates that we want to see the package information.

❑ In Step 6, we used -qa. The a indicates that we are querying *all* currently-installed packages.

137

❑   In Step 7, we used -qf. The f indicates that we wish to query the package that owns the specified file.

❑   Finally, in Step 8, we used -ql. The l indicates that we wish to query the list of files contained in the specified package.

RPM Package Security

RPM has had a number of releases over the years, and the latest versions (one of which is bundled with your system) have a few new features. One new feature of interest to us is that RPM now checks the **signature** of a package when querying, installing, or upgrading it.

Checking the signature of a package allows you to ensure that it is from a trustworthy source. All official Red Hat Packages are signed by Red Hat using its GnuPG key, and RPM checks the package's GnuPG signature against the Red Hat GnuPG key to make sure the package is what it claims to be. If you do not have an appropriate key installed to verify the signature, then you will get a warning message like this (we mentioned it earlier, remember?):

```
warning: lynx-2.8.5-11.i386.rpm: V3 DSA signature: NOKEY, key ID db42a60e
```

The exact content of the warning message depends on the situation. For example, If RPM cannot verify the GnuPG signature of the package then you will see the following
error message:

```
error: V3 DSA signature: BAD, key ID 0352860f
```

By contrast, if RPM cannot find the appropriate key to verify the signature of a package, you will get this warning:

```
warning: V3 DSA signature: NOKEY, key ID 0352860f
```

GnuPG signatures are digital signatures that are very hard to forge. Signatures are created with a unique secret key *and can be verified by their recipient using a* public key. *A digital signature timestamps a document so that if anyone tries to tamper or modify it, the verification of the signature will fail.*

Red Hat GNU Privacy Guard (GPG) Keys

To install Red Hat's GPG keys on your installed system, issue the following command:

```
# rpm --import /usr/share/rhn/RPM-GPG-KEY
```

or, use the following, to install them from CD-ROM (make sure you've got the right one in the drive):

```
# rpm --import /mnt/cdrom/RPM-GPG-KEY
```

These commands will install Red Hat's public GPG keys onto your system. You can also import other vendors, GnuPG keys in much the same way; just change the name of the file to the one that they've supplied to you.

To display a list of all GnuPG keys installed for RPM package verification on your system, issue the following command:

```
# rpm -qa gpg-pubkey*
gpg-pubkey-db42a60e-37ea5438
```

This will return a list of results. If you've installed the Red Hat key, you should see the following listed amongst them:

```
gpg-pubkey-db42a60e-37ea5438
```

We can get even more complete details of a Red Hat GPG key by executing the following command:

```
# rpm -qi gpg-pubkey-db42a60e-37ea5438
```

In the above command, note that gpg-pubkey-db42a60e-37ea5438 *is the name of the Red Hat GnuPG key, gathered from the output of the command* rpm -qa gpg-pubkey*.

This produces the following response – quite detailed isn't it? Most importantly it reveals the vendor's name and signing date, which is handy if you've got a key on your system, but aren't sure who it's from, or if it is still in date:

```
Name          : gpg-pubkey              Relocations: (not relocateable)
Version       : db42a60e                     Vendor: (none)
Release       : 37ea5438                  Build Date: Sun 20 Apr 2003
14:10:53 BST
Install Date: Sun 20 Apr 2003 14:10:53 BST      Build Host: localhost
Group         : Public Keys              Source RPM: (none)
Size          : 0                           License: pubkey
Signature     : (none)
Summary       : gpg(Red Hat, Inc <security@redhat.com>)
Description :
-----BEGIN PGP PUBLIC KEY BLOCK-----
Version: rpm-4.1 (beecrypt-2.2.0)

mQGiBDfqVDgRBADBKr3Bl6PO8BQ0H8sJoD6p9U7Yyl7pjtZqioviPwXP+DCWd4u8HQzcxAZ5
7m8ssA1LK1Fx93coJhDzM130+p5BG9mYSWShLabR3N1KXdXQYYcowTOMGxdwYRGr1Spw8Qyd
LhjVfU1VSl4xt6bupPbWJbyjkg5Z3P7BlUOUJmrx3wCgobNVEDGaWYJcch5z5Blof/41G8kE
AKii6q7Gu/vhXXnLS6m15oNnPVybyngiw/23dKjSZVG7rKANEK2mxg1VB+vc/uUc4k49UxJJ
fCZglgu1sPFV3GSa+Y/7jsiLktQvCiLPlncQt1dV+ENmHR5BdIDPWDzKBVbgWnSDnqQ6KrZ7
T6AlZ74VMpjGxxkWU6vV2xsWXCLPA/9P/vtImA8CZN3jxGgtK5GGtDNJ/cMhhuv5tnfwFg4b
/VGo2Jr8mhLUqoIbE6zeGAmZbUpdckDco8D5fiFmqTf5+++pCEpJLJkkzel/32N2w4qzPrcR
MCiBURESPjCLd4Y5rPoU8E4kOHc/4BuHN903tiCsCPloCrWsQZ7UdxfQ5LQiUmVkIEhhdCwg
SW5jIDxzZWN1cml0eUByZWRoYXQuY29tPohVBBMRAgAVBQI361Q4AwsKAwMVAwAwIDFgIBAheA
AAoJECGRgM3bQqYOsBQAnRVtg7B25Hm11PHcpa8FpeddKiq2AJ9aO8sBXmLDmPOEFI75mpTr
KYHF6rkCDQQ361RyEAgAokgI2xJ+3bZsk8jRA8ORIX8DH05UlMH27qFYzLbT6npXwXYIOtVn
0K2/iMDj+oEB1Aa2au4OnddYaLWp06v3d+XyS0t+5ab2ZfIQzdh7wCwxqRkzR+/H5TLYbMG+
hvtTdylfqIX0WEfoOXMtWEGSVwyUsnM3Jy3LOi48rQQSCKtCAUdV20FoIGWhwnb/gHU1BnmE
S6UdQujFBE6EANqPhp0coYoIhHJ2oI08ujQItvvNaU88j/s/izQv5e7MXOgVSjKe/WX3s2Jt
B/tW7utpy12wh1J+JsFdbLV/t8CozUTpJgx5mVA3RKlxjTA+On+1IEUWioB+iVfT7Ov/0kcA
zwADBQf9E4SKCWRand8K0XloMYgmipxMhJNnWDMLkokvbMNTUoNpSfRoQJ9EheXDxwMpTPwK
ti/PYrrL2J11P2ed0x7zm8v3gLrY0cue1iSba+8glY+p31ZPOr5ogaJw7ZARgoS8BwjyRymX
Qp+8Dete0TELKOL2/itDOPGHW07SsVWOR6cmX4VlRRcWB5KejaNvdrE54XFtOd04NMgWI63u
qZc4zkRa+kwEZtmbz3tHSdRCCE+Y7YVP6IUf/w6YPQFQriWYFiA6fD10eB+BlIUqIw80Vgjs
BKmCwvKkn4jg8kibXgj4/TzQSx77uYokw1EqQ2wkOZoaEtcubsNMquuLCMWijYhGBBgRAgAG
BQI361RyAAoJECGRgM3bQqYOhyYAnj7hVDY/FJAGqmtZpwVp9IlitW5tAJ4xQApr/jNFZCTk
snI+4O1765F7tA==
=3AHZ
-----END PGP PUBLIC KEY BLOCK-----
```

Verifying Red Hat Signed Packages

Having installed Red Hat's GPG keys, we can then verify official Red Hat packages as being authentic. As an example, let's verify the Lynx package that we looked at earlier:

```
# rpm -K lynx-2.8.5-11.i386.rpm
lynx-2.8.5-11.i386.rpm: (sha1) dsa sha1 md5 gpg OK
```

If all goes well you will see an MD5 gpg OK message. This proves that the signature of the package has been verified and that it has not been corrupted or altered.

Installing Packages

RPM provides other advantages over the Package Management Tool), as it can install packages from *any* source – including Red Hat distribution CDs, network locations, FTP, and HTTP.

The syntax for installing a package looks like this:

```
rpm -i [options] <package_filename>
```

As an example, let's look at the installation of a couple of packages, and their dependencies, now.

Try It Out   **Installing Packages using RPM**

1. First, let's install the Lynx web browser that we've just verified is OK. You should already be logged in with root privileges, with the terminal window open and still in the Red Hat/RPMS directory of your mounted CDROM. From there, type in the following at the command line:

```
# rpm -ivh lynx-2.8.5-11.i386.rpm
```

The output you get depends on whether the Lynx browser is already installed. If it's not, then you'll see the following:

```
Preparing...                ######################################### [100%]
   1:lynx                    ######################################### [100%]
```

But, if it's already on your machine then RPM won't attempt to install it again. Instead, you will get the following message:

```
Preparing...                ######################################### [100%]
        package lynx-2.8.5-11 is already installed
```

2. That went quite easily, didn't it? Now, let's perform another installation example, installing a package that has dependencies. The **balsa** package is a GNOME e-mail client. If we try to install this using the same technique as we did before, we get a **failed dependencies** error message. Try it if you like:

```
# rpm -ivh balsa-2.0.6-1.i386.rpm
error: Failed dependencies:
        libesmtp.so.5 is needed by balsa-2.0.6-1
```

3. As you can see from the output, RPM fails to install the package. Instead, it shows an

141

error message indicating that the package balsa-2.0.6-1.i386.rpm has a dependency that is not met – namely, the package `libesmtp.so.5` is not installed. RPM provides the file name of the dependency but does not provide the package name to resolve it. This isn't very helpful, but fortunately Red Hat provides an extra package that can be installed to get suggestions about package filenames to resolve dependencies.

The package in question is currently called *rpmdb-redhat-9-0.20030313.i386.rpm* but the name may differ slightly in your version (just look on your CDROM for a filename beginning `rpmdb-` and that'll be it). Simply install it as you installed the previous packages:

```
#rpm -ivh rpmdb-redhat-9-0.20030313.i386.rpm
Preparing...              ########################################### [100%]
1:rpmdb-Red Hat           ########################################### [100%]
```

4. Now if we try to install the balsa package again we will get a message suggesting the location of the dependent file:

```
# rpm -ivh balsa-2.0.6-1.i386.rpm
error: Failed dependencies:
        libesmtp.so.5 is needed by balsa-2.0.6-1
    Suggested resolutions:
        libesmtp-0.8.12-5.i386.rpm
```

5. So, let's try again. This time, install the suggested package `libesmtp-0.8.12-5.i386.rpm` first:

```
# rpm -ivh libesmtp-0.8.12-5.i386.rpm
Preparing...              ########################################### [100%]
    1:libesmtp            ########################################### [100%]
```

6. When that's complete, you can install the balsa package as follows:

```
# rpm -ivh balsa-2.0.6-1.i386.rpm
Preparing...              ########################################### [100%]
    1:balsa               ########################################### [100%]
```

Alternatively, you could have installed them together on the same line, like this:

```
# rpm -ivh balsa-2.0.6-1.i386.rpm libesmtp-0.8.12-5.i386.rpm
Preparing...              ########################################### [100%]
    1:libesmtp            ########################################### [ 50%]
2:balsa                   ########################################### [100%]
```

7. Finally, it's worth mentioning that RPM packages can be installed directly from the Internet. We can use HTTP or FTP addresses to install directly. If you wanted to install say the vnc-server directly from the Red Hat web site, you'd type this:

```
# rpm -ivh
http://ftp.redhat.com/pub/redhat/linux/9/en/os/i386/RedHat/RPMS/vnc-server-
3.3.3r2-47.i386.rpm
```

How It Works

We've used the RPM command for installation, much as we did for querying earlier, this time, however, the options are slightly different. Each of the three install commands used the option -ivh here, which translates as follows:

- ❑ i indicates that we intend to perform an installation

- ❑ v indicates that we want RPM to display "additional information". For example to display package file names while performing multiple package installation with one rpm command.

- ❑ h indicates that we want RPM to print hash (#) marks during the installation process to show the progress of the installation.

Removing Packages

Removing unwanted packages from your system is an important task. RPM makes package removal easy. It keeps record of all the files installed by each package, so we can easily clean our system by removing all the files associated with an unwanted package.

Try It Out   Removing Packages using the RPM

OK, so we probably don't actually need the vnc-server, lynx, and balsa packages on our system. So, here's how we go about removing them:

1. First, type the following to remove the vnc-server package:

```
# rpm -e vnc-server
```

2. That was pretty easy; now do it again for Lynx:

```
# rpm -e lynx
```

3. All OK, so far. Now, how about balsa? Ah, we've got dependencies here, so we need to progress carefully. If we try to remove `libesmtp-0.8.12-2.i386.rpm` before we remove `balsa-1.2.4-7.i386.rpm` then we'll get an error:

```
# rpm -e libesmtp
error: Failed dependencies:
        libesmtp.so.5 is needed by (installed) balsa-2.0.6-1
```

This is because (as we learned in the previous example) `balsa-2.0.6-1` is dependent on `libesmtp.so.5`. So, if RPM were to remove `libesmtp.so.5`, then `balsa-2.0.6-1` wouldn't work anymore. So RPM protects us from this: any attempt to remove the `libesmtp` package throws an error.

We can, however, *force* RPM to remove `libesmtp`, even with balsa still installed. To do this, specify the –nodeps option in the RPM command:

```
# rpm --nodeps -e libesmtp
# rpm -e balsa
```

And it will remove the packages regardless. Let's look at the logic behind how this works.

How It Works

We used the `rpm` command to remove installed packages; this time using the `-e` option to indicate that we're using RPM to *remove* a package.

> Note that we didn't specify the full package file names (`vnc-server-3.3.3r2-47.i386.rpm` and `lynx-2.8.5-11.i386.rpm`) in the commands above; instead, we used the names of the packages themselves (`vnc-server` and `lynx`):

```
# rpm -e vnc-server
# rpm -e lynx
```

We also used the –nodeps option to remove the `libesmtp` package. It is not really recommended to use this option for the installation or removal of packages, as the newly installed package will not work without having all of its dependent files installed. However it's worth knowing about it in case you're confronted with a broken or corrupted package that you need to remove from your machine.

Upgrading Packages

Upgrading a package is similar to installing one. The only difference is in the processing that goes on in the background. When it upgrades a package, RPM *uninstalls* the old package and then *installs* a new one. It copies the new configuration file with an `.rpmnew` extension without touching the existing configuration file, if the existing configuration file has been changed since it was first created (that is to say if you, the user, have changed it from its defaults).

The syntax for a package upgrade using RPM is this:

```
rpm -U [options] <package_filename>
```

Let's go through the steps of upgrading the fetchmail remote mail retrieval and forwarding utility.

To upgrade the fetchmail package with latest version (assuming that you've queried it and are satisfied that it is what it claims to be):

```
# rpm -Uvh fetchmail-6.2.0-3.i386.rpm
Preparing...                ########################################### [100%]
   1:fetchmail              ########################################### [100%]

Latest version of the Red Hat packages can be downloaded from www.RedHat.com
website.
```

Verifying Package Integrity

RPM provides one more useful piece of functionality it – allows us to compare information about our installed files with the same information from the original package. This helps when we need to check a file for changes, deletions, or data corruption.

Let's look at a few example of how to verify a package:

❑   To verify a particular file contained in a package:

```
# rpm -Vf /usr/bin/vncviewer
```

If the package owning the file has not been changed, corrupted, or deleted then you will not see any message.

❑   To verify an installed package against the RPM file:

```
# rpm -Vp vnc-3.3.3r2-47.i386.rpm
```

Again, if everything is OK then you will not see any message.

❑   If you try to verify a package which is *not installed* on the system, you will see a message such as the one in the example below:

```
# rpm -Vp lynx-2.8.5-11.i386.rpm
missing   c /etc/lynx.cfg
missing   c /etc/lynx.cfg.cs
...
missing     /usr/share/locale/sv/LC_MESSAGES/lynx.mo
missing   d /usr/share/man/man1/lynx.1.gz
```

❑   To verify all installed packages on your system:

```
# rpm -Va
```

This command will compare all files installed by packages with the original packages.

> **For more details about RPM, see the project's web page at http://www.rpm.org/max-rpm/.**

Package Installation in TAR Format

While RPM is an excellent, feature-rich, technology, it's not used universally, and you may occasionally find yourself needing to deal with binary packages in TAR format.

> *A **binary package** is a pre-compiled package, and hence comes ready to install. By contrast, you may also come across source code packages – these contain uncompiled code, and must be compiled before installation.*

A TAR file is an archive file created using the TAR command on a Linux system. TAR stands for **Tape ARchive**. TAR archives were initially used to store files on magnetic tape but now commonly occur on all storage media.

TAR files are simply a method of sticking a number of smaller files together, so that a collection of files becomes one larger (easier to handle) file. This larger file can then be compressed using a program like gzip to reduce its size. (This is similar to the way that Windows creates ZIP files.)

Here's a summary of the advantages and disadvantages of using TAR files:

Advantages of using TAR:

❑   Not all software is available in RPM format. There is more chance of pre-compiled (binary) software being available in TAR.

❏ TAR files work on all Linux and Unix flavors, while not all Linux machines (such as Debian machines) can deal with RPM files by default.

Disadvantages of TAR format:

❏ Difficult to keep track of files installed by a TAR file package

❏ Difficult to check for file corruption or modification

Try It Out   **Installing a Binary Package in TAR Format**

In order to help us understand how to deal with TAR packages we'll demonstrate the installation of a small file package that tells us what kind of web server a web site is running on.

1. Firstly we downloaded the file chkwww-0.4.3.tar.gz from www.sourceforge.net, and placed it in our /usr/local directory (though we could have put it anywhere).

2. Next we to the /usr/local directory and uncompress the TAR file (you can tell it's been compressed using GZIP, as it has a .gz suffix. (*This step isn't always necessary*).

```
# gzip -dv pychkwww_0.4.TAR.gz
pychkwww_0.4.TAR.gz:    81.6% -- replaced with pychkwww_0.4.TAR
```

The -dv options mean:

❏ -d This decompresses the file.

❏ -v This uses verbose mode, so it prints its progress to the screen.

❏ -f This option forces the overwriting of old (existing) files with their newer counterparts.

This creates an uncompressed TAR file called chkwww-0.4.3.tar

3. Now we 'unTAR' the package to release the files with it. This is done with the following command. You'll see a list of the files released:

```
# TAR -xvf pychkwww_0.4.TAR
pychkwww/
pychkwww/CVS/
......
pychkwww/README
pychkwww/TODO
pychkwww/VERSION
```

147

```
pychkwww/pychkwww.py
pychkwww/Makefile
pychkwww/changelog
```

The `-xvf` options mean:

❑   `-x` This option extracts the files.

❑   `-v` This uses verbose mode, so it prints its progress to the screen.

❑   `-f` This option forces the overwriting of old (existing) files with their newer counterparts.

4.   That's it. Our software should now be installed. We'll check the directory created by unTARring the package, to make sure it worked:

```
# ls -al pychkwww
total 64
drwxrwxr-x    4 1000      1000        4096 May 18  2002 .
drwxr-xr-x   13 root      root        4096 Feb 12 00:40 ..
...
-rw-rw-r--    1 1000      1000         480 Mar 27  2002 Makefile
-rwxr-xr-x    1 1000      1000        6841 May 18  2002 pychkwww.py
-rw-rw-r--    1 1000      1000         164 Mar 27  2002 README
-rw-rw-r--    1 1000      1000          46 Mar 27  2002 TODO
```

It's full of files, so it looks promising.

5.   Finally the acid test – we move into the `pychwww` directory, and try to run the software:

```
# cd pychkwww
# ./pychkwww.py
```

6.   If you've got your Internet connection running, try feeding it the following URL to make sure the software is working properly:

```
# ./pychkwww.py www.linux4biz.net
```
www.linux4biz.net (66.103.135.76): Apache/1.3.27 (Unix) mod_log_bytes/1.2
mod_bwlimited/1.0 PHP/4.3.0 FrontPage/5.0.2.2510 mod_ssl/2.8.12 OpenSSL/0.9.6b

Summary

This chapter has aimed to equip you with the knowledge you need to confidently add, remove, and upgrade packages on your system. You should now be able to do the following:

❑ Customize the packages installed on your system using the Package Management Tool

❑ Install additional software directly from the .rpm file, using the Package Manager

❑ Query, Install, Remove, Upgrade, and Verify .rpm files using the RPM command line interface

❑ Ensure update .rpm files you receive from Red Hat are the real thing by checking their GnuPG signature file

❑ Understand the basic principals behind uncompressing and installing TAR files on your system, so you'll know how to proceed when an .rpm file is not available.

This chapter has aimed to give you a taster, and good working knowledge of Red Hat's package management software. If you're interested in learning more, the following resources will be helpful:

❑ Red Hat RPM Documentation:
http://www.redhat.com/docs/manuals/linux/RHL-9-Manual/custom-guide/

❑ Max RPM: http://www.rpm.org/max-rpm/

❑ Open source software portal: http://freshmeat.net/

❑ RPM search portal: http://rpmfind.net/linux/RPM/

In the next chapter, we'll take a look at some of the many applications that are package with your Red Hat Linux 9 distribution, that you're likely to find useful on a day-to-day basis.

5

Everyday Applications

You've installed your Red Hat Linux 9 operating system; you've connected to the Internet; and maybe you've installed a few packages. Now, what about those everyday tasks? How do you set about using your new operating system to do all those important jobs like e-mailing, and creating documents and spreadsheets (and even some of the more fun jobs like manipulating graphics, listening to music, and even developing applications)?

In this chapter we'll survey some of the many applications available within the Red Hat Linux 9 distribution. Red Hat Linux 9 comes with a bewildering array of applications, and to cover them *all* in a single chapter would be impractical; but we'll show you the applications that we think you're most likely to need in order to complete those vital everyday tasks, and to have some fun too.

We'll group the applications in this chapter into the following sections:

- ❑ Office applications
- ❑ Internet applications
- ❑ Personal information management applications
- ❑ Multimedia applications
- ❑ System applications

Within each section, we'll discuss what's required in order to install the application (if it hasn't already been installed by default), and how to configure the installation to suit your requirements. We'll also point out some of the similarities and differences between these applications and other applications that you may be familiar with – such as those found on the Microsoft operating system.

We'll also cover emulator technologies – which are able to emulate the Microsoft Windows operating system, or interpret Windows applications and allow them to run on Linux. These will be of interest if, for example, you're thinking of developing a cross-platform application and you want to check its compatibility with both Linux *and* Windows operating systems.

As a survey, this chapter is designed to show you what's available, rather than to act as a user guide for individual applications. For most of these applications, the online help is comprehensive and well written, and can be accessed from the application's Help menu. In addition, we'll give you URLs of web sites that provide further documentation and support.

Office Applications

While it's not necessarily the most exciting topic, there's no denying that most of us will spend at least some of our time creating and maintaining office documents such as documents, spreadsheets, and presentations. Therefore, we'll start this chapter with an introduction to the **office productivity** applications available within Linux. (As a reward, we'll look at the Internet applications in the next section!)

Because these office tasks are so important, Red Hat Linux 9 comes with a number of different office applications. Some of these applications are rich in functionality and compare with the likes of Microsoft Office, while others are smaller in size but still worthy of mention. These applications should be enough to meet your requirements – and if not, there are even more office application suites for Linux available via the Internet.

We'll start this section with a brief survey of all the office application suites that are included with Red Hat Linux 9. We can't cover them all in depth, because there isn't room; but we will give you an idea of what you can achieve by taking a closer look at *OpenOffice*, the standard office suite in Red Hat Linux 9.

Red Hat Linux and Office Applications

The following office application suites are all available with Red Hat Linux 9:

❑ The **OpenOffice** suite is the office suite that's installed when you install Red Hat Linux 9 using the default settings. OpenOffice consists of a number of applications, including the following:

❑ OpenWriter (for word processing)

❑ OpenCalc (for spreadsheets)

❑ OpenDraw (for graphics)

❑ OpenImpress (for presentations)

OpenOffice is the most functionally capable of the suites listed here, and we'll return to study it in more detail in a moment.

❏ The **StarOffice** suite is arguably one of the most popular office suites on the market for Linux. The latest release at the time of writing is **StarOffice 6.0**. This is a commercial product, with a complete support arrangement (including helpdesk support), and includes extra functionality licensed from third-party vendors. There's more about the latest release of StarOffice at http://www.sun.com/staroffice.

Red Hat's Publisher's Edition, included within this book, includes OpenOffice which shares the same codebase as StarOffice 6.0. For more information on OpenOffice take a look at http://www.openoffice.org.

❏ The **Koffice** suite is one of the original office suites. It's completely integrated, and available for the K Desktop Environment (KDE). It offers a number of applications, including:

❏ KWord (for word processing)

❏ KSpread (for spreadsheets)

❏ KPresenter (for presentations)

❏ Kivio (for flowcharting)

❏ Krita (for graphical applications)

You can get a free download of Koffice from http://www.koffice.org. It is at version 1.2.1 at the time of writing.

❏ The **GNOME Office** suite of office applications also consists of a number of applications, including:

❏ AbiWord (for word processing)

❏ Gnumeric (for spreadsheets)

❏ Gimp (for graphics)

❏ MrProject (for project management)

However, it should be noted that GNOME Office is not as tightly integrated as the OpenOffice suite. More information can be found at http://www.gnome.org/gnome-office.

The development of OpenOffice continues as an Open Source project, under the banner of OpenOffice.org. While OpenOffice is built on the original StarOffice code base, the code developed for OpenOffice will be incorporated into future releases of the StarOffice product suite.

In addition, Sun Microsystems has incorporated OpenOffice into the Gnome Office suite. If you're comparing applications, this will explain any similarities you may come across!

Installing Office Applications

Most of the packages for the default office and productivity applications are listed within the Office/Productivity package group, which you'll find under the Applications category of the Red Hat Package Management (RPM) application that we discussed in Chapter 4. (There are one or two exceptions; for example, GIMP is listed in the Graphics package group.)

You can see which office components are currently installed on your machine by starting the RPM now. To do this, select Main Menu | System Settings | Add/Remove Applications (you'll be prompted for the root password, unless you're already logged in as root), scroll down to the Applications category, find the Office/Productivity package group, and click on the Details button. You should see something like this:

As you can see, the Office/Productivity package consists of 12 packages, including one for the OpenOffice suite, one for the Koffice suite, and a number of packages that make up part of the GNOME suite. Four of these packages (including the OpenOffice suite) are installed by default installation when you install Red Hat Linux 9 in any of its versions:

Package Name	Description
ggv	This is GNOME Ghostview – a user interface for any postscript files created using tools such as Ghostscript. For more on this, see http://www.cs.wisc.edu/~ghost/gv/index.htm
mrproject	This is a graphical project management tool. It's similar to Microsoft Project, allowing you to plan project tasks and resources
openoffice	This is the OpenOffice.org office suite. As we've already mentioned, it's a set of office productivity applications.
xpdf	This is a PDF file viewer for the X Window system.

You can safely install any (or all) of the remaining packages alongside OpenOffice, simply by selecting the packages you wish to install and clicking the **Update** button, just as we described in Chapter 4. (You'll need the distribution disks in order to complete the installation.) Thus, you can experiment with these applications at your leisure, choose your favorites, and (if you wish) uninstall the others later on.

For more on installing and uninstalling packages with the RPM, see Chapter 4.

We'll spend the remainder of this section looking at some of the applications in the OpenOffice suite. It's worth noting that the latest information and downloads for OpenOffice can be found at http://www.openoffice.org. In particular, you'll find that you can run OpenOffice on a number of different platforms, as well as Linux – this site has OpenOffice downloads for a variety of platforms including Linux, Windows, and Mac OS X. You'll also find localized dictionaries, documentation, and support facilities to help you get the most from these applications.

Starting an OpenOffice Application

As soon as OpenOffice is installed (either by default as part of the operating system installation, or manually by adding the package via the RPM), it is ready for you to use. You can start any of the OpenOffice applications from the **Main Menu** | Office menu:

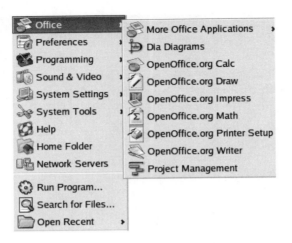

In addition to the menu shortcuts, the OpenOffice installation process also places three shortcut icons within the taskbar at the bottom of the screen; these are for the **Writer**, **Impress**, and **Calc** applications respectively. To invoke any of these applications, just click on the icon:

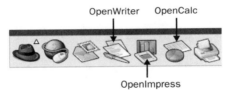

It is also possible to run the office applications from the command line interface. By default, the executable files are installed into the /usr/bin directory, which is part of the $PATH environment variable. This means that we can run any of these applications simply by typing its name at the command line. For example, the following command starts the OpenCalc application:

```
$ oocalc
```

Here are the commands for some other applications in the OpenOffice suite:

Executable	Application
oocalc	Spreadsheet application
oodraw	Drawing application
oomath	Mathematical formula composer

Executable	Application
ooimpress	Presentation application
oowriter	Word processor
ooffice	The default OpenOffice window, for creating any OpenOffice document
oopadmin	For setting up printers for OpenOffice applications
oosetup	The OpenOffice set-up application

Common Functionality

To begin, let's take a look at some of the elements that are common to all the applications in the OpenOffice suite:

❑   The **layout** of main window of each application will be familiar to you if you've ever used applications such as Microsoft Word. The top part of the application displays the **menu toolbar** and a **function toolbar**. Beneath this is the **object toolbar** and the **ruler**, with the main working area below that. The **status toolbar** is at the bottom of the window, and behaves like Microsoft Word's status bar. To the side of the main word area is the **main toolbar**. The diagram below demonstrates these areas as visible within an OpenOffice application:

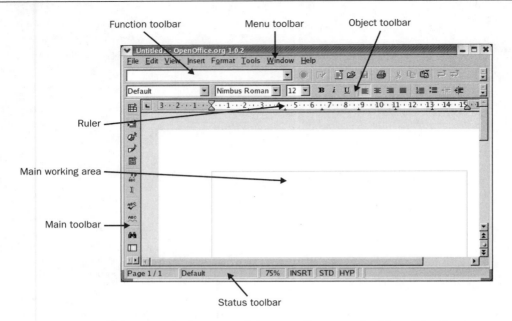

Function toolbar   Menu toolbar   Object toolbar

Ruler

Main working area

Main toolbar

Status toolbar

- ❑ You can choose to hide some of these toolbars via the View | Toolbars menu option. Unlike Microsoft Word, OpenOffice doesn't allow you to undock the toolbars or move them around the screen. However, we can customize the contents of a toolbar – either by right-clicking on a toolbar and selecting Customize, or by selecting View | Toolbars | Customize... from the menu. The toolbars vary from application to application, although the Function, Object, and Main toolbars are common to all the OpenOffice applications.

- ❑ The menu structure also varies from application to application, and therefore it would be impractical to try and explain all the options here. If you've used Microsoft Office then you'll notice some familiar menu options. Even if you're unfamiliar with MS Office, you'll find these quite self-explanatory. For example:

  - ❑ The File menu allows you to open, save, and close files, and offers other features such as printer and page-reviewing options.

  - ❑ The Tools menu allows access to tools that are either incorporated into the application or added via plug-ins. In addition, this menu also usually offers the opportunity to configure various application-specific options.

  - ❑ The Window menu allows you to switch between different documents that you have open in the application at the same time.

  - ❑ The Help menu provides access to the in-built help system (which, incidentally, is extremely comprehensive, and should be the first port of call for any problems or information you require).

Compatibility with Microsoft Office

One thing that many first-time Linux users worry about is whether their MS Office documents are compatible with OpenOffice. For example, is it possible to:

❑ Create a document in Microsoft Word, and then edit it using OpenOffice?

❑ Save a spreadsheet in OpenOffice, and then use it at work within Microsoft Excel?

These are very valid questions, and the answer to both is "Yes!" OpenOffice's built-in **interoperability** features allow you to use OpenOffice applications to load and save documents using file formats that are compatible with other applications (such as those in Microsoft Office). The way in which OpenOffice handles features such as object embedding (and other features that are native to Microsoft Office) must also be configured – to ensure their behavior is as you would expect.

You can configure these options by accessing the Options dialog from **Tools | Options** menu from any OpenOffice application:

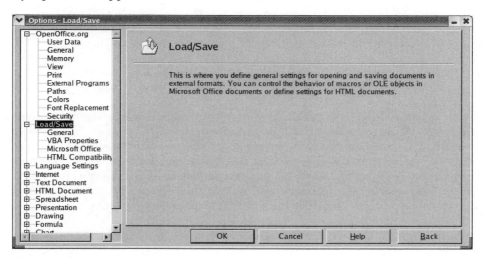

Not all OpenOffice applications support specific conversion features (those that do are discussed here), but they all support the ability to load and save between different file formats. You can find out more by looking at each application's documentation.

Of particular interest here are the options found under the Load/Save node on the left of this dialog. We won't cover all the options here, but we will cover those associated with compatibility with Microsoft Office.

General Loading and Saving Options

The option of interest here is the default File Format that is used when you save a document. You can see this option at the foot of the General tab:

It is here that you can select the default format that the application will use whenever you ask it to save your document to disk (say, using File | Save). As you can see from the screenshot above, when you first install OpenOffice this default document type is set to the OpenOffice.org.1.0 format.

If you want to work with Microsoft Office file formats only, then it is here that you should change this default setting. This can be particularly useful if you transfer files between home and work often, and you don't want to forget to save in the correct format. For example, suppose you use Microsoft Word XP at your place of work, and OpenOffice's OpenWriter at home. If you regularly create documents at home for use at work, you can configure OpenWriter to save your documents in **Microsoft Word 97/2000/XP** format by default, so that these documents are compatible with the software at your place of work.

VBA Options

It is possible that your documents contain code written using **Visual Basic for Applications (VBA)**. OpenOffice applications can handle VBA code in a number of different ways, but support is limited to documents that originated in Microsoft Word 97/2000, Microsoft Excel 97/2000, and Microsoft PowerPoint 97/2000.

OpenOffice supports VBA through the dialog box below:

There are two options for each of the three office applications that support VBA code embedding. These options are:

Option	Description
Load Basic code to edit	When this option is selected, the application will load the VBA code from the original document and embed it into a special Basic module within OpenOffice. This module will preserve the code and allow you to edit it through the application's interface or IDE.
Save Original Basic Code again	When this option is selected, the application will save the code as preserved in the Basic module in the format expected of the Office application, so the code will continue to work as expected (assuming its syntax is correct).

It is beyond the scope of this chapter to cover BASIC within OpenOffice. If you want to know more, take a look at http://www.engineering.usu.edu/cee/faculty/gurro/ Software_Calculators/StarOffice_Docs/StarOfficeBasicManual.zip. StarOffice Basic is very similar to OpenOffice Basic, and you can switch between OpenOffice and VBA Help (if you run Windows) to find assistance.

Microsoft Office Options

Microsoft Office's applications also allow users to embed objects of one type within another. For example, if you wanted to show some sales data from a spreadsheet within your sales report, then you can easily embed your Excel spreadsheet within your Word document. In Microsoft parlance, this is known as **Object Linking and Embedding** (or **OLE**). With OLE, the embedded object inherits the functionality of the application it was created in (so in the example cited here, the embedded Excel spreadsheet inherits the functionality of MS Excel, even though it is embedded into an MS Word file).

The **Options** dialog box in OpenOffice allows us to select which objects are converted (if at all) and at which stage – either when the object is loaded into OpenOffice and/or saving from OpenOffice into a Microsoft format:

The checkboxes in the [L] (for "load") column indicate that an object of the specified type should be converted into an OpenOffice object when a Microsoft document is loaded. The checkboxes in the [S] (for "save") column indicate that the object should be converted to the specified Microsoft Object when the document is saved to a Microsoft file format. (So, if you leave the [S] checkbox unchecked, the objects will *not* be converted and will be absent from the resulting file.)

As you can see from the screenshot above, there are four object types supported, including Microsoft Word (**WinWord**), Microsoft Excel, Microsoft PowerPoint, and MathType.

> *MathType is an application used for representing mathematical formulae. For more on this application, see* http://www.mathtype.com/mathtype.

HTML Compatibility Options

This dialog doesn't offer any features for converting between versions of Microsoft Office, but it does contain the setting that indicates what browser is targeted when exporting a document from an OpenOffice application in **HTML format**. OpenOffice supports a number of formats, including:

❑ Netscape Navigator (version 3.0 and 4.0)

❑ Microsoft Internet Explorer (version 4.0)

❑ HTML 3.2 (most browsers support this)

File Format Options

In addition to the settings within the Options dialog, OpenOffice's ability to load from (and save to) different file formats is integral to the applications themselves. These options vary according to the context of the application, and so they are covered within the OpenOffice applications themselves.

However, it's also worth noting the existence of a generic document conversion tool called AutoPilot, which is accessible from all OpenOffice applications. If you select File | AutoPilot | Document Converter, you'll see a dialog box like the one shown below:

AutoPilot is actually a batch tool, for which OpenOffice provides a shortcut.

This dialog provides you with options to convert from StarOffice or Microsoft Office file formats to the new OpenOffice XML (eXtended Markup Language) format. In the screenshot above, we're concentrating on Microsoft Office file formats and a Word document we have to convert, so we've marked the Word documents option.

After pressing Next, you'll see the dialog box shown below. It prompts us to say whether we wish to convert templates, documents, or both, and whether we are to include sub-directories in our conversion process. In this case, we're converting only Word documents from our working directory and placing the converted files in the same directory:

When you click the Next button again, you'll see a confirmation dialog box. If you're happy that everything is present and correct, select the Convert button and the conversion process will begin:

When the conversion is complete, the Progress screen will display the results of the conversion process.

Note that this conversion process will render any VBA code invalid. If your documents contain VBA code that you wish to preserve, you should avoid this method.

Conversion Quality and Considerations

It's worth mentioning that the conversion quality between different file formats (especially Microsoft Office) is excellent. The only caveats are that the conversion process from OpenOffice to Microsoft Office can lead to files larger that their original file sizes due to the lack of compression. However, this is likely to change in future releases.

It's worth experimenting with the Rich Text Format or RTF file format – this will help to avoid potential conversion errors, although at the expense of certain formatting capabilities. Another option is to link your graphics to external files instead of embedding them within your documents.

Using OpenWriter for Word Processing

When you start OpenOffice's **OpenWriter** (or just **Writer**) word processing application (which you can do using Main Menu | Office | OpenOffice.org Writer or the shortcut icon from the task bar), you are presented with a window like the one below:

OpenWriter provides the wealth of features that one would normally expect to find in a commercial word processing application. We won't list them all here; like the other applications in the suite, it would warrant a book in its own right. However, we will highlight some of the key features included and also describe how interoperability with other applications such as Microsoft Office is achieved. Some of the key features present are:

- ❑ Styles and style galleries
- ❑ Thesaurus
- ❑ Spell checker
- ❑ Clipart
- ❑ Support for other file formats, such as Microsoft Word, StarWriter, and so on

As we've seen, OpenWriter is compatible with Microsoft Word. In particular, it is capable of loading and saving documents and templates in a number of Word file formats, including Microsoft Word 97/2000/XP and Microsoft Word 6.0/95. You can load and save between OpenOffice's native version and any of the other versions listed, simply by using the File | Open and File | Save dialogs. The File Type drop-down box allows you to choose the appropriate format:

Using OpenCalc for Spreadsheets

OpenOffice's **OpenCalc** (or **Calc**) application again provides numerous features that you would expect of a commercial application and is comparable with Microsoft Excel, the spreadsheet application within Microsoft Office. Some of the key features present are:

❑   Ability to handle multiple spreadsheets simultaneously

❑   Embedded graphics and charts

❑   Cell security

❑   External data sources

❑   Data Pilot (this is similar to PivotTables in Excel)

OpenCalc also supports compatibility with Excel, in its ability to load and save spreadsheets and templates in a number of Excel file formats, including Microsoft Excel 97/2000/XP and Microsoft Excel 4.x–5.0. Other interoperability features include the handling of VBA code and embedded objects (as we mentioned earlier in this chapter).

There are other, more specific options that mimic the behavior of MS Excel, and help to make users with an MS Excel background feel more comfortable. One specific such option is the ability to indicate that OpenCalc's searching capability should behave in the same manner as Excel's. This option can be found in the Tools | Options dialog box, in the Spreadsheet | Calculate tab:

Note the Search criteria = and <> must apply to whole cells option in this dialog. When this option is selected, OpenCalc handles searches in the same way as Microsoft Excel, in that the search criteria entered are specific and must match the whole cell. When the option is unselected, the search criteria are matched against *any* position within the cell.

Using OpenImpress for Presentations

OpenOffice's **OpenImpress** (or **Impress**) application again provides many of the kind of features that you would expect of a commercial application, and is comparable with Microsoft's PowerPoint, the presentation management application within Microsoft Office. The key features of OpenImpress include:

- ❏ Master templates
- ❏ Slide animation and transition effects
- ❏ Notes against slides
- ❏ Timing rehearsals

OpenImpress supports compatibility with Microsoft's PowerPoint, in its ability to load and save presentations and templates in PowerPoint's file format (namely PowerPoint 97/2000/XP).

There are a number of other applications installed within the OpenOffice suite that we haven't covered in this chapter. It's worth experimenting with the applications installed, to learn more about what they're capable of doing – here's a brief summary of each:

- ❏ The diagramming tool, **Dia**, is launched through Main Menu | Office | Dia Diagrams. This application is used for drawing diagrams based on a variety of templates – from simple boxes and lines to circuit diagrams. It's very similar to a primitive version of Microsoft's Visio diagram application. See http://www.lysator.liu.se/~alla/dia/dia.html for more information.

- ❏ The **Draw** application, launched via Main Menu | Office | Openoffice.org Draw, can be used to generate drawings that are of a more graphical nature. It allows you to insert clipart from its internal library or external sources. It draws its influence from Microsoft's Draw application.

- ❏ The **Printer Setup** application (Main Menu | Office | Openoffice.org Printer Setup) simply allows you to confirm printer devices that may be available to you, and direct output from applications such as OpenOffice to your printers. Its closest Windows cousin is the Printers option found within the Windows Control Panel.

Internet Applications

The existence of the Internet is at the heart of many of Linux's most exciting applications. Therefore, as promised, in this section we'll take a look at Linux's Internet-related applications.

The default installation of Red Hat Linux 9 includes a number of applications contained in the Graphical Internet package. All these applications have a **graphical user interface (GUI)** to make the user's life easier. The package group contains some 14 applications (of which eight are installed by default). In this section we will concentrate on just two of them:

- ❑ The **Mozilla** application – a web browser that provides similar functionality to Netscape's Navigator or Microsoft's Internet Explorer browsers. Mozilla is a fully functional web browser, and also supports extensions to add further functionality (such as mail).

- ❑ The **GAIM** client – an Instant Messaging client similar to Microsoft's Instant Messenger and capable of interfacing with a number of messaging protocols (such as AIM, ICQ, Yahoo!, MSN, IRC, and others) used by various messaging clients.

We'll take a look at these applications in more detail, and discuss their history and interoperability features; and then you'll be in a position to explore at your leisure.

The Mozilla Web Browser

The Netscape browser's core source code, known as **mozilla**, was released to the public under the Netscape Public License (NPL) in 1998. The Mozilla project (a group set up to continue Netscape Communicator as an Open Source application) used this code as the basis for its own commercial-level browser. The current version of Mozilla is released under the NPL license for modifications of the core mozilla code and the Mozilla Public License (MPL) for any new additions.

The Mozilla web browser is the primary browser for Red Hat Linux, and is an X Window System application that provides a very similar look and feel to the Netscape Navigator and Internet Explorer applications. To take a look, fire it up now by clicking the Web Browser icon on the bottom left of your desktop (next to the Main Menu button), or by selecting Main Menu | Internet | Mozilla Web Browser:

The layout of the application is likely familiar to you. The **menu bar** contains all the familiar menus, and the **navigation toolbar** allows you to type in a URL, move back and forward between recently visited pages, reload a page, and stop a page from loading. The above screenshot also shows a **personal toolbar folder**, which contains shortcuts to your favorite websites – you can control the shortcuts on your personal toolbar folder by using the Manage Bookmarks option (which you'll find under the Bookmarks menu):

The features provided by Mozilla (and the look and feel of those features) will be familiar if you've used Internet Explorer, and more especially if you've used Netscape Navigator (because Mozilla and Navigator are derived from the same original source code).

The Mozilla Mail Client

In addition to its core functionality as a web browser, we can extend Mozilla's base featureset by installing additional functionality (known as **plug-ins**) such as the Mozilla-based **mail client**. In fact, the mail client plug-in is installed as a default extension to Mozilla.

The mail client is accessible from the Mozilla application by selecting the Window | Mail & Newsgroups option from the menu bar. When you first use this, you'll be prompted to create a default account using the information provided by your ISP or network administrator. When you've successfully entered that information, the main application will start with the following screen:

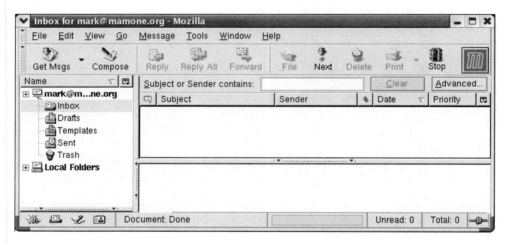

This has very similar functionality to that of Microsoft's Outlook Express – providing folders for your e-mail and for any newsgroups that you're subscribed to. By default, Mozilla includes support for Internet Security Standards such as SSL (Secure Sockets Layer), which provides encryption of information over the Internet.

Let's have a look at some of the specific interoperability features within Mozilla's mail.

Importing from Other Clients

If you have been using another mail client such as Netscape Communicator, Microsoft Outlook, or Microsoft Outlook Express, you may import your mail messages into Mozilla mail by using the features provided from the Tools | Import menu option. This option presents you with the following dialog:

This feature will guide you through the process of importing **mail settings**, and **messages**, or an **address book** from another mail client – you simply select the appropriate option and follow the wizard.

It's also possible to *export* an address book to a variety of formats (including Outlook and Outlook Express). To do this, select Window | Address Book, then the address book you want to export, and then click the Tools | Export menu option.

The GAIM Instant Messenger Application

So you can browse the Internet and correspond using e-mail; what about chatting? This technology has suffered from the number of different protocols used by different organizations for transmitting information. However, in true Linux tradition, **GAIM** is flexible enough to cope with this and offers an elegant solution.

As we mentioned in Chapter 3, GAIM is a utility for supporting online chats; it's similar to things like the AOL Instant Messenger application. It provides a single front-end for multiple protocols (including ICQ, IRC, and Yahoo) and so can interoperate with other Instant Messenger applications.

The first thing to do (if you haven't done so already) is create an account with an Internet messaging service (there are plenty around – MSN and Yahoo! are just two examples). Then, start GAIM (by selecting Main Menu | Internet | Instant Messenger or type gaim at the command line):

By default, only two protocols are installed with GAIM – AIM/ICQ and TOC. It's quite possible that your messaging service uses a different protocol – for example, MSN Messenger and Yahoo! both use their own protocols. GAIM supports many such protocols; to install the protocol support you need, click the Plugins button and use the Load option to load the plug-ins you require for each protocol:

When you've done that, you can tell GAIM about your account – to do that, you click the Accounts button, and supply the information about your account and the protocol used.

When you've done that, you can sign in and start chatting:

The latest updates, documentation and additional plug-ins to extend the functionality of GAIM can be found at its web site at http://gaim.sourceforge.net.

Personal Information Management

As if the Mozilla plug-ins for tasks such as e-mail management weren't enough, an application to manage e-mails, contacts and related things is available in the form of Ximian's **Evolution**. The Evolution application is a groupware program, similar to Microsoft Outlook, that provides access to personal information such as e-mail, a calendar, contacts, and so on. Management of this type of information is often known as **personal information management** (or **PIM**). Programs like Evolution (and Outlook) allow you to manage all of this personal information within a single application.

Installing Evolution

If you look in the RPM GUI, you'll find the Evolution package under the Graphical Internet package group (which is within the Applications category). In fact, it is installed by default as part of the default installation of Red Hat Linux 9 excluding the Server edition for obvious reasons.

Once installed, you can start the Evolution application by selecting Main Menu | Internet | Evolution Email, or by clicking the Evolution Email shortcut that you'll find on the taskbar at the bottom left corner of the desktop (near the Main Menu button).

Setting up Evolution

If you are starting Evolution for the first time, the setup wizard will guide you through completing the information to establish a connection with your mail server through your Internet Service Provider (ISP). The screen below shows one of the early screens in the Evolution Setup Assistant, which starts up the first time you run the application:

Alternatively, you can set up your mailbox properties once the application has started properly. To do this, select Tools | Settings (this is the starting point for changing most of Evolution's settings), and then select the Mail Accounts tab, which allows you to add new accounts and edit the properties of your existing accounts:

The wizard guides you through process of entering the information that is provided by your ISP to gain access to your Internet account and e-mail subscription: your name, e-mail address, and the name of the server and username assigned by your ISP.

Using Evolution

Selecting this option will start the setup wizard, and when the wizard is complete you'll see the Summary screen by default. You can move to other areas of the application by selecting the icons on the left hand side of the window. For example, selecting the InBox icon will display the following screen:

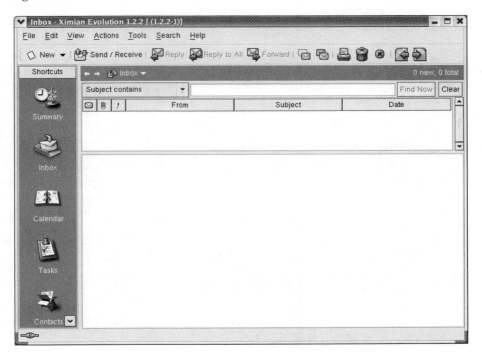

The layout of the window consists of the usual **menu bar** and a context sensitive **toolbar**. The toolbar's icons reflect the application's current mode (Summary, Inbox, Calendar, Tasks, or Contacts). These modes are accessed via the **shortcut toolbar** that runs down the left hand side of the application:

❑ The Summary feature provides a summary screen, similar to Outlook's Today screen. It provides a summary of your Mail Box, indicating the number of e-mail messages in your Inbox and Outbox with counters for each. A list of current Appointments and Tasks is shown along with the ability to capture the current Weather forecast and News Feeds from the Internet.

177

❑ The Inbox (shown above) provides access to your e-mail account, allowing you to send, receive, and manage your e-mails using such features and folders.

❑ The Calendar allows you to manage your schedule, adding forthcoming appointments between one or more people and attaching reminders so you don't forget!

❑ The Tasks feature provides a simple task database, allowing you to record tasks and assign Due Dates. In addition, you can categorize your tasks for more flexibility when managing them.

❑ The Contacts feature allows you to store your contacts in an address book, which may then be used when sending e-mails. However, it allows you to store far more information than simply an e-mail address such as their address, web pages, a variety of telephone numbers, company information, and more!

Again, we'll avoid trying to provide a user guide here; that would take too much room, and the online documentation is more than sufficient to take you through the details of individual tasks. Instead, we'll concentrate on the *key* features of the application, we'll note some similarities with Microsoft Outlook, and we'll also cover some of the features for interoperability with other applications (particularly Microsoft Outlook).

The Summary Feature

As mentioned, this feature is very similar to the Today screen in Microsoft Outlook, or the Summary screen in Microsoft Outlook Express. It summarizes the information held within the application, and includes useful features for gathering information from various sources on the Internet.

To modify the settings that apply to this screen, you can use Tools | Settings to bring up the Evolution Settings dialog, and then select the Summary Preferences tab:

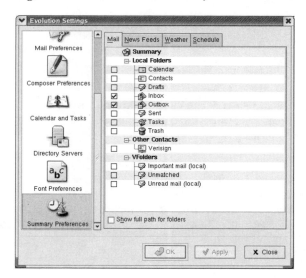

This dialog contains four tabs, which allow you to customize the contents of the Evolution Summary screen:

Tab	Description
Mail	Allows you to add shortcuts to each of your local mail folders (including subfolders) – including the Inbox, Outbox, Sent, and Drafts folders, and any other folders you create using the Inbox mode. If you add a shortcut to a folder, the Summary also shows you a count of the number of items in that folder.
News Feeds	Allows you to add links to news feeds. The News Feeds tab contains a number of predefined news feeds to choose from – the Red Hat Linux Update Watch (https://rhn.redhat.com/rpc/recent-errata.pxt) is displayed by default. You can also use the News Feeds tab to create your own.
Weather	Allows you to retrieve the current weather forecasts from a recognized source. For example, the Met Office (in the UK) is used as the source for weather forecasts most of the main cities within the UK.
Schedule	Allows you to manage the display of calendar and task summaries in the Summary display. You can choose how many days of your calendar to be displayed at once (choose from one day, five days, one week, or one month). You can also choose to whether to display *all* tasks in the Summary, or only those tasks that are "due today".

The Inbox Feature

The Inbox screen provides an interface not only to your Inbox folder, but to all your local mail folders. When you first open the Inbox screen, you get to see the Inbox folder, with a list of messages shown in the top panel and the content of the currently selected message shown underneath in the preview panel. The toolbar contains shortcuts to the most popular features – creating, replying, and deleting messages, printing, navigation, and so on.

The folder bar is a particularly useful feature that's not shown by default. To make it appear, select View | Folder Bar:

Folder bar   Contents of folder   Contents of message (preview pane)

As you can see, the folder bar makes it much easier to find your way around your local mail folders. In addition, you can use the folder bar to manage your folders – creating, deleting, moving, copying, renaming folders and so on. For example, to create a new subfolder you simply select the parent folder in the folder bar and *either* select File | New | Folder *or* right-click and select Create New Folder.

Evolution also provides the usual search facilities, which are very similar to those in Microsoft's Outlook. You can apply search criteria against fields held in e-mails, such as the subject or body.

The Calendar Feature

The Calendar function provides you with a view that represents a certain time period. It can display a single day, a week (including or excluding weekends), or a month. You can change this setting via the View | Current View menu item. The example below shows the Working Week view:

It is within these views that you can create **Appointments** that holds information such as **Summary, Location, Start Date/Time, Classification,** and so on. You can even add a **Reminder** to your appointment, and you can create recurring reminders over a period of days, weeks, months, or years. In the screenshot above you can see that I had a couple of appointments, including a visit to the dentist (oh joy!) and a meeting with the publisher...

The Tasks Feature

The **Tasks** screen is a simple but effective list of jobs. To enter a task, you can use the **New | Task** button or the **Click to add a task** textbox. If you want, you can also assign a **Due Date**, and when the task is complete, you can mark it as finished.

The screen below shows an example of the **Tasks** screen with some tasks entered to show you some of the features described:

You can see three tasks in this screenshot. I cleaned the car last Friday, and afterwards I marked the task as complete by clicking the checkbox next to that task. We're having a dinner party tomorrow (Tuesday), so I have to buy some food – the application is showing that task in bold because I have to buy that food today! The final task shows that I have until February 26 to submit this chapter to the Publisher.

Remember that these tasks can also be displayed on your **Summary** *screen to act as a reminder for you.*

The Contacts Feature

The **Contacts** screen acts as an address book. The screen presents columnar list of contacts that exist within your address book. The screen below shows the contact screen with just a few contacts already entered:

You can see here that I have added a few contacts. I've added contact entries for all the co-authors of this book, and for two companies (**Wrox Press** and **Red Hat**). I've also added a **distribution list**, which I've called Beg RHL9 Authors. This entry has a table icon to the right of it, to indicate that it's a distribution list; it contains a list of the entries for the other authors.

To add a contact, you can use the New | Contact button or the File | New | Contact menu option. When you do so, you get a dialog box in which to enter your information:

Creating distribution lists is equally simple – you use the New | Contact List button or the File | New | Contact List menu option to bring up the dialog, supply a name, and then use your mouse to drag-and-drop contacts into the list.

To the right of the window you'll notice a list of shortcut buttons. Each button acts as a filter on the contacts. So if I selected the W button, only those contacts beginning with W would be shown – in this case only Simon Whiting and Wrox Press.

Importing E-mail from other Systems

If you are familiar with Microsoft Outlook (or Outlook Express), then you will find Evolution very familiar and comfortable. In fact, you can use Evolution either to import data from a recognized format in the form of a data file or to connect to an e-mail account already held on Microsoft Exchange such as one within your corporate environment or even at home.

Importing from Outlook and Other Formats

The File | Import option from the menu starts the Evolution Importer Assistant. Step 1 of the assistant invites you to indicate whether you want to import from an older program, or from a file. If you're importing from a file, Step 2 looks like this:

You can import from any of six formats listed in the drop-down list shown in the screenshot. When you've selected the data file you wish to convert, move to Step 3 using the Next button, and select the Import button to begin the import process.

> *You cannot use this technique when importing information from Microsoft Outlook or Outlook Express version 4 (or later). However, you can convert these files into the standard mbox format that **is** supported by the above method (you can perform this conversion using another mail application such as Mozilla Mail). Alternatively you can use the Outport Tool. For more information, see http://outport.sourceforge.net and http://support.ximian.com/cgi-bin/ximian.cfg/php/enduser/std_adp.php?p_faqid=59.*

Connecting to a Microsoft Exchange Mail Server

Connecting your Evolution client to a Microsoft Exchange server is fairly simple, as long as you have purchased the Ximian Connector for Microsoft Exchange. Instructions for setting up accounts using this feature can be found within the online documentation, or at the Ximian support desk (try http://support.ximian.com/cgi-bin/ximian.cfg/php/enduser/popup_adp.php?p_faqid=148).

Further information on the Ximian Connector can be found at http://www.ximian.com/products/connector, which describes in more detail the features within the product and the costs associated with it.

Multimedia Applications

The category of multimedia applications encompasses a wide variety of applications from playing CDs, to creating your own music library using MP3 files, to creating your own videos! This section covers some of these applications that tackle audio or graphical file formats.

Red Hat Linux 9 ships with no less than 19 packages packed full of multimedia applications. You'll find these packages in the Sound and Video package group (under the Applications category) in the RPM. Aside from the three standard package groups, there are 11 other package groups installed by default – these applications cover a variety of audio and graphical functionality:

Package Group	Description
cdda2wav	Utility for copying `.wav` files from audio Cds
cdlabelgen	CD case designer
cdp	Text application for playing audio Cds
cdparanoia	Compact disc digital audio (CDDA) extraction tool (also known as a **ripper**)
cdrecord	Command line based CD recording program
dvdrecord	Command line based CD and DVD recording program
grip	Graphical CD ripper and MP3 encoder
gtoaster	CD Recording package for both sound and data
mikmod	MOD file player
xawtv	TV application for suitably compliant devices

xmms	Multimedia player

We'll deal with these two types of applications in the following two subsections.

Audio Applications

As well as just allowing you to play CDs, Red Hat Linux provides a load of other utilities – from creating special effects in XMMS to converting them into MP3 files and labeling them. We can't cover all of the audio applications in the **Sound and Video** package group, so we'll concentrate on the most useful and user-friendly applications, and some of which are included in other packages such as the GNOME desktop:

❑ Playing audio CDs with Gnome-CD

❑ Playing multimedia files with Xmms

❑ Burning (writing) and ripping (extracting from) music CDs with cdparanoia, grip, and other utilities

Playing Audio CDs

The default application for playing your audio CDs is **Gnome-CD**. You can run Gnome-CD by selecting **Main Menu | Sound & Video | CD Player** or by typing gnome-cd at the command line, but you'll find that the application starts automatically if you put an audio CD into your CD drive. It presents you with the following screen:

This will automatically extract the track list and duration from the CD. From here you can play, skip forward, skip backward, and adjust the volume, and so on, just as you would on a standard CD player.

The two buttons on the left (just below the words **Unknown Album** in the screenshot) lead to the **Track Editor** and **Preferences** dialogs. The **Preferences** dialog is particularly useful, because it allows you to choose the CD player device and to control the behavior of the application when you start it and close it:

Playing Multimedia Files

Red Hat Linux 9 ships with a copy of **Xmms** (version 1.2.7), which is a cross-platform multimedia player very similar to the popular WinAmp on the Windows platform. To start Xmms, you can select Main Menu | Sound & Video | Audio Player, or run xmms from the command line. Either way, you are presented with the following screen:

As you will notice, the interface is small and concise, relying on separate windows to encapsulate further features that you may decide to switch on. You can access the xmms main menu by right-clicking on the title bar of the window. This provides you with a menu that allows access to the following:

- ❑ Play options (File, Directory, Location)
- ❑ Window displayed (Main Window, Playlist Editor, or Graphical Equalizer)
- ❑ An Options sub-menu
- ❑ A Playback sub-menu
- ❑ A Visualization sub-menu

In the screenshot below, you can see the Main Window, Playlist Editor, and Graphical Equalizer all together. The application has retrieved the tracks from a CD by using the Play Directory option, and selecting /mnt/cdrom as the location. You can also see that Track 2 has been selected and is currently playing:

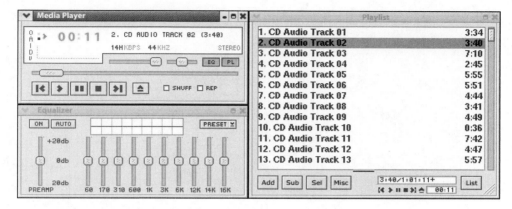

Support for Various Audio and Video Formats

So, the xmms application can be used to play audio CDs in the same way as Gnome-CD. The real benefits come from using the application to play other audio and video formats, such as MP3s, which may exist on media other than a CD. For example, you may keep your MP3 collection on your hard disk, in which case you may use the Play Directory feature of XMMS.

> NOTE: By default Red Hat has disabled the ability for XMMS to play MP3 files; however, this capability can be reinstated and is discussed later on in this section.

You can extend the capabilities of the xmms application using plug-ins, which can be enabled and configured using the Preferences dialog. To get to the Preferences dialog, right-click on the main xmms window and select Options | Preferences:

You'll notice that the dialog contains a number of tabs – these tabs allow you to configure various plug-ins and include **Audio**, **Visualization**, and **General** options. We'll concentrate on **Audio** plug-ins and allow you to play with the others. There are a number of plug-ins already installed, and these plug-ins cover the following audio sources:

❏   Audio CD-ROMs (using `libcaudio.so`)

❏   `.mod` files (using `libmikmod.so`)

❏   `.wav` files (using `libwav.so`)

❏   `.ogg` files (using `libvorbis.so`)

Support for MP3s

You'll notice that MP3 is missing. Red Hat decided to disable MP3 support by default, in view of legal concerns surrounding patents and licensing. However, you can reinstate such features by installing the XMMS MP3 update from various Internet sites. You simply need to install the **xmms-mp3** RPM, which consists of the following two files:

❏   `/usr/lib/xmms/Input/libmpg123.la`

❏   `/usr/lib/xmms/Input/libmpg123.so`

Also provided is the source or SRPM from which the binary RPM was built. This is the same SRPM shipped with Red Hat Linux 9 except that it uses the unrestricted XMMS source (i.e. has MP3 support), and has been modified to create the xmms-mp3 sub package. The package can be downloaded from http://www.gurulabs.com/downloads.html.

You would then install the RPM using a command line similar to the following, depending on the package name:

```
rpm -Uvh xmms-mp3-1.2.7-13.p.i386.rpm
```

Finally (although we won't discuss them here), it's worth noting that there are xmms extensions that provide a number of other features, including visualization, skins, and effect plug-ins (for simulating echo, stereo, and other effects).

CD Burning and Ripping Utilities

This section covers some of the utilities that Red Hat Linux provides for writing data to CDs and DVDs (a process known as **burning**). We'll also cover the utilities for taking digital data from the audio tracks of a CD (known as **ripping**) and turning them into MP3 files (known as **encoding**). The MP3 files can then be stored on your hard disk and played through the XMMS application that we discussed earlier.

Extracting Audio Files from CD to MP3

First, let's consider the task of extracting audio files from CD into MP3 format. The utility of choice for this task is cdparanoia, which is installed by default within Red Hat 9. It can be run only from the command line, but it is very flexible and you can have a lot of fun learning what all the different parameters are for. To find out about all the different parameters, just type the application name at the command line:

```
$ cdparanoia
...
USAGE:
  cdparanoia [options] <span> [outfile]
OPTIONS:
 -v --verbose            : extra verbose operation
 -q --quiet              : quiet operation
 -e --stderr-progress    : force output of progress information to
                           stderr (for wrapper scripts)
...
```

In its simplest form, the following command line will extract all the tracks on a CD and store them in separate files in the current working directory:

```
$ cdparanoia -B -w "1-"
```

Here's how to interpret the parameters in this command:

Parameter	Meaning
-B	Indicates that this is a batch and each track will be extracted to a separate file
-w	Indicates that the output file is to be a Microsoft .wav file

| `"1-"` | Indicates that you wish to extract from the first track to the end of the disc |

You can find out more about cdparanoia *at* http://www.xiph.org/paranoia/.

A GUI for CD Rippers and MP3 Encoders

To make your CD ripping and MP3 encoding activities easier, Red Hat Linux 9 includes the **grip** utility. You can fire up this GUI by selecting Main Menu | Extras | Sound & Video | grip. By default, it's configured to use cdparanoia for extracting the audio files (as .wav files) and the lame executable for encoding the files into MP3 format.

As we've mentioned, the lame encoder is not included by default in Red Hat Linux 9, due to its decision to not support MP3 out of the box. However, you can download the lame encoder from http://rpmfind.net/linux/freshrpms/redhat-8.0/lame, and you can get the bladeenc encoder from http://bladeenc.mp3.no.

The interface of the grip utility is intuitive and fairly easy to use. The main screen is shown below:

More information can be found at the Grip's web site at http://nostatic.org/grip/.

Recording Files onto CD

The **cdrecord** utility is a command line utility for recording files onto writable CDs using an appropriate CD-Writer drive (CD-R or CD/RW). It is installed by default in Red Hat Linux 9, and its web site can be found at http://www.fokus.gmd.de/research/cc/glone/employees/joerg.schilling/private/cdrecord.html.

Like `cdparanoia`, the `cdrecord` utility is a very flexible program and as such has a large number of parameters. The parameters you need vary according to the type of CD format you are writing (for example, whether you're creating an audio CD or a data CD). For a full list of parameters, you can check the website or type the application's name at the command line:

```
$ cdrecord
...
Options:
    -version        print version information and exit
    dev-target      SCSI target to use as CD/DVD-Recorder
    ...
```

The example command below records an audio CD by writing the `.wav` files created by using the `cdparanoia` utility:

```
$ cdrecord -v dev=2,0 -dao *.wav
```

This example assumes that the `.wav` files are located in the current directory, and that a blank CD-R or CD-RW is in the drive. Here's how the parameters used here affect the application's behavior:

Parameter	Meaning
`-v`	Indicates that progress is displayed via the verbose switch
`-dev`	Indicates the SCSI target for the device identified. Each SCSI device is assigned an ID; in this case it's 2,0.
`-dao`	Indicates that a single session is to be written to the CD and closed when finished
`*.wav`	Indicates that all files matching this specification should be written to the CD

You can also use the `dvdrecord` utility to record information on writable DVD drives such as DVD-RAM. There's more information on this at http://www.nongnu.org/dvdrtools/.

GnomeToaster

If you find all this command line stuff too daunting, you could use the **GnomeToaster** application. GnomeToaster is a graphical CD recording utility written for the GNOME environment. You can start this application by selecting Main Menu | System Tools | More System Tools | CD Writer, or by typing `gtoaster` at the command line:

We won't dwell on this application, but we'll note that the user interface is again easy to use and provides a simpler (if less flexible) alternative to the `cdrecord` option. You simply use the top part of the dialog to locate the files you want to record, drag them across to the bottom part of the dialog (which represents the CD-ROM drive), and select the Record option.

Graphics Applications

There are numerous graphical applications installed within Red Hat Linux; some exist as part of KDE or GNOME. Others can be found within application suites such as OpenDraw (which is included within OpenOffice), and yet others are standalone applications written for the sole purpose of manipulating images.

In this chapter, we'll concentrate on the applications that are installed by default with Red Hat Linux 9: The GIMP, PDF Viewer, GQView, and OpenDraw. Most of these are contained within the Graphics package group (which you'll find under the Applications category of the RPM), and can be found in the Main Menu | Graphics menu.

The GIMP

The **GNU Image Manipulation Program** (or **GIMP**, as it's affectionately known) is a very powerful piece of software used for graphic manipulation and is equally at home as a simple paint program as it is at retouching photographic images you may have. It may be extended using the plug-in technology common to a number of Linux applications but may also be enhanced by using the internal scripting interface that allows you to automate tasks.

The GIMP has been released under the GNU General Public license and as such is freely distributed software. It is installed by default within Red Hat Linux 9 and it has a web site at http://www.gimp.org/, where you'll find documentation, support, and downloads.

You can start the application by selecting **Main Menu | Graphics | The GIMP**, or by typing gimp at the command line. A variety of configuration and control windows appear when you start the application, and you can control which dialogs are open at any given time by using the **File | Dialogs** menu of the main GIMP window (which is the top-left of the three windows shown below):

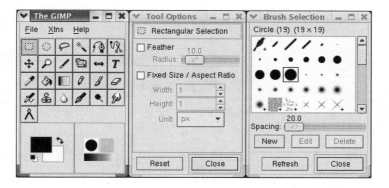

As you can see, the GIMP application is a discrete window containing a menu, an icon toolbar, and color information. Each new image is seen in its own separate window (not shown here), which carries its own menu (accessed by right-clicking on the image).

The application is considerably more powerful than Microsoft Paint, and its features are more closely aligned with applications such as Photoshop or Paint Shop Pro. For example, it supports:

❑ Numerous paint tools

❑ Support for layers and channels

❑ Advanced scripting and plug-in capabilities

❑ Gradient editor and blend tools

❑ Transformation support such as rotate and scale

❑ Multiple file formats

The GIMP's features are too numerous to list in detail, and again we will leave you to play with the application. The online documentation (found at http://www.gimp.org/docs.html) is very thorough and this can be supplemented by the documentation found at its main web site (at http://www.gimp.org/). In addition, a large collection of resources, available from the web site, covers patterns, palettes, brushes, gradients, scripts, and fonts, and contains links to other important web sites for The GIMP (such as a plug-in registry at http://registry.gimp.org/index.jsp and the very useful **GIMP User Group** – or GimpForce – at http://gug.sunsite.dk/).

GQView

GQView is a simple application that allows you to view a number of graphical images simultaneously. You start by selecting the directory in which the graphic files exist, and then either selecting the file from the left-hand pane with its image being displayed in the right hand pane or using the Slideshow feature available on the View menu.

To start this application, select Main Menu | Graphics | More Graphical Applications | GQView Image Viewer or run gqview from the command line. The screenshot below shows the utility being used to display screenshots from the Red Hat Linux installation process that we covered back in Chapter 1:

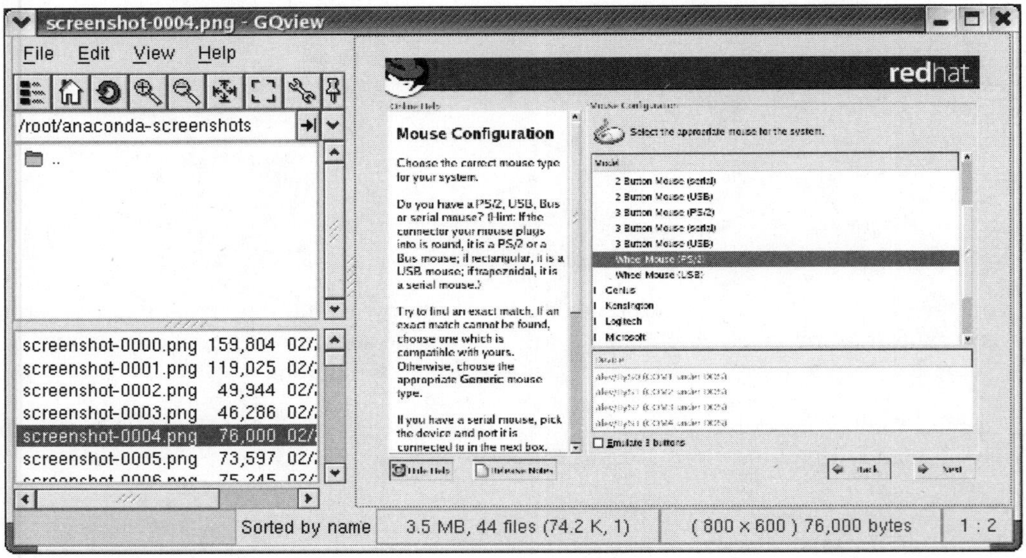

PDF Viewer

The **PDF Viewer** is another simple application, whose functionality is limited to viewing PDF files on-screen. To start the PDF Viewer, select Main Menu | Graphics | PDF Viewer or run the xpdf application from the command line. To access a file, use the right-hand mouse button and select Open from the menu.

From the command line you can view a PDF document, specifying it as the first parameter on the command line. If we wanted to display the file chapter05.pdf, we would use the following command:

```
$ xpdf chapter05.pdf
```

If you want to convert a document into PDF format, there are a number of ways to achieve this. In essence it involves converting to the postscript file format, and then using a utility to convert to the PDF file format using the **PS2PDF** converter supplied with Ghostscript. For more information, see http://www.pathcom.com/~kujira/pdf_idx.htm.

OpenDraw

The **OpenDraw** application is installed as part of the OpenOffice suite, and is similar to the Microsoft Draw application that is now embedded within Microsoft Word. It allows you to draw diagrams using a variety of 2D- and 3D-objects and shapes, group and color them, and then embed your diagrams into your OpenOffice documents. It also supports the generation of graphs and the manipulation of text within your image.

System Applications

There are numerous other applications available and installed with Red Hat 9. Half the fun of a new operating system is exploring all these applications. There is much that isn't installed by default, but is available on the Internet as freeware.

In this section of the chapter we'll talk about some of the handy system utilities and bread-and-butter applications that are usually not so exciting but are there to make your life easier. The applications we'll examine here are the file managers, file compression utilities, and emulators.

A Simple Text Editor

For many users, the way in which tasks are accomplished primarily via GUI-based applications is a big attraction. Unix has always been associated with command line input, and it was not until the X-Windows system provided a GUI front-end that things become easier. One application that lends itself to this method of input is the simple text editor.

Of course, you could use editors such as OpenWriter to edit such documents, but the formatting and functionality provided with applications like OpenWriter is really overkill for configuration files and similar documents. This is where **gedit** is very useful.

The gedit application is similar to Notepad or Wordpad in MS Windows, and is an effective text editor with a nice graphical user interface. To launch gedit, choose Main Menu | Accessories | Text Editor, or type `gedit` at the command line:

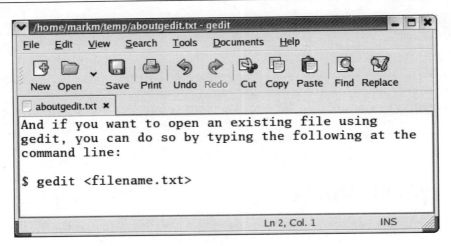

A File Management Application

A **file manager** is a GUI that allows you to manage and navigate the various drive types and directory structures on your system and network. Given the size of hard disks today (60GB is normal), and the capacity of CD-ROM drives, DVD-ROM drives, not to mention your local area network, the ability to quickly navigate and manage the files of such devices is extremely important.

To start you off navigating your file system, Red Hat Linux places a link to your home directory (/home/<username>) on your desktop – mine is labeled **Mark's Home**. This shortcut fires up the favored file manager of Red Hat Linux 9 – the **Nautilus** application – and hence allows you to manage your files and file system easily via Nautilus's graphical user interface.

Alternatively, you can start Nautilus by typing `nautilus` at the command line. For example, to start exploring the /usr directory you would type:

```
$ nautilus /usr
```

Let's take a look at the Nautilus GUI:

This application is very similar to the Windows Explorer application you find in Microsoft's Windows operating systems. It allows you to move up and down directory trees by double-clicking the icons. It also allows you to create new folders, move files, and cut and paste directories and files.

A File Compression and Archiving Application

While Nautilus allows you to manage your files, you'll also find times when you need to archive files into a single compressed file in the style of PkZip. The **File Roller** application provides a graphical user interface to compressed files, allowing you to archive files and extract items from existing archives. It's very similar to the WinZip utility for Microsoft Windows, which also provides a graphical interface to the PkZip utility.

To start the File Roller application, select Main Menu | Accessories | File Roller or type file-roller at the command line:

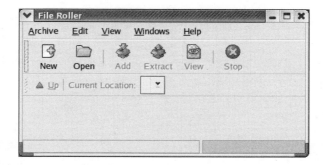

File Roller supports a number of compressed file formats including .zip, .lzh, and so on. It can be used to create new archives using the Archive | New menu option, to open existing archives, and to extract files from these archives.

For example, to create a new .zip archive, select the Archive | New menu option and enter a filename in the field provided (here, I'm creating a new file called /home/markm/screenshots.zip):

Then you can add files using the Add shortcut icon or the Edit | Add Files menu item. This will prompt you to select the files you wish to add. The screenshot below shows the window after adding all the files from the /root/anaconda-screenshots directory, that we took while writing Chapter 1:

This starts the process of adding the files to the archive, compressing as we go.

Emulators

We've discussed various interoperability features of the applications in this chapter. For example, we've seen how OpenOffice is able to load and save files in formats like the Microsoft Office formats, and other non-native formats. In addition to these features, there are a number of **emulators** in existence. An emulator implements another (virtual) operating system within Linux, and hence you can run executables that are native to that operating system.

Hence, we can (for example) run an emulator application that simulates the Microsoft Windows operating system running within Linux, and hence allows us to run Microsoft Windows Applications (binary files) untouched in their native format – from within Linux!

The concept of emulators is not new, and they're not unique to Linux. There have been many different emulators, for lots of platforms – mainly targeted at those who wish to recapture their youth or take a trip down memory lane. Among the most common emulators are those that simulate 8-bit home computers like the Sinclair ZX Spectrum. However, what's far more impressive is the fact that emulators are available for simulating complex operating systems such as Microsoft Windows.

In this section of the chapter we will discuss some of the emulators available. We won't cover emulators in detail – it's a large and complex topic, and the online documentation provided by the suppliers of some of these emulators is more than sufficient to get you started. But we will mention a couple of emulators, so you can start to get an idea of what they're about.

VMWare

The VMWare application is an Enterprise Class virtual machine that can run multiple versions of an operating system on a single computer. For example, you could run multiple versions of the Windows operating system on a single Linux machine. More information can be found at http://www.vmware.com/. An example screen is shown below, demonstrating Windows XP running under VMWare on a Linux box:

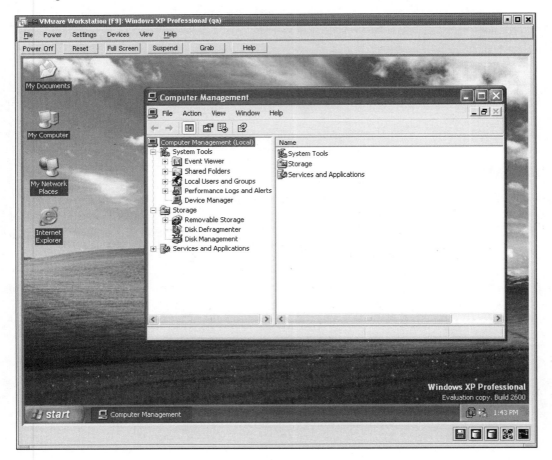

Wine

Wine is an application that implements the Windows Application Programming Interface (API) on top of the native X Window System that is used by the GNOME and KDE graphical environments. It's more of a compatibility layer than an emulator, but it does allow Windows applications to run. The latest version and more information can be found at Wine's web site at http://www.winehq.com/.

Most recent release of the Wine RPM packages can be found at http://mecano.gme .usherb.ca/~vberon/wine/, and the instructions for installing Wine and troubleshooting problems that you encounter can be found within the *Wine User Guide*, at http://www.winehq.com/Docs/wine-user/.

Summary

In this chapter we've touched on a variety of applications installed by default in Red Hat Linux 9. In some cases, we've discussed how they can be extended to provide yet further functionality. In fact, there are thousands of quality applications that are available either within the Red Hat Linux distribution or via the Internet, in some cases freeware thanks to the Open Source Foundation and the GNU Project. In other cases, shareware is available at a small cost, again via the Internet.

We started by covering the OpenOffice suite of applications commonly used for office productivity. We touched on a couple of Internet applications – the Mozilla browser and the GAIM Instant Messenger application – and the Evolution personal information management tool. We skipped through a number of multimedia applications, which provided various audio and graphical facilities, and took a look at some of the more essential system tools – the gedit text editor, the Nautilus file manager, the File Roller compression tool, and the VMWare emulator.

There is such a wealth of functionality available that you shouldn't have trouble finding the application you need to do the job you want – whether it's included in the Red Hat Linux 9 distribution or out there on the Internet somewhere. We'll cover some more applications in Chapter 13. And if there's nothing out there that fits your requirements, you could always start off your own Open Source project. In the end, you can achieve in Linux everything that you'd expect to be able to achieve on other platforms.

6

The Shell

Before graphical user interfaces came into vogue, the only way to interact with an operating system was via the **command line shell** (often known simply as the **shell**). The shell allows users to type in commands for the operating system and the operating system to display the output that results from the execution of these commands.

Despite the rise of GUIs like GNOME and KDE and predictions of the complete demise of the command line shell, the shell has held steady as the user interface of choice for a large number of users – sometimes as a last resort when the GUI fails, but often simply because it is a very flexible and powerful tool. In fact, the shell has evolved into a tool that allows users to do pretty much *all* that can be done using the operating system – far beyond what a GUI would permit.

In this chapter, we'll be discussing the following:

- ❑ The concepts of a command line shell and its background
- ❑ Shell commands, shortcut keys, and aliases
- ❑ The command line syntax
- ❑ Managing multiple tasks at the same time
- ❑ Using the shell as a scripting language

The Shell as a Command Line Interface

An operating system such as the Linux kernel consists of code written mostly in the low-level programming language C. The kernel is loaded into memory at the time the machine boots up, and sits there awaiting instructions.

There are a number of ways for us to pass instructions to the kernel. One of the most important is to write programs that interact with it – once a program is written, you may compile and execute it to accomplish the task.

Since programs written to interact with the kernel often have several tasks in common, there is usually a library of these common tasks, which is a collection of C subroutines (or functions as some might call them) organized into a library. This is simply known as the *C library* or the *libc*. While programs that use the C library are powerful and flexible, it is often cumbersome, if not downright impractical, to write a program, compile it, and run it every time we need to do something as simple as copying a file.

This is where the shell comes in. The shell is a **declarative and parameterized** mechanism for executing common tasks. What this means is that the shell allows us to execute programs that are generic enough to take parameters. For example, by using the file copy program cp, supplying a source file and a destination file as parameters (also known as arguments), it is possible to copy a file from one location to another in the file system. The power of the shell comes from the wide gamut of programs that can be executed from it. These programs are what are commonly known as *UNIX commands*. As some readers might have guessed by now, the shell itself is another program.

As well as allowing us to simply execute commands, the shell enables us to *manage* the execution of commands. It allows users to define shortcuts and abbreviations to refer to these commands and even to serve as a handy tool for knitting together commands to create conglomerates that function as new commands (they're called scripts).

In terms of flexibility, performance, task automation, and repetitive processing of tasks, the shell in the hands of a knowledgeable user still beats a GUI hands down.

Different Types of Shell

The earliest versions of UNIX came with what is today known as the **Bourne shell** (also known as sh), named after its inventor, Steve Bourne. Since then a variety of shell flavors have emerged. However, the core functionality and basic syntax of all of these shells has changed very little.

The **C-shell** (or csh), distributed as part of BSD UNIX, was the next popular flavor of the shell to arrive. The C-shell syntax resembles the C programming language (particularly when it comes to writing shell scripts), hence its name. This aspect of the C-shell was intended to popularize it among the UNIX users, who at that time were largely C programmers.

Other popular shells soon arrived – each with more features than the last, while all being backward compatible for the most part. Among them were the **Korn shell** (or ksh), which was written by David Korn of AT&T Bell Laboratories, and **tcsh** or the C-shell with command-completion features – that is, the shell 'intuitively' completes the commands when we type them in.

The **Born Again shell** (or **Bash**) is one of the newer flavors of the shell, and is almost completely compatible with its ancestor, the Bourne shell.

It is interesting to note that most Unix systems have sh available apart from a preferred flavor of the shell for that Unix system. In fact, some Unix systems make several shells available, and the user may switch between them at will. As far as Linux (and therefore Red Hat Linux 9) is concerned, Bash is the preferred shell, although users may switch to other shell flavors (for example, you can switch to the C-shell by typing csh at the Bash prompt). The choice of a shell is often dictated by personal preference, sometimes by the fact that a user started of with a particular flavor, or sometimes, as in the case of the C-shell, the programming language the user is comfortable with. In this chapter we focus on using the default shell, Bash, to illustrate features of the shell.

Let's begin the chapter by trying to find out what your current shell is. We can figure this out by typing the ps command in any terminal window at the command prompt. The ps command lists the processes – that is to say, the currently executing programs on your system:

The command prompt is depicted as $ for brevity, it is usually [user@localhost current directory] by default. We shall learn more on setting the prompt later in this chapter.

```
$ ps
  PID TTY          TIME CMD
 5355 pts/0    00:00:00 bash
 5381 pts/0    00:00:00 ps
```

On executing the ps command, we should see an output similar to the one above. On the last column of the second line of the output we see bash. If we were to switch to a different shell, say csh, we would see csh in the output beside the Bash shell, which was used to launch it. Try it out by typing csh, followed by ps:

```
$ csh
$ ps
  PID TTY          TIME CMD
 5355 pts/0    00:00:00 bash
 5389 pts/0    00:00:00 csh
 5409 pts/0    00:00:00 ps
```

It should be noted that when we say that we 'switch' to another shell, we do not actually exit Bash and start csh; rather we use bash as the launchpad to start another shell, in this case csh. We'll be looking at the ps command in more detail in the next section.

Built-in Programs and External Programs

There are two different types of command that can be executed from a shell. They are **built-in programs** and **external programs**:

❑   Built-in programs are inherently built into the shell:

- ❑ All shells share a common set of built-in programs, such as the cd command, which enables us to change directory.

- ❑ In addition, there are other built-in commands that are specific to *certain* flavors of the shell. For instance, the amend method for setting environment variables usually varies from one flavor of the shell to another. We shall see more on setting environment variables later in this chapter.

❑ External commands are those that are independent of the flavor of shell. They can be executed from any shell and yield more or less the same result. For instance, the date command would output the date no matter what shell it is executed from.

For the purpose of our discussion, we shall refer to both built-in commands and external commands by the generic term, *command*.

Checking Compatibility of a Command with a Shell

Of course, when we're working within a particular shell, we can use only the built-in commands that are valid for that flavor of shell. As we'll see later, this is particularly important when we write a shell script – a file that contains a sequence of shell commands. If we run a shell script within a particular shell, then it should contain only commands that are valid for the shell in question.

To this end, it is useful to be able to check whether a given command is a built-in or an external command. For this, we can use the type command. This command tells us whether it is a built-in command within the current shell, or (if it is an external program) the location of the command.

For example, in the Bash shell, if you use type to query the nature of the date and cd commands, you'll find that the former is external and the latter is built-in:

```
$ type date
date is /bin/date
$ type cd
cd is a shell builtin
```

We will be talking more about shell scripts toward the end of this chapter.

Some Common Shell Commands

In this section we'll examine some of the commands that we could use to find our way around Red Hat Linux 9 using the command line shell. There are different categories of command:

- ❑ File system commands, used for navigating and manipulating the file system

- ❑ Process management commands, used to manage processes

- ❑ Administrative commands

In this section we'll take a look at these three categories of commands and examine some frequently used examples of each.

File System Commands

File system commands allow us to access and manipulate various parts of the Unix file system tree. In Unix, the file system is organized as a tree structure, in much the same way as in other operating systems (each directory can contain files and sub-directories). For each machine, there is always one **root directory**; this is the topmost directory, and contains sub-directories and files. We refer to the root directory by using the forward slash (/).

From this basic structure, there are a number of tasks that we may need to do, such as changing the working directory, establishing the contents of a particular directory, or creating, copying, moving, and deleting files and directories.

Changing and Establishing the Working Directory

The **working directory** is the directory we're currently working in. To change the working directory (that is, to select a particular directory to be the working directory), we use the `cd` (change directory) command.

For example, to select the root directory to be the working directory, we would type the following:

```
$ cd /
```

To select the directory /home/deepakt (the home directory of the user deepakt) to be the working directory, we could type this:

```
$ cd /home/deepakt
```

Absolute and Relative Paths

In both of the above examples, we've specified the absolute path of the directory in question. We can also use relative paths. For example, if we wanted to change the working directory from /home/deepakt to its parent directory, /home, we could use the absolute path like this:

```
$ cd /home
```

or the relative path, like this:

```
$ cd ..
```

We can use `cd` to change the working directory to any directory that the system allows us to. If you use the `cd` command with no arguments, then it will always set the working directory to be the directory that we logged into (often this is /home/*<username>*).

This is different from the Microsoft DOS command prompt, where the cd command with no arguments merely prints the absolute path of the present directory.

We'll deal with aspects of the file system in more detail in the next chapter.

Determining the Working Directory

Now comes the question of how to determine our current directory. For this, we use the pwd (print working directory) command, which outputs the absolute path of the present working directory. For example:

```
$ cd /home/deepakt
$ pwd
/home/deepakt
```

Listing the Contents of a Directory

We can list the contents of a directory by using the ls (list directory contents) command. If we don't specify a directory, then ls will list the contents of the present working directory:

```
$ ls -al
total 288
drwxr-xr-x    3 deepakt  users        4096 Jan 16 14:29 .
drwxr-xr-x   11 deepakt  users       16384 Jan 16 14:27 ..
-rw-r--r--    1 deepakt  users       49714 Jan 16 14:27 f.html
-rw-r--r--    1 deepakt  users       22696 Jan 16 14:29 ff.html
drwxr-xr-x    2 deepakt  users           0 Jan 16 17:10 foo
-rw-r--r--    1 deepakt  users      131498 Jan 16 14:20 showthread.php.html
```

The ls command has a multitude of options. In the example above, we've used two options:

❑   The -l option requests that the output is the "long form" – that is, with more details than just the name of the file.

❑   The -a option lists all the files – including those beginning with a dot (.). Files beginning with a dot are usually configuration files. For those of us familiar with Microsoft operating systems, they are vaguely analogous to hidden files in DOS.

Don't worry if the output above doesn't make a great deal of sense – we'll be discussing file attributes in detail in Chapter 7. For now, it's enough to know that each item is either a file or a directory, and that a directory is denoted by a d in the first position of the 10-character code in the first column. In the above output, there are three directories listed – foo, the present working directory (denoted .), and the parent directory (denoted ..). We'll discuss more options of the ls command in the next chapter.

Also, the man command (denotes manual) describes most commands. To display the manual pages of the ls command, we could type man ls at the command line.

Creating, Moving, and Removing Files and Directories

When it comes to creation and removal, directories and files are handled differently, so we'll take a couple of subsections to explain.

Creating and Removing Directories

We use mkdir (make directory) and rmdir (remove directory) respectively to create or remove directories. The following example creates a subdirectory under the present working directory, called grapple:

```
$ mkdir grapple
```

It's also possible to create an entire hierarchy of directories at one go. To do this, we use the –p option. For example, this command would create the directory 4wds (as a subdirectory of the vehicles/cars directory), but it would *also* create the vehicles and cars directories if they did not already exist:

```
$ mkdir -p vehicles/cars/4wds
```

By default, the rmdir command can remove only an empty directory – that is, one that has no files in it. This is designed to help us avoid deleting files that we didn't necessarily know were there:

```
$ rmdir grapple
```

To remove a directory and its contents recursively including the sub-directories, we could use the rm -r command:

```
$ rm -r vehicles
```

Creating and Removing Files

A quick way to create a file is to use the touch command. The actual purpose of the touch command is to update the timestamp of an existing file (the idea being that if you touch the file, then the OS should update its timestamp). A side effect of this is that if you specify the path of a file that does not yet exist, then Linux will also create an empty file:

```
$ touch tigers.txt
```

To remove a file, we use the rm (remove) command:

```
$ rm tigers.txt
```

Moving Files and Directories

To move a file or directory, we use the mv (move) command. This requires two arguments – the file or directory to be moved, and the destination:

```
$ mv squidgy.txt squeezy.txt
```

This is a classic example of "moving a file". In this example, we're using mv not to move the file to a different directory but simply to *change the name* of the file. In Linux, "moving" a file really means "changing its path".

It's also possible to move multiple files at the same time. For example, this command moves the files squeezy.txt and stodgy.txt from the present working directory to the directory /etc/textures:

```
mv squeezy.txt stodgy.txt /etc/textures
```

Try It Out   Creating, Moving, and Removing Files and Directories

Let's step through a simple example in which we create a directory with a file in it, then rename the file. Once we are done experimenting, we will clean everything up by deleting both the file and the directory.

1. Change the present working directory to your home directory. For example, if you were logged in with the username deepakt, then you would simply type this:

```
$ cd
```

2. Just to check that the above step worked, use pwd to check the present working directory:

```
$ pwd
/home/deepakt
```

3. Now create a subdirectory called test, and make it the working directory:

```
$ mkdir test
$ cd test
```

4. Now create a new file called nomme.txt:

```
$ touch nomme.txt
```

5. To prove that the touch command really did create a new file, you can use the ls command to list the contents of the test directory:

```
$ ls -al
total 4
drwxr-xr-x    2 deepakt  users            0 Jan 16 17:29 .
drwxr-xr-x    3 deepakt  users         4096 Jan 16 17:29 ..
-rw-r--r--    1 deepakt  users            0 Jan 16 17:29 nomme.txt
```

6. Now use mv to change the name of the file, and use ls again to check the change:

```
$ mv nomme.txt name.txt; ls -al
total 4
drwxr-xr-x    2 deepakt  users            0 Jan 16 17:29 .
drwxr-xr-x    3 deepakt  users         4096 Jan 16 17:29 ..
-rw-r--r--    1 deepakt  users            0 Jan 16 17:29 name.txt
```

Note that we used a semicolon (;) after the mv command and typed in the ls command.
A semicolon is used to separate multiple commands on the same line.

7. Next, we'll start the cleanup. Use rm to remove the file name.txt, and use ls to check it:

```
$ rm name.txt
$ ls -al
total 4
drwxr-xr-x    2 deepakt  users            0 Jan 16 17:29 .
drwxr-xr-x    3 deepakt  users         4096 Jan 16 17:29 ..
```

8. Now move back to the parent directory (that is, make your user's home directory the working directory):

```
$ cd ..
$ pwd
/home/deepakt
```

9. Finally, remove the test directory that we created right at the beginning:

```
$ rmdir test
```

Summary of Filesystem Commands

Here's a quick summary of common commands necessary for getting around the filesystem:

cd	Change directory. Without arguments this command changes the current working directory to the home directory of the user. When a directory name is supplied as an argument, it changes the current working directory to that directory.
pwd	Prints the current working directory.
mkdir	Creates new directories. Creates one or more directories as specified by arguments to this command. When a hierarchy is specified, the -p option creates intermediate directories if they are missing.
rmdir	Removes an empty directory.
cat	Concatenates the contents of a file. May be used in conjunction with the > operator to create a file or the >> operator to append to a file (see later section on I/O redirection for details).
rm	Removes a file. The -i option prompts the user to confirm whether to proceed with deletion. The -f option is the silent remove option. It attempts to remove the file without seeking confirmation; if it is unsuccessful in removing the file, it does not report an error.
mv	Move one or more files or directories supplied as arguments to another directory.
ls	Lists the contents of one or more directories supplied as arguments to it. The -l option lists the details of a file. The --color option lists files with color-coding describing the type of file. The -t option lists the timestamps of files and directories. The -R option recursively lists the contents of a directory. Several more of the important ls options are discussed in the next chapter.
touch	Modifies the timestamp of files or directories supplied as arguments. If a specified argument does not exist, touch creates an empty file by that name in the current directory.

Process Management Commands

Unix (and therefore Linux) has the notion of processes that are essentially tasks running on the operating system infrastructure. Each time a command is invoked, the invocation results in one or more **processes** being spawned. Processes belong to users, and in general are insulated from each other. Often, the only time general users of the system are concerned with processes is when a one refuses to respond; this is commonly referred to as a **program hang**.

Listing Processes

To list the current processes spawned, that is started from a particular shell or its parent shell, we can use the ps (processes spawned) command:

```
$ ps
PID TTY          TIME CMD
 5355 pts/0    00:00:00 bash
 5381 pts/0    00:00:00 ps
```

To list *all* the processes on the system, we can use the ps command with the –A option:

```
$ ps -A
  PID TTY          TIME CMD
    1 ?        00:00:04 init
    2 ?        00:00:00 keventd
    3 ?        00:00:03 kapmd
    4 ?        00:00:00 ksoftirqd_CPU0
    5 ?        00:00:03 kswapd
    6 ?        00:00:00 bdflush
    7 ?        00:00:00 kupdated
    8 ?        00:00:00 mdrecoveryd
    ...
```

Note that this option is case-sensitive (as are most Linux commands).

Getting the Complete Command Line

We do know that processes represent commands that were executed. But what ps does not tell us (at least not easily) is what the complete command line was when the process was invoked. Sometimes, we need to know what arguments were passed to the command and what options were invoked. To see the complete command line of a process with the name of the owner of the process against it, we can coax the ps command with the –auxww options:

```
$ ps -auxww

USER       PID %CPU %MEM   VSZ   RSS TTY      STAT START   TIME COMMAND
root         1  0.0  0.2  1336   428 ?        S    Jan15   0:04 init
...
root       449  0.0  0.3  2056   756 ?        S    Jan15   0:00 /sbin/dhclient -1 -q -lf
/var/lib/dhcp/dhclient-eth0.leases -pf /var/run/dhclient-eth0.pid -cf /etc/dhclient-eth0.conf eth0
root       619  0.0  0.2  1328   412 ?        S    Jan15   0:00 /usr/sbin/apmd -p 10 -w 5 -W -P
/etc/sysconfig/apm-scripts/apmscript
ident      657  0.0  0.3 27032   708 ?        S    Jan15   0:00 identd
root       671  0.0  0.4  3276   860 ?        S    Jan15   0:00 /usr/sbin/sshd
root       685  0.0  0.3  2096   752 ?        S    Jan15   0:00 xinetd -stayalive -reuse -pidfile
/var/run/xinetd.pid
deepakt   5270  0.0  3.1 16436  5952 ?        S    12:03   0:04 /usr/bin/gnome-session
deepakt   5313  0.0  0.3  2900   724 ?        S    12:03   0:00 /usr/bin/ssh-agent /etc/X11/xinit/Xclients
```

Now, the final column gives the complete command used. For example, the lines shown in bold show the complete command used to invoke the DHCP client daemon. The thing to note in all of these cases is the presence of the PID column. The **Process ID (PID)** is a number that is used to uniquely identify a process at any given time.

Terminating a Process

The kill command can be used to send a signal to a process – by specifying the signal to be sent and the Process ID. The signal that most general users are interested in is the SIGTERM signal, which terminates the process. This is particularly useful for dealing with a process that is hanging or has run amok:

```
$ ps
PID TTY          TIME CMD
 5355 pts/0    00:00:00 bash
 5365 pts/0    00:00:00 haywire
 5381 pts/0    00:00:00 ps
$ kill -s SIGTERM 5365
$ ps
PID TTY          TIME CMD
 5355 pts/0    00:00:00 bash
 5381 pts/0    00:00:00 ps
```

The SIGTERM signal can be *handled* by processes in that it allows processes to *clean up* before exiting; for example, the process may want to close the files it has opened before exiting. If the safer option of SIGTERM does not work, then we may resort to SIGKILL. The SIGKILL signal forces a process to terminate immediately – it does not allow it to exit gracefully. The man 7 signal command lists and describes the complete set of signals.

Watching System Processes

The top command allows us to see which processes consume maximum resources on the system. The top command refreshes the screen periodically since the resource consumption on a system usually fluctuates rapidly.

Administrative Commands

It is Linux's **administrative commands** that set it apart from GUI-based operating systems. These commands are as numerous as they are powerful. In this section, we examine only the most important administrative commands (in terms of day-to-day use). More commands will be introduced in later chapters, especially in Chapter 10.

Switching Identities

For day-to-day activity on your Linux system, it's generally a good idea to log in using a regular user account – that is, one that has no administrative privileges. (For example, this protects you from the dangers of accidentally deleting or changing important files and configuration.)

However, to perform certain privileged tasks, such as shutting down the system, you need to assume the identity of an administrator (or root user, in Unix parlance). In these situations, it's rather inconvenient to have to log out of the system and log back in as a root user. For this reason, there is a simpler alternative – you can use the su command (with no arguments) and supply the root user's password. This will provide you with a shell that has the privileges of the root user. When you've completed your administrative tasks, you can switch back to the safety of non-admin privileges by exiting the root shell – typing exit or *Ctrl-D*.

The su command can also be used to switch identities between two non-root users. The id command prints the current user ID of the user:

```
$ id
uid=500(brucewayne) gid=513(users) groups=513(users)
$ su
Password:
bash# id
uid=0(root) gid=0(root) groups=0(root), 1(bin), 2(daemon)
bash# exit
$ id
uid=500(brucewayne) gid=513(users) groups=513(users)
$ su batman
Password:
$ id
uid=800(batman) gid=513(users) groups=513(users)
```

The uid field indicates the user ID of the user, which is a unique number, assigned to each and every user on the system. gid is the group ID of the *primary group* that a user belongs to. A group is essentially a collection of users who have some common set of privileges. For instance, all members of the engineering group may have access to say, the blueprints directory on a machine. Each user belongs to at least one group, which is known as the primary group. In addition, they may also belong to other groups as indicated by the groups field. Groups like users have a number associated with them; 513 in this case denotes the group ID of the users group.

Shutting Down and Rebooting

The shutdown command shuts down the system. This command is restricted to root users only. Shutdown can be immediate (in which case the now argument is passed), or it can be delayed (by *n* seconds by passing the -t *n* option).

If we need to *reboot* rather than *shut down* the system, the reboot command comes in handy. It is usually a good idea to run the sync command before rebooting or shutting down the system. The sync command ensures that file system objects are in a consistent state.

Disk Usage

The df command displays a partition-by-partition summary of disk usage. We can supply arguments such as -k to indicate to df that it should report disk usage in increments of kilobytes, as shown here:

```
$ df -k
Filesystem              1K-blocks      Used Available Use% Mounted on
/dev/hda2                 5716172   3424988   2000812  64% /
/dev/hda1                  101089     19137     76733  20% /boot
none                        94752         0     94752   0% /dev/shm
/dev/cdrom                 659488    659488         0 100% /mnt/cdrom
```

The `Available` column indicates remaining disk space. In this case, roughly 2Gb of disk space remains free on the root partition.

> *The next chapter, Chapter 7, will deal with file systems in more detail.*

Mounting Disks and Media

Often we need to read from CD-ROM discs, and to read from and write to floppy disks. Since Linux treats all peripheral devices as file systems, we need to **mount** or associate these physical devices to a file system **mount point** – essentially a directory. The `mount` command can be used to mount such media. We need to have root user privileges to mount and unmount devices.

Here's an example. Start by trying to use `ls` to list the contents of `/mnt/cdrom`:

```
# ls /mnt/cdrom
```

At this stage, no files are listed since there is no device associated with the `/mnt/cdrom` mount point. Now put a disc in, mount the CD-ROM device to the `/mnt/cdrom` mount point, and list the contents again:

```
# mount /dev/cdrom /mnt/cdrom
# ls /mnt/cdrom
RedHat
Autorun
README
```

The exact listing you get depends on which CD is in your CD-ROM drive.

The complementary command is the `umount` command, which *disassociates* a device from a file system mount point:

```
# umount /mnt/cdrom
```

The `eject` command is also handy for CD-ROM devices, since it un-mounts the device and pops the tray open (on condition that the underlying CD-ROM drive supports this operation).

> *On RedHat Linux 9, when we insert a CD into the drive the system automatically mounts the CD. The commands above may be used to do this manually. Again, there is more on this topic in the next chapter.*

Listing Users

Often, administrators (and even regular users) need to see the list of users currently logged on to the system. (This is a little counter-intuitive to users familiar with desktop operating systems, since the Unix model allows users to connect to a system remotely using programs such as `telnet` and `rlogin`.)

You can achieve this with the `who` command, which lists all users currently logged on to a machine:

```
# who
deepakt     :0              Jan 13 12:03
hbatman     192.168.1.100   Jan 11 11:30
```

The `finger` command goes one step further, listing users logged on to a remote system somewhere on the network. For `finger` to work, the remote server should have the `fingerd` daemon running; this is becoming rarer by the day in these times of increased system security.

Special Keys and Shortcuts

The Bash shell comes with numerous special keys and clever shortcuts, which are designed to make our life at the keyboard faster and more efficient. Some of these control process execution, while others simply make it easier to enter in our next command.

Control Keystrokes

Many of the following keystrokes are used to interrupt the execution of a process:

- ❑ *Ctrl-C* sends a SIGINT signal to the currently executing process, causing the process to be interrupted from whatever it was doing. This is useful when a program runs into a condition such as an infinite loop and we decide to terminate the execution of the command.

- ❑ *Ctrl-* sends a SIGSEGV signal to the currently executing process. By default, the SIGSEGV signal causes a process to write the memory image of itself to the disk, often to a file called `core`. Some programmers find this useful because it allows them to interrupt execution of a (possibly faulty) program and then examine its memory image in the core file – and thus determine what the program was doing.

  At other times, *Ctrl-* comes in handy while attempting to terminate programs that do not terminate on *Ctrl-C*. Such programs may actually be handling the SIGINT signal for a legitimate purpose, but in a hang state, this prevents the graceful termination of the process.

- ❑ *Ctrl-Z* is used to suspend a process that is currently executing. This causes the process to relinquish control, and the shell prompt is returned. In a later section on job control, we shall see more about this behavior.

- Ctrl-D is used to indicate the end of input. For instance, if a program was coded to read in data until it encountered an end-of-file condition, Ctrl-D can be used to simulate the end-of-file when a user is typing in the input for the program.

  The classic example for this is the shell itself. If you type Ctrl-D at the command prompt, the shell assumes that you have reached the end of your input into the shell, and that you have decided to exit. In fact, for the shell, Ctrl-D is synonymous with the exit command.

- Ctrl-V does not have anything to do with process management, but it is used to input literal values of Ctrl keystrokes. For example, if we need to type the character corresponding to Ctrl-D, we would type Ctrl-V Ctrl-D.

- The erase keystrokes (Ctrl-W and Ctrl-U) come in handy when editing the command line (a topic that we will cover in the next section of this chapter). Ctrl-W erases the entire word to the left of the cursor, and Ctrl-U erases everything to the left of the cursor.

- The navigation keystrokes (Ctrl-A and Ctrl-E) move the cursor to the start and end of the command line, respectively.

- Ctrl-R can be used to invoke an interactive search of the history.

Cursor Keys

The **cursor keys** are those that allow us to manipulate the input cursor of the shell. Using the Up and Down arrow keys, it is possible to scroll through a history of commands that were executed, and hence execute them again (the Up arrow key allows you to scroll backward through the history of commands, while the Down arrow key allows you to scroll forward through them).

Often we want to execute a command that is only slightly different from a previous command. In this case, we can use the Up and Down arrow keys to retrieve the previous command, and then use a number of different keys to position the cursor and edit the command:

- We can use the Left and Right arrow keys to position the input cursor within the command.

- As we mentioned earlier, we can also use Ctrl-A to jump to the start of the command line and Ctrl-E to jump to the end.

- We can use the Backspace key to delete characters, and enter new characters simply by typing them in.

- When we are finished, we hit Enter to execute the command.

The history Command

While we're on the subject of the command history, it's worth taking a look at the history command. The history command prints a history of the commands executed, with a sequential number next to each command in the history:

```
$ history
    1  ls -al
    2  date
    3  pwd
    4  who
    5  touch cellar/maze/labyrinth/passage/foo.txt
$ !2
date
Tue Jan 14 23:03:43  2003
$
```

A previous command at position n can be referred to as !n. So in order to execute the date command again, we could simply type in !2 (as shown above). While this does not sound like much of a saving, it is a great help when we're working with very lengthy commands.

Other Related Keyboard Shortcuts from the Shell's History

Here are some more useful shortcuts that may be used to invoke commands from the history:

❑ The double-exclamation mark (!!) has the effect of telling Bash to execute the last command once again. For example, if we execute the date command, and then enter !!, the date command will be executed again:

```
$ date
Tue Jan 14 23:03:43  2003
$ !!
Tue Jan 14 23:03:45  2003
```

❑ An exclamation mark (!), followed by some text, has the effect of executing the command from the shell's history that begins with that text and has the closest match to it. For example, given the history of five commands shown above, the command !p would result in the pwd command being executed. If there was another command starting with the letter p in the history (say, ps), then we would have to supply a closer match (such as !pw) to execute the pwd command.

❑ The !$ shortcut allows us to reuse the last argument of the previous command. For example, in the fifth command of the above history, we have created a file named foo.txt under a deep directory structure. Suppose that we wanted to remove it immediately after: we could do this by typing in rm !$ as the next command:

```
$ touch cellar/maze/labyrinth/passage/foo.txt
$ rm !$
rm cellar/maze/labyrinth/passage/foo.txt
$
```

The Bash shell automatically substitutes !$ with the last argument of the previous command, so that the rm command with the gray background above is equivalent to the one shown with the white background after it.

219

❏ An extension of the !$ shortcut is the !* shortcut. This simply translates into *all* of the arguments of the previous command. For example, the following commands create two files and then delete them again:

```
$ touch foo.txt bar.txt
$ rm !*
rm foo.txt bar.txt
$
```

❏ As we mentioned earlier, the *Ctrl-R* keystroke can be used to invoke an interactive search of the history. After typing in *Ctrl-R*, we could type in the minimal set of characters that uniquely match the start of a command in history:

```
$ history
    1   ls -al
    2   date
    3   pwd
    4   ps
    5   touch cellar/maze/labyrinth/passage/foo.txt
$ Ctrl-R
(reverse-i-search)'pw': pwd
```

The act of typing in the letters pw uniquely matches the pwd command, successfully distinguishing it from the ps command, which also starts with the letter p.

Auto-completion

In the previous section we looked at shortcuts that helped us to quickly ferret out commands from the history and execute them as such or modify them before executing them. In this section, we explore shortcuts to reference commands and objects in the file system. The *Tab* key is our ally in this quest.

Command Completion

In order to appreciate command completion, we first need to understand how, when we type in a command at the prompt, the shell knows where to look for that command on the file system. For instance, when we type in the date command the shell seems to know that we are referring to the date program residing in the /bin directory.

In fact, when Bash starts up it consults a **startup script**. The startup script contains an environment variable called PATH, the value of which is a list of directories that contain programs. Then, when we type in a command and hit *Enter*, Bash automatically searches the directories in this list, in an attempt to locate a program whose name is the same as the command we typed in.

We'll discuss environment variables, and startup variables, more as we progress through the chapter.

If we type in just the first few letters of a command at the Bash prompt, and then hit the *Tab* key, Bash starts searching the PATH (the list of directories) for a unique command that matches the starting letters that we typed in:

❑   If it finds an exact match, it completes the command automatically:

```
$ da<Tab>
date
Tue Jan 14 23:03:43 2003
```

❑   If it finds *more* than one match, it beeps and awaits user input. If we hit the *Tab* key again, it displays a list of all matches. At this point, we need to type in more letters and hit the *Tab* key again to narrow down the search to the command that we are interested in:

```
$ ta<Tab>
tac tack tail talk tar
tal<Tab>
$ talk
```

❑   If Bash does not find a single match, it simply beeps every time we hit the *Tab* key. So, going by the previous cases, if Bash beeps twice in a row with no choices to display, it is trying to tell us that it found no match for what we typed in.

Filename Completion

Apart from automatically matching and completing the commands to be executed, Bash also features automatic completion of the names of files and directories. For example, the following creates two directories called cistern and cavern, and then a file called water.txt. Then, in the third command, we move the file into the cistern directory using the mv command, by specifying just enough of the cistern directory name followed by the *Tab*:

```
$ mkdir cistern cavern
$ touch water.txt
$ mv water.txt ci<Tab>stern
```

The *Tab* keystroke causes Bash to look for a unique match, and in this case it finds one – the cistern directory – and thus completes the directory name.

The same rule applies to files too. The first command here changes the working directory to cistern, and the second removes the file water.txt (which we specify simply by typing w and letting *Tab* and the shell do the rest!):

```
$ cd ci<Tab>stern
$ rm w<Tab>ater.txt
```

221

Command Line Syntax

So far in this chapter, we've been exploring techniques that make our lives easier working with Bash. In this section, we shall explore the syntax of the command line, including details of what makes Bash such an expressive interface to the operating system. This section will also contain several building block concepts that we will use when we program using the shell in the last section.

File Globbing

Often, we want to deal with not one but several files at a time: for example, if we want to copy all the files in a directory to another directory, or if we want to copy just a group of files with a certain extension into another directory. To do this, we need a way to address files (and directories) as a group, based on certain characteristics of their names. This is where **file globbing** comes in. *File globbing* is a loose term that describes the technique of grouping files together using simple wildcard or metacharacter expressions.

There are three metacharacters available:

❑ The asterisk (*) represents zero or more matches of any characters.

❑ The question mark (?) represents a match of exactly one character.

❑ The square brackets ([ ]) match any one of the characters between them. The characters to match may also be specified as a hyphen-separated range of characters to match against.

We can also use the exclamation mark (!). When we apply ! to an expression, it indicates that we are looking for the complement of the expression match resulting from the parentheses metacharacters (that is, all results *except* those that match the expression).

Try It Out   **File Globbing**

Perhaps the easiest way to understand the type of things that file globbing allows us to do is to look at an example. So, in this example we'll create a number of files and then use different globbing expressions to select different subsets of the files for listing.

1. Create a temporary folder called `numberfiles`, and then set it to be the current working directory:

```
$ mkdir /home/<username>/numberfiles
$ cd /home/<username>/numberfiles
```

2. Now create ten files, named after the Italian words for the numbers 1 to 10. Use the `touch` command to do this:

```
$ touch uno due tre quattro cinque sei sette otto nove dieci
```

❑ Use the `ls` command just to list them all (by default, it lists them by name in alphabetical order):

```
$ ls
cinque  dieci  due  nove  otto  quattro  sei  sette  tre  uno
```

3. Now let's group them in a number of different ways, using the metacharacters we just mentioned. First, list all the files that start with the letter `s`:

```
$ ls s*
sei  sette
```

4. Next, use the `?` metacharacter to select all files whose name consists of exactly three characters:

```
$ ls ???
due  sei  tre  uno
```

5. Next, select all the files whose name starts with a vowel:

```
$ ls [aeiou]*
otto  uno
```

6. Next, select all the files whose name starts with any character in the range `a` to `f`:

```
$ ls [a-f]*
cinque  dieci  due
```

7. Finally, select all the files whose name *does not* start with a vowel. The exclamation operator must be within the square parentheses.

```
$ ls [!aeiou]*
cinque  dieci  due  nove  quattro  sei  sette  tre
```

How It Works

We've used the `ls` command here to demonstrate file globbing, because the output from `ls` shows the effects of the globbing very clearly. However, you should note that we can use file globbing with any command that expects filename or directory-name arguments. Let's look at each of the globbing expressions here.

We used the expression s* to match all files that begin with the letter s:

```
$ ls s*
```

This expression matches the file names sei and sette, and would even match a file called s if there were one, because the * matches any string of any length (including the 0-length string).

To match filenames with *exactly* three characters, we use a ? to represent each character:

```
$ ls ???
```

We used the expression [aeiou]* to pick up all filenames starting with a vowel. The * works in the same way as in the s* example, matching any string of any length, so files matching this expression begin with a character a, e, i, o, or u, followed by any other sequence of characters:

```
$ ls [aeiou]*
```

A similar approach applies for the expression [a-f]*, except that we use a hyphen (-) within the parentheses to express any one of the characters in a **range**:

```
$ ls [a-f]*
```

Using a range implies that the characters have an assumed order. In fact, this encompasses all alphanumeric characters, with numbers (0–9) preceding letters (a–z). (Hence the expression [0-z]* would match all filenames that start with either a number or a letter.)

Finally, we use the exclamation mark (!) within the square parentheses to negate the result of the vowel-matching expression, thereby arriving at all filenames that start with a consonant:

```
$ ls [!aeiou]*
```

Aliases

Aliases are our first step toward customizing Bash. In its simplest form, an **alias** functions as an abbreviation for a commonly used command. In more complex cases, aliases can define completely new functionality. An alias is easily defined using the notation *<alias_name>=<alias_value>*. When we need it, we invoked it using *<alias_name>* – the shell substitutes *<alias_name>* with *<alias_value>*.

In fact, the standard Red Hat Linux 9 shell already has several aliases defined. We could list the existing aliases using the alias command:

```
$ alias
alias l.='ls -d .* --color=tty'
alias ll='ls -l --color=tty'
alias ls='ls --color=tty'
alias vi='vim'
alias which='alias | /usr/bin/which --tty-only --read-alias --show-dot --
show-tilde'
```

Some of the common aliases include aliases for the `ls` command, to include our favorite options. If you use the `ls` command without any options then it would simply print the list of files and sub-directories under the current working directory. However, in this case the `ls` command is aliased to itself, with the `--color` option, which allows `ls` to indicate different file types with different colors.

Aliases may be defined for the lifetime of a shell by specifying the alias mapping at the command line or in a startup file (discussed in a later section) so that the aliases are available every time the shell starts up.

Environment Variables

Like aliases, **environment variables** are name-value pairs that are defined either on the shell prompt or in startup files. A process may also set its own environment variables programmatically (that is, from within the program, rather than declared in a file or as arguments).

Environment variables are most often used either by the shell or by other programs to communicate settings. Some programs communicate information through environment variables to programs that they spawn. There are several environment variables set for us in advance. To list all of them that are currently set, you can use the `env` command, which should display an output similar to that below:

```
$ env
HOSTNAME=localhost.localdomain
SHELL=/bin/bash
TERM=xterm
HISTSIZE=1000
USER=deepakt

MAIL=/var/spool/mail/deepakt
PATH=/usr/local/bin:/usr/bin:/bin:/usr/X11R6/bin:/home/deepakt/bin

...
```

As you can see, the `PATH` variable is one of the environment variables listed here. As we described earlier in this chapter, Bash uses the value of the `PATH` variable to search for commands. The `MAIL` variable, also listed here, is used by mail reading software to determine the location of a user's mailbox.

System-defined Variables and User-defined Variables

We may set our own environment variables or modify existing ones:

```
$ echo $PATH
PATH=/usr/local/bin:/usr/bin:/bin:/usr/X11R6/bin:/home/deepakt/bin
$ export MYHOME=/home/deepakt
$ export PATH=$PATH:$MYHOME/mybin
$ echo $PATH
PATH=/usr/local/bin:/usr/bin:/bin:/usr/X11R6/bin:/home/deepakt/bin:/home/
deepakt/mybin
```

While user-defined variables (also known as local variables) can be set as
MYHOME=/home/deepakt, these variables will not be available to any of the commands
spawned by this shell. For local variables to be available to child processes spawned by a
process (the shell in this case), we need to use the export command. However, to achieve
persistence for variables even after we log out and log back in, we need to save these settings in
startup files.

Environment variables are defined either interactively or in a startup file such as .bashrc.
These variables are automatically made available to a new shell. Examples of environment
variables are PATH, PRINTER, and DISPLAY.

However, local variables do not get automatically propogated to a new shell when it is created.
The MYHOME variable is an example of a local variable.

The echo command, followed by the name of a variable prefixed with a dollar ($) symbol,
prints the value of the environment variable.

I/O Redirection

Earlier in the chapter, we referred to the file system and how we can use file system commands
to manipulate files and directories and process management commands such as ps to manage
processes. The shell provides us with a powerful set of operators that allow us to manage input,
output, and errors while working with files and processes.

I/O Streams

If a process needs to perform any I/O operation, it has to happen through an abstraction
known as an **I/O stream**. The process has three streams associated with it – **standard input**,
standard output, and **standard error**. The process may read input from its standard input, write
its output to standard output, and write error messages to its standard error stream.

By default, the standard input is associated with the keyboard; output and error are associated with the terminal, in our case mostly an xterm. Sometimes, we may not want processes to write to or read from a terminal; we may want the process to write to another location, such as a file. In this case we need to associate the process's standard output (and possibly the standard error) with the file in question. The process is oblivious to this, and continues to read from the standard input and write to the standard output, which in this case happens to be the files we specify. The I/O redirection operators of the shell make this redirection of the streams from the terminal to files extremely simple.

The < Operator

The **< operator** allows programs that read from the standard input to read input from a file. For instance, let us consider the wc (word count) program, which reads input from the keyboard (until a *Ctrl-D* is encountered) and then prints the number of lines, words, and characters that were input:

```
$ wc -l
12345
67890
12345
^D
3
```

Note that we've used the −l option here, which has wc print the number of lines only.

Now consider a case in which we have the input to wc available in a file, called 3linefile.txt. In this case the following command will produce the same result:

```
$ wc -l < 3linefile.txt
3
```

In this case the standard input is redirected from the keyboard to the file.

The > Operator

The **> operator** is similar to the < operator. Its purpose is to redirect the standard output from the terminal to a file. Let us consider the following example:

```
$ date > date.txt
```

The date command writes its output to the standard output, which is usually the terminal. Here, the > operator indicates to the shell that the output should instead be redirected to a file.

When we write the file out to the terminal (using the cat command), we can see the output of the date command displayed:

```
$ cat date.txt
Tue Jan 14 23:03:43 2003
```

Try It Out   Redirecting Output

Based on what we have learned so far, let us create a file with some contents in it:

```
$ cat > test.txt
The quick brown fox jumped over the rubber chicken
^D
$ cat test.txt
The quick brown fox jumped over the rubber chicken
```

This way of using cat to creating a file is similar to using the Microsoft DOS command COPY CON TEST.TXT .

How It Works

The cat command, used without any options, is supposed to echo back to the standard output anything that it reads from the standard input. In this case, the > operator redirects the standard output of the cat command to the file test.txt. Thus whatever was typed in on the keyboard (standard input) ended up in the file test.txt (standard output redirected by the shell).

The >> Operator

The >> **operator** is essentially the same as the > operator, the only difference being that it does not overwrite an existing file, instead it appends to it.

```
$ cat >> test.txt
Since rubber chicken makes bad nuggets
^D
$ cat test.txt
The quick brown fox jumped over the rubber chicken
Since rubber chicken makes bad nuggets
```

The | Operator

The | operator is used to feed the output of one command to the input of another command.

```
$ cat test.txt | wc -l
2
$wc -l test.txt
2
```

The output of the cat command – that is, the contents of the file test.txt – is fed by the shell to the wc command. It is the equivalent of running the wc -l command against the test.txt file. It is also possible to chain multiple commands this way, for example *command1 | command2 | command3*.

Configuring the Shell

As we saw in the section about aliases, most of us are likely to have our own preferences about how the shell should function. Bash is a highly customizable shell that allows us to set the values of environment variables that change its default behavior. Among other things, users like to change their prompt, their list of aliases and even perhaps add a welcome message when they log in:

```
$ echo $PS1
$
$ export PS1="Grandpoobah > "
Grandpoobah >
```

Bash uses the value of the PS1 environment variable to display its prompt. Therefore we could simply change this environment variable to whatever pleases us. However, to ensure that our brand new prompt is still available to us the next time we log in to the system, we need to add the PS1 setting to the .bashrc file.

Try It Out

Let us add some entries to our .bashrc file (save a backup copy first, so you can put it back to normal when you're done):

```
export PS1="Grandpoobah> "
alias ls='ls -al'
banner "Good day"
```

When we log in, we see a banner that displays the silly Good day message. If we list our aliases and environment variables, we see that our new settings have taken effect.

How It Works

When a user logs in, Bash reads the /etc/bashrc file (which is a common startup file for all users of the system). Then it reads the .bashrc file in the user's home directory and executes all commands in it, including creating aliases, setting up environment variables, and running programs (the banner program in this case).

Since the user's .bashrc is read after the system-wide configuration file, this is a good place to override any default settings that may not be to the user's liking.

A user can also create a .bashrc_logout script in their home directory, and add programs to it. When the user logs out, Bash reads and executes the commands in the .bashrc_logout file. Therefore, this is a good location to add that parting message or reminder, and simple housekeeping tasks.

229

A Sample .bashrc

Let us take a look at a sample .bashrc file.

```
export PS1='foobar$ '
export PATH=$PATH:/home/deepakt/games

alias rm='rm -i'
alias psc='ps -auxww'
alias d='date'
alias cls='clear'
alias jump='cd /home/deepakt/dungeon/maze/labyrinth/deep/down'
```

Setting the PS1 environment variable changes the command prompt. We may have a separate directory in which we store a number of games. We also add this directory to the PATH environment variable. In the aliases section, we alias the rm command to itself with the -i option. The -i option forces the rm command to confirm with the user if it is all right to delete a file or directory. This is often a useful setting for novice users to prevent accidental deletion of files or directories. We also abbreviate the ps command and arguments to display the entire command line of processes with the psc alias. The date command is abbreviated as d. Finally, to save on typing the complete path to a deeply nested directory, we create jump, an alias to the cd command that changes our current working directory to the deeply nested directory.

As we saw in an earlier section, the su command switches the identity of a user to that of another user. By default, when the switch happens, the new user's .bashrc file is not executed. However, if we use the - option to su, the new user's .bashrc is executed and the current directory is changed to that of the new user:

```
$ su - jmillionaire
```

Managing Tasks

The Linux operating system was designed to be a multitasking operating system – that is, to allow multiple tasks to be executed together. Until a few years ago, end users of the system were not directly exposed to this aspect of the operating system.

As far as Linux is concerned, the job-control features of Bash allow users to take advantage of the multitasking features of the operating system. In this section, we shall look at managing multiple tasks, both attended and unattended, starting with an overview of how processes work in Linux.

Processes

Processes, as we saw earlier, are programs executing in memory. A process may be associated with a terminal (for example, the date command is associated with the terminal since it prints it standard output to the terminal). The association of a process with a terminal also means that all the signals delivered to terminal's group of processes will be delivered to the process in question.

Some processes, such as servers (or daemons), are seldom associated with a terminal. These processes are typically started as part of the system boot process, and they run during the entire time that the system is up and write output to log files. When a user starts a process (that is, when the user runs a command), the command is associated with the terminal and is therefore also described as running in the foreground.

While a process is running in the foreground, the shell does not return a prompt until the process has completed execution. However, a process may also be started such that the prompt is returned immediately; in this case, the process is called a background process.

To run a process as a background process, we use the ampersand (&) character after the command:

```
$bash ls -R / &
```

This indicates to the shell that the process must be disassociated from the terminal and executed as a background process. Its output continues to be written to the terminal.

Job Control

Job control is a feature of Bash that allows the user to start and manage multiple programs at the same time rather than sequence their execution. We can suspend a program using the *Ctrl-Z* key, and we can send it to the background or foreground (using the bg and fg commands) or even leave it suspended. It is also possible to list all of the jobs (processes) started and terminate some of them.

Try It Out

Let us try using job control to manage a long-running process, say the ls -R / command, which recursively lists all the files and directories on the system:

```
$ ls -R /
^Z
[1]+  Stopped        ls -R /

$ jobs
[1]+  Stopped        ls -R /
```

```
$ bg %1
[1]+   ls -R / &

$ fg %1
ls -R /
^Z
[1]+   Stopped      ls -R /

$ kill -s SIGKILL %1

$
[1]+   Killed       ls -R /
```

How It Works

We start the program `ls` with the `-R` option. After a while, we decide to suspend the program using the *Ctrl-Z* key. The `jobs` command displays the current jobs and their status.

We use the `bg` command to send the process to the background. After a while, we decide to bring the process back to the foreground, for which we use the `fg` command. Both `bg` and `fg` take an argument that indicates the job number. The `%1` argument indicates that we are referring to job number 1.

Finally, having had enough of the process, we suspend it once again and kill it (using the `kill` command).

Note that the job control commands are built-in commands, and not external commands.

Scheduling Tasks

Often, it is not necessary (or not possible) for the user to be present when a task needs to execute. For example, if a user wants to have a certain script executed at midnight to take advantage of the spare CPU cycles, then what they need is a mechanism by which the task can be **scheduled** and executed unattended. Alternatively, if a certain task takes hours to complete and may not require any user input, it is not necessary for the user to remain logged on until the task is complete.

Scheduling Processes

We can use the `cron` utility to execute tasks automatically at arbitrary times, and even repeatedly if required. The `cron` daemon is a system process that runs at all times in the background, checking to see if any processes need to be started on behalf of users. We can schedule tasks for `cron` by editing the `crontab` file.

Try It Out   Scheduling a Task

Let's schedule a `cron` job that needs to be started every Monday and Thursday at 11:55 PM to back up our system:

```
$ crontab -e
No crontab for deepakt - using an empty one
```

This brings up an editor (`vi` by default), using which we add our `crontab` entry:

```
55  23  *  *  1,4  /home/deepakt/mybackup >/home/deepakt/mybackup.out 2>&1
```

We need to save the file and exit the editor:

```
crontab: installing new crontab
$ crontab -l
# DO NOT EDIT THIS FILE - edit the master and reinstall.
# (/tmp/crontab.6642 installed on Fri Jan 17 05:09:37 2003)
# (Cron version -- $Id: crontab.c,v 2.13 1994/01/17 03:20:37 vixie Exp $)
55     23     *     *     1,4     /home/deepakt/mybackup
/home/deepakt/mybackup.out 2>&1
```

How It Works

We need to use the `crontab` command to create new `cron` jobs. The `-e` option pops up the `vi` editor that allows us to add the new `cron` job. The entry for a `cron` job consists of six columns:

- ❑ The first five columns indicate the time at which the job should execute and the frequency – the minute (0–59), the hour (0–23), the day of the month (1–31), the month of the year (1–12), and the day of the week (0–6, with 0 indicating Sunday). An asterisk represents all logical values, hence we have asterisks for the day of the month and the month of the year (job needs to run during all months of the year).

- ❑ The last column indicates the actual command to be invoked at these times. We need to specify the full command, with the complete path leading to our backup program and also redirect the output to a log file.

  The `2>&1` indicates that the standard error is also redirected to the same log file.

Allowing a Process to Continue after Logout

The nohup command can be used to execute tasks that need to continue to execute even after
the user has logged out:

```
$ nohup ls -R / &
```

The nohup command is quite straightforward, in that it takes the program to be executed as the
argument. We need to send the whole process to the background by using the & operator. The
standard output and error of the nohup command will be written to the user's home directory
in a file called nohup.out.

Shell Scripting

As we've seen in this chapter, the shell has extensive capabilities when it comes to providing
tools for finding our way around the operating system and getting our job done. But the true
power of the shell is in its capacity as a scripting language.

To capture this, we use **shell scripts**. Essentially, a shell script is a sequence of commands and
operators listed one after another, stored in a file, and executed as a single entity.

Shell scripting in Bash is a topic that deserves a book by itself. Our objective in this short
section is simply to touch upon the salient features of scripting using Bash.

Bash shell script files start with the command interpreter, in this case bash itself:

```
#!/bin/bash
```

or:

```
#!/bin/sh
```

Variables

Like most other programming languages, Bash scripting requires variables to store its data in
during the course of execution. Shell scripts' variables are essentially the same as regular
environment variables. In fact they are set and retrieved the same way as environment
variables. Certain variables have special meanings:

- ❑ $n indicates the nth argument to the script. Therefore $1 would indicate the first
  argument to the script.

- ❑ $0 indicates the name of the script itself

- ❑ $* prints the complete command line

Let's try out a program that prints the values of special variables n and $*$:

```
#!/bin/sh

echo "Script name: $0"
echo "First argument: $1"
echo "Second argument: $2"
echo "All arguments : $*"
```

The echo command (in our shell script) has the effect of interpreting and writing its arguments to the standard output.

We need to save this in a file called testcmd.sh:

```
$ chmod +x testcmd.sh

$ ./testcmd.sh foo bar

Script name: ./testcmd.sh
First argument: foo
Second argument: bar
All arguments : foo bar
```

We run the command testcmd.sh as ./testcmd.sh because this indicates the full path of the shell script or in other words, we indicate that the testcmd.sh script residing in the current directory needs to be executed. Alternatively we could add the current working directory to our PATH:

```
$ export PATH=$PATH:.
```

Literal Usage of Special Characters

Over the course of the chapter we've seen that the shell uses several special characters. Often, we may need to use these special characters literally. In this situation, we use **quotation characters** to protect these special characters from being interpreted by the shell or the shell script.

We often use **single quote** (') characters to protect a string:

```
$ touch 'foo*bar'
```

This creates a file called foo*bar on the disk. Without the single quotes the * character would have been interpreted as a wildcard metacharacter.

We use **double quote** characters when referencing variables. All characters, including \ and ',
are interpreted literally except for dollar ($) which is used to refer to the value of a variable:

```
$ foo="foo/'"
$ bar="'\bar"
$ echo "$foo$bar"
foo/''\bar
```

The double quotes protected the single quotes and the slashes (both forward and backslashes)
when the strings were assigned to variables `foo` and `bar`. As expected, when $foo and $bar
are enclosed in double quotes in the last command, the $ is interpreted, and the two variables
expanded to their values.

The **backquote** (`) is used to execute commands. The backquote is convenient when the output
of a certain command needs to be assigned to a variable:

```
$ datevar=`date`
$ echo $datevar
Tue Jan 14 23:03:43  2003
```

Conditional Constructs

Finally, we'll look at ways to specify the execution path of our code based on conditions. This is
more complex than the ideas we've looked at so far, but with that complexity comes a great
deal of added flexibility. You can use conditional constructs to create extremely flexible scripts
that automate many common tasks upon your system.

We will begin by looking at the `if then .. else .. fi` conditional construct used for testing
and branching. This command is useful when we needed to execute a certain set of statements,
i.e. commands if a particular condition is met and a certain other set of commands if the
condition is not satisfied.

We could type the example below into a file using our favorite editor and save it as a shell
script, say `testif.sh`:

```
#!/bin/sh
x=10
y=5

if [ "$x" -eq "$y" ]
then
  echo x and y are equal
else
  echo x and y are not equal
fi
```

Then issue the following command:

```
$ chmod +x testif.sh; ./testif.sh
```

The chmod command sets execution permissions for the shell script; in other words, it makes the script executable. The next chapter, on filesystems, contains detailed information on setting various permissions for files. The ./testif.sh command executes the script. We see the following output:

```
x and y are not equal
```

As an aside, it is not necessary to type a shell script into a file. We could type it in at the command line itself:

```
$ x=10; y=5
$ if [ "$x" -eq "$y" ]
> then
> echo x and y are equal
> else
> echo x and y are not equal
> fi
x and y are not equal
$
```

Note that the shell prompt changes into a > sign since the shell expects more input.

The if then ... else ... fi statement has the following syntax:

```
if expression
then
   statement 1
   statement 2
...
   statement n
else
   statement 1'
   statement 2'
...
    statement n'
fi
```

If the value of the expression turns out to be true, the statements from *statement 1* to *statement n* are executed. If it evaluates to false, the statements from statement 1' to *statement n'* are executed. The expression can be formed using operators, in this case the -eq operator. The -eq operator tests for equality of numbers. It evaluates to true if two numbers are equal and false if they are not.

237

A shorter form of this construct is the `if then .. fi` construct shown below:

```
if expression
then
   statement 1
   statement 2
   ...
   statement n
fi
```

This construct is useful when we need to execute certain statements only if a certain condition is met. Below is a sample script that uses the `if then .. fi` form:

```
#!/bin/sh
x=10
y=5

if [ "$x" -eq "$y" ]
then
   echo "The two numbers are equal"
fi
```

Note that in both cases the statements are indented only to make the code more readable and this is not a requirement.

Loops

In this section we shall look at looping constructs that allow us to conditionally execute a set of statements repeatedly.

The `for` loop is essentially a simple looping construct that allows us to specify a set of statements that need to be executed a certain number of times:

```
#!/bin/sh
for fil in `ls *.txt`
do
   cat $fil >> complete.txt
done
```

The script above concatenates all the text files in the current directory into one large text file.

```
#!/bin/sh
for number in 1 2 3 4 5
do
   echo $
done
```

The script above produces the following output:

```
1
2
3
4
5
```

The syntax of the for construct is:

```
for variable in word
do
   statement 1
   statement 2
   ...
   statement n
done
```

Here word is a set of items that get assigned to the variable one at a time for each iteration of the loop. The loop therefore executes as many times as there are items in the word.

The while looping construct tests a logical condition for continuing the looping:

```
#!/bin/sh
x=10
y=5

while [ "$x" -ge "$y" ]
do
   echo $y
   y=`expr $y + 1`
done
```

The script above displays the output:

```
5
6
10
```

The syntax of the while construct is below:

```
while expression
do
   statement 1
   statement 2
   .
   .
   statement n
done
```

The `while` loop continues as long as the expression evaluates to be true.

Going Further

We've given you only a taste of the functionality that your Bash shell has to offer. There are very many good books on the subject that you can consult if you wish to learn more about its more complex functionality.

Summary

This chapter has aimed to give you a working knowledge of the Bash command line shell. It began with a brief history of where the shell came from, before moving on to explore some simple yet useful commands to manage processes, the file system, and some administrative tasks. We also looked at some shortcuts and control keys that abbreviate many common tasks. We also explored the command line syntax, environment variables, I/O redirection, and shell configuration, before moving on to look at managing multiple tasks, and scheduling unattended tasks. Finally we briefly went through the concepts, and some of the important constructs, of shell scripting.

The File System

In Chapter 6, as we explored the shell, we touched upon several aspects of the file system. In this chapter, we take our understanding further by discussing the file system in greater depth. In very simple terms, the file system is that part of the operating system that takes care of organizing files and directories. Of course, the file system does much more than that and in this chapter we explore the following aspects of the file system:

- ❑ Various file and directory attributes and how they relate to our everyday tasks
- ❑ File system hierarchy and the location of various useful programs
- ❑ The concept of supporting multiple file systems
- ❑ Managing and maintaining the file system

What Is the File System?

What does the file system do for the end-user? Besides organizing our data files and useful programs, it also manages configuration information required for the operating system to provide us a consistent environment every time we restart the computer. It also enforces security and allows us to control access to our files. Processes may read, write, append, delete, move, or rename files and directories. The file system defines the rules of the game when such operations are performed.

The shell, combined with a host of other programs, allows us to navigate the file system and get our tasks done. Depending on the distribution and installed software, we may also use file managers to navigate the file system; in the case of Red Hat Linux 9, we may use the **Nautilus** file manager.

However, one of the most interesting aspects of the file system (and one that is not immediately obvious) is the fact that Linux treats almost *all* devices as **files**. Hard disks, terminals, printers, and floppy disk drives are all devices – devices that can be read from and written to (mostly). In fact, with the **proc** file system, Linux goes so far as to provide a file system abstraction to running processes. We shall see more about this later. But the thing to note is that treating devices as files allows Linux to deal with them in a consistent manner.

Linux supports a wide variety of file system types including Microsoft Windows file system types. Some first-time Linux users find it interesting that it is possible to copy a file from a Microsoft Windows file system onto a floppy and edit it on a Linux machine and take it back to Windows. In fact, Linux even allows remote Windows-shared file systems to be accessed locally using Samba (we'll see more of this in Chapter 9).

The Anatomy of a File

To understand the file system better, we'll start off with a close examination of an individual file. Let's start off by creating a file with a line of data in it:

```
$ cat >dissectme.txt
Innards of this file
^D
$ ls -l dissectme.txt
```

Now that we have created our file, let's list it with the ls command:

```
-rw-r--r--    1 deepakt   users          21 Jan 19 18:40 dissectme.txt
```

In fact the ls command is our close ally in the exploration of the file system. It is a veritable *swiss army knife* when it comes to examining the various attributes of a file. By attributes, we mean the various characteristics of the file including its name, date of creation, permissions to access it, and so on. We also need to remember that file and directory names in Linux are case-sensitive – that is, bluecurve.txt, Bluecurve.txt, and BLUECURVE.txt are all different file names.

File Types

We start off by analyzing the output of the ls command. The first column (that is, the -rw-r--r-- segment) has information about the type of the file and the permissions to access it. The first '–' symbol indicates that the file is a regular file and not a directory or other type of file. The first character of the ls -l listing always indicates the type of the file, to tell us whether it is a regular file, a directory, a FIFO (a mechanism by which programs communicate with each other), a character device (such as a terminal), or a block device (such as a hard disk).

Let's try to list the various types of files to understand how they differ from a regular file. In the listing for the /etc directory, we see that the first letter indicating the type of the file is the letter 'd', confirming that /etc is indeed a directory:

```
$ ls -ld /etc
drwxr-xr-x    59 root      root          8192 Jan 19 18:32 /etc
```

In the next two listings, we initially list one of the first hard disks on the system, /dev/hda in this case. We see the letter b, which indicates that this is a block device. While listing the terminal device /dev/tty, we see that the letter c indicates a character device:

```
$ ls -l /dev/hda
brw-rw----    1 root      disk       3,   0 Aug 30 16:31 /dev/hda
$ ls -l /dev/tty
crw-rw-rw-    1 root      root       5,   0 Aug 30 16:31 /dev/tty
```

A **block device** performs input and output in blocks of data; for example, when we read a file from the hard disk, data is read in multiples of a block of (say) 4096 bytes. By contrast, a **character device** (such as a terminal) reads and writes data one character at a time.

We shall see more about device files in the /dev directory in later sections of this chapter.

When we list the bash shell executable in the /bin directory, we see that sh is actually a symbolic link to the Bash shell (/bin/bash):

```
$ ls -l /bin/sh
lrwxrwxrwx    1 root      root          4 Oct 30 14:46 /bin/sh -> bash
```

A **link** is not really a file by itself; rather, it is a pointer to another file. We shall see more about links in the course of the chapter.

The last two listings, below, are rather exotic from a user's perspective, since the user rarely (if ever) deals with them directly. Here, we create a FIFO called myfifo, using the mknod command; and then we list it. The letter 'p' indicates that this is a FIFO:

```
$ mknod myfifo p
$ ls -l myfifo
prw-r--r--    1 deepakt   users         0 Jan 19 19:09 myfifo
$ ls -l /tmp/ssh*
/tmp/ssh-XXiVoKic:
total 0
srwxr-xr-x    1 deepakt   users         0 Jan 19 18:40 agent.996
```

A FIFO is a mechanism used by processes to talk to each other, therefore known as an inter-process communication mechanism or IPC. FIFO is an acronym for "First In, First Out". Programmers, rather than end-users, deal with FIFOs.

On listing the Secure Shell (SSH) directories in /tmp, we see a file whose listing begins with the letter s. This indicates that the file is a **socket**, another IPC mechanism that is often used by processes on remote machines to talk to each other.

243

SSH comprises of a set of programs that are intended to provide a secure alternative to Unix remote access programs that transmit information including passwords in clear-text.

Another command that is useful in checking the type of files is the `file` command. It does more than just list the type of the file; it is often able to distinguish between files of the same type. That is, it can differentiate between a regular text file and a program file:

```
$ file /etc /dev/hda /dev/tty /bin/sh /bin/bash dissectme.txt myfifo
/tmp/ssh-*/*
/etc:                      directory
/dev/hda:                  block special (3/0)
/dev/tty:                  character special (5/0)
/bin/sh:                   symbolic link to bash
/bin/bash:                 ELF 32-bit LSB executable, Intel 80386,
                           version 1 (SYSV), dynamically linked (uses
                           shared libs), stripped
dissectme.txt:             ASCII text
myfifo:                    fifo (named pipe)
/tmp/ssh-XXiVoKic/agent.996: socket
```

Note the entry for /bin/bash, which indicates that this file is an executable, compiled to execute on an Intel processor. We shall see more about dynamically linked executables in a later section.

Linux treats files as a 'stream of bytes', without record boundaries; that is, there are no special characters used by the system to distinguish, say, one line from the next. On the other hand, even though files on Microsoft Windows operating systems also do not have explicit record boundaries, the operating system uses the convention that text files have a *carriage return–line feed* pair at the end of lines. The operating system also uses different modes for opening files as *text* or *binary* files.

Unix does not use filename extensions in the way that Windows does. All associations between filenames and extensions are merely based on convention. Typically, Unix executable files don't have extensions like `.com` or `.exe`.

Links

When we listed the `/bin/sh` file, we noted that it is in fact a **link** to the file `/bin/bash`. In other words, `/bin/sh` is not really a file in itself, but anyone executing `/bin/sh` is actually executing `/bin/bash`. Actually, this is quite fine since Bash is a replacement for the sh shell, and is nearly 100% backward compatible with sh.

To illustrate the usage of links, let us consider a hypothetical program `foo` which has two different modes of operation; in mode one, it copies files, and in mode two, it renames files. One way to switch between the modes of the program is to pass it an option, say `foo -c file1 file2` would create a copy of `file1` named `file2`. If we pass it the `-m` option (that is, `foo -m file1 file2`), it would create a copy of `file1` named `file2` but would also remove `file1` (therefore effectively renaming it).

244

Another way to switch modes would be to create two links to the file `foo`, one named `copy` and the other named `rename`. Now the program `foo` needs to figure out only the name it was invoked with to switch to the appropriate mode. In other words, if it was invoked with the name `copy`, `foo` would copy the file, and if it was invoked with the name `rename`, it would copy the file and remove the original.

The concept of a link is analogous to that of a shortcut in Microsoft Windows. A link allows us to refer to a file (or directory) by a different name, even from a different directory altogether. This leads us to another use of links – version management of software. Let us take the case of a program that refers to the `libc.so.6` library in the `/lib` directory. Simply put, a **library** contains common functions that may be used by several programs:

```
$ ls -al /lib/libc.so.6
lrwxrwxrwx  1 root  root  14 Oct 30 14:45 /lib/libc.so.6 -> libc-2.2.93.so
```

Here, we can see that `libc.so.6` is actually a symbolic link to the actual library `libc-2.2.93.so`. This means that if the library is upgraded from version `2.2.93` to (say) `2.2.94`, the upgrade process removes the link between `libc.so.6` and `libc-2.2.93.so` and creates a new link between `libc.so.6` and `libc-2.2.94.so`. This ensures that the programs referring to `libc.so.6` need not be modified every time a library they refer to is changed.

This applies not just to libraries, but also to executable programs. Users typically refer to the program by a link, while system administrators can replace the actual executable with a newer version unbeknownst to the user.

Hard Links and Symbolic Links

Links come in two flavors: **hard links** and **symbolic links** (also known as **soft links**). Before we learn more about each of these, we need to understand the concept of **inodes**. Inodes are essentially an indexing mechanism – a number by which the operating system refers to a file. The file name is for us mortals; the operating system mostly refers to a file by its inode number.

> *Linux hard disks are divided into partitions. Partitions allow us to divide the disk into file systems that have different functionality and are often managed independently of each other. For instance, a system may have a **root partition** housing all the operating system commands and configuration files and a **user partition** that houses the directories and files of individual users. We shall see more about partitions in a later section of this chapter.*

The inode number is unique only within a disk partition. In other words, it is possible for two files on different partitions (say, one on the `/boot` partition and another on the `/` partition) to have the same inode number. The `df` command can be used to list the partitions on our system. To see the inode number of a file, we could use the `ls` command again, this time with the `-i` option:

```
$ ls -li /etc
total 2012
 226972 -rw-r--r--   1 root   root    15228 Aug  5 03:14 a2ps.cfg
```

245

```
226602 -rw-r--r--    1 root    root    2562 Aug  5 03:14 a2ps-site.cfg
226336 -rw-r--r--    1 root    root      47 Jan 19 04:00 adjtime
  . . .
```

The inode number is listed in the first column. Each file has a unique inode number. While both hard links and symbolic links are used to refer to another file, the real difference is in the inode number:

❑   Hard links have the same inode number as the original file.

❑   Symbolic links have their own unique inode number.

Let's create both hard links and symbolic links to see how they work:

```
$ ln dissectme.txt hard.txt
$ ln -s dissectme.txt soft.txt
```

Both hard links and symbolic links can be created using the `ln` command. While the `-s` option of the `ln` command creates a symbolic link, with no options it creates a hard link. Initially, we create a hard link to the file `dissectme.txt` with the name `hard.txt`. We then create a symbolic link to the same file, called `soft.txt`:

```
$ ls -li dissectme.txt hard.txt soft.txt
131524 -rw-r--r--    2 deepakt  users  21 Jan 19 18:40 dissectme.txt
131524 -rw-r--r--    2 deepakt  users  21 Jan 19 18:40 hard.txt
131528 lrwxrwxrwx    1 deepakt  users  13 Jan 19 20:23 soft.txt ->
                                                       dissectme.txt
```

When we list all three files with the `-i` option of `ls`, we see that inode numbers of the hard link and the inode number of the actual file are the same:

```
$ cat dissectme.txt hard.txt soft.txt
Innards of this file
Innards of this file
Innards of this file
```

When we list the contents of the file and the links, we see that output is just the same, indicating that all three are actually referring to the same file.

Now let's try something else:

```
$ pwd
/home/deepakt
$ ln /boot/boot.b boot.b_hard
ln: creating hard link `boot.b_hard' to `/boot/boot.b': Invalid cross-device
link
```

```
$ ln -s /boot/boot.b boot.b_soft
$ ls -al boot.b_soft
lrwxrwxrwx  1 deepakt  users    12 Jan 19 20:21 boot.b_soft -> /boot/boot.b
```

When we attempt to create a hard link to a file on a different partition, the operating system does not allow us to do so. This is because inode numbers are unique only within a partition and a hard link requires the same inode number as the link target, which may not be possible on a different partition. However, we are able to successfully create a symbolic link to a file on a different partition.

Links are commonly used for organizing shared directories. For instance, a project group may choose to share files in a directory called /var/documents. Users who wish to share documents may choose to leave the documents in any subdirectory under their own home for ease of maintenance. This is how a typical directory structure would look like in this case:

```
$ ls -l /var/documents
total 0
lrwxrwxrwx    1 deepakt   users    22 Feb 23 23:54 deepakt ->
                                                    /home/deepakt/joe_docs
lrwxrwxrwx    1 zora      users    18 Feb 23 23:55 zora ->
                                                    /home/zora/work/blueprints
lrwxrwxrwx    1 sarah     users    18 Feb 23 23:55 sarah ->
                                                    /home/sarah/deep/down/mydocs
```

Members of the group may choose to maintain their documents in any sub-directory under their home directory. They still have the convenience of referring to a colleague's shared documents by accessing /var/documents/<user name>. A new project member, say with the user name apprentice, would typically execute the following command to add her document directory to this scheme of things:

```
$ ln -s mydocdir /var/documents/apprentice
```

For this scheme to work, the owner of the /var/documents directory should allow members of the project group write permissions for the /var/documents directory. We shall see more about groups and permissions in the next section.

Ownership of Files

Every file stored on a Linux system has an **owner** – this indicates the creator of the file. Each file also has the notion of a **group** associated with it. A group is essentially a group of *users* (a number of groups exist on the system by default – including the groups users, administrators, and daemon). The file /etc/group has a complete list of available groups on the system:

```
$ cat /etc/group
root:x:0:root
bin:x:1:root,bin,daemon
daemon:x:2:root,bin,daemon
sys:x:3:root,bin,adm
...
users:x:100:deepakt
ntp:x:38:
...
```

The first column indicates the name of the group; the second column indicated by an x character is the password column; the third column is the group ID of the group which is a unique number for the group. The last column is a list of users who belong to the group. In this case, the group `users` has a group id of `100` and the user `deepakt` belongs to it.

Let's go back to the listing of the `dissectme.txt` file again:

```
-rw-r--r--    1 deepakt  users          21 Jan 19 18:40 dissectme.txt
```

In the output here, the third column (`deepakt`) indicates that the owner of this file is a user called `deepakt`. The fourth column shows that the file belongs to a group called `users`.

It is possible to assign access control based on group membership. For instance, we can arrange for all the members of a certain project to belong to the same group, and set up group access permissions for that group to all the project-related documents on our Linux system. This way, we could allow access to these documents for all users belonging to that group and to no other users. This becomes clear when we learn about permissions in the next section.

By default, the group of the file is the same as the group that the creator of the file belongs to. However, it is possible to change a file's group so that it is different from that of its owner. To change the ownership of a file, we use the `chown` command; to change its group, we use the `chgrp` command.

File Permissions

In the `ls` listing above, the `-rw-r--r--` part of the output indicates the **permissions** associated with a file. The **permissions block** is split into three parts:

- ❑ The first part indicates the read, write, and execute permissions for the owner.

- ❑ The second indicates the read, write, and execute permissions for the group.

- ❑ The last part indicates the read, write, and execute permissions for the rest of the world (that is, users who do not belong to the group of this file).

There are a number of different characters we use here to reflect permissions:

- ❏ An r indicates read permission
- ❏ A w indicates write permission
- ❏ An x indicates execute permission
- ❏ A hyphen (-) indicates that a particular permission is denied

Execute permissions for a file do not automatically mean that a file can be executed – the file also has to be of an executable format (like an executable binary or a shell script).

Therefore in the example above, we see that the owner has permissions to read and write (that is, modify) the file, but no permissions to execute it. Other members of the users group may only read the file, but they may not modify or execute it. The same permissions also hold for the "rest of the world".

Directory Permissions

For a directory, "read", "write", and "execute" have slightly different meanings:

- ❏ The "read" permission refers to the ability to list the files and subdirectories contained in that directory.
- ❏ The "write" permission refers to the ability to create and remove files and subdirectories within it.
- ❏ The "execute" permission refers to the ability to enter the directory using the cd command (in other words, change the current working directory to be this directory).

We can use the chmod command to change permissions for a file – by specifying the permissions for the owner, group, and others. An easy way to interpret permissions in the context of directories is to think of directories also as files, the only difference being that these files contain names of files or other directories. Therefore listing a directory is analogous to reading the contents of a file, and adding or removing contents of a directory is analogous to writing and deleting content from a file.

So what are the default permissions when we create a file? This is controlled by the default file creation mask, which can be set using the umask command.

A File and Directory Permissions Experiment

Let's create a file and a directory and experiment with changing permissions and ownership. First, we'll list the current file mask:

```
$ umask -S
u=rwx,g=rw,o=rw
```

249

Here the -S option prints out the default file mask in rwx form. This mask allows owners to read, write, and execute files; it allows the group and others read and write permissions, but no execute permissions.

Now, let's modify the file mask:

```
$ umask u=rwx,g=r,o=r
$ umask -S
u=rwx,g=r,o=r
```

We do this using the umask command supplying the desired file mask. Our new mask allows the owner read, write, and execute, while the group and others have just read permissions. A newly created file reflects the current file mask:

```
$ mkdir widgets
$ ls -ld widgets
drwxr--r--      2 deepakt   users           4096 Jan 20 01:05 widgets
$ cd widgets
$ touch foowidget
$ ls -al
total 8
drwxr--r--      2 deepakt   users           4096 Jan 20 01:05 .
drwx------     13 deepakt   users           4096 Jan 20 01:05 ..
-rw-r--r--      1 deepakt   users              0 Jan 20 01:05 foowidget
```

Here we should notice that (as intended) the foowidget file has just read permissions for the group and others: However, you may note that while the file mask reads u=rwx,g=r,o=r, the owner of this file does *not* have execute permissions! This is because foowidget is interpreted by the shell as a text file, and execute permission does not make sense for text files in general. Shell scripts or other text files of scripting languages such as Perl are therefore treated as text files but need to be manually assigned execute permissions for them to run. (If we were to compile a program to create an executable, we would notice that execute permission for the owner is enabled. Execute permissions are also enabled by default for the owner when creating a directory since the execute permissions for a directory is necessary to allow users to execute the cd command to enter the directory.)

Now, let's modify the files permissions again:

```
$ chmod u=rwx,g=rw,o=rw foowidget
$ ls -al foowidget
-rwxrw-rw-      1 deepakt   users              0 Jan 20 01:05 foowidget
```

This command modifies the permissions of the foowidget file such that the group and others are now allowed to both read and write the file and the owner is allowed to read, write, and execute it. The file list confirms that the permissions have indeed changed.

Now, let's switch to the root user and change the ownership of the file:

```
$ su
  Password:
# chown nobody:nobody widgets
```

To change the ownership of the widget directory, we use the chown command. The chown command is restricted to the root user only, so we switch to the root user using the su command and *then* change the owner and group of the file to nobody and nobody respectively.

The chown command takes the name of the new owner followed by the file name. Optionally, we can also modify the group by specifying the name of the new group after the owner, separated by a colon ':' character. In this case the owner is nobody and the group is also named nobody. Both the user and group of name nobody are used to assign minimum privileges to programs that are often exposed to the external world such as daemon (or server) processes.

Now we switch back to being a normal user by typing exit in the shell, and try to list the widget directory:

```
# exit
$ ls -al widgets
ls: widgets/.: Permission denied
ls: widgets/..: Permission denied
ls: widgets/foowidget: Permission denied
 total 0
```

Now we can check the impact of the changed ownership of the directory. Without the root user's privileges, it's not possible to enter the directory, although the read permission still allows us to see that the file foowidget exists inside the directory.

Finally, let's finish up by trying to remedy this situation. Switch once again to the root user and change the group ownership of the directory to grant permissions for the group, before changing back to a normal user again:

```
$ ls -ld widgets
drwxr--r--    2 nobody    nobody        4096 Jan 20 01:05 widgets/
$ su
Password:
# chgrp users widgets
# chmod g=rwx widgets
# exit
```

The new group ownership and group permissions once again allow us access to the directory:

```
$ ls -ld widgets
drwxrwxr--    2 nobody    users         4096 Jan 20 01:05 widgets
$ cd widgets
```

Ordinary Users with Extraordinary Privileges

We've already seen in this chapter that when a program executes, it needs to have permissions for performing its tasks (see the attempt in the previous section to list the widgets directory). Often non-root users need to perform functions that may be restricted to root users only. This applies not just to the root and non-root user case; in fact it applies to any user or the group the user belongs to that may not have the permission to perform a certain operation.

Fortunately, there is a way to set permissions so that this can happen, *without* actually elevating the non-privileged user to a privileged status. If a certain command requires root privileges, the super-user can set the `setuid` execute permissions for this program. Once the `setuid` bit has been set, it is possible for non-privileged users to execute the program and have it behave as if it were run by root.

The `passwd` program is a typical example of such a program. Regular users can use this program to modify the password they use for logging in. By default on Red Hat Linux 9, passwords are encrypted and stored in the file `/etc/shadow` that can be modified only by the root user. From what we have seen so far, when a user executes the `passwd` program, the program would assume just the privileges assigned to that user. So how does the password program modify this file to update it with the new password? The trick lies in setting the `setuid` bit:

```
$ ls -al /usr/bin/passwd
-r-s--x--x    1 root      root          15368 May 28  2002 /usr/bin/passwd
```

The s indicates the `setuid` bit for this program. Thus when the `passwd` program executes, it assumes the privileges of the root user. Since it is restricted to just updating the `/etc/shadow` file, there is not much of a risk involved. In simple terms, assigning the `setuid` bit by a privileged user to a program owned by them indicates that other users may execute the program with the same privileges as the owner. Along the lines of the `setuid` bit is the `setgid` bit. When set, the program executes with the privileges of the group it belongs to.

Of course, it is not advisable to assign the `setuid` bit arbitrarily to programs. System administrators and programmers must carefully review the program before assigning the `setuid` bit to prevent malicious users from using `setuid` bit-enabled program to compromise system security. The `setuid` and `setgid` bits can be assigned via the `chmod` command:

```
$ chmod u=rws treasure_key.txt (setting the setuid bit)
$ chmod g=rws treasure_key.txt (setting the setgid bit)
```

Time Attributes

Any file has associated with it three different **time attributes**:

❑   **mtime** is the time at which the file was last modified

❑   **atime** is the time at which the file was last accessed

❑   **ctime** is the time at which the *attributes* of the file were last changed

When we list a directory using the `ls -l` command, the output includes the `mtime` (the modification timestamp) of each file. The `ls` command also has a `--time` option; this option takes the argument values `atime` or `ctime` and displays the other two time attributes accordingly. The `touch` command (with a filename as the argument) can be used to update a file's `mtime` and `atime`.

Try It Out   Exploring Time Attributes

Let's create a file and perform a few operations on it. After each operation, we'll check the file's `mtime`, `atime`, and `ctime` to determine how they have been affected by the operation.

1. Let us start by creating a new text file, called `time.txt`. We can use the `cat` command to create the file and to put some text into it. Put in as much text as you like, and use *Ctrl-D* to end the input. Then, use three `ls` command calls to check the `mtime`, `atime`, and `ctime` (as described above):

```
$ cat > time.txt
Test of time
^D
$ ls -l time.txt; ls -l --time=atime time.txt; ls -l --time=ctime time.txt
-rw-r--r--    1 deepakt   users          13 Jan 20 03:49 time.txt
-rw-r--r--    1 deepakt   users          13 Jan 20 03:49 time.txt
-rw-r--r--    1 deepakt   users          13 Jan 20 03:49 time.txt
```

We can see that they are all the same. Here, the file was created at 03:49. The file was accessed and modified at that time, and its attributes were all set at that time, so the `mtime`, `atime`, and `ctime` are all the same. Pause for a minute or so before moving onto Step 2.

2. Now, let's modify the content of the `time.txt` file, by overwriting the existing content with some new content. We can use the `cat` command again, and use *Ctrl-D* to end the input. Then, look at the `mtime`, `atime`, and `ctime` again:

```
$ cat > time.txt
Sands of time
^D
$ ls -l time.txt; ls -l --time=atime time.txt; ls -l --time=ctime time.txt
-rw-r--r--    1 deepakt   users          14 Jan 20 03:51 time.txt
-rw-r--r--    1 deepakt   users          14 Jan 20 03:49 time.txt
-rw-r--r--    1 deepakt   users          14 Jan 20 03:51 time.txt
```

You can see from this output that the `mtime` (modification time) attribute has changed, as we'd expect, because we've just modified the file. More surprisingly, the `ctime` (attribute change timestamp) has *also* changed – this is because the modification altered the size of the file.

Also, note that the `atime` didn't change, because we have not accessed (that is, read) the contents of the file in the time since we first created it. Again, pause for a minute before moving onto Step 3.

3. Now, let's use `cat` again, but this time to read and list the contents of the file (note the slightly different usage). Then, look at the `mtime`, `atime`, and `ctime` again:

```
$ cat time.txt
Sands of time
$ ls -l time.txt; ls -l --time=atime time.txt; ls -l --time=ctime time.txt
-rw-r--r--    1 deepakt   users          14 Jan 20 03:51 time.txt
-rw-r--r--    1 deepakt   users          14 Jan 20 03:52 time.txt
-rw-r--r--    1 deepakt   users          14 Jan 20 03:51 time.txt
```

This time we can see that only the `atime` has changed, reflecting the fact that we accessed the file but we didn't change it (or its attributes) in any way. Pause once more, before moving to Step 4.

4. Finally, use `chmod` to change the permissions of the file. Then, look at the `mtime`, `atime`, and `ctime` one more time:

```
$ chmod u=rwx time.txt
$ ls -l time.txt; ls -l --time=atime time.txt; ls -l --time=ctime time.txt
-rwxr--r--    1 deepakt   users          14 Jan 20 03:51 time.txt
-rwxr--r--    1 deepakt   users          14 Jan 20 03:52 time.txt
-rwxr--r--    1 deepakt   users          14 Jan 20 03:53 time.txt
```

This time, only the `ctime` has changed – because we changed the attributes but did not access or modify the file.

5. Finally we shall use the `touch` command to modify time-stamps of a file. The `touch` command can be used to change both the modification and access times of a file or directory:

```
$ ls -l time.txt; ls -l --time=atime time.txt; ls -l --time=ctime time.txt
-rwxr--r--    1 deepakt   users          14 Jan 20 03:51 time.txt
-rwxr--r--    1 deepakt   users          14 Jan 20 03:52 time.txt
-rwxr--r--    1 deepakt   users          14 Jan 20 03:53 time.txt
```

The command above displays the time-stamps (`mtime`, `atime`, and `ctime` respectively) of the file. Execute the commands below:

```
$ touch -m time.txt
$ ls -l time.txt; ls -l --time=atime time.txt; ls -l --time=ctime time.txt
-rwxr--r--    1 deepakt   users          14 Jan 20 03:54 time.txt
-rwxr--r--    1 deepakt   users          14 Jan 20 03:52 time.txt
-rwxr--r--    1 deepakt   users          14 Jan 20 03:54 time.txt
```

The modification time has changed since the –m option to the touch changed the modification time (atime). We also notice that as with the cat > command, the ctime also changed. We pause for a minute and execute the commands below:

```
$ touch -a time.txt
$ ls -l time.txt; ls -l --time=atime time.txt; ls -l --time=ctime time.txt
-rwxr--r--    1 deepakt   users             14 Jan 20 03:54 time.txt
-rwxr--r--    1 deepakt   users             14 Jan 20 03:55 time.txt
-rwxr--r--    1 deepakt   users             14 Jan 20 03:55 time.txt
```

As seen above, using the –a option to touch, we can modify the access time (atime) of the file. Consequently, the ctime also has changed.

The difference between using touch and cat (or a text editor) is clearer when it comes to modifying the access time. When changing the atime with touch, the ctime is also modified whereas it is unchanged when using the cat > command.

File Size

The **size** of a file is indicated in the file listing with the –l option in bytes:

```
$ ls -al dissectme.txt
-rw-r--r--    1 deepakt   users             21 Jan 19 18:40 dissectme.txt
```

To obtain the size of the contents of a directory, we could use the du command. The –h option prints the size in a human-readable format, i.e. in bytes, kilobytes, megabytes, etc. The –s option summarizes the output rather than list the sizes of each of the files and directories in each of the subdirectories:

```
$ du -sh /home/deepakt/
153M /home/deepakt
```

File Names

The ls command always displays file names, regardless of what options you choose. The –F option indicates the various file types with symbols, such as:

❑ A slash (/) next to a directory

❑ An asterisk (*) next to an executable file

❑ A pipe (|) next to a FIFO

❑ An @ next to a symbolic link

For example:

```
$ ls -F
a.out*          dissectme.txt   foo.txt    new2   ps_auxww.txt   whataboutme.txt@
boot.b_soft@    downloads/      hard.txt   new3   ps.txt         which.txt
crontab.txt     env.txt         hello.c    new4   soft.txt@      widgets/
csh.txt         foobar          myfifo|    new5   testcmd.sh*
```

This command lists a typical directory with all of the different file types in it. Of course, to see the same output, you'd have to create these files using the commands described earlier (that is, mkdir for a directory, chmod for setting execute permissions on a file, mknod for a FIFO, and ln for creating a symbolic link).

When the -d option is used with a directory name as the argument, the ls command prints information *only* about the directory and not about its subdirectories and the files it contains. Another useful option for color terminals is the --color option of ls which lists files of each type with a different color.

White Space in File Names

Linux does away with the traditional Unix restriction that file names cannot have white space characters in them. The following example creates a file called filename with white spaces.txt:

```
$ cat > "filename with white spaces.txt"
This file has white spaces in its name
```

To read the contents of this file, we can refer to the filename using the slash-space-escape sequence for a white space character:

```
$ cat filename\ with\ white\ spaces.txt
This file has white spaces in its name
```

In fact we could interchangeably use double quotes or backslashes irrespective of whether we are creating the file or listing its contents. Also, if we use the bash shell, using the *Tab* key for command completion automatically adds the slashes to the filename.

File Search Utilities

Over time, most users tend to accumulate quite a large number of files, so much so that that it becomes impractical to search for files merely by listing directories. At other times, we may be trying to execute a program and not finding it since it is not in a directory listed in our PATH environment variable. We obviously need something more powerful than ls when we're searching for files.

Searching with the locate Command

The quickest and simplest way of locating files on Linux is to use the `locate` command. It maintains an index of files on the file system and is able to return partial and exact matches very quickly. We may specify a complete file name or an expression that uses metacharacters as search criteria for the locate command. The `locate` command can also perform case-insensitive searches for file names.

Try It Out   Elementary Searching Using locate

Let's try using the `locate` command to search for a few files.

1. First, let's try out the `locate` command with no options. Search on the string `moon`, like this:

```
$ locate moon
/usr/share/icons/Bluecurve/16x16/apps/kmoon.png
/usr/share/backgrounds/images/space/clem_full_moon_strtrk.jpg
/usr/share/backgrounds/images/space/gal_earth_moon.jpg
...
```

As you can see, this searches the system for partial and exact matches, and so the output here includes any file whose name contains the string `moon`.

2. Now let's try searching with an expression that uses a metacharacter. The following command uses the `*` character as a wildcard:

```
$ locate "*.conf"
/etc/sysconfig/networking/profiles/default/resolv.conf
/etc/X11/gdm/factory-gdm.conf
/etc/X11/gdm/gdm.conf
...
```

This returns any file whose name ends with the `.conf` extension.

3. Now try an example using the `-i` option, to see the difference between case-sensitive and case-insensitive searches. First, without the `-i` option, we have a case-sensitive search:

```
$ locate bluecurve
/usr/lib/gtk-2.0/2.0.0/engines/libbluecurve.la
/usr/lib/gtk-2.0/2.0.0/engines/libbluecurve.so
/usr/lib/gtk/themes/engines/libbluecurve.la
...
```

Now, run the same command with the -i option, to specify case-insensitivity:

```
$ locate -i bluecurve
/usr/lib/gtk-2.0/2.0.0/engines/libbluecurve.la
/usr/lib/gtk-2.0/2.0.0/engines/libbluecurve.so
/usr/lib/gtk/themes/engines/libbluecurve.la
...
/usr/share/pixmaps/nautilus/Bluecurve
/usr/share/pixmaps/nautilus/Bluecurve/desktop-home.png
/usr/share/pixmaps/nautilus/Bluecurve/Bluecurve.xml
...
```

We can see that the search results are different – for example, the second search picked up the file Bluecurve.xml, while the first did not.

4. The locate command maintains an index of files on the system which is used to quickly look up file names. This index is updated periodically (automatically) with new files. However, the –u option can also be used to update the index explicitly.

To demonstrate, we first create a file called new_file.txt using the touch command:

```
$ touch new_file.txt
```

We then attempt to search for the file, but it returns no results even though the file has been created in the current directory. This is because the new file has not yet been added to the index of files:

```
$ locate new_file.txt
$
```

Now we change user to be the root user so that we have privileges to update the locate command's index. We run the locate command this time with the –u option, which updates the index:

```
$ su -
Password: <not displayed>
# locate -u
# exit
```

Now we try to locate the file again from the revised index. This time the locate command is able to locate the file new_file.txt since it has been added to the index of files by the –u option above:

```
$ locate new_file.txt
/home/deepakt/new_file.txt
```

Searching with the find Command

While the `locate` command is very useful for finding files quickly anywhere on the system, the search criteria that can be specified with `locate` are quite rudimentary. The `find` command has a much richer array of options. With the `find` command it is possible to search for files and sub-directories under a certain hierarchy, or specify various criteria such as the access time of the file, the size of the file, and so on. It is also possible to use `find` to execute other commands on files that meet the search criteria. Therefore, while `locate` is very fast with fewer features, `find` is more feature-packed while being slower.

Try It Out   Advanced Searching Using find

Let's experiment with the `find` command to execute a number of searches for files, specifying various criteria. The following examples will give us a taste of what is possible with `find`.

We start off by searching for files under the `/etc` directory that end with the `.conf` extension:

```
$ find /etc -name "*.conf" -print
/etc/sysconfig/networking/profiles/default/resolv.conf
/etc/X11/gdm/factory-gdm.conf
/etc/X11/gdm/gdm.conf
```

The first argument to `find` is the directory below which to search for files. Other arguments specify the search criteria to be utilized. In this case, we specify the `-name` option, which takes an expression representing a file or set of files as its argument. The search string may be a simple metacharacter expression or it can be the exact name of the file. Note that we use double quotes to specify the search string; this prevents the shell from interpreting the asterisk literally. Finally, we could specify the action to be performed once the search criteria are met. The `-print` option specifies the action; it indicates that the name of the files or directories matching the criteria should be displayed.

In the next search example, we look for all directories under `/tmp` whose name starts with the string `ssh`:

```
$ find /tmp -type d -name "ssh*" 2>/dev/null
/tmp/ssh-XX18hvoD
/tmp/ssh-XXzdTPki
/tmp/ssh-XX4DYEB5
/tmp/ssh-XX7KJPAN
```

These are temporary directories created by the `ssh` programs run by various users. The `-type` option specifies the type to search for, in this case `d`, indicating a directory. (Similarly, `f` indicates a file.) We may have permission to list only those SSH temporary directories that belong to us. Hence to redirect permission errors, we use the shell redirection to redirect the error to the `/dev/null` device. The `/dev/null` device is actually a pseudo device that acts as a black hole, accepting input and discarding it at the same time.

This next search is based on the time of last access – we do this by specifying the −amin option:

```
$ mkdir foobar
$ date
Mon Jan 20 22:41:29 PST 2003
$ find . -type d -name "foo*" -amin -10 -print
./foobar
$ ls -ld --time=atime foobar/
drwxr-xr-x    2 deepakt  users             4096 Jan 20 22:41 foobar/
```

The −10 option combined with the −amin option specifies a search for files that have been accessed in the last 10 minutes. Therefore we are actually searching for files with names that begin with foo that have been accessed in the last 10 minutes. A +10 option would result in a search for files last accessed more than 10 minutes ago.

In the next example, we combine the −amin option with the −or option:

```
$ mkdir bar
$ find . -type d -name "foo*" -amin -10 -or -name "*bar"
./foobar
./bar
```

The −or option is actually the logical OR operator that can be used to combine two specified criteria. In this case we search for files called foo* that have either been accessed in the last 10 minutes, or files with names ending in bar. (The −and option allows us to combine two of the specified criteria in a logical AND expression.)

We can also search by file size, using the −size option. By specifying the size with a plus (+) or minus (−) sign before it, we indicate that the file should be greater or smaller in size than the specified number:

```
$ find . -size -20k -and -size +10
./.viminfo
./downloads/nop.txt
./downloads/p.txt
./downloads/curl
./downloads/curl/p.txt
   ...
```

In this case, we search for files whose size is between lesser than 10B and 20KB (note that we've used the −and option to achieve this!).

In the last search, we demonstrate the −exec flag, which allows us to execute a command when the search criteria are met:

```
$ find /tmp -type f -atime +1000 -exec rm {} \; 2>/dev/null
```

The -exec option is followed by the command to be executed and optionally a pair of curly braces. The command is executed for each file that matches the criteria. The curly braces indicate the matched file. The semicolon (;) indicates the end of the command; it is escaped (by a preceding \ character) to prevent the shell from interpreting it. In this case, we search and delete all files under the /tmp directory that have not been accessed in the last 1000 minutes.

Searching with the GNOME Search Tool

The GNOME search tool is a graphical front-end to the locate and find commands. It may be invoked from the Main Menu by clicking on Search for Files:

File names can be entered in the **File is named** field, and a directory in which to start the search can be specified in the **Look in folder** field. In the example above, we search for the file `hosts` in the `/etc` directory.

Wildcard searches are also possible using the expression syntax we used for `locate`. For instance, `host*` would search for all files starting with the characters `host` (and followed by one or more characters), and would therefore match `hosts`, `hosts.deny`, `hosts.accept`, and so on.

Clicking on the **Additional Options** label presents an advanced search interface using rules, as we described in Chapter 2.

Text Searches

Combining file searches with text searches within files allows us to quickly pinpoint the files that have the text we are looking for. We know how to search for a file by its filename (and also by its location); but how do we search the file system for files that contain a particular string of text? This type of search is very useful, but quite different from what we can achieve using `locate` or `find`.

The `grep` command is the most common way to search for a string in a file. In fact it can search multiple files at the same time. The `grep` command, by default, performs a case-sensitive search, though it can perform a case-insensitive search if required.

The `xargs` command reads its standard input and feeds it as arguments to any command that is supplied as an argument to it. In other words, `xargs` will dynamically create the arguments for a command. This makes it particularly useful for chaining commands using the pipe (|) shell operator. As illustrated in Chapter 6, simply using a pipe operator feeds the output of a command as input to another command. The `xargs` command in conjunction with the pipe operator feeds the output of a command as arguments to another command. The following example illustrates its use.

Try It Out   Using grep and xargs

Let us try out some grep searches and combine them with the xargs and find search utilities.

The grep command takes the string or expression to match as the first argument followed by one or more files to search. In the following example, grep searches for the string nobody in the files /etc/passwd and /etc/group:

```
$ grep nobody /etc/passwd /etc/group
/etc/passwd:nobody:x:99:99:Nobody:/:/sbin/nologin
/etc/passwd:nfsnobody:x:65534:65534:Anonymous NFS
User:/var/lib/nfs:/sbin/nologin
/etc/group:nobody:x:99:
/etc/group:nfsnobody:x:65534:
```

The grep command prints the names of the files in which the string was found, followed by a colon character (:) and the occurrence of the string within those files.

The -i option causes grep to search for the string or expression ignoring case. In the next example, the line corresponding to the Deepak Thomas user is displayed as a match since the string Deepak Thomas matches a case-insensitive search for the expression de*:

```
$ grep -i "de*" /etc/passwd
deepakt:x:501:100:Deepak Thomas:/home/deepakt:/bin/bash
```

Finally, we look at the combination of the find, xargs, and grep commands to search for files in the /etc directory that contain the string farfalla (which, in this case, happens to be the name of the machine the command is run on):

```
$ find /etc -type f 2>/dev/null |xargs grep farfalla 2>/dev/null
/etc/sysconfig/networking/profiles/default/network:HOSTNAME=farfalla
/etc/sysconfig/network:HOSTNAME=farfalla
/etc/hosts:127.0.0.1     farfalla        localhost
```

The find command locates all the files in the /etc directory. This list is piped as the input to the xargs command. The xargs command in this case has one argument – the grep command. The grep command also has an argument, i.e. the string to search for. Internally the xargs command constructs a command line that looks like this:

```
grep farfalla file1 file2 ... filen
```

Here, *file1*, *file2*, ..., *filen* are the results of the search by the find utility.

Other Text Searching Tools – awk and sed

There are other, more sophisticated text searching tools in existence. For example, the awk command is considered to be a language in itself, and allows for rich expressions and control flow. Another command, sed (the **stream editor**), is intended to transform input text streams, typically files or the output of commands.

The following awk script prints the login names and the actual names of users on the local system:

```
$ awk -F: '{print $1, "-", $5}' /etc/passwd
root - root
bin - bin
daemon - daemon
ftp - FTP User
nobody - Nobody
rpc - Portmapper RPC user
vcsa - virtual console memory owner
nscd - NSCD Daemon
sshd - Privilege-separated SSH
nfsnobody - Anonymous NFS User
xfs - X Font Server
ident - pident user
apache - Apache
webalizer - Webalizer
deepakt - Deepak Thomas
```

The -F option here indicates the field separator. In this case, it is the colon (:) character that is used to separate fields in the /etc/passwd file. The awk action prints the first and fifth columns of the file to the standard output (that is, the terminal), with a hyphen (-) character separating column entries on each line.

The following sed command line transforms a string in the seashells.txt file. The expression 's;sells;shells;' indicates that the pattern sells should be substituted with the pattern shells (the letter s indicates substitution):

```
$ cat >seashells.txt
She sells sea shells on the sea shore
^D
$ sed -e 's;sells;shells;' seashells.txt
She shells sea shells on the sea shore
```

The commands awk and sed do not modify the input file directly. Instead, they treat the file as a stream of input and write the output to the standard output (in this case, the terminal).

Navigating the File System

In this section we shall look at the file organization of Red Hat Linux 9 in general, based on the various utilities that are available and also the location of configuration files. The root file system is indicated by the /. Let us list the contents of the root file system:

```
$ ls -F /
bin/    dev/    home/    lib/          misc/    opt/     root/    tftpboot/    usr/
boot/   etc/    initrd/  lost+found/   mnt/     proc/    sbin/    tmp/         var/
```

The end-user utility programs are organized under the /bin, /usr/bin, and /usr/local/bin directories. The tables below list some of the common programs under these directories. It is very useful to ensure that these directories are set in the PATH environment variable.

> *Remember, you can get full information on each of these by querying their man pages, and abridged details by typing the command followed by - -help.*

Let's look at each of these directories in some detail.

Commands Found in the /bin Directory

The following are all commands, located in the /bin directory:

Command	Description
awk	Pattern scanning and processing language
bash	The Bourne-again shell
cat	Concatenates files and prints on to standard output
chgrp	Changes the group ownership
chmod	Changes file access permissions
chown	Changes file ownership permissions
cp	Copies files and directories
cpio	Copies files to and from archives
csh	C-shell

cut	Removes sections from each line of input
date	Prints the current date and timestamp. Super user may set the date and time
dd	Converts and copies files
df	Displays disk usage for file systems
dmesg	Displays startup messages
echo	Displays a line of text
ed	An old text editor
grep	Regular expression matching program
gzip	GNU zip program for compressing files
kill	Terminates running processes
ln	Creates links to files and directories
ls	Lists files
mail	Command-line mail client
mkdir	Creates a directory
more	Paginates a file
mount	Maps a file system to a directory
mv	Moves a file from one location to another; same as re-naming a file
netstat	Prints network statistics
ping	Checks for the network reachability of other machines on the network.
ps	Lists currently running processes
pwd	Displays current working directory
rm	Removes files
rmdir	Removes directories

sed	Stream editor can be used to edit files, output of programs etc.
sh	Bourne shell
sleep	Delays for a specific amount of time
sort	Sorts the lines of input
su	Changes identity of a user
tar	Archiving program
tcsh	Enhanced C shell
touch	Updates the time-stamp on a file
umount	Unmount a currently mounted file system
uname	Prints system information
vi	A text editor

Commands Found in the /usr/bin Directory

The following are also commands, and they're located in the /usr/bin directory:

Command	Description
at	Queue jobs for later execution
bc	A bench calculator
cc	C-compiler. This command is a symbolic link to the GNU C-compiler gcc.
clear	Clears the screen
crontab	Maintains a list of tasks to be performed later
du	Reports disk usage for a directory and sub-directories
emacs	An editor
F77	Fortran compiler
file	Prints file type

267

Command	Description
find	File-searching utility
finger	Looks up user information
ftp	File transfer program
gcc	GNU C-compiler
gdb	GNU debugger
gftp	Graphical FTP client
gimp	GNU Image manipulation and painting program
gmake	Maintains a group of programs. This command is a symbolic link to the GNU make command gmake.
head	Displays the first few lines of a file
ispell	Interactive spell checker
lpr	Spools print jobs
man	Displays manual pages for commands
nslookup	Looks up DNS information of a host
passwd	Changes the password of a user
telnet	Telnet client allows remote logins
wall	Sends a message to the terminals of all users currently logged on
wc	Counts words, lines and characters of input text
which	Displays the full path of commands
who	Displays the list of users currently logged on to the system

System Configuration Files Found in the /etc Directory

The next batch of files are system configuration files, located in the /etc directory and its subdirectories. This table contains some of the more commonly modified ones:

File	Description
exports	Lists the file systems to be exported via NFS
ftpaccess	Configuration file for ftpd
group	Lists the various groups on the system and each of their members
hosts	Lists the hostname and IP addresses of machines
host.conf	Used by the DNS resolver library
motd	Contains the message of the day
passwd	Contains user information for all users on the system
shadow	Contains the encrypted passwords of the user
xinetd.conf	Configuration file for the xinetd daemon

Administrative Binaries Found in the /sbin and /usr/sbin Directories

Administrative binaries can be found under /sbin and /usr/sbin. Below is a list of commands from the /sbin directory.

Binary	Description
arp	Prints the ARP (Address Resolution protocol) table of a machine.
cardmgr	PCMCIA device manager
chkconfig	Manages runlevel information for system services
debugfs	Ext2 File system debugging utility
dhclient	DHCP client
e2fsck	Ext file system diagnosis and repair tool
fdisk	Disk partitioning utility
fuser	Displays the ids of processes using the specified files

ifconfig	Configures network interfaces
insmod	Installs loadable kernel modules
lspci	Lists all PCI devices on this systems
lspnp	Lists all PNP devices on this system
mkfs	Creates a new file system on a partition
modprobe	Detects and manages loadable modules.
route	Display and sets system routing table
sysctl	Displays or changes system parameters

The following list contains some of the files from the /usr/sbin directory:

adduser	Creates a new user
automount	Configures mount points for autofs
chpasswd	Updates password file in batch mode
chroot	Runs command with the root set to a new root
gpm	Mouse-based cut and paste utility for virtual consoles
groupadd	Adds a new group
in.fingerd	Finger daemon
in.ftpd	FTP daemon
in.identd	identd daemon
in.telnetd	Telnet daemon
kudzu	Configures new hardware
pppd	PPP daemon
squid	HTTP caching server
tcpdump	TCP/IP diagnostics tool

Binary	Description
vipw	Password file editor
zdump	Dumps timezone information

Other Important Files

The /usr/local/bin directory usually houses new programs as and when they are installed.

Shared libraries (that is, libraries that contain common functions used by multiple programs at the same time without multiple in-memory copies) reside in the /lib, /usr/lib, and /usr/local/lib directories. It is often a good idea to ensure that the LD_LIBRARY_PATH environment variable contains these directories. This variable is not set by default, although it can be set in the .bashrc file or other startup files.

The /boot directory contains bootable images of Linux kernels. Below is an extract from a typical listing (here, the vmlinuz entries are the kernel binaries):

```
$ ls /boot
boot.b
chain.b
config-2.4.18-14
config-2.4.18-17.8.0
...
vmlinuz-2.4.18-14
vmlinuz-2.4.18-17.8.0
vmlinuz-2.4.18-19.8.0
```

Transient and temporary files can be found under /var/tmp and /tmp. The /tmp directory is cleaned up by startup scripts after every reboot, whereas the /var/tmp directory is not. This behavior may dictate for some programmers the choice of using /var/tmp as opposed to /tmp.

Files related to peripherals such as devices can be found under the /dev directory. By convention, various peripherals such as CD-ROM drives and floppy drives are mounted under the /mnt directory. We shall see more on this directory in a later section.

The /proc directory provides a file system abstraction to the processes currently running on the system. Each process has a directory assigned to it and several files under it which contain information about the process. For more details you should refer to the proc manual page by invoking the command man proc.

And finally, as we first discovered in Chapter 2, the users' home directories are typically created under /home.

Managing Drives and Partitions

Now that we have seen several aspects of the file system from an end user's perspective, we will look at some of the administrative aspects of the file system such as the different drives on a system and its partitions. Apart from the hard disks on a system, there is almost always a floppy disk drive and a CD-ROM drive, both of which are treated as file system drives. In addition, certain other peripheral devices such as digital cameras or removable storage devices may present the storage available on them as file system drives. A drive may be **mounted** – that is, made available for use by the file system. The drive may also be **unmounted**, making it unavailable for the file system to use.

We can list the currently mounted drives on a system using the df or mount commands. Let us look at the output of the df command:

```
$ df -k
File system          1K-blocks       Used Available Use% Mounted on
/dev/hda2             5716172     3426868   1998932  64% /
/dev/hda1              101089       19137     76733  20% /boot
none                   94752           0     94752   0% /dev/shm
/dev/fd0                1423         105      1318   8% /mnt/floppy
/dev/cdrom             661728      661728         0 100% /mnt/cdrom
```

The -k option to df causes it to report partition sizes in kilobytes.

In the listing above, we see that:

❑ The first IDE hard disk /dev/hda has two partitions, /dev/hda1 and /dev/hda2

❑ The floppy drive is the /dev/fd0 drive

❑ The /dev/cdrom drive represents a CD-ROM drive.

In addition, there is a drive marked none which (in this case) represents a temporary file system (tmpfs) necessary for certain shared-memory operations.

With the other drives, besides the space usage numbers on each of them, the thing to note is the Mounted on column. This represents the directory that these file systems are mapped on to. Therefore:

❑ The /dev/hda2 partition contains a file system that is mapped on to the / or the root directory.

❑ The /dev/hda1 partition contains another file system that is mapped on to the /boot directory.

What this means is that each time we execute the cd / command or the cd /etc command, we are actually accessing a file system on the second partition of the only hard disk on this system. Also, executing ls -l /mnt/cdrom will list the top-level files and subdirectories of the currently mounted CD in the CD-ROM drive.

Mounting Drives

A device such as a floppy drive may be detected by the operating system when it boots up. However, for the floppy drive to be *usable*, it needs to be mounted first (this is like grafting the drive onto a file system entry point).

To mount a drive, we need to first create a directory (or use the already available /mnt/floppy and /mnt/cdrom directories for floppy disks and CD-ROMs respectively). We then mount the floppy drive /dev/fd0 to that directory. Drives may be mounted in two different ways:

❏ Automatic mounting of the drive at the boot time

❏ Manual mounting at any time after the system has come up

For a drive to be mounted automatically by the system, we need to make an entry for it in the file /etc/fstab or the file system table file. Here is a typical /etc/fstab file:

```
LABEL=/           /            ext3    defaults           1 1
LABEL=/boot       /boot        ext3    defaults           1 2
none              /dev/pts     devpts  gid=5,mode=620     0 0
none              /proc        proc    defaults           0 0
none              /dev/shm     tmpfs   defaults           0 0
/dev/hda3         swap         swap    defaults           0 0
/dev/cdrom        /mnt/cdrom   iso9660 noauto,owner,kudzu,ro 0 0
/dev/fd0          /mnt/floppy  auto    noauto,owner,kudzu 0 0
```

Notice that there are more entries in this file than were listed by the df command. This is because there are drives of several other types that do not have true file system characteristics. For instance, disk usage of the proc file system does not make much sense since the proc file system actually represents a set of processes currently executing on the system. Similarly, the /dev/pts entry indicates a pseudo-terminal device, which is not really associated with commonly used files and directories; rather it is used for managing terminal-based input and output. However, these special types of file systems are also listed in /etc/fstab so that they may be mounted automatically at boot time.

Also, notice that besides the floppy and CD-ROM drives, there is also a swap device: this is a device used by the operating system to juggle processes and chunks of memory content between the RAM and the hard disk, therefore allowing arbitrarily large programs to be loaded and be executed. In general, swap partitions are critical to the operating system since they are necessary for multi-tasking – that is, running multiple tasks at (almost) the same time.

The Hardware Browser

Another way to check for the hard disks on a system and their partitions is using the Hardware Browser application, which you'll find under the Main | System Tools menu. When you're there, select the Hardware Browser option to view the hard drives on your system:

In the screenshot above, you can see that on this machine the disk /dev/hda has three partitions, and that one of them is a Linux swap partition.

Mounting Drives Manually

We can mount a drive (such as the CD-ROM drive) manually by using the mount command. To unmount a drive manually, we use the umount command.

We can also use the Bluecurve desktop to mount disks such as floppies and CD-ROMs. To do this, right-click on the workspace and choose Disks from the context menu, and then select the required drive to be mounted (floppy, CD-ROM, or both):

As a demonstration, we'll try to mount a floppy disk using the mount command and later unmount it to understand how the process of mounting and unmounting drives works (you'll need a floppy disk for this).

We start out by trying to list the /mnt/floppy directory. No files are listed since the floppy drive device has not yet been mounted to /mnt/floppy:

```
$ ls /mnt/floppy/        before mounting the floppy drive
no files listed
```

We attempt to mount floppy drive device /dev/fd0 to /mnt/floppy. However, we are prevented from doing so since this is a privileged operation allowed only for administrators or programs that have the setuid bit set. So we switch to the root user and try to mount the drive. This time we succeed in mounting the /dev/fd0 device to /mnt/floppy:

```
$ mount /dev/fd0 /mnt/floppy
mount: only root can do that
$ su
Password:
# mount /dev/fd0 /mnt/floppy
# df -k|grep floppy
/dev/fd0                    1423       105       1318    8% /mnt/floppy
```

The mount command minimally takes two arguments. The first is the name of the device containing a file system to mount, and the second is a directory to map the device on to. We verify this using the df command whose output is piped to the grep command which searches for the string 'floppy' and sure enough, the drive is listed as being mounted to /mnt/floppy.

Once this is done, non-root users may also access the /mnt/floppy directory. We can exit from the root shell and assume our previous identity of a regular user:

```
# exit
$ ls /mnt/floppy/
aliases.txt  df.txt   ff.html      ps_A.txt        testcmd.sh  which.txt
crontab.txt  env.txt  parted.txt   ps_auxww.txt    top.jpeg
```

Now, as a normal user, we can list the files under the /mnt/floppy directory:

```
$ umount /dev/fd0
umount: only root can unmount /dev/fd0 from /mnt/floppy
$ su
Password:
# umount /dev/fd0
# exit
exit
$ ls /mnt/floppy/
bash$
```

However, as a regular user, we are not permitted to unmount the device. To do this, we once again assume the identity of the root user and run the umount command. The umount command takes the name of the device, /dev/fd0 in this case. Once the device is unmounted, the ls listing is not available any more since there is no device with files and sub-directories grafted to the file system at this point.

Partitions

We can use partitions to divide a disk drive into a number of file systems. For example, consider the hard disk we discussed earlier, which had one partition dedicated to the root file system (/), another for the /boot directory (which houses the various kernels that can be used to boot up the system), and the swap partition.

On **dual boot systems**, partitions allow us to dedicate certain partitions to one operating system and the remaining to a second operating system. The partitions are indicated as numbers next to the disk drive – for example, /dev/hda1, /dev/hda2 (and so on), or /dev/sda1, /dev/sda2 (and so on). The first IDE hard disk is usually named as /dev/hda, the second one as /dev/hdb, and so on. SCSI hard disks are named in the order /dev/sda, /dev/sdb, and so on.

The partition information of a disk is stored in a partition table that is read by the operating system. Later in this chapter, we'll look at the tools that we can use to manipulate the partition table to change partition information on hard disks.

Supported File System Types

Now that we know how disks are organized into partitions, we can venture out to the topic of **file system types**. Various operating systems have their own notion of how data should be organized on disk partitions. For instance, Microsoft DOS uses the **FAT** (**file allocation table**) file system to organize files on the disk. Later on, with the advent of Windows NT, **NTFS** (**NT file system**) became another file system supported by Microsoft operating systems.

The *de facto* file system on Linux is the **ext** (or **extended**) file system. A second version of this file system was called **ext2**; Red Hat Linux 9 supports the latest version, **ext3**. Usually when a system is shut down abruptly, i.e. without allowing it to save all of the in-memory file system data, the operating system performs a lengthy sanity check of the disk and sometimes also repairs the disk. With ext3, the time taken for the check (and repair) in such an event is significantly reduced due to a new feature supported by ext3 known as *journaling* which maintains disk consistency by constantly logging disk activity.

Red Hat Linux 9 currently supports a host of file systems, and many simultaneously. For example, it is possible to have a system with one FAT partition and the remaining partitions in the ext3 format. The file /proc/filesystems contains a list of the file systems supported on a particular machine:

```
$ cat /proc/filesystems
nodev    rootfs
nodev    bdev
```

```
nodev    proc
nodev    sockfs
nodev    tmpfs
nodev    shm
nodev    pipefs
         ext2
nodev    ramfs
         iso9660
nodev    devpts
         ext3
nodev    usbdevfs
nodev    usbfs
nodev    autofs
         vfat
```

The nodev entry against a file system type indicates that there is currently no device using that file system type (although the file system type itself is supported). In the sample listing above, the file system types currently used by devices are: the extended file system types – ext2 and ext3 used by the Linux partitions, the CD-ROM file system ISO-9660 for the CD-ROM device, and the VFAT file system for the floppy device.

Support for additional file systems can be compiled into the kernel or loaded as a kernel module. Chapter 10 has information on recompiling the kernel and setting up loadable kernel modules.

Compatibility of File Systems

How is it possible for a file residing on a Linux ext3 partition to be copied onto a floppy that uses the VFAT file system? Historically file systems have been designed with a certain operating system or certain class of operating systems in mind. For this reason, file system types are subject to the idiosyncrasies of the operating systems. However, Linux handles a multitude of file systems, several of which have been designed with other operating systems in mind. How is this possible? Do programmers who write programs on Linux write code to handle each and every supported file system that Linux supports? If that was true, wouldn't these programs break when a new file system type is supported?

The answer is no (this would make most programs way too complex and non-maintainable, besides being very hard to extend when a new file system type is supported by the operating system!). The way this is handled is by using the **Virtual File system** (**VFS**). VFS is not really a file system in itself; rather, it is a way to abstract the common aspects of most file system types.

For example, almost all of the operations that relate to the manipulation of files can be reduced to a few basic actions: *create, delete, rename, open, read, write,* and *close.* The VFS layer in the kernel supports these generic interfaces in the form of functions that higher-level programs can use. Internally, VFS figures out the real implementation to invoke.

For example, while attempting to copy a file from a FAT partition to an ext3 partition, the copy program would invoke *system calls* (among other things) such as read() and write(). Since the VFS layer understands that the target file system type is FAT, it ends up invoking a fat_read(), and since the destination file system type is ext3, it invokes ext3_write():

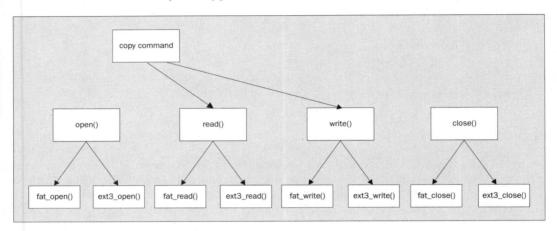

In the above diagram, the copy command invokes the read() system call. The read() internally translates into the appropriate file system specific call, say fat_read().

Managing Partitions

In this section we shall see how to manipulate a partition table – to create, verify, delete, and resize partitions and to manage partitions in general. It is inevitable that most people will have to deal with the task of partitioning or re-partitioning hard disks, either as part of a fresh installation or a disk upgrade, sooner or later.

Fortunately, we have several tools at our disposal for the task at hand. The fdisk command is the oldest of this genre of tools, though these days the parted command seems to be the preference of an increasing number of users. The cfdisk and sfdisk commands are other partition manipulation tools that are available as part of the Red Hat Linux 9 distribution. The **disk druid** utility is also supplied by Red Hat, and can be employed if the user chooses to perform custom partitioning

Try It Out   Editing Partitions with parted

Since parted is fast emerging as the popular choice for editing partitions, we'll use it here to experiment with partition management. The parted program unlike fdisk does not gather all the modifications during an editing session and apply changes to the partition table at the end.

Inexperienced users of `parted` need to be aware of the following:

❏   `parted` writes changes immediately to the partition table, and hence users are warned against curious experimentation using `parted` on disks containing any information of significance.

❏   When resizing a partition, the partition in question must not be in use. That is, it must be unmounted using the `umount` command.

Having said that, `parted` is definitely much more function-packed and user-friendly in comparison to `fdisk`.

In our example below, since we will be resizing the root partition, we cannot have the root partition mounted. Therefore we need to run `parted` from a boot disk as described below:

1.   A boot disk image with `parted` is available at the URL ftp://ftp.gnu.org/gnu/parted/bootdisk/partboot.img. Download a copy if you're not confident about making a boot disk yourself.

2.   Save the image as the file `partboot.img`. The image file needs to be written on to a floppy disk (as the root user) by running the `dd` command as shown below from the same directory as the file:

```
# dd if=partboot.img of=/dev/fd0 bs=1440k
```

This step prepares the book disk. For more information about this, please refer to the Parted manual:

http://www.auth.gr/mirrors/gnu/manual/parted-1.6.1/html_mono/parted.html.

3.   The system needs to be shut down and restarted by booting from this boot disk.

4.   Once the system comes up, run the `parted` command from the boot disk as below. When editing partitions other than the `root` or `boot` partitions, we need not use a boot disk. We simply need to ensure that the partition is **unmounted** and invoke `parted` as `/sbin/parted`.

```
# parted /dev/hda
```

5.   We start `parted` as the root user, specifying the hard disk whose partition table we wish to modify. The `parted` command allows us to edit the partition table interactively:

```
(parted) print
Disk geometry for /dev/hda: 0.000-6149.882 megabytes
Disk label type: msdos
Minor     Start      End     Type     File system  Flags
1          0.031    101.975  primary  ext3         boot
```

```
2         101.975    5773.359    primary    ext3
3        5773.359    6149.882    primary    linux-swap
```

6. The `print` command prints the current disk geometry with the partition information. Note that `parted` can specify the size of partitions as a size range, i.e. 0 to about 100Mb for partition 1 and roughly 101Mb to about 5773Mb for partition 2. This is a marked improvement over some of the earlier programs that required us to manually calculate disk geometry using cylinders, sectors, etc. Here, we see that we have two extended file system partitions and one `swap` partition:

```
(parted) resize 2 101.975 5000
(parted) print
```

```
Disk geometry for /dev/hda: 0.000-6149.882 megabytes
Disk label type: msdos
Minor    Start       End       Type       File system   Flags
1          0.031    101.975    primary    ext3          boot
2        101.975   4996.779    primary    ext3
3       5773.359   6149.882    primary    linux-swap
```

7. The first thing we do is attempt to resize the biggest partition of the three (that is, the second partition), which currently extends from 101.975 Mb to 5773.359 Mb. We use the `resize` command by specifying the partition to resize (Partition 2), and the new size range (101.975 to 5000). With this resizing, we shrank the partition by 773.395 Mb (that is 5773.359 Mb – 5000 Mb). On printing the partition table, the new disk geometry is evident:

```
(parted) mkpartfs primary ext2 4996.779 5773.359
(parted) print
```

```
Disk geometry for /dev/hda: 0.000-6149.882 megabytes
Disk label type: msdos
Minor    Start       End       Type       File system   Flags
1          0.031    101.975    primary    ext3          boot
2        101.975   4996.779    primary    ext3
4       4996.780   5773.359    primary    ext2
3       5773.359   6149.882    primary    linux-swap
```

8. We now proceed to create a *new* partition, using the space that we took from Partition 2. We use the `mkpartfs` command to do this, indicating that this is a primary partition (partitions can be primary, extended, or logical). We also indicate that this is a partition that will house an ext2 file system since ext3 is not yet supported by `parted`. We specify the new partition range from 4996.779 Mb to 5773.359 Mb. Printing the partition table confirms that the new partition has been created:

```
(parted) rm 4
(parted) resize 2 101.975 5773.359
```

9. Now that we have learned to resize partitions, we can try and restore things to their original state (at the start of this example). We delete the newly created partition using the rm command, specifying the partition number of the partition we wish to remove. Finally, we resize Partition 2 to its original size:

```
(parted) print
Disk geometry for /dev/hda: 0.000-6149.882 megabytes
Disk label type: msdos
Minor    Start       End     Type      File system  Flags
1          0.031    101.975  primary   ext3            boot
2        101.975   5773.359  primary   ext3
3       5773.359   6149.882  primary   linux-swap
(parted) quit
```

10. The print command confirms our latest attempt to resize the partition. Once we are done experimenting, we exit the parted program using the quit command.

Adding a New Hard Disk

Regardless of the hard disk real estate that we start out with, it is very likely that most of us will run out of disk space before the end of the lifecycle of our machines. This is when we will most likely get a disk upgrade by purchasing an additional hard disk or replace the current disk with one that has more storage capacity.

When we first installed Red Hat Linux 9 on the system, we did not have to bother about explicitly setting up our hard disk – the installer took care of this behind the scenes. But if we need to add a disk ourselves, there are a few manual steps that we need to perform.

Detecting the Hard Disk

After hooking up the new hard disk to the system, and before going any further, it is necessary to ensure that the disk has been recognized by the operating system. Usually, Red Hat's **kudzu** configuration tool will allow us to configure our new hardware when it is detected during the bootup process.

To ensure that the new disk has been recognized, we need to examine the kernel startup messages – these messages can be viewed using the dmesg command. We need to look for detection messages corresponding to our new hard disk. Here is a typical dmesg line, which indicates that the new hard disk has been detected:

```
$ dmesg | grep -i maxtor
hdb: Maxtor 90651U2, ATA DISK drive
```

281

*An alternative is to list the contents of /proc/partitions, which lists all the currently available partitions including those that have not been mounted yet. Here is the listing of a typical /proc/partitions file. For our purposes, it is sufficient to look for a new row in the table and note the name column, in this case **hdb**.*

```
$ cat /proc/partitions
major minor #blocks name  rio   rmerge rsect  ruse   wio   wmerge wsect  wuse   running use     aveq
22    0     661728 hdb   40    32     280    500    0     0     0      0      -24865  2297424 1939878
3     0     6297480 hda   17031 21392 305170 253707 11959 16564 228632 422367 -1     6577905 2337991
3     1     104391 hda1  35    85     240    408    14    6     40     244    0       636     652
3     2     5807497 hda2  16967 21086 304394 252974 11788 14238 208776 250927 0       188263  503912
3     3     385560 hda3  9     25     104    146    157   2320  19816  171195 0       3453    171341
```

If there are no kernel startup messages or listings in /proc/partitions, then it is quite likely that the disk was not detected. There are several possible reasons for the system's failure to detect the disk. To eliminate the possibility of a hardware setup problem, we should check all hardware settings such as the master–slave mode settings of the hard disk and compare them with the manufacturer's recommended settings. It's possible that the detection failure may have occurred because the correct driver is missing from the kernel; this problem can be remedied by re-compiling a kernel, or by using a dynamically loadable kernel module that has support for the new hard disk. Chapter 10 has details on how to perform these steps.

Partitioning the Hard Disk

Once the disk has been detected, it is usually assigned a /dev name (such as /dev/hdb) automatically by the system. Once we know what this name is, as can be seen from the dmesg output or the /proc/partitions file, we need to partition the device.

If we intend to create a swap partition on this disk, the rule of thumb is to create a partition that is at least 2.5 times the size of the available physical RAM. We may use parted, fdisk, sfdisk (or another similar command) to partition the new drive. During the partitioning process, it is necessary to specify the intended file system for this hard disk.

Formatting the Hard Disk

After partitioning, the next logical step is to format the disk. The formatting process prepares the partition for a certain file system type to create files and directories. During this process several file system-specific information may be created on the partitions. Formatting is very much specific to the file system that will be installed on the partition. For instance, to format the first partition of the /dev/hdb disk to use the ext3 file system, the following command is used:

```
#  mkfs.ext3 -c /dev/hdb1
```

The −c option forces a check for disk errors.

Mounting the Hard Disk

Now that we have partitioned and formatted the disk, it is ready for use and needs to be mounted to a file system mount point. For example, suppose we intend to mount the new partition to the directory /public. For this, we can use the following command:

```
# mount -t ext3 /dev/hdb1 /public
```

Although this command mounts the partition for now, it is *not* enough to mount the partition automatically when the system reboots. For **automatic mounting**, we need to add an entry to the /etc/fstab file. A typical entry would look like the one below:

```
/dev/hdb1          /public               ext3     defaults        1 1
```

The first entry (/dev/hdb1) represents the partition containing the file system to be mounted. The second entry (/public) represents the directory that this file system should be mounted to. The third entry (ext3) indicates the file system type. The fourth entry indicates the permissions for the device; permissions determine the type of operations that may be performed on the file system. In this case, the default permissions (that is, allowing both read and write access) is in effect. The last two entries indicate operating system parameters (dump frequency and parallel fsck number) that may be left set to 1.

> The parted command has a copy command that enables entire file systems to be copied from one partition to another. This is particularly useful during disk upgrades that involve the replacement of an existing disk with a larger one. It is possible to add the new disk to the system without removing the older disk – possibly in a master–slave configuration. If you want to set this up, you should look at the disk manufacturer's documentation.
>
> Once both disks are hooked up to the system, we could use the parted copy command to copy the old file systems to the new partitions. Once the copy is complete, the old disk may be removed from the system or re-used (even perhaps as a swap disk) on the same system.

From this point, we are ready to use the /public directory (in this case) just like any other directory on the system.

File System Maintenance

For deriving optimum performance out of the file system, and to guard against data corruption, we need to ensure proper maintenance of the system in general and the file system in particular as it manages the persistent part of the operating system.

Precautions

When it comes to file system maintenance, there are a number of simple precautions that help in preventing costly mishaps. It is extremely important that the system be properly shu tdown before restarting the machine. This is because on a running system, usually a significant part of the file system is always being worked upon in memory. In fact, if possible, it is a good idea to run the `sync` command before shutting down the machine, as this will flush unwritten file system blocks in memory to the disk – and hence avoid boot time file system inconsistencies.

As you'll recall from Chapter 1, during the Red Hat Linux 9 installation we are prompted to create a boot disk. It is always a good idea to create a boot disk. This is particularly useful if the partition containing the bootable image of the kernel becomes corrupted. With a boot disk it is possible to boot up to a minimal shell and run diagnostics and repair tools.

If you have important data on your system, it is always a good idea to use some form of backup utility to back up the system periodically. We look at this in more detail in Chapter 10.

Running fsck

Most Unix file system partitions contain a **super block**, which is essentially a 'book-keeping section' of that partition . When a system is shut down gracefully (that is, without errors), a flag is set to indicate the graceful shutdown. When the system comes up the next time, it examines this flag to see if the shutdown was graceful or not. If not, the system may require us to run diagnostic and repair tools on that partition.

The most popular diagnostics and repair utility on Linux (and in the UNIX world) is **fsck**. Running `fsck` with the `y` option allows `fsck` to proceed with any repairs that need to be performed in the course of diagnostic analysis. The `N` option to `fsck` would perform a dry run, i.e. the actual repair routines would not be performed but only printed out. Here is a typical output with the `N` option on a partition with a corrupted superblock.

```
$ /sbin/fsck -N /dev/hda
fsck 1.27 (8-Mar-2002)
[/sbin/fsck.ext3 (1) -- /dev/had] fsck.ext3 /dev/hda
$ /sbin/fsck -y /dev/hda
fsck 1.27 (8-Mar-2002)
e2fsck 1.27 (8-Mar-2002)
Couldn't find ext3 superblock, trying backup blocks...
fsck.ext3: Bad magic number in super-block while trying to open /dev/hda

The superblock could not be read or does not describe a correct ext3
file system.  If the device is valid and it really contains an ext3
file system (and not swap or ufs or something else), then the superblock
is corrupt, and you might try running e2fsck with an alternate superblock:
    e2fsck -b 8193 <device>
```

Tuning the File System

The tune2fs command allows us to set various tunable parameters on the ext2 file system partitions. It is commonly used to control the frequency at which fsck is automatically run on a file system:

❑ The fsck utility could be run once every few days, weeks, or months by specifying the -i option. For example, the following command would force an execution of fsck once every two weeks:

```
$ tune2fs -i 2w
```

❑ The -c option controls the running of fsck based on the number of reboots. For example, -c 10 indicates that the fsck will be run once in every 10 system reboots

```
$ tune2fs -c 10
```

Summary

In this chapter we explored the Red Hat Linux 9 file system in some detail. In summary, our focus was on the following areas:

❑ File system concepts and the need for a file system.

❑ The various attributes of a file such as the types of files, ownership, permissions, access privileges, time stamps, file sizes, and file names. We also explored the concept of hard links and symbolic links.

❑ Various utilities such as find and locate to search for files on the file system and also utilities such as awk and sed used in conjunction with xargs and the find command to search for strings in files.

❑ The organization of the file system in terms of directories, configuration files, and executables.

❑ Creating and formatting partitions and file systems, and mounting file systems on to directories on the system.

❑ We also learned how to add a new hard disk to the system, as well as format and partition it correctly.

❑ Finally, we also dealt with the topics of maintaining the file system by taking certain precautions, as well as diagnosing and repairing file systems using fsck and tuning the file system using tune2fs.

In the next chapter, we're going to take a closer look at how Linux deals with users, groups, permissions, and related issues.

8

Managing Your User Accounts

Unix has always supported the notion of multiple users working independently and simultaneously on the same computer – right back to the earliest Unix operating systems, born at the end of the 1960s. Each user in possession of a valid user account could log in to the computer (by supplying a username and a password) and hence work with the desired applications. Users would access the system via a **system console** (which was normally reserved for administrative tasks such as backups) or from one of a number of **serial terminals** (these usually consisted of a keyboard and a monitor, or perhaps even a line printer). Even though networking wasn't part of the original Unix design, it became available quite early, giving users the ability to interact with a Unix system from anywhere: locally, via the telephone system and a modem, via a network connection.

Linux has inherited its multi-user nature from those first Unix systems, just as it has inherited a surprising number of other capabilities, such as permissions and file protection. These features haven't changed much over time. What *has* changed is the toolset – tasks like adding a new user account are now easier than they've ever been. The traditional techniques (using command line tools, or even employing a text editor to alter the relevant configuration files) have been enriched with graphical tools that greatly simplify our administrative chores. Red Hat Linux is just one of a number of Linux distributions that have made developments in this direction.

If you have a single machine that is meant mostly for exclusive use, and you're not planning to share its resources with anyone else, then the world of administering user accounts and permissions may seem a little irrelevant to you. However, the notion of multiple user accounts is quite important in Linux, as it is in many other modern operating systems (such as Mac OS X, other Unix derivatives like the BSD family, and Microsoft Windows NT, 2000, or XP).

Whether you share your machine with other users, or it's exclusively for your own personal use, each action you request of it will be denied or allowed in accordance with specific policies. For example, some user accounts will be allowed to install applications, execute certain programs, and access devices such as a CD-ROM drive, while other accounts will not.

Understanding how to manage user accounts and control permissions is a definite advantage when learning Linux. For example, it will allow you to share your computer with other people without compromising privacy; it will help you to protect yourself from accidental damage (like accidental deletion of system files); it will help you to avoid virus problems; and it will help you prevent secondary users from cluttering the system with unnecessary software installations.

In this chapter, we will:

❑   Formally introduce the notion of the root user, and normal users, groups, and home directories

❑   Demonstrate how to create, modify, and delete users and groups

❑   Look at various strategies for granting and denying access to resources

❑   Review a number of valuable commands that are particularly useful when dealing with user accounts

❑   See how to configure your Red Hat Linux installation so that you can carry out certain administrative tasks via a "non-administrator" user account

Let's start with an overview of the main concepts.

The Purpose of Different User Accounts

By now, you've probably become used to the fact that, in order to access your computer through Linux, the first thing to do is to **log in** – by providing a **user name** and the corresponding **password**. That's the same for each user; every user of the system is able to identify themselves by their own unique username.

The existence of different user accounts on a system has a number of important and useful consequences:

❑   That only authorized users are able to access the system. This is because the operating system allows entry to those users who supply the correct **credentials** (a username and a matching password).

❑   **Access** to resources like files and devices will be granted accordingly. For example, any authorized user is able to *read* the "message of the day" contained in the /etc/motd file (try it!), but only some users are permitted to *change* the contents of that file.

❑   Each user is assigned a separate directory, called their **home directory**, for storing personal data.

- ❑ Linux can be configured to execute user-specific setup procedures at the time that user logs in. For example, it might run a program that notifies the user of the arrival of new mail.

- ❑ Every program started by the user is associated to that user's account, and can be identified afterward. Moreover, each program will have access only to those resources that the owner can access.

Superusers and Normal Users

Many large systems make a distinction between an **administrator** (or **superuser**) and a **normal user**. In particular, a user is prevented from performing special (often sensitive) tasks, such as the following, unless that user has administrator privileges:

- ❑ Global maintenance, personalization, and upgrade of the system

- ❑ Global installation of applications, devices, and their drivers

- ❑ Periodic backup of data

- ❑ User account management

It is the administrator's work that leaves normal users free to carry out their day-to-day tasks. Indeed, in very large environments with many thousands of users, system administration is a full-time job. In these environments, it's easy to see why it makes sense to differentiate between superusers and normal users. If administration were left down to the individual users, regardless of their expertise or authority, then the lack of policy and control could be catastrophic – risking the stability of the system, performance levels, security violations, and so on.

In fact, the distinction between superusers and normal users is also enforced in *all* Linux installations – even on small Linux computers that are used by only one person. Why? Well, many of the same arguments that apply on large networks *also* apply on the smallest installations! For example, while the superuser account is very useful for performing certain tasks, it's definitely a mistake to work as superuser when you're performing more "everyday" tasks like reading e-mails. It's not only that you don't *need* superuser privileges to read your e-mail – it's also about protecting yourself from accidentally damaging your system integrity.

The administrator account in Red Hat Linux (as in almost every other operating system of Unix heritage) is called **root**. The power of root is so extensive that almost no task is forbidden for this account. While it's impossible for a normal user to delete system files, root is able to delete them all too easily.

For this reason, the root account should be used with great care. Red Hat recommends that you create a personal account as part of the Linux installation, and we did that back in Chapter 1. If you are currently logged into your Linux system using the root account, it is a good idea to log out now and log back in with a normal (non-root) account.

> In general, don't use the root account unless you need to use it.

If you're worried about the hassle of logging in and out of different accounts, then worry no more. Linux allows you to run a root shell from within your normal account, so that you can do most of your work under the normal account and switch to the root shell for those sensitive administration-level activities. We'll talk about that later in this chapter.

The Red Hat User Manager

In this section, we'll have a look at some of the most common tasks in user account management: creating user accounts and groups, and adding a user account to a group. We'll use the graphical **Red Hat User Manager** tool to step through some examples. Then, in the next section, we'll look at what's happening under the covers – we'll check the impact of our actions on the relevant configuration files and learn how to perform the same (and other) operations via the command line.

To try the **Red Hat User Manager**, we'll need to use the root account (and to be extra careful!) at each step. We'll assume that you're logged in with a non-root account, which (as we've already mentioned) is the safest way to use your operating system.

When you launch any of Red Hat Linux's graphical administration tools from a non-root account, Linux will (if necessary) prompt you to enter the password to the root account. The figure below shows the window you'll see every time the root password is required by a graphical tool:

If the password is accepted, a key-shaped icon will appear in the notification area at the bottom right corner of the screen. As long as that icon remains displayed, you can start other Red Hat Linux graphical administration tools without being asked again for the root password. The key icon does not mean that all actions are undertaken with root privileges; it simply means that when an administration tool requires the root account to run, it may skip this step because the user has already provided the password.

Creating a User Account

Let's step through the process of creating user accounts for some of the authors of this book. We'll assume that one normal user account (**eziodm**, the account for Pancrazio 'Ezio' de Mauro) was created during the installation process; we'll add a couple more accounts, **kapils** and **deepakt**, over the course of the following steps.

Try It Out   Creating User Accounts

1. Launch the **Red Hat User Manager** (do this by selecting **Main Menu | System Settings | User and Groups**, or by typing `redhat-config-users` at a command line). Enter the root password if you're prompted to do so. After this, you'll see the **Red Hat User Manager** interface, which looks like this:

    Each line contains the details of one user account. By default, system accounts are not shown. If you want to see the system accounts, you can do so by selecting the **Preferences** menu and disabling the **Filter system users and groups** option.

2. Click on **Add User**. This will open the **Create New User** window:

291

As you can see, this looks rather similar to the **Add a User Account** dialog we saw back in Chapter 1, when we were installing Red Hat Linux. Fill the necessary values, so that the dialog looks something like the one shown above. There are a few points to note as you fill in the fields here:

❑ Remember to choose a unique name for the new account.

❑ The **Login Shell** list is taken directly from the /etc/shells file. It is possible to type in the location of a shell that doesn't appear in this list. However, the values commonly used here are /bin/bash or /bin/tcsh. If you don't know the difference between the two, stick to /bin/bash – it tends to be more popular.

❑ You should create a **Home Directory**, unless the account is for a program and not a person.

❑ It is a good idea to create a **private group** for the user at the same time, because this will help in setting up good protection schemes. This is the default for Red Hat Linux and shouldn't be changed without good reason.

❑ Finally, it is best *not* to specify a **user ID** manually, but to allow the tool to generate one.

After clicking **OK**, the new user will be created and the account will be visible on the main window.

3. Click on the new account, then on the **Properties** button to review the information just entered and check that it's correct. With the three tabs (**Account Info**, **Password Info**, and **Groups**) it is possible to enable account expiration date, lock the account temporarily, enable password expiration, and assign the account to some of the existing groups. Click on **OK** when you're done reviewing or changing.

4. Congratulations! The new account has been created. Now repeat the procedure above from Step 2 to create as many more accounts as you like. Here's what the **User Manager** looks like after creating accounts called **kapils** and **deepakt**:

User Name	User ID ▼	Primary Group	Full Name	Login Shell	Home Directory
eziodm	500	eziodm	Pancrazio 'Ezio' de Mauro	/bin/bash	/home/eziodm
kapils	501	kapils	Kapil Sharma	/bin/bash	/home/kapils
deepakt	502	deepakt	Deepak Thomas	/bin/bash	/home/deepakt

Creating a Group

Groups are useful when we need to treat a number of different users the same way. For example, if we want to grant a group of users access to a particular file or directory, we add the users to a group and grant the permission to the group (instead of to the individual user accounts). We'll see more of this later, but first we need to see how to create a group.

We have some user accounts for some of the authors on this book. Let's create a group called authors, and then we'll add these accounts to that group.

Try It Out   **Creating a new Group**

1. We can use the Red Hat User Manager GUI to manage our groups too. Once you've launched the GUI, press the Groups tab to see which groups are present:

Again, the GUI's default behavior is to hide the system groups. You can reveal them selecting the Preferences menu and then disabling the Filter system users and groups option. In the screenshot above you can see a group for each of the user accounts we created earlier on: this is the effect of the Create a private group for the user option we selected when adding the accounts.

2. Now click the Add Group button, to create a new group. In the resulting Create New Group dialog, type the name of the new group. If you know what you're doing, you can specify a certain group identification number; otherwise, you should let the system decide:

Once you're done, press the OK button.

3. Now you'll see that the authors group has been created, and is shown in the main User Manager screen. You can create more groups if you like, simply repeating Step 2.

Managing Group Members

Once we've created our new group, we can start adding the relevant user accounts to it. Then, when we specify the access rights for our group later on in this chapter, the access rights we set will apply to every member of that particular group.

Group membership is not set in stone when the group is created: we can add accounts to the group, and remove members from the group, at any time. In fact, there are two ways to manage group membership:

❏ We can modify a *user's* properties, by specifying which groups that user is a member of

❏ We can modify a *group's* properties, by specifying which users belong to that group

In the following example we'll add the users eziodm, kapils, and deepakt to the authors group. In the process, we'll see both of the techniques listed above.

Try it Out　　　**Managing Group Membership**

1. First, we'll modify the membership properties of the eziodm account. In the Red Hat User Manager, select the Users tab, and then select the eziodm user. Then click the Properties button, and select the Groups tab in the newly created window.

2. In the Groups tab, we can see which groups this user belongs to, just by looking at the checkboxes. We can also add the user to (and remove them from) groups simply by clicking on the group names:

In this case, we're managing the **eziodm** user account's membership of the various system and custom groups that exist on the system. This user is already a member of the private group of the same name, and by clicking on the checkbox next to the **authors** group, we can add the user to that group too. Click the **OK** button to confirm.

3. Now let's add the other two users to the **authors** group. Back in the **User Manager** dialog, select the **Groups** tag and then the **authors** group, and then click on **Properties**. In the resulting **Group Properties** dialog, select the **Group Users** tab.

You should find that the **eziodm** user is already checked, because we added this user to the group a moment ago. To add the other two users, we just check the checkboxes next to those usernames:

4. When you submit this, the User Manager will confirm the three new members of the **authors** group:

How Linux Stores User Account Information

As you've seen, the Red Hat User Manager makes it really easy to create user accounts and groups, and to define group membership. Having seen it in action, it's a good time to see where account information is stored in the file system. By taking a quick look at these files, we'll get a better understanding of what we achieved in the examples above, and will prepare us for using the command line tools that we'll see later in this chapter.

Linux stores its local user account information in the following text configuration files:

Configuration File	Purpose
/etc/passwd	Contains a list of local users and their data
/etc/shadow	Contains encrypted passwords, and bookkeeping information such as account expiry
/etc/group	Defines groups and associated accounts

> *There is a fourth file, /etc/gshadow, that we will not cover extensively here. It stores encrypted **group passwords**. You can find out more by reading the HOWTO file on this subject, which (in the current release) can be found at /usr/share/doc/shadow-utils-20000902/HOWTO.*

User Accounts and their Properties (the /etc/passwd File)

To examine in better detail the properties of a user account on your system, you can take a look at your /etc/passwd file (using a text editor such as gedit or a CLI command such as cat). The /etc/passwd file is essentially the **user account database** in which Linux stores valid accounts and related information about these accounts.

Here's an example, which includes details of the accounts we just created using the User Manager. Your /etc/passwd will be similar in structure to the file excerpt shown here, though the exact details may be a little different:

```
root:x:0:0:Super User:/root:/bin/bash
halt:x:7:0:Stop the System:/sbin:/sbin/halt
eziodm:x:500:500:Pancrazio 'Ezio' de Mauro:/home/eziodm:/bin/bash
kapils:x:501:501:Kapil Sharma:/home/kapils:/bin/bash
deepakt:x:502:502:Deepak Thomas:/home/deepakt:/bin/bash
```

Each line of the /etc/passwd file is a single **record** in the user database, and represents a single user. The administrator (root) account is usually the first user account defined in the file; it's followed by a number of **system accounts**, and finally the ordinary user accounts (like the eziodm, kapils, and deepakt accounts here).

As you can see, each record is composed of a number of **fields**, which describe the properties of the user account. In this file, adjacent fields are separated by a colon (:) character. To get a better understanding of the purpose of each field, let's look, for example, at the third record:

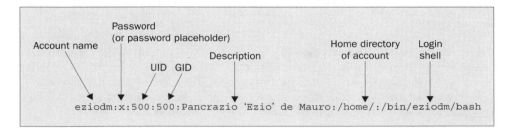

- ❏ The first field contains the **username** (also known as the **account name** or **login name**). When the user logs in, submitting a user name, Linux looks up the specified user name in this table. Usernames usually begin with an alphabetic character, and can be up to 32 characters long, although some older programs can accept only the first eight characters.

  In fact, the eight-character limit for account names is an historic Unix thing. Sticking to this maximum length is still considered the safest choice, especially when networking with older Unix computers.

- ❏ The second field contains a placeholder for the **password**. In older versions of Linux, this field used to contain an encrypted version of the password itself. For reasons of security, passwords are now stored in the /etc/shadow file (they're still stored in encrypted form); we'll return to this issue in the next section.

- ❏ The third field contains the account's **user identification number** (or **UID**). The UID identifies the user account – each UID is unique to exactly one account within the system. In Red Hat Linux, UIDs below 500 are reserved for system accounts; for example, the UID 0 (zero) is reserved for the superuser, root. If the UID 0 is assigned to another account, it will grant administration rights to that account. Needless to say, that is a very dangerous thing to do!

- ❏ The fourth field contains the **group identification number** (or **GID**) of the account's **primary group**. A GID is unique to exactly one group within the system. An account belongs to at least one group (and it may belong to more than one), but the one specified here is the primary group with which the user is associated, and is usually the private group we created at the same time as the account.

  Once again, the GID 0 (zero) should be reserved for root, even though it's not as dangerous as the UID zero.

297

An account's UID and primary group GID are not necessarily the same values; the example above is slightly special. As we mentioned, UIDs and GIDs below 500 are reserved for the system; and eziodm *was the first non-system account created on this machine. So, when the system created this account, it set the UID to the first available UID value (which was 500), and it assigned the GID of the associated group to the first available GID value (which was also 500).*

❏ The fifth field is the **description** of the user account. In general, the description can be any string. For example, when the account is for a particular person, it usually makes sense to use that person's name for the account description (like the accounts for Ezio, Deepak, and Kapil above); when the account is designed to fill a specific role, then a description of the role is suitable (like the halt account above).

Later in the chapter, we'll see how the User Information dialog allows a user to enter a name and contact information associated to their account. When they do so, the information is stored in this field, in comma-separated format.

❏ The sixth field contains the account's **home directory**. This is most commonly used for personal accounts, and provides the user with a directory within which they can store their own personal files. By default, a user's home directory is created under the /home directory (for example, eziodm's home directory is /home/eziodm), but in fact, it is possible to place a user's home directory anywhere on the system.

There is one notable exception: the root account's home directory is always /root (or even / itself in old systems). This design is to ensure that the directory will be available for use even if /home is not available after booting (for example, if the /home file system lies on a separate partition to the rest of the file system, and a disk error prevents Linux from mounting it).

For an account that is associated with a function or a software program, rather than a user, the notion of using the home directory field to store "personal files" is somewhat lost. In this scenario, the home directory field is sometimes used to specify the directory in which the software is located, or it may point to a general location place like the /bin directory.

❏ The seventh and final field contains the **login shell** associated with the account. We saw in Chapter 6 that the shell is in charge of executing user commands. The system runs the login shell whenever you log in using text mode, or open a terminal window using graphical mode. A list of valid shells is normally kept in /etc/shells (although any program can be used as a login shell). There are programs that check the contents of /etc/shells to find out whether a user account is an ordinary account (with a shell listed in /etc/shells) or a special account. One special account is the halt user above: if you log in using the halt account and you supply the correct password, the system will initiate the shutdown sequence to switch the computer off.

You can get more information with the man 5 passwd and man 5 shells commands from your terminal window or console screen.

User Account Passwords (the /etc/shadow File)

As it happens, any user has read access to the /etc/passwd file – indeed, this access is handy if, say, you need to match an account name to its UID. But as we mentioned above, older versions of Linux stored account passwords in encrypted format in the second field of the /etc/passwd file. A consequence of this was that it was easy for users to access the encrypted versions of the passwords of other users.

Initially, this was not considered a security issue because the passwords were encrypted. However, the storage of encrypted passwords in /etc/passwd is no longer considered safe; as we'll see in a moment, techniques now exist that make it much easier to guess a user's password given its encrypted form and knowledge of the encryption algorithm.

To plug this security hole, Red Hat Linux 9 stores encrypted passwords is a different file – /etc/shadow. This file is accessible to root only. While normal users can still read from /etc/passwd, they do not have permission to read from /etc/shadow, and thus do not have access to encrypted passwords.

Password Encryption

While the account passwords are now stored safely in the restricted access /etc/shadow file, Red Hat Linux *still* takes the precaution of storing them in encrypted format.

Let's see what an encrypted password looks like. If you use root privileges to examine the contents of the /etc/shadow file, you'd see each encrypted password stored as an incomprehensible string of characters like this:

```
$1$mWzQxFuT$EWnSiX5hmxiERbUpfwR5V0
```

Red Hat Linux *never* stores passwords in the clear text form in which the user enters them. Rather, it always encrypts them before storing them or working with them, in such a way that it is not easily possible (or even feasible) to decipher the encrypted version and find out the original.

In fact, once the password has been encrypted and stored in /etc/shadow, there will never be the need to decrypt it ever again. This is a key point: when a user logs in, the operating system verifies their identity by *encrypting* the submitted password and comparing it with the encrypted string contained in the /etc/shadow. If the two strings match, access is granted. It is this process that enables Red Hat Linux to avoid ever having to decrypt passwords.

A Technique for Guessing Passwords

Unfortunately, the fact that a password is encrypted before storage is not enough to guarantee that it can't be discovered by other means. While it's very difficult to use decryption techniques to discover the original passwords, it is quite possible to use a *brute force* method to find out "weak" passwords. The power of modern computer hardware makes it possible to take large numbers of common passwords, encrypt them using the same algorithm used by the operating system, and check if the encrypted version is the same as the one stored in the password file.

This technique is often called a dictionary attack, because the attacker can take large numbers of candidate passwords from a dictionary. A surprising number of passwords can be cracked in this way – indeed, in Chapter 12 we'll take a look at a program called `crack`, which uses this technique to crack passwords.

The existence of such techniques is the motivating factor behind the decision to place passwords in `/etc/shadow`, rather than `/etc/passwd`. Thus, users are prevented from stealing encrypted passwords, and then trying to "break" the weak ones via a dictionary attack.

> *Further discussion of cryptographic techniques is outside of the scope of this chapter. However, cryptography is a fascinating science. If you're interested, you could start experimenting with **GnuPG** (the GNU Privacy Guard) – install the gnupg package on your system, then have a look at the gpg command. The gpg manual page will certainly be useful, providing information and lists of other documents.*

A Sample /etc/shadow File

Let's examine a few lines from a sample `/etc/shadow` file. This example contains the entries for the accounts we via using the **User Manager**, earlier in this chapter. Once again, your `/etc/shadow` will probably differ from this, although its structure will be similar:

```
root:$1$eÂúkæÛAÈ$Kv55YOaIHDcPlI1q6igoQ0:11961:0:99999:7:::
halt:*:11961:0:99999:7:::
eziodm:$1$W/RgbXrI$OP9t9IyVmQyvPfxNLUFwQ1:12100:0:99999:7:::
kapils:!!$1$68Q7Ci4g$CqbN8rdCBw4GmxDlouQ2q/:12100:0:99999:7:::
deepakt:$1$sUejrHGF$I3cSo2TRmKIbN55wfLgfB1:12100:0:99999:7:::
```

Just like `/etc/passwd`, each line (or *record*) represents a user, and adjacent fields are separated by "`:`". Again, to understand the purpose of the fields in this file, let's look at the third line:

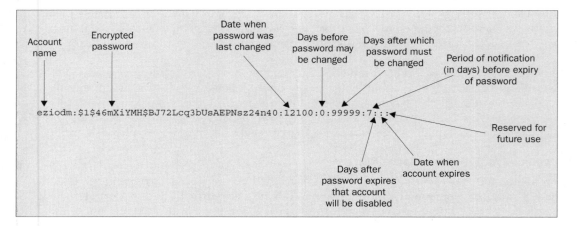

❑   The first field contains the account name. It must match the name found in /etc/passwd.

❑   The second field contains the encrypted password. A * character here indicates that the account is disabled (that is, the user cannot log in), while a ! ! sequence here (followed by the original encrypted password) indicates that the account is temporarily locked.

❑   The third field indicates the date when the password was last changed. It is expressed as the number of days elapsed since January 1, 1970. It is very typical, in systems of Unix descent, to count the number of days or seconds since this date. In the example above, we can see that eziodm's password was last changed 12100 days after January 1, 1970.

❑   The fourth field contains a count of the number of days before the password *may* next be changed. The value zero or an empty field (as in the examples above) means that it can be changed anytime.

❑   The fifth field contains a count of the number of days after which the password *must* be changed. This default value means that the password can stay in its place for almost 274 years, which is probably long enough!

❑   The sixth field specifies how many days warning the user will get that their password is about to expire.

❑   The seventh field specifies after how many days the account is disabled if its owner does not change the password when requested to.

❑   The eighth field is the date when the account will be unconditionally disabled, expressed in days since January 1, 1970.

❑   Finally, at the end of the line there is one more empty field, reserved for future use.

To get more information about /etc/shadow, you can consult its manual page, by typing man 5 shadow at your shell prompt.

Groups (the /etc/group File)

A user can belong to many groups, but as we've seen, /etc/passwd allows only membership of one group (the **primary group**). Membership of additional groups must be specified in the /etc/groups file. Unsurprisingly, this file is very similar in structure to the two we've already seen. The following example shows the groups we created earlier in this chapter:

```
root:x:0:root
bin:x:1:root,bin,daemon
daemon:x:2:root,bin,daemon
eziodm:x:500:
kapils:x:501:
```

```
deepakt:x:502:
authors:x:503:eziodm,kapils,deepakt
```

The structure is quite simple. Let's study the second line of this file to understand the fields:

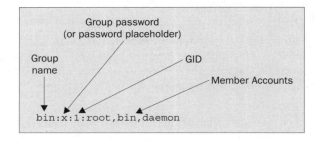

❑   The first field contains the group name

❑   The second field contains a placeholder for an optional **group password**. The password, if present, is stored in /etc/gshadow. Group passwords are rarely used so we won't discuss them here

❑   The third field contains the group identification number (GID). As we've mentioned, every group on the system must have its own unique GID. Recall that /etc/passwd refers to primary groups by number, not by name; so when it's necessary, this field is used to match a group number with its corresponding group name

❑   The last field contains the **list of user accounts** that belong to this group.

For more information about /etc/group, you can type man 5 group at your shell prompt.

Advanced User Account Management

We've also seen how to manage user accounts and groups via the Red Hat User Manager, and we've seen how Red Hat Linux stores this user information in the configuration files /etc/passwd, /etc/shadow, and /etc/group.

It's evident that these configuration files are just plain text files, and its perhaps tempting to put aside the User Manager and edit those files manually, using a text editor such as gedit. It is quite possible to manage your user information this way, but it is safer to use the User Manager or the CLI commands instead:

❑   First, the files are of critical importance to the successful execution of your Red Hat Linux installation, and their integrity must be ensured at all times. The tools are designed to ensure the integrity of these files, but if you edit them manually then you are on your own.

❑ Second, the tools they carry out proper **file locking**. This is a mechanism that prevents overwriting problems in a situation where several administrators try to manage users at the same time.

It is definitely convenient to be able to examine these configuration files, but when you need to make adjustments to them, it's safest to use the designated tools – the graphical User Manager interface that we've already seen, and the command line tools that we'll examine next.

Some Useful Command Line Tools

If you plan to use the command line tools to manage your users and groups, then you'll need to do so in the context of the root account. Having fired up a terminal window, there are a few clues to remind you which account you're logged in as – remember that the typical root shell prompt is denoted with the # character, while the prompt for an ordinary user account is denoted with $ or >.

You can also use the id command to check your identity:

```
$ id
uid=500(eziodm) gid=500(eziodm) groups=500(eziodm),503(authors)
```

The output above shows that the user is logged in as the eziodm account. (Note that it also confirms information about the account's group membership – in particular, that its primary group is also called eziodm and that the user is a member of two groups, eziodm and authors.)

To run in the context of the root account in a terminal window, simply execute the su (switch user) command at the command line:

```
$ su -
Password:
```

You'll be prompted to type the root password, as shown above. The effect of the su command is to execute a new shell under a different user account. Note that the new shell doesn't *substitute* the existing shell. Instead, the new shell runs *on top of* the existing shell. To demonstrate this point, take a look at the following screenshot, which shows a user switching from eziodm to root, using the root shell and then leaving it:

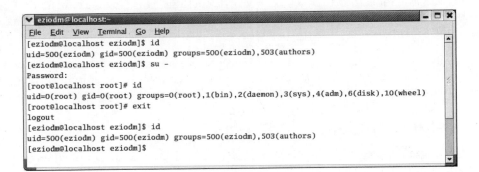

```
[eziodm@localhost eziodm]$ id
uid=500(eziodm) gid=500(eziodm) groups=500(eziodm),503(authors)
[eziodm@localhost eziodm]$ su -
Password:
[root@localhost root]# id
uid=0(root) gid=0(root) groups=0(root),1(bin),2(daemon),3(sys),4(adm),6(disk),10(wheel)
[root@localhost root]# exit
logout
[eziodm@localhost eziodm]$ id
uid=500(eziodm) gid=500(eziodm) groups=500(eziodm),503(authors)
[eziodm@localhost eziodm]$
```

As you can see, new (root) shell terminates (via the exit command), the terminal window remains open and reverts to the context of the original account.

Note that the su command here is accompanied by a – symbol. This ensures that the new shell is treated just like any other login shell. In particular, it means that the login scripts associated to the user account (root in this case) will be executed just as if root were logging in from a terminal. These scripts have a number of effects. For example, in this case:

❑ They set the current working directory to be that of root's home directory

❑ They set the $PATH environment variable (the search path for executable programs) to the value associated with the root user – by adding the directories /sbin and /usr/sbin. These two directories contain administrative programs that are used only by administrative accounts.

If the – character is omitted, the su command will execute a shell but will not execute the login scripts.

If you use su to switch to the root account, and then find that various administrative commands are "missing", then it could be that you omitted the – switch: that is, you typed just su instead of su –.

Note also that you can use su to execute a shell with an account other than root, for example:

```
$ su kapils
$ su - kapils
```

We're now ready to add new users to the system using the command line.

Adding Users at the Command Line

Adding users can be a straightforward task on a stand-alone PC, but when you're a professional system administrator with a lot of settings to get through, the graphical User Manager tool can make the task a time-consuming one.

Hence, it sometimes makes more sense to make use of command line tools instead. Once you've got the hang of the command line tools, it's easy to include them in automated scripts, and hence perform complex or lengthy operations more quickly. As you'd expect, the command line tools also have lots of options and are rather more flexible than their GUI counterparts.

Try It Out   **Adding Users with the Command Line Interface**

In its simplest form, here's the sequence of commands that replicates the behavior of the graphical tool, using default values when possible.

1. At a *root shell* prompt, type the following command to add a new user taking all the defaults:

```
# useradd -c 'Mark Mamone' -s /bin/bash markm
```

2. Before proceeding, use the gedit text editor to examine the configuration files. First, in /etc/passwd, you should find the following new entry, for the account you've just created:

```
. . .
eziodm:x:500:500:Pancrazio 'Ezio' de Mauro:/home/eziodm:/bin/bash
kapils:x:501:501:Kapil Sharma:/home/kapils:/bin/bash
deepakt:x:502:502:Deepak Thomas:/home/deepakt:/bin/bash
markm:x:503:504:Mark Mamone:/home/markm:/bin/bash
```

The UID is 503 and the primary, private GID is 504. Next, from /etc/group, we read:

```
. . .
eziodm:x:500:
kapils:x:501:
deepakt:x:502:
authors:x:503:eziodm,kapils,deepakt
markm:x:504:
```

From this, we can deduce that the group with GID 504 is called markm. Finally, there's a new line in /etc/shadow:

```
. . .
eziodm:$1$W/RgbXrI$OP9t9IyVmQyvPfxNLUFwQ1:12100:0:99999:7:::
kapils:!!$1$68Q7Ci4g$CqbN8rdCBw4GmxDlouQ2q/:12100:0:99999:7:::
deepakt:$1$sUejrHGF$I3cSo2TRmKIbN55wfLgfB1:12100:0:99999:7:::
markm:!!:12100:0:99999:7:::
```

The !! in the second field means that the account is disabled. In fact, this is the default behavior of useradd – it creates disabled accounts.

3. To enable the newly created account, we must assign a password. Still using the root account, use the `passwd` command to assign a password for `markm`:

```
# passwd markm
Changing password for user markm.
New password: (password not shown)
Retype new password: (password not shown)
passwd: all authentication tokens updated successfully.
```

4. Now refresh your view of the `/etc/shadow`, to see what has changed:

```
...
eziodm:$1$W/RgbXrI$OP9t9IyVmQyvPfxNLUFwQ1:12100:0:99999:7:::
kapils:!!$1$68Q7Ci4g$CqbN8rdCBw4GmxDlouQ2q/:12100:0:99999:7:::
deepakt:$1$sUejrHGF$I3cSo2TRmKIbN55wfLgfB1:12100:0:99999:7:::
markm:$1$3afRsVjz$mg9zGakhspD.fcpDwx4wv0:12100:0:99999:7:::
```

Now the `markm` account has a password, and is fully operative.

5. To test out the `markm` account, open a new terminal window as a normal user. Then use the `su` command to verify that the account works:

```
$ su - markm
Password: (password not shown)
$ id
uid=503(markm) gid=504(markm) groups=504(markm)
```

As you can see, the new user identity is now `markm`. The new current directory is `/home/markm`, because we used the `su –` form:

```
$ pwd
/home/markm
$ ls -a
.    ..    .bash_logout    .bash_profile    .bashrc    .emacs    .gtkrc
```

How It Works

The `useradd` command creates a new user called `markm`. The description, `Mark Mamone`, is delimited by single quotation marks to instruct the shell to keep it as a single parameter. The shell is `/bin/bash`:

```
# useradd -c 'Mark Mamone' -s /bin/bash markm
```

The `passwd` command assigns a password to the account. The password is to be accepted but not displayed:

```
# passwd markm
```

Other aspects of the account are determined automatically from the system defaults and from the arguments we've specified. By default, the home directory will be /home/markm; the UID and GID will be the first available (in our case 503 and 504 respectively), and the account and password expiration data are taken from /etc/login.defs and /etc/default/useradd.

You might be surprised to find that the newly created home directory is not empty. Its content is copied from the /etc/skel directory, which contains the files and directories that should be added to a new home directory whenever a new user account is created. This is a particularly handy feature for the system administrator: if every user needs a similar setup, it is sufficient to put the desired files in /etc/skel.

Other defaults, like password-aging values, are taken from /etc/login.defs.

More on the useradd and passwd Commands

The useradd command has several options that you can use when the defaults are not appropriate. More details are available by typing man useradd in a terminal. Here's a list of the most commonly used options:

Option	Purpose
-d	Allows you to specify the user's home directory
-e	Allows you to specify the expiration date of the account in the format DD-MM-YYYY (two digits for the day, two for the month, four for the year)
-f	If the password expires, the operating system will wait a number of days before permanently disabling the account. This option allows you to specify the number of days between these two events
-g	Allows you to specify the GID of this account
-G	Allows you to specify a comma-separated list of other groups to which the user belongs
-M	Allows you to omit the creation of a home directory
-u	Allows you to specify the UID of this account

The passwd command can be used whenever a password needs to be changed or initialized. Of course, normal (non-root) users are allowed to change only their *own* passwords – they can do this via the passwd command. Root can change *anyone*'s password, and to do that they can specify the passwd command followed by the account name (as we saw in Step 3 of the example above).

307

Modifying One's Own User Account

Once a user account has been created, its owner has a certain degree of control over it. Not surprisingly, Red Hat Linux has graphical and command line tools and account owners can change things like the password, account description, and shell.

Modifying One's Own Password

As you'll see in the two examples below, the basic steps for changing your password are identical whether you use the GUI or the command line procedure.

To change your password via the graphical interface, select **Main Menu | Preferences | Password** or type `userpasswd` in a terminal window. The following dialog will appear. For security reasons, you'll have to type your old password first:

Then you'll be prompted twice for the new password:

If you type the same password twice, and it is not too short or based on a dictionary word, the new password will be accepted. Remember, it is a good idea to change your password regularly, especially if your computer is shared with somebody else, even if the system does not enforce password expiration.

To change your password via the command line, you can use the `passwd` command, which we've already met. You'll first be challenged to enter your current password – again, this is to ensure you have the right to change it:

```
$ passwd
Changing password for user eziodm.
Changing password for eziodm
(current) UNIX password: (password not shown)
```

Then you're asked to enter the new password. We can take this opportunity to find out the sort of passwords that are acceptable. Try typing ape5 as your new password:

```
New password: (password not shown)
BAD PASSWORD: it is too short
```

Since ape5 is too short, try elephant6 instead:

```
New password: (password not shown)
BAD PASSWORD: it is based on a dictionary word
```

The passwd command won't accept dictionary-based passwords either: it has an inbuilt mechanism that prevents you from choosing passwords that can be easily guessed. Try something a little more complex, like e!eph4nt:

```
New password: (password not shown)
Retype new password: (password not shown)
passwd: all authentication tokens updated successfully.
```

As you can see, the steps in the command line procedure are identical to those of the GUI-based procedure.

> *Finally, remember that if a normal user, like eziodm, forgets their password, root can run the following command to reset it to a known value:*

```
# passwd eziodm
```

Changing Your Own Account Description and Shell

Red Hat Linux also provides GUI and CLI utilities that allow a user to control other aspects of their account. You can launch the GUI utility by selecting Main Menu | Preferences | About Myself or by typing userinfo at the command line. This will bring up the User Information dialog:

With this dialog, you can edit the system's record of your name, and add contact information if you wish. All this information is then stored (in comma-separated format) in the *description* field of the record in /etc/passwd like this:

```
eziodm:x:500:500:Pancrazio 'Ezio' de Mauro,,212 555-
4343,:/home/eziodm:/bin/bash
```

You can also use this dialog to change your login shell. Note that it is not possible to choose a shell that is not in the list. When you're finished, you just click **Apply** to confirm (if you want to discard your changes, click **Close** instead). If you modify and confirm anything, the tool will ask your password to verify your identity.

Changing Your Account Description via the Command Line

From the command line, you can use chfn to change your personal information and chsh to change your shell. Here's an example in which the user eziodm uses chfn to change the personal information:

```
$ chfn
Changing finger information for eziodm.
Password: (password not shown)
Name [Pancrazio 'Ezio' de Mauro]: Pancrazio de Mauro
Office []:
Office Phone [212 555-4343]: +44 20 1234 5678
Home Phone []: +39 02 1234 5678
Finger information changed.
```

The result achieved by this is very similar to that achieved by using the **User Information** dialog we saw a moment ago. You can see that this user was first required to enter the password (to identify themselves), and then changed the account's Name and Office and Home phone numbers.

To change the login shell, you can use the chsh command – which works in a very similar way:

```
$ chsh
Changing shell for eziodm.
Password: (password not shown)
New shell [/bin/bash]: /bin/tcsh
Shell changed.
```

If you want to return to your previous shell, just run chsh again and specify the original one:

```
$ chsh
Changing shell for eziodm.
Password: (password not shown)
New shell [/bin/tcsh]: /bin/bash
Shell changed.
```

You can find out more about chfn and chsh by consulting their manuals from a terminal with man chfn and man chsh.

Using the root Account to Modify Another User Account

When we need to adopt the root account and apply changes to another account, the best tool to use is dependent on the changes we need to make. Some of the more *common* operations (like account or password expiry) are easy to perform, using the **Red Hat User Manager** (we select the account and then press the **Properties** button).

However, if we need to make more major changes to an account (such as changing the UID), the **Red Hat User Manager** is not enough. In fact, we can't even use the CLI-based commands like passwd, chfn, and chsh utilities to change the UID of an account.

If you absolutely *must* change an account home directory, UID, GID, or even login name, here's how to do it using usermod on the command line. Remember, you have to be logged in as root to do this! Let's suppose we have the following user in /etc/passwd:

```
eziodm:x:500:500:Pancrazio 'Ezio' de Mauro:/home/eziodm:/bin/bash
```

If we want to rename the account from eziodm to eziod, we can run usermod like this:

```
# usermod -l eziod eziodm
```

We've used the -l option to indicate that we want to change the login name, and we specify the *new* login name before the existing one. As a result, the record for this user in /etc/passwd changes to:

```
eziod:x:500:500:Pancrazio 'Ezio' de Mauro:/home/eziodm:/bin/bash
```

As you can see, the account has preserved its UID, description, home directory, and so on. If you want to change the location of the user's home directory, you can run this command after the previous one:

```
# usermod -d /home/eziod -m eziod
```

Here's how to read this command:

- ❑ The -d /home/eziod option specifies the new home directory.

- ❑ The -m option instructs usermod to *move* the contents of the old directory to the new one. After the move, the old home directory will not be visible anymore.

- ❑ The username (eziod) specified at the end of the command is the account on which usermod must operate.

You can change an account's UID and GID via usermod, using the -u and -g options respectively. However, this operation can create undesirable side effects if the user has files outside his or her home directory. In particular, the command does not update the *ownership* of those files accordingly – and they have to be changed manually (perhaps with the help of other utilities, like find). The manual page of usermod (man usermod in a terminal) warns about this and other critical points.

To get a list of files whose owner or group does not exist in /etc/passwd or /etc/group, you can use the following command as root:

```
# find / -nouser -o -nogroup
```

The find command is a very powerful and useful command. You can check other options with man find in a terminal. There's more about it in Chapters 2 and 7.

Deleting User Accounts

Deleting user accounts is all too easy. In the **Red Hat User Manager** graphical interface, you can delete a user simply by selecting the user in the **Users** tab, and then clicking on the **Delete** button.

*Be very careful when deleting accounts via the **Red Hat User Manager**: there will be no confirmation! However, the user's home directory will not be destroyed. So, in cases of accidental deletion it is possible to recover the files and create an account with the same properties of the one just deleted.*

From the root command line, you can run userdel. Using the command like this will erase the account called test from /etc/passwd, but the associated home directory will not be deleted:

```
# userdel markm
```

If you also specify the -r option, the account information, home directory, and mailbox will also be destroyed:

```
# userdel -r markm
```

Advanced Group Management

As we've seen, each user account belongs to a primary group (specified in the /etc/passwd file) and can be assigned to other groups during the account creation or whenever necessary. Groups are useful when setting permissions on files or directories. We've already seen how to create groups and manage group membership via the Red Hat User Manager, now we'll perform some similar tasks, and more, with the command line. The following commands will directly affect /etc/groups.

Creating Groups via the Command Line

You need to be logged in as root in order to create a new group from the command line. The command is groupadd, followed by the group name:

```
# groupadd editors
```

Optionally, you can specify the GID, like this:

```
# groupadd -g 1973 editors
```

For further information, you can browse the manual page by executing man groupadd from a terminal.

Managing Group Membership from the Command Line

From the command line and with the appropriate permissions, even ordinary users can administer groups and decide which users belong to them. This authorization comes from root, via the gpasswd command:

```
# gpasswd -a eziodm authors
Adding user eziodm to group authors
# gpasswd -A eziodm authors
```

The first command uses the -a option to ensure the eziodm account is added to the authors group. The second command uses the -A option to grant eziodm the administration rights for the authors group.

Now, the eziodm user account is permitted to add new users to the authors group, like this:

```
$ gpasswd -a markm authors
Adding user markm to group authors
```

He can also remove users from that group:

```
$ gpasswd -d deepakt authors
Removing user deepakt from group authors
```

Revoking a User's Permission to Manage Membership of a Group

Finally, we can see what happens when root revokes administration rights for eziodm. This can be done passing an empty list to the -A option:

```
# gpasswd -A '' authors
```

To test that this command has indeed revoked eziodm's right to manage the authors group, we can switch users to eziodm and use that account context to try to reinsert deepakt as a member of the authors group:

```
# su - eziodm
$ gpasswd -a deepakt authors
Permission denied.
```

As you can see, eziodm no longer has the rights to add members to the authors group.

If you want to find out something more about gpasswd, you can check its manual page with man gpasswd at your shell prompt.

> *When you add new members to a group, or remove members from a group, your changes are not visible until the next login, either via su – or by logging out completely and logging back in. If you use su – followed by your account name (or even newgrp followed by a group you've just been given access to), only commands you type in that shell (try for example id) will be affected by the new membership.*

Deleting Groups

It is advisable to delete a group only when it doesn't contain any members. It is possible to delete secondary groups with user accounts still associated to it. Moreover, deleting a group (just like deleting a user account) could leave "stale" files whose group no longer exists. You can run the following command periodically as root on your system, to identify these files:

```
# find / -nouser -o -nogroup
```

From there, you can reassign these files to valid users or groups.

To delete a group via the Red Hat User Manager GUI utility, you need to select the group, and click the Delete button.

> **Beware: the group is deleted immediately, and *without confirmation*!**

Deleting Groups via the Command Line

From the command line, as root, use the `groupdel` command followed by the group name:

```
# groupdel authors
```

Just like the graphical tool, `groupdel` will not ask for confirmation.

You can check the manual page for this command via `man groupdel`.

Users, Groups, and File System Permissions

With the help of groups, it is possible to implement some very sophisticated access policies. You'll recall from Chapter 7 that every file or directory in the file system defines access rights for three different sets of users (the *owner*, the *group*, and *others*) via a system of access modes that you can see when you use `ls`:

```
$ls -l
drwxr-xr-x    4 eziodm    eziodm      4096  Feb 12 17.40  backup_images
-rw-r--r--    4 eziodm    eziodm   1037238  Feb 12 17.25  picture1.bmp
-rw-r--r--    4 eziodm    eziodm    262314  Feb 12 17.29  picture2.bmp
-rw-r--r--    4 eziodm    eziodm     58398  Feb 12 17.37  picture3.bmp
```

When it comes to user groups, the behavior of Red Hat Linux is notably different from that of many other Unix variants, including other Linux distributions. By default, every user belongs to its own **private group**, which is not shared with anyone else. Earlier in this chapter, we saw that whenever we create a new user account, the system tools also create a private group for that account which has the same name.

Together with this user/private group scheme, Red Hat Linux also ensures that the default creation mode for files (the **umask**) grants write permissions to the group. Since the group (like the user account) is private, this does not compromise the security of files that are owned by the user. However, this mechanism becomes quite an advantage, when sharing files among users.

In this section we'll see six use cases regarding file protection and file sharing. You can regard them as suggestions on how to set up several protection schemes that suit normal files, directories, or executable programs:

- ❏ You can apply these techniques to files, to control which documents can be accessed by which accounts and groups.

- ❏ You can apply the techniques to directories, to control which accounts can access that directory, add files to it, or list its contents.

- ❏ You can apply the techniques to executable programs, to control which accounts have the rights to execute certain pieces of software on your computer.

First Scenario: Private Files

In this scenario, a user wants to keep his or her files private. Groups are not really relevant here: it is sufficient to remove read, write, and execute permissions for others. The permissions for the group don't really matter, since in Red Hat Linux the primary group is assigned to its primary user only. Thus, a directory with its permissions set as below guarantees privacy of its contents – that is, the directory's content can't be read, written, or executed by users other than the owner:

Once again, it is important to note that group permissions (**Read, Write, Execute**) are safe because the group in question is the group called `eziodm` – and the only member of this group is the user called `eziodm`.

Second Scenario: Public Read-only Files

This scenario is quite simple to implement. We want to give public access to the file, and we want this public access to be read-only. Therefore, all we need to do is to ensure that the **Write** permission for **Others** is denied:

The screenshot above shows the permissions applied to a *directory*. We can tell this because the Text view starts with d (it's **drwxrwxr-x** here). When applied to a *directory*, the Execute permission refers to the user's authority to *search* files in that directory.

Third Scenario: Restricted Read-Only

In this scenario, we want to keep our files private, and open up the possibility of viewing the files to a *limited* number of users. This is where groups start to make sense:

The screenshot shows the permissions for a directory that belongs to the **authors** group. However, group members won't have Write access to the folder. All other users (that is, users who are *not* members of the **authors** group) are completely barred. To complete our access policy on this directory, all we need to do is add the appropriate users to the **authors** group. It is a good idea to repeat this for each file contained in the directory. It is a tedious task with the graphical tool, but it can be quickly achieved with the command line:

```
$ chmod -R u=rwx,g=rx,o-rwx restricted_files
```

In this command, -R (remember that –R and –r are not the same thing!) instructs chmod to update the restricted_files directory and its *entire* contents, as follows:

- ❑ Setting the owner's permissions to Read, Write, Execute (u=rwx)
- ❑ Setting group permissions to Read, Execute (g=rx)
- ❑ Taking away Read, Write, Execute permissions for all others (o-rwx).

For additional techniques for specifying permissions, you may want to review the chmod command syntax with man chmod in a terminal.

Fourth Scenario: Restricted Write

As we gain confidence in the members of the **authors** group, we now want to give them Write access to the directory and its contents. This is not as trivial as it seems: we have to remember that each user has a different, personal, primary group. If we don't set up the directory properly, we'll end up with a rather messy situation: each newly created file will be assigned to the user's primary group, not to **authors**. This makes file sharing a bit difficult, but still possible.

The solution is to add the **Set GID Bit** to the shared directory. The Set GID Bit is a special access right conceived exactly for this scenario: every file created in the directory will belong to the *directory*'s group, not to the user's private group. To activate the Set GID Bit on a directory and fully benefit from it, the owner can create and initialize it with these commands:

```
$ mkdir restricted_directory
$ chgrp authors restricted_directory
$ chmod ug+rwx restricted_directory
$ chmod o-rwx restricted_directory
$ chmod g+s restricted_directory
```

The mkdir command creates a directory called restricted_directory, and then the chgrp command changes its group to authors. Then there are three chmod commands:

- ❑ The first (ug+rwx) ensures that user and group have read, write, and execute permissions
- ❑ The second (o-rwx) clears all permissions for others
- ❑ The third (g+s) activates the Set GID Bit

Now we can copy files into the directory, or create files directly in it. No matter what method is used, the group will always be correctly set. This is what the directory looks like in the file manager:

Note that the Text view field specifies the letter s (instead of x) in the group permissions, and in the Number view field, the Set GID Bit appears as a 2 in front of the usual three digits.

Fifth Scenario: Restricted Write, Public Read

To achieve this result, and have a directory that is shared in read-write mode among a restricted group of users and viewable read-only for the public, we only need to add Read and Execute permissions for Others:

Sixth Scenario: Restricted Write, Restricted Read

In this last scenario, we want the contents of the book directory to have different permissions for different groups:

❑ We want to grant Read, Write, Execute for the authors group (they need to *write* the contents).

❑ We want to grant Read, Execute rights to the lecturers group (they need to *read* the contents to prepare lectures).

❑ We don't want any other accounts to be able to access the directory (for example, we don't want students to peek at exercises, and solutions).

The difficulty here is that we can't set up different protections for different groups *on the same directory*, because only one owner and group can be specified. On the other hand, we don't want to rely on Others for our protection scheme, because that would include students as well.

Here's a possible way to get around it. We can create a group called course, which inherits all the users from authors and lecturers. Then we proceed with creating a material directory that is Read, Write, Execute accessible by the owner (probably a lead author) and Read, Execute accessible by the course group. Other users must not have access to it. Here's a possible example:

```
drwxr-x---   2 eziodm    course    4096 Jan 19 11:03 material
```

This means that everyone belonging to the **course** group, and who *also* belongs to **authors** or **lecturers**, will be able to access the `material` directory. No other accounts will be able to access the directory.

Now, we can create the `book` directory as a subdirectory of the `material` directory. The `book` directory will be Read, Write, Execute accessible by the owner and the **authors** group. Other users will have only Read, Execute access. This is exactly what we want, because the `material` folder immediately above protects the `book` folder from unwanted access by students, so it is safe to leave Read and Execute access for others: in our case, others can *only* be the `lecturers` group. We must not forget to activate the **Set GID Bit** on the folder, in order to allow our writers to cooperate nicely. So, these are the permissions for the `book` directory:

```
drwxrwsr-x     2 eziodm     writers      4096 Jan 19 11:04 book
```

When root Is Not Necessary

We've mentioned already that the protection offered by Linux when working as a normal user is a definite advantage. Certainly, working as root all the time is one of the worst habits that a novice Linux user can develop. For example, suppose you're working as the root user, and you're cleaning up some unwanted files in your home directory, so you want to execute the following command:

```
# rm -rf /home/eziodm/tmp/redundant
```

Now, consider what happens if you accidentally insert a space character, like this:

```
# rm -rf /home /eziodm/tmp/redundant
```

Please **don't** try this out for yourself! The extra space character is almost invisible, but it completely changes the meaning of the command. The first of these commands will attempt to delete only the directory `/home/eziodm/tmp/redundant` and its contents. But the second command will attempt to seek out and destroy the contents of every home directory on the system!

If you're working as root, then there's no protection – root is allowed to delete these directories, and they'll be wiped out in an instant.

You can protect yourself from accidents like this by working as a normal user. Normal users are prevented from deleting such important directories, and this is what happens when you try:

```
$ rm -rf /home /eziodm/rmp/redundant
rm: cannot remove '/home': Permission denied
```

321

So, the message is clear: use the root account only when it is really necessary. This generally applied policy has so far prevented viruses from spreading wildly in Linux (and Unix in general): it's impossible for an ordinary user to infect an executable in the /bin directory, quite simply because ordinary users don't have Write access to those files.

In addition, it's also possible to protect personal files and directories by disabling write permissions to prevent accidental deletion.

You don't need the root account for those daily tasks such as surfing the net, and you won't miss root's authority. Most of the time, there is simply no advantage in working as root. In general:

> **It is good practice to work as an ordinary (non-root) user whenever possible.**

Naturally, there are times when administration rights are required – for example, when adding new users, changing a forgotten password, connecting to the Internet, setting up a local area network connection, formatting a floppy disk, and so on. Red Hat Linux comes with an excellent set of tools to perform these tasks graphically – and as we've seen, the system asks you to enter the root password when necessary, so there's no need to be root all the time.

Here are some other tips to improve your normal user experience.

Mounting Devices

Thanks to technologies like USB, FireWire, and PCMCIA (or PC Card) devices, we have several removable storage media to plug into our computer. In Linux, plugging these devices in can be quite a tedious job – because each device must be mounted, and mounting a device requires administration privileges.

The solution is to update /etc/fstab once and for all as root with the correct information. Once you've done this, normal users will be able to mount removable (or fixed) media, either graphically or via the command line.

Try It Out   Mounting Devices with Normal User Accounts

Let's suppose we have a CompactFlash card containing pictures taken with a digital camera. Once inserted, Red Hat Linux supports this medium, which is considered just as if it were an ordinary hard disk.

1. If you don't know the name of the device associated to your removable media, try to plug it in and have a look at the system logs. To do this, select Main Menu | System Tools | System Logs, or type redhat-logviewer from a terminal window. Authenticate if necessary, and then choose System Log and insert your card. You should see something like this:

You can see the same lines in a root terminal by using the following command:

```
# tail -f /var/log/messages
```

In the output above, we can tell that the device has been recognized as an IDE disk, `hde`, with only one partition (`hde1`). Thus, `/dev/hde1` is the device we want to mount.

2. Now we have to choose a **mount point** in the file system. `/mnt/flash` is an appropriate mount point. We can create `/mnt/flash` from the file manager, or from a root shell using the following command:

```
# mkdir /mnt/flash
```

3. The final step to make this device available to normal users is to edit the file `/etc/fstab`. This file contains a list of mountable devices and relative options. As root, open `/etc/fstab` using a text editor such as `gedit`. Add the following (highlighted) line at the end of the file:

```
...
/dev/cdrom      /mnt/cdrom      iso9660  noauto,user,kudzu,ro 0    0
/dev/fd0        /mnt/floppy     auto     noauto,user,kudzu    0    0
/dev/hde1       /mnt/flash      auto     noauto,user,kudzu    0    0
```

This is how to read the line:

❑ The first field (`/dev/hde1`) is the device to be mounted

❑ The second field (`/mnt/flash`) is the mount point

❑ The third field (`auto`) will try to detect automatically the **file system type** on the device, for example `vfat` (very likely) or `ext3`

❑ In the fourth field, `noauto` prevents the device from being mounted automatically when the system is started. Also, `user` is the *crucial* option: it is this setting that allows normal users to mount the device

The rest of the line is not relevant to our example and can be ignored. You can find out more with `man fstab`.

4. Congratulations! Now the CompactFlash card can be mounted and unmounted by normal users without root's intervention. To test this out, log in as a normal user and select **Main Menu | System Tools | Disk Management**. The **User Mount Tool** dialog will appear with the newly added device:

Device	Directory	Filesystem
/dev/hde1	/mnt/flash	auto
/dev/fd0	/mnt/floppy	auto
/dev/cdrom	/mnt/cdrom	iso9660

X Close   Format   Unmount

At this point you can mount or unmount it pressing the appropriate button and browse its contents through the file manager.

5. You can try from a normal user terminal as well:

```
$ mount /mnt/flash
$ ls -l /mnt/flash
total 2
drwxrwxr-x    4 eziodm       eziodm          2048 Nov   9 12:35 dcim
$ umount /mnt/flash
```

As an extra bonus, files stored in the CompactFlash card are owned by the user who mounted the device.

Using the su Command

We've already used the su (switch user) command quite extensively to change the user account context within a terminal window. If you need to perform a lot of administrative work, then it makes sense to open a terminal window open, execute su - in it (to log in as root), and then keep that window open, just for admin tasks, for as long as you need it. Every time you need to run a command as root, just type it into *that* window, while you do all your other non-admin work in another window, as a normal user.

If you take this approach, it helps if you have some way to make the root shell terminal window visually distinct from the non-root shell window. This is effective, and it's very easy – you can create a special **root shell terminal** on your desktop, and give it distinctive features, like a different title and color scheme.

Try It Out   Creating a Root Shell Launcher

First of all, while using a normal account, we need to create a new terminal profile called root. We'll give it a red background and a permanent "root shell" title.

1. Open a terminal window (choose Main Menu | System Tools | Terminal).

2. From the Edit menu, choose Profiles..., then click on the New button and type root as the new profile name:

Press Create to confirm.

3. Now, back in the Edit Profiles window, select the root profile and press the Edit button. Now you can use your creativity to personalize the window used for root shells. For example, you can change window title to root shell, and set the color scheme to white-on-red, as shown below:

Whatever you decide to do, you *must* select the Run a custom command instead of my shell checkbox in the Title and Command tab, and the command *must* be su -. It is this that ensures that, whenever this profile is activated in the terminal, Linux will execute su -, and not your habitual shell.

By choosing a colored background, you create a root shell window that is clearly distinct from the others. Moreover, the title of this window will always contain the phrase root shell, even if the application changes it.

4. If you don't want to create a special launcher on your desktop or bottom panel, that's it: whenever you open a terminal window, you can choose File | New Window or File | New Tab and select the root profile instead of Default. Naturally, before having access to the root shell, you'll need to type the root password (no matter how acquainted you get with your Linux system, it will never trust you completely...)

5. If you want to create a **launcher** (that is, a personalized icon), then click with the right mouse button on the desktop background and choose New Launcher from the menu that pops up. The Create Launcher dialog will appear:

Fill in the window that will appear as shown above. It's important to get the spacing and double-hyphen right in the **Command** line:

gnome-terminal --window-with-profile=root

There is no need to go to the **Advanced** tab. The key here is that we start a new gnome-terminal with the `root` profile that we've just created. Therefore this window will be different than the others.

When you press **OK**, a new icon will be created on the desktop.

6. Whenever you double-click the icon, a terminal window will appear with the title and color scheme that you specified in Step 3 (mine has white text on a red background). You'll need to type the root password. Once you're authenticated as root, you will be able to use this terminal to issue root commands:

7. You can also drag the icon on the bottom panel, so that it is always available. Be careful and administer your powers wisely!

Compiling, Installing, and Running Software

We'll finish this section with a few words about software compilation, installation, and execution. We won't talk about RPM packages here, because we've already learned about them in Chapter 4 and you have seen **tarballs** (archives of possibly compressed files of the form .tar) as well.

If you need to compile software then it's usually sufficient to compile it as a normal user. Any well-behaved piece of software that requires compilation by a root user should warn you of such a requirement. The advice generally offered when extracting and compiling tarballs is to do so within the context of a normal account.

Extracting and compiling from within a normal (non-root) account is also a good *security* measure. For example, extracting from an archive from within the root account can get you into problems if the archive contains *absolute paths* instead of *relative* ones. Consider a tarball that contains, say, a file called /etc/passwd: if you extract it as root, you could be in serious trouble, because it will overwrite your user account file! But if you extract from the safety of a normal user, then you're using an account that is not allowed to overwrite the file, and so you're protected from such disasters.

> *Better yet, you can extract and compile software with a non-root, non-personal account —
> and then you won't even risk the possibility of messing up your home directory.*

Immediately before the compiling phase, most modern programs require you to run a configure script. If this is the case (you can almost always find a README or INSTALL file or equivalent to get instructions from), installing the program with a non-root account becomes quite easy. Just run the script with the --prefix option, like this:

```
$ tar xzvf program_name-1.0.tar.gz
$ cd program_name-1.0
$ ./configure --prefix=$HOME/software/program_name-1.0
$ make
$ make install
```

If the program is well behaved, it will compile itself knowing that the installation directory is different than the default, typically /usr/local, /usr, or /opt. This will allow you to install the necessary files to a place that you can write to.

If the program doesn't have a configure script, the solution may not be straightforward. In this case, read carefully the documentation that is included with the package (INSTALL and README files are good starting points) and, if all else fails, you may need to ask around or even contact the original developer.

Finally, we come to the first execution of the much sought after program. One thing is really important:

> **Never run newly installed and unknown software as root!**

This is especially important if you haven't read the source code of the program and you're not certain about its features. At worst, you might damage your operating system installation, either by accidentally misusing the program or because the software you run has not been carefully written. In some extreme cases, it could even happen that the software you downloaded is *not* the one you wanted, or it will not behave as advertised.

For test-driving newly installed software, you can create a special user, for example called `swtest`, and switch to that account every time you run a new program for the first time. You'll have a chance to see the program in action, and possibly check `swtest`'s home directory for added configuration files.

Who Is Logged In?

We know now that Linux is a multi-user system, and consequently it is possible for many remote users to be logged in to our Linux machine simultaneously, with each using their own account. But from where?

Back in the old times, a traditional Unix system would often have a (sometimes huge) number of **serial terminals** connected to it. Each terminal was basically just a screen with an attached keyboard (or maybe just a printer), capable of sending characters to the Unix host and displaying characters received from it. Does this sound familiar? That term *terminal* is still used today to identify a window in which users run shells and type commands.

Although serial terminals can still be seen today, they've been largely replaced by network connections. Besides the computer itself, the **network** is the place from which most login requests are likely to come. In subsequent chapters of this book you'll see how to manage networking and services that allow remote login. This feature in particular is really empowering and useful, but sometimes not desirable.

The following table contains a list of commands that we can use to find out who logs into our system and what they are doing when they're there. Even though these commands are some of the oldest of all Unix commands, they are still very much in use today:

Command	Description
who	Used to check who is logged in, and from where
w	Used to check who is logged in, and what they are doing (that is, what program they are running at the moment)

Table continued on following page

Command	Description
whoami	Displays the user name of the invoking user
last	Used to check who logged in in the past
lastb	If /var/log/btmp exists, shows a list of failed login attempts. It is disabled by default

For further details, each command has its own manual page, accessible through the man command, for example with man whoami.

Summary

User accounts and groups play an important role in Red Hat Linux, just as they do in most other modern operating systems. We've seen in this chapter how the notion of a user account can be employed to provide many different users with simultaneous access to a system – each user having their own identity. Each user can have their own personal home directory, which (by default) is a subdirectory of /home.

From there, we can also devise systems of access rights, explicitly allowing or denying access to a file, directory, or executable, depending on the identity of the user. Indeed, we single out a special user account called root (which has very free administrative rights), and any number of other system accounts; and we are encouraged to create personal accounts for the people who use our system.

With a system that has a number of users, it becomes convenient to create groups of users and assign permissions to the groups. This makes the task of access management much more manageable and flexible. For example, we can set the access rights to a file to be dependent on the identity of the user. We can also assign special privileges to a group of users, and change the members of that group as often as necessary.

The information that describes all the users and groups on a system is contained in the files /etc/passwd, /etc/shadow, and /etc/group. There are a number of tools for managing the users and groups on the system – in particular, the graphical **User Manager** interface and the **User Information Tool**, and an array of flexible command line utilities:

❑ su and id for changing user and checking the user's identity

❑ useradd, passwd, chfn, chsh, usermod, and userdel for managing user accounts

❑ groupadd, groupdel, and gpasswd to managing groups

Having established the basics of users and groups (and having practiced creating and manipulating some users and groups), it's natural to examine how they can be used to implement some access policies. In this chapter we examined six strategies of file protection and sharing, starting with some simple scenarios and building up to a situation in which different groups of users require different access rights to the same set of files.

We stressed the advantages of working under a normal user account. We saw how easy it is to make errors when performing regular (seemingly harmless) tasks, and how these errors can cause a lot of damage if you're working as root. Working under as a normal user account affords us some protection, and so it's worth avoiding the root wherever possible. We looked at how to carry out administrative tasks in a normal user environment: mounting disks, executing sporadic root commands, and compiling and installing software locally.

Finally, we noted a number of useful commands designed to check users activity on a Linux machine: who, w, whoami, last, and lastb.

The next chapter will further expand the limits of your Red Hat Linux computer by connecting it to a network and making it fully interoperable with other servers.

9

Building Networks

If we're going to share resources among computers efficiently, then the use of networks is essential. Networking is a potentially complex topic, but it's powerful, and these days it's indispensable. For example:

- ❑ At work, it's hard for many corporations to imagine life without the large networks that make files and services accessible to their employees.

- ❑ At home, if you've got a couple of computers then the convenience of having them networked together for sharing files is immeasurable. (There are plenty of network professionals who started out by tinkering with small home networks.)

- ❑ Networking is also what makes the Internet possible.

Linux is a popular choice these days when it comes to enterprise networking solutions. Linux networks are fast, reliable, secure, and cost effective. Google (http://www.google.com) provides one of the best examples of enterprise Linux networks. Google's search engine comprises more than 10,000 servers networked together to form world's one of the biggest distributed computing systems, and the world's largest commercial Linux cluster. The Stone SouperComputer is another (rather different) example of what is possible with Linux-based networking (see http://stonesoup.esd.ornl.gov/).

We'll begin this chapter with a general discussion of networks, and the advantages of using Linux for building networks. Then, we'll devote sections to each of the following services:

- ❑ Setting up a web server, for hosting web sites (or, if you're planning to develop web sites, to test your sites as you build them)

- ❑ Setting up an FTP server – a place from which users can download files, and/or upload files

- ❑ Setting up a print server, to manage printers and enable them to be shared among multiple users

- ❑ Setting up a file server, to share files (for example, between Windows and Linux systems)

- ❑ Setting up a mail server, for delivering e-mail to its final destination (for example, you could use an e-mail client on a Windows 2000 laptop and configure it to send and receive e-mail via a local Linux mail server)

- ❑ Setting up a DHCP server, which automatically assigns network settings to connected systems

You may choose not to read all of this chapter, but only the sections that relate to the services you're interested in. You probably won't need all these services on your Linux machine, and you're not obliged to set them all up! (In fact, there are good security reasons for choosing not to set up a service unless and until you *need* it to be there. We'll discuss this more in Chapter 12.)

Moreover, these services all work independently of one another, so (for example) you don't have to set up an FTP server in order for your web server to work. You can enable and disable any service just at the time you need it.

By default Red Hat Linux 9 setup provides you the option to configure the firewall. If the firewall has been configured then you might face some problems accessing the services setup in this chapter. After setting up or configuring any of the services discussed in this chapter, you should always check the firewall settings and if needed, open the ports to enable access to those services. Please refer to Chapter 12 of this book for more information about setting and configuring the firewall.

Networking

These days, networking is part of our daily life. Whether we are sending email from our desktop PCs or using Internet for shopping, networking is at the heart of what we're doing. In fact, there are a number of different types of network. For example:

- ❑ A local area network (LAN) is a network that covers a limited geographical area

- ❑ A metropolitan area network (MAN) covers a geographic area such as a city or suburb

- ❑ A wide area network (WAN) may span a wide geographic area, spread over many states or countries. The Internet is an example of a WAN.

To facilitate communication across these networks, we have **protocols**. A protocol is a standard language by which two (possibly dissimilar) systems can communicate. For example, TCP/IP is the protocol that allows different machines to participate together to make the Internet work.

For more information about Networking protocols such as TCP/IP, AppleTalk, X.25, Frame Relay, ISDN, PPP, SLIP, PLIP, and so on, try http://www.tldp.org/LDP/nag2/index.html *and* http://www.tldp.org/HOWTO/Networking-Overview-HOWTO.html.

Red Hat Linux and Networking

Red Hat Linux 9 comes bundled with lots of networking applications and utilities that will help you meet your networking requirements. We can categorize and list the networking applications that come with Red Hat Linux 9 as follows:

Application Type	Applications
Web server	`httpd` – the widely used Apache HTTP server
FTP server	`vsftp` – a very secure ftp server
File server	`samba` – the SAMBA server, which provides file sharing between SMB-enabled machines (such as Windows and Linux machines)
	`samba-client` – the SAMBA client programs, designed to access SMB shares
Print server	`cups` – CUPS printing service and the drivers to use it
Mail server	`sendmail` – a widely used mail transport agent
DHCP server	`dhcp` – a DHCP server and relay agent

Over the course of this chapter, we will discuss some of these applications and help you to get your Linux machine acting as a full-fledged network server.

Why Is Linux Good for Networking?

Once of the most significant factors in choosing the hardware and software for a network is the **total cost of ownership** (TCO). This is the cost of purchase, setup and configuration, and also maintenance. If you sit down and analyze the requirements of different parts of network architecture, you'll quickly find that the free, open nature of Linux systems lends itself better to some parts of network than others.

Linux is a particularly good choice for supporting network applications (such as file servers, web servers, and mail servers):

❏ Of course, the cost of purchase (both of the operating system and the software itself) is low. Cost of setup should generally also be favorable, particularly given the advances both in recent releases of network applications and in Red Hat Linux 9 itself, and the vast body of knowledge in the open source community that is available via web sites, news groups and local Linux users' groups. (Many enterprise level solutions companies like Red Hat, IBM, Hewlett Packard, and Sun Microsystems have also started providing commercial level support for Linux servers.)

- ❑ The stability and reliability of the operating system is also influential, because an unstable or unreliable system brings maintenance costs. Linux is a good choice for network applications because it makes the grade in these areas. Moreover, Linux is ready for high-availability environments (see http://www.ibiblio.org/pub/Linux/ALPHA/linux-ha).

- ❑ Other factors influencing TCO include the scalability, flexibility, and security of the system:

  - ❑ By choosing a Linux operating system and open source networking applications, you have access to the source code of both the system and the application. This puts you in a position to adapt the applications to achieve whatever aims you need.

  - ❑ We've already seen evidence, earlier in this chapter, that Linux is capable of being deployed in both small- and large-scale networks.

  - ❑ Red Hat Linux installs by default with a minimum of good-practice security, and (as we'll see in Chapter 12) can be further enhanced with a combination of open source security tools and good practice.

Linux is also great for services that can be replicated (for example, DNS). You can configure such machines cheaply, and replicate them. Then, if one machine fails, it doesn't matter; it should be possible to replace it cheaply. In the meantime, the replicate servers keep on working to provide the service.

By contrast, Linux is not a common choice for basic infrastructure, such as routers, hubs, and switches. While Linux is capable in this area, it's desirable only when the low cost of cheap (or cast off) PCs is the major selection criteria. In a more business critical role, where reliability will count for more than minimum purchase price, dedicated hardware is still the most popular choice.

You can find more information about TCO comparison between Red Hat Linux and other Unix flavors at http://www.redhat.com/whitepapers/services/tco.pdf.

Assumptions for Network Setup

In the demonstrations in this chapter, we've used a network setup that may not be the same as your own environment. You can choose your own server, connectivity devices (switch, hub, and direct cable connection), IP address scheme, and hostname to set up networking in a way that suits your own requirements. In this section, we'll note the network settings that we've used. In order to facilitate, we'll begin with an explanation of the terms that we'll use.

The **network topology** refers to the shape or layout of the network. It defines how different systems in a network are connected and communicate with each other. The ideal topology of a network depends on the size of the network, the requirements of its users, and the policies of the company or organization.

The following diagram shows an ideal network topology:

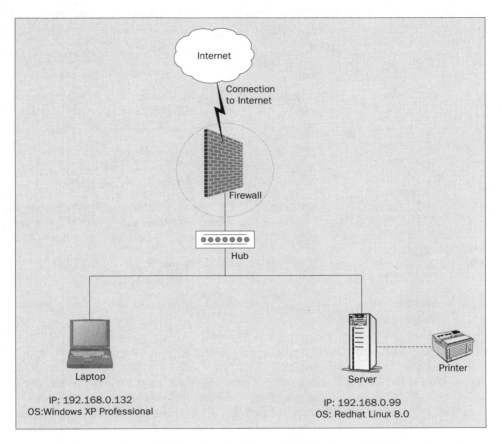

This diagram shows a client machine (in the form of a Windows 2000 laptop), and a server (running Red Hat Linux 9, and supporting some of the services described in this chapter). They are connected via an internal network, and protected from the Internet by a hub and a firewall. Of course, your network topology might look different than this.

For example, if you have a smaller network, then it's possible that you don't have a hub, and that your firewall is not a dedicated machine but a piece of software hosted by your Linux server machine. If you have only a single machine, then it can double as both the server and client machines in this diagram (being a client of its own services!). We've used a topology like this one in this chapter.

Note that both the end-user's laptop and the server machine have been assigned an **IP address** – this is used to uniquely identify the computer (or other device) within a TCP/IP network. An IP address is a 32-bit binary address in the form of four decimal values. Each of these four decimals represents an 8-bit value (an octet), and hence is in the range 0 to 255. This format is known as **dotted quad notation**.

337

In fact, the TCP/IP network is divided into different class networks. The important classes are defined below:

Class	Values	Description
Class A	1.x.x.x to 127.x.x.x	The first octet specifies the network number, and the remaining octets specify the host within the network. This class supports about 1.6 million hosts per network.
Class B	128.0.x.x to 191.255.x.x	The first two octets specify the network number, and the remaining octets specify the host within the network. This class supports 16,320 networks with 65,024 hosts each.
Class C	192.0.0.x to 223.255.255.x	The first three octets specify the network number, and the remaining octets specify the host within the network. This class supports nearly two million networks with up to 254 hosts each.
Class D	224.0.0.0 to 239.255.255.255	These are reserved for multicast groups
Class E	240.0.0.0 to 254.255.255.254	These are reserved for special purpose use.

The TCP/IP networks can also be divided by public and private IP addresses:

❑ Your public IP address is assigned to you by your Internet service provider (ISP). In fact, this IP address is allocated to the ISP by the Internet Assigned Numbers Authority (IANA – http://www.iana.org). It's your public IP address that identifies you on the Internet.

❑ Private IP addresses are those (like the addresses used in the diagram above) that identify a device within a private or non-Internet connected network. There are three TCP/IP network address ranges reserved for use in private networks: 10.0.0.0– 10.255.255.255, 172.16.0.0–172.31.255.255, and 192.168.0.0–192.168.255.255.

A **netmask** is a 32-bit string that hides the network part of an IP address, so that only the host (computer) part of the address remains. For example, the netmask 255.255.255.0 looks like an IP address, but in fact hides the first 24 bits of the IP address so that only the last 8 bits remain (recall that 255 is the decimal representation of the binary 11111111). Hence, the netmask 255.255.255.0 is commonly used for Class C IP addresses to reveal the specific host computer address publicly.

There are a few more definitions that will be useful here:

❑ A **gateway** is a host that is connected to two or more physical networks, and hence allows messages to switch between them.

❑ The term **hostname** refers to the unique name of the machine, so that it can identify itself on the network.

❑ Finally, the **domain name system** (or **DNS**) is a distributed database that translates domain names into IP addresses and vice versa. For example, DNS translates the domain name www.linux4biz.net to the IP address 212.69.200.83.

With all that in mind, let's return to those two machines on our network – the Red Hat Linux 9 server machine and the Windows 2000 client laptop machine. Here are the network configuration settings we used for those two machines in this chapter.

The Red Hat Linux 9 server machine is set up as a firewall and router, and has Internet connectivity. Over the course of the chapter we'll show how it can be configured as a file server, printer server, DHCP server, FTP server, web server, or mail server:

Server	Value
Operating system	Red Hat Linux 9
IP address	192.168.0.99
Netmask	255.255.255.0
Hostname	linux4biz

The laptop is a simple client machine, designed for an end-user and (potentially) sharing resources with other similar machines on the network:

Setting	Value
Purpose	A Client laptop system to be used to share resources configured on Linux server
Operating system	Windows 2000 Professional
IP address	192.168.0.132
Netmask	255.255.255.0
Hostname	Win

As we've said, your network topology, and the network configuration of your machine(s), may be different; but many of the principles in this chapter remain the same, and you should be able to get any of these services going regardless of your own environment.

We will assume that you have root access to the Red Hat Linux server. Throughout the chapter, we'll use the terms *Linux server* and *client* to refer to the Red Hat Linux 9 server machine and the Microsoft Windows 2000 client machine respectively.

Setting up a Web Server

When we want to publish web pages on the Internet (or on an intranet), we use a web server. In essence, a **web server** is an application that does two things:

❑   It listens for page requests.

❑   When it receives a page request, it examines the request and responds with the page that was requested.

For example, when you use a web browser to browse http://www.wrox.com, the browser turns this into a **request** message and sends it across the Internet to Wrox's own web server. When the web server receives this request, it processes it, works out what page you requested, puts that page together from whatever resources are necessary, and sends the page back to your browser, in the form of a **response** message.

Of course, there are many different web browsers in existence (including Mozilla, Opera, Internet Explorer, and others), and there are also a great many types of web server software. To enable a browser to request pages from a web server, they communicate using **Hypertext Transfer Protocol** (**HTTP**) – this is the standard protocol for the Internet. The request and response messages are composed using HTTP, and this is what allows *any* browser to request web pages from *any* type of web server.

> *By default, all web servers listen for HTTP requests on port 80. Web servers also use port 443 to listen for requests made through secure HTTP connections, over SSL (secure sockets layer), through a protocol called HTTPS.*

So, if you want to publish your own web site, you'll need a machine with some web server software. However, the chances are that if you build your own web site, you probably won't want to expose it to the Internet from your *own* machine. There are security and maintenance issues to manage, and you'd need to buy enough hardware and bandwidth to handle all the page requests. More likely, you'd choose an Internet service provider (ISP), and use their web servers to host your web site for you.

So, why would you want to install a web server on your Red Hat Linux machine? Well, here are two scenarios:

❏ First, if you're building a web site, then you'll need a web server so that you can test your site as you're developing it

❏ Second, although you might not host an Internet site from your own machine, you might host an intranet site – a private web site available only to other machines inside your private network. The demand for intranet pages is much more predictable than for Internet pages, and the security risks are not so significant.

So, in this section, we'll show you how to set up a web server on your machine, configure it, and publish pages on it. From there, you'll soon be developing your own sites.

The Apache Web Server

As we've mentioned, there are a number of commercial and freely available web servers in existence. Among the commercial web servers are offerings from Netscape, IPlanet, SunONE, Microsoft (the Internet Information Server, or IIS), and Zeus. Among the open source web servers, we can list Apache, thttpd, and Redhat TUX.

Of all these, **Apache** is most widely used. At the time of writing, 66% of all web sites are hosted on Apache web servers (according to the Netcraft Web Server Survey, http://www.netcraft.com/survey) – the vast majority of them running on Linux or Unix operating systems. Apache's popularity is due not only of its open source pedigree, but also to its highly competitive levels of performance, functionality, stability, flexibility, and security:

❏ Apache's flexibility comes from the fact that it is a **modular** web server. That means that you can meet your requirements by plugging any number of external modules into the core httpd daemon. Of course, being open source software, you also have access to Apache's source code, which you can customize to fit your needs.

Apache is also very scalable. You can run Apache on high-end hardware, and it's possible to increase the capacity of Apache web servers by sharing the load across any number of servers. It's also very portable, being available for a number of operating systems.

❏ Apache's security is very good in comparison to other web servers. Moreover, the Apache Foundation is extremely active in the continued defense of Apache from security problems – particularly in the form of announcements and patches.

❏ Apache performs very well – it boasts a highly optimized daemon for serving static content which dramatically outperforms its nearest rivals. Moreover, it rarely crashes and achieves extremely long up-times.

❏ Apache comes with detailed documentation, which helps to make the setup and configuration easy. And of course, because it's so popular there's a wide network of support for Apache, in the form of mailing lists, newsgroups, and commercial vendors like Red Hat.

❏ Apache development is active. The Apache Foundation is actively involved in development of new modules; new versions of Apache to make it reliable stable and secure.

Since you've already got Red Hat Linux 9, there's another good reason for choosing Apache as your web server software – it's included as part of the Red Hat Linux 9 distribution! At the time of writing, the latest version of Apache is 2.0.44.

Installing Apache

As we've alredy noted, Apache is a *modular* server – the core server provides the basic functionality, with extended features available in various modules. This makes it very flexible and easy to configure, becuase you need to configure only the modules you need. So, it's worth looking at how to control the installation and removal of these modules.

In fact, the different modules are contained in the different packages that we can install via the Red Hat Package Manager (RPM). Recall that to start RPM's graphical interface, you can select **Main Menu | System Settings | Add/Remove Applications**, or type the following command at the command line:

```
$ redhat-config-packages
```

The Apache web server packages are listed in the **Web Server** package group, which is found under the **Applications** category in the RPM. If you look at the details of this package group now, you'll see that there are 17 packages listed:

Only one of these packages in the group is a **Standard Package** – that's the **httpd** package that contains the base Apache web server functionality. The remaining 16 packages are all optional packages (the RPM calls them **Extra Packages**). The important packages are explained below:

Package	Description
httpd-manual	Contains the documentation for the Apache web server. After installation, you can access this documentation from the command line by typing `man httpd`
hwcrypto	Provides support for hardware SSL acceleration cards. This package should be installed if you have hardware SSL acceleration cards like Ncipher Nforce on your server
mod_ssl	Provides an SSL interface to the HTTPS web server, and hence enables the Apache web server to support SSL. This package should be installed if you want to provide secure connections to your clients
php	Provides the PHP module for Apache, which enables the web server to serve PHP web pages. This package is required if you if you want to host web sites which contain pages written with the PHP scripting language
webalizer	Provides programs for web server log file analysis. This package enables you to generate HTML usage reports for your website

You can find out more about other Apache modules at the Apache web site,
http://httpd.apache.org/docs-2.0/mod.

You can choose whichever extra packages fit your requirements; it's definitely worth installing the httpd-manual package, and then you should choose whatever other packages fit your own requirements. Remember that you can re-launch the RPM at any time, and add or remove packages, as you need them.

When you've selected the packages you need, click the **Close** button to dismiss the **Web Server Package Details** window, and then click the **Update** button on the on main **Package Management** window to begin the installation. During the installation, you'll be prompted to insert the distribution discs, as they're required. The RPM will also inform you of any conflict between package dependencies.

The Apache Configuration Files

Apache's configuration information is contained in a select bunch of configuration files:

❑ The `/etc/httpd/httpd.conf` file is Apache's main configuration file.

❑ The `/etc/httpd/conf.d` directory contains configuration files for any installed modules (such as PHP, SSL, and so on).

- ❏ The /etc/httpd/logs directory is a symbolic link to /var/log/httpd directory, which contains all the Apache log files.

- ❏ The /etc/httpd/modules directory is a symbolic link to /usr/lib/httpd/modules directory, which contains all the Apache modules configured as dynamic shared objects.

  Dynamic shared objects (or DSOs) are modules that are compiled separately from the Apache httpd binary. They are so-called because they can be loaded on demand. There's more information on DSOs at http://httpd.apache.org/docs-2.0/mod.

- ❏ The /etc/httpd/run directory is a symbolic link to /var/run, which contains the process ID file (httpd.pid) of the httpd process.

- ❏ /etc/rc.d/init.d/httpd is a shell script, used for starting and stopping the Apache web server.

Starting Apache for the First Time

You can start Apache using the Red Hat **Service Configuration** GUI dialog, or via the command line. Here's how to start Apache from the **Service Configuration** dialog:

1. First, you need to fire up the GUI. To do this, click on **Main Menu | System Settings | Server Settings | Services** or type the following at the command line:

```
$ redhat-config-services
```

It will ask for root password if you started it as a normal user. When you do this, you get the **Service Configuration** dialog:

This dialog contains a list of all the services that are supported on your computer. The checkboxes indicate which of these services are started automatically when the machine boots up (as part of the cron). There are also Start, Stop, and Restart buttons so that we can start and stop services manually.

2. Scroll down the list on the left of the dialog, and select the entry for httpd. As we said, the httpd service is the Apache web server service. Check the status of the httpd service, in the bottom-right of the dialog; if it is stopped (as above), then click the Start button to start it.

If you want it to start automatically next time you reboot your machine, check the checkbox too. Then select File | Save Changes to save the new settings. That's it; you can close the Service Configuration dialog by selecting File | Quit.

To control the Apache web server from the command line, we can use the service command to fire the httpd script. Here's how we use it to start the web server:

```
# service httpd start
Starting httpd:                                              [  OK  ]
```

If there are difficulties in starting the web server, then you'll find out about it here. For example, if you attempt to do this without root privileges, then you'll get a message telling you that permission is denied. And here's another example:

```
# service httpd start
Starting httpd: httpd: Could not determine the server's fully qualified
domain name, using 192.168.0.99 for ServerName
                                                             [  OK  ]
```

Here, the message explains that the server's fully qualified domain name (FQDN) couldn't be determined, and that it's using the IP address (192.168.0.99) instead. If you get this message, it's because you have neither setup a FQDN for your Linux server, nor configured the ServerName configuration directive in the httpd.conf configuration file.

An FQDN is a unique name, consisting of hostname and domain name, which can be resolved to an IP address. For example, www.linux4biz.net is a fully qualified domain name.

Returning to the httpd script itself, there are similar switches for stopping or restarting the service:

```
# service httpd restart
Stopping httpd:                                              [  OK  ]
Starting httpd:                                              [  OK  ]
# service httpd stop
Stopping httpd:                                              [  OK  ]
```

There are a few other options you can use with the `httpd` script. If you run the script without an option, the resulting usage message reveals all the available options:

```
# service httpd
Usage: httpd
{start|stop|restart|condrestart|reload|status|fullstatus|graceful|
           help|configtest}
```

The `configtest` option is a particularly useful one. The configuration file is quite complex, and so it's useful to check it for errors after you make changes to it. To do this, you use the `configtest` option:

```
# service httpd configtest
Syntax OK
```

Testing the Apache Web Server

Once you've started the Apache web server, you should test it to see if it's working properly. To do that, we'll use a web browser to request a web page from our server! There's a page provided by default for this purpose, and you can request it via the URL http://localhost. So, launch a web browser (Main Menu | Internet | Mozilla Web Browser), and type this URL into the address box:

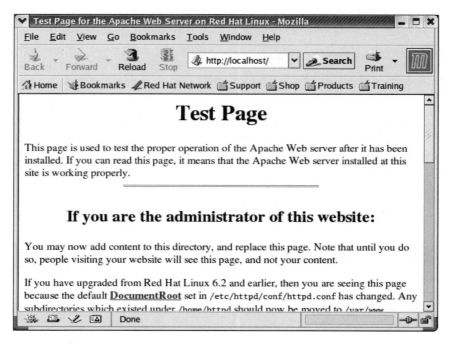

Configuring your Web Server

It's a good idea to configure your web server. Red Hat does provide a GUI tool, `apacheconf`, for configuring Apache, but it does not format the configuration file very well. Webmin (http://www.webmin.com – see Chapter 13) is an alternative web-based software that can be used to manage most of the Linux services, including the Apache web server. However, in this section we'll show you how to do some basic configuration by editing the `httpd.conf` Apache configuration file directly.

Try It Out   **Configuring Your Web Server**

We're going to configure the web server by adjusting a couple of the settings to suit our needs.

1. Launch the gedit text editor (by selecting Main Menu | Accessories | Text Editor), or your favorite text editor. Use it to open the file /etc/httpd/conf/httpd.conf.

2. Select Search | Find and use the resulting dialog to find the word **ServerAdmin** in the file. The first occurrence should be the `ServerAdmin` directive, which looks like this:

```
# ServerAdmin: Your server address, where problems with the server should be
# e-mailed. This address appears on some server-generated pages, such
# as error documents. e.g. admin@your-domain.com
ServerAdmin root@localhost
```

As you can see, the configuration file describes this directive very well. Change the email address to your own email address, or an address that you may have set up for web site administration. For example:

```
# ServerAdmin: Your server address, where problems with the server should be
# e-mailed. This address appears on some server-generated pages, such
# as error documents. e.g. admin@your-domain.com
ServerAdmin webmaster@linux4biz.net
```

3. Now use the same technique to find the `ServerName` directive (you'll probably find that it's right after the `ServerAdmin` directive). Change this directive first by removing the leading # character. Then, if you have a registered DNS name, add it here (in place of the DNS name `test.linux4biz.net`, which I'm using here to demonstrate):

```
# ServerName gives the name and port that the server uses to identify itself.
# ...
ServerName test.linux4biz.net
```

347

The server name you specify should be a FQDN (because it will need to be resolved to an IP address by DNS). If you haven't setup a DNS, then you can enter the IP address allocated to the Linux server instead, like this:

```
ServerName 192.168.0.99
```

4. Save the httpd.conf file, and close it.

5. Restart the httpd daemon to reflect the changes. To do this, use Red Hat **Services Configuration** GUI, or the httpd command line script as described earlier in this chapter:

```
# service httpd restart
Stopping httpd:                                        [  OK  ]
Starting httpd:                                        [  OK  ]
```

Now browse to http://localhost again, to check that the web server is still serving web pages. You should see the Apache **Test Page** that we saw earlier in this section.

There are many configuration settings that you can control via the httpd.conf configuration file. For more information, refer to the Apache web server documentation at http://httpd.apache.org/docs-2.0/.

Setting up Your First Web Site

In the remainder of this section, we'll set up a simple web site, which will be accessible on the network. This will involve creating a simple HTML web page, and saving it to a location on the hard disk that is used by the web server to store published web pages. Then, when a user requests the page, the web server will be able to respond by retrieving it from this location and sending it to the requestor.

Try It Out   Publishing Your First Web Page

1. Launch an editor (you can use a dedicated web page editor such as Mozilla Composer if you have it installed; alternatively, **gedit** will do). Create a new file – call it index.html and save it in the directory /var/www/html.

2. Type some HTML into the file. For example:

```
<html>
<head>
  <title>Beginning Red Hat Linux - Apache Test Page</title>
</head>
<body>
  <center>
    <h1>Beginning Red Hat Linux - Apache Test Page</h1>
    This is the first page of your web site!
```

```
    </center>
 </body>
 </html>
```

3. Now open a browser and browse to the page using your server's FQDN address or IP address. (For example, I'm using the URL http://test.linux4biz.net/index.html below to match my DNS name, but you might use something like http://192.168.0.99/index.html.) Your browser will send this request to the web server listening for connections on port 80 by default. Web server will serve the default web site pages. The following screenshot shows the output you should see:

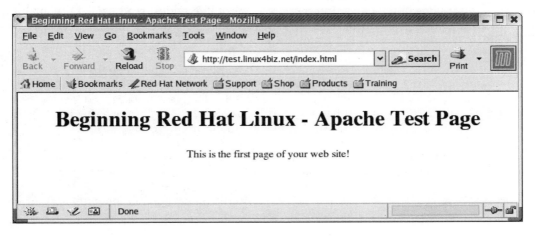

How It Works

In this example, we set up a simple web page under Apache web server's default root directory, /var/www/html, and tested it on an internal network. You can add more pages and directories under the /var/www/html directory as explained in the previous example.

If you want to make your web site available on the Internet, then you'd need to connect your web server to the Internet and assign it a public IP address, so that external users send page requests to it. You can also register a DNS so that your website as a memorable name (so users don't need to refer to your web site by its IP address!).

By default, your Apache web server hosts just one web site (whose root is at /var/www/html). However, you can configure your Apache web server to host as many web sites as you like, and specify the root directory of each site to be whatever folder you wish.

If you want more information about acquiring and using Apache, try http://httpd.apache.org/, or *Professional Apache 2.0* and *Professional Apache Security*.

Setting up an FTP Server

If you want to enable other users to download files from a location on your server's hard disk, and/or to upload files to that location, then one solution is to install an **FTP server**. You can think of an FTP server essentially as an area of disk space that is used for storing files, plus the software and configuration required to allow other users to upload and download files. When users want to upload or download from your FTP server, they use a program called an **FTP client**.

These communications between FTP server and FTP client take place using the **File Transfer Protocol** (**FTP**). FTP is a TCP protocol that is designed specifically for the transfer of files over a network, and it's one of the oldest Internet protocols still in widespread use. The availability of so many different FTP client programs, and the fact that many operating systems come with FTP software pre-installed, are indications of how relevant FTP still is today.

FTP is not considered a secure protocol, because communication between the FTP client and server are unencrypted. Consequently, **Secure FTP** (**SFTP**) is also becoming popular (and, indeed, is part of the openssh package that comes with Red Hat Linux 9), and it's also possible to configure your FTP server in other ways, for example by forcing users to log in, or by using access control lists (ACLs) to allow different rights to different groups of users.

> *You need to take careful security precautions if you plan to expose your FTP server on the Internet. We'll talk about how to minimize the security implications of supporting an FTP server in Chapter 12. There's also information on this subject, and on the FTP protocol in general, at RFCs 959 and 2577 (ftp://ftp.rfc-editor.org/in-notes/rfc959.txt and ftp://ftp.rfc-editor.org/in-notes/rfc2577.txt).*

In fact, many FTP servers still allow **anonymous FTP access**, which means that the FTP server allows any user to access its disk space and download its files. Anonymous FTP access is used mostly to enable users to access freely available documents and files via the Internet without access control.

In spite of the security issues, FTP remains popular – it's fast and easy to use, and it is the Internet standard protocol for file transfer.

FTP Servers in the Red Hat Linux Distribution

There are a number of FTP servers available for Red Hat Linux 9 For example:

- ❏ **vsftpd** is a simplified FTP server implementation. It is designed to be a very secure FTP server, and can also be configured to allow anonymous access. We'll explore vsftpd in this section.

- ❏ **TUX** is a kernel-based, threaded, extremely high performance HTTP server, which also has FTP capabilities. TUX is perhaps the best in terms of performance, but offers less functionality than other FTP server software. TUX is installed by default with Red Hat Linux 9.

❑ **wu-ftpd** is a highly configurable and full-featured FTP daemon, which was popular in earlier versions of Red Hat Linux but has since given way to the more security-conscious vsftpd.

❑ **gssftpd** is a kerberized FTP daemon, which means that it is suitable for use with the Kerberos authentication system.

All of these FTP servers ship as part of the Red Hat Linux 9 distribution. However, we will consider only the first of these, vsftpd, here.

Installing the vsftpd FTP Server

The easiest way to install the vsftpd FTP Server package is via the RPM GUI tool. Once you've started the tool (for example, by selecting Main Menu | System Settings | Add/Remove Applications), find the FTP Server package group, which is listed under the Servers category. Check the checkbox for this package group.

If you want, you can click on Details to see the package details. You will see that the package group contains only one package vsftpd – it's under the Standard Packages banner.

Click on Close when you've finished.

Back in the Package Management window, click on Update to start the installation. You'll be prompted to insert the Red Hat Linux 9 installation disks as necessary.

Starting Your FTP Server

To start the FTP service (and hence enable users to upload and download files), we can use the Service Configuration tool. To launch the tool, select Main Menu | System Settings | Server Settings | Services, or type the following command at the command line:

```
$ redhat-config-services
```

Again, you'll be prompted for the root password, unless you're already logged on as root. To start the vsftpd FTP Server, select the vsftpd entry in the list and then click the Start button:

Again, if you want the FTP service to start automatically next time you reboot your machine, then check the checkbox too. Then click on File | Save Changes to save your new settings.

Unsurprisingly, it's also possible to start and stop these FTP services from the command line, using the `service` command to start and stop the `vsftpd` script:

```
# service vsftpd start
Starting vsftpd:                                              [  OK  ]
# service vsftpd stop
Stopping vsftpd:                                              [  OK  ]
```

Again, if you run the script without an option, the resulting usage message reveals all the available options:

```
# service vsftpd
Usage: vsftpd {start|stop|restart|condrestart|status}
```

Testing Your FTP Server

Now you've set up your FTP server and started the service, we'll adopt the role of the client to quickly test that the service is working. From a command line, issue the `ftp` command to start an FTP session, naming your FTP server as the server that you want to connect to:

```
$ ftp 192.168.0.99
Connected to 192.168.0.99 (192.168.0.99).
220 (vsFTPd 1.1.3)
Name (192.168.0.99:none):
```

In the above, recall that `192.168.0.99` is the IP address of the Linux server. You should get a `Name` login prompt like the one shown above – this is enough to confirm to us that the vsftpd server is running. Press *Ctrl-C* to terminate this FTP session and return to the command line.

Using Your FTP Server

Having installed and (briefly) tested our FTP server, we can begin to use it, and in this section we'll demonstrate a few uses. As we go, there are a number of configurations issues to consider, and in this section we'll take a look at five important configuration issues:

- ❏ Configuring for anonymous FTP server file download
- ❏ Configuring for anonymous FTP server file upload
- ❏ Creating a system account for per-user access to the FTP server
- ❏ Disabling local system user accounts
- ❏ Blocking FTP access for user accounts

We'll also show you how to configure an FTP greeting banner.

Configuring an Anonymous FTP Server for File Download

Anonymous users cannot read from just *any* directory on your Linux server. By default, the vsftpd package creates a directory tree starting at /var/ftp, and enables 'anonymous read access' to this directory and the directory structure beneath it.

To demonstrate this, we'll start by placing a test file on the FTP server so that other users can download it. Then, we'll adopt the role of one of these users, and run a client FTP session to access the FTP server, examine the contents of the FTP site, and download a copy of the test file.

Setting up the FTP Server

All we need to do here is place some test content somewhere under the /var/ftp directory, so that other users can access it. The owner of the /var/ftp is the root account, and by default is the only one with permission to write to the directory (recall from Chapter 8 that the *owner*, *group*, and *others* can all have different privileges on a directory or file).

353

So to start, use a command line to switch to the root user:

```
$ su -
Password:
```

Then you can place whatever content you want under the /var/ftp directory. For example, you can easily use a command such as echo to create a simple test file:

```
# cd /var/ftp/pub
# echo "This is the contents of a test file!" > test.txt
```

Here, we've created the file test.txt and placed it in the /pub subdirectory.

Using an FTP Client to Test Anonymous Read Access

Now you can test for anonymous read access, by using an FTP client to try to grab a copy of this test file via an FTP connection. You can use any FTP client, and you can test from a Windows or Linux machine – provided the client machine can see the FTP server across a network. (You can even use your Linux server as a client, if you have only one machine.)

For example, in both Windows and Linux you can use the ftp program at the command line. In the following, we'll use the ftp program as FTP client to connect to the FTP server, examine the contents of the FTP site, and then download the file test.txt:

1. Start by connecting to the FTP server. When you're prompted for a username, specify anonymous (as shown below) or ftp to indicate that you want anonymous access:

```
$ ftp 192.168.0.99
Connected to 192.168.0.99 (192.168.0.99).
220 (vsFTPd 1.1.3)
Name (192.168.0.99:none): anonymous
331 Please specify the password.
Password:
230 Login successful. Have fun.
Remote system type is UNIX.
Using binary mode to transfer files.
```

2. Now, we can start to examine the contents of the FTP site that are available to users with anonymous access. For example, here we'll use the ls command to examine the contents of the FTP root directory (which happens to be the directory /var/ftp on the server):

```
ftp>ls
227 Entering Passive Mode (192,168,0,99,69,34)
150 Here comes the directory listing.
drwxr-r-x    2 0        0            4096 Feb 28 13:40 pub
226 Directory send OK.
```

This shows that the root directory contains just one subdirectory, called pub. Now we'll use cd to change to this directory, and we'll list its contents:

```
ftp> cd pub
250 Directory successfully changed.
ftp> ls -al
227 Entering Passive Mode (192,168,0,99,56,125)
150 Here comes the directory listing.
drwxr-xr--x    2   0          0                 4096 Feb 28 13:40 .
drwxr-xr-x     3   0          0                 4096 Feb 27 19:15 ..
-rw-r--r--     1   0          0                   22 Feb 28 13:30 test.txt
226 Directory send OK.
```

3. Now, we'll attempt to download the test.txt file we've just located. To do this, we'll use the get command:

```
ftp> get test.txt
local: test.txt remote: test.txt
227 Entering Passive Mode (192,168,0,99,98,207)
150 Opening BINARY mode data connection for test.txt (22 bytes).
226 File send OK.
```

When the file is successfully downloaded, you should find it in your present working directory.

4. Finally, we'll end the session:

```
ftp> bye
221 Goodbye.
$
```

For more information about anonymous ftp, please refer to RFC 1635, which can be found at ftp://ftp.rfc-editor.org/in-notes/rfc1635.txt.

Configuring an Anonymous FTP Server for File Upload

In much the same way, anonymous FTP users can write only to the directories that we *allow* them to write to. By default, vsftpd does not allow users to upload to the FTP server at all; we must first configure the server to allow anonymous users write access to some directory.

So, we'll set up the FTP server for anonymous write access first; then we'll test it again using an FTP client.

Setting up the FTP Server for Anonymous Write Access

There are four steps here. We'll need to create the folder, set the appropriate permissions, and then enable uploading in the FTP server configuration:

1. First, we need to create a writeable directory. Again, you'll need the root account for this. Let's create a directory called /upload (in the /var/ftp/pub directory):

```
# cd /var/ftp/pub
# mkdir upload
```

2. Next, we need to set the permission of the upload directory so that it allows write-only access to anonymous FTP users (so that they can write to the directory but not to download from it – this restricts file sharing among FTP users). To do this, we'll first use the chgrp command to change the group associated with the upload directory:

```
# chgrp ftp upload
```

Now, the *owner* of the folder is still root, but the directory's group is ftp – the set of FTP users. Now we'll use the chmod command to assign read/write/execute access to the owner, write/access only to the group, and deny access to other users:

```
# chmod -R u=rwx,g=wx,o-rxw upload
```

3. Finally, we must configure the vsftpd server to allow anonymous upload. To do this, we simply edit the configuration file, /etc/vsftpd/vsftpd.conf. Open this file using gedit (or your favorite text editor), and locate the following lines:

```
# Uncomment this to allow the anonymous FTP user to upload files. This only
# has an effect if the above global write enable is activated. Also, you will
# obviously need to create a directory writable by the FTP user.
#anon_upload_enable=YES
```

Just remove the leading # character in the last line, and save the file:

```
anon_upload_enable=YES
```

4. Finally, restart the vsftpd service by using the **Restart** button in the **Server Configuration** dialog, or typing the following at the command line:

```
# service vsftpd restart
```

That's it. Now we're ready to test this configuration.

Using an FTP Client to Test Anonymous Write Access

So, let's test our configuration with another simple session on our FTP client:

1. Connect to the client and log in (using the username `anonymous` or `ftp`) as you did before:

```
$ ftp 192.168.0.99
Connected to 192.168.0.99 (192.168.0.99).
220 (vsFTPd 1.1.3)
Name (192.168.0.99:none): anonymous
331 Please specify the password.
Password:
230 Login successful. Have fun.
Remote system type is UNIX.
Using binary mode to transfer files.
```

2. Change directory to the `pub/upload` directory. Try to list its contents – you'll find that you can't, because that's the way we configured the permissions on the `upload` directory:

```
ftp> cd /pub/upload
250 Directory successfully changed.
ftp> ls
227 Entering Passive Mode (192,168,0,99,95,148)
150 Here comes the directory listing.
226 Transfer done (but failed to open directory).
```

3. However, you can upload a file. To prove it, use the `put` command to upload a simple file like this:

```
ftp> put uploadtest.txt
local: uploadtest.txt remote: uploadtest.txt
227 Entering Passive Mode (192,168,0,99,133,229)
150 Ok to send data.
226 File receive OK.
40 bytes send in 0.000101 secs (2.1e+02 Kbytes/sec)
```

4. That's it. Now you can close the FTP session:

```
ftp> bye
221 Goodbye.
#
```

Now you can go back to your FTP server and check the contents of the /var/ftp/pub/upload directory. You should find the uploadtest.txt file that was just uploaded from the client.

FTP Authentication via System Accounts

We've seen some examples using anonymous access to the vsftpd FTP server (via the anonymous or `ftp` username), but what happens if a user has a system account and tries to gain access? Well, by default, vsftpd allows this, and gives the user access to their home directory this way. For example, suppose your system has an account for the user called `eziodm`. This user can use an FTP client to log in and gain access to their home directory, `/home/eziodm`, via vsftpd like this:

```
# ftp 192.168.0.99
Connected to 192.168.0.99 (192.168.0.99).
220 (vsFTPd 1.1.3)
Name (192.168.0.99:none): eziodm
331 Please specify the password.
Password:
230 Login successful. Have fun.
Remote system type is UNIX.
Using binary mode to transfer files.
ftp> ls
      ...lists contents of /home/eziodm directory...
```

This can be useful, if your situation demands it. For example, you could set a machine up as a dedicated FTP server and create an account for each user that needs to perform FTP:

```
# useradd -m -d /home/eddiew
# passwd eddiew
Changing password for user eddiew.
New password:
Retype new password:
passwd: all authentication tokens updated successfully.
```

Thereby you assign each user their own individual FTP space.

Disabling Local System User Accounts for FTP

By default, these users would have the same permissions to read, write, and execute the contents of their home directory via FTP that they would have if they were accessing the directory by sitting at the computer. More importantly, authentication via FTP is not encrypted, so allowing FTP access via user accounts is actually *not* a good way to allow access to your system if you've got anything sensitive to protect.

Therefore, in most situations it's recommended that you *disable* FTP access via user accounts. This is easy to do – you just change the appropriate setting in the configuration file, `/etc/vsftpd/vsftpd.conf`. When you open the file, locate the following lines:

```
# Uncomment this to allow local users to log in.
local_enable=YES
```

Change the directive to read as follows:

```
local_enable=NO
```

Then restart the vsftpd service using the **Server Configuration** dialog, or typing the following at the command line:

```
# service vsftpd restart
```

Now, if you try using an FTP client to gain FTP access via a system user account, you'll be refused:

```
$ ftp 192.168.0.99
Connected to 192.168.0.99 (192.168.0.99).
220 (vsFTPd 1.1.3)
Name (192.168.0.99:none): eziodm
530 This FTP server is anonymous only.
Login failed.
```

Blocking FTP Access for User Accounts

Alternatively, we can deny FTP access to individual users (rather than to all users). We control this using the file /etc/vsftpd.ftpusers file, which contains the list of users that are *not* allowed FTP access to the server.

To try this, first change the local_enable directive back from NO to YES, in /etc/vsftpd/vsftpd.conf, to enable FTP access via system accounts:

```
# Uncomment this to allow local users to log in.
local_enable=YES
```

Then, open the /etc/vsftpd.ftpusers file (using root privileges), add an account name at the bottom, and save the file. There's no need to restart the vsftpd service; changes to the /etc/vsftpd.ftpusers file take effect immediately.

Then use the account to try to gain FTP access via an FTP client:

```
# ftp 192.168.0.99
Connected to 192.168.0.99 (192.168.0.99).
220 (vsFTPd 1.1.3)
Name (192.168.0.99:none): eziodm
331 Please specify the password.
Password:
530 Login incorrect.
Login failed.
```

Configuring an FTP Greeting Banner

Once you've installed the vsftpd FTP server, there are all sorts of ways you can configure it to behave as you want. Here's a simple example. We can change the default greeting message that the FTP server issues to clients on connection, simply by changing the value of the `ftpd_banner` directive in `/etc/vsftpd/vsftpd.conf`: For example, try changing it to this:

```
# You may fully customize the login banner string:
ftpd_banner=Welcome to the Wrox Press FTP service.
```

Then restart the vsftpd service, so that the change takes effect. Now use your FTP client to log in to the FTP server, and you'll be greeted with this new message:

```
$ ftp 192.168.0.99
Connected to 192.168.0.99 (192.168.0.99).
220 Welcome to the Wrox Press FTP service.
...
```

For more information about the vsftpd FTP server, and all the configuration possibilities, refer to the man pages by typing `man vsftpd` and `man vsftpd.conf`. You can find also more information about the vsftpd FTP server at http://vsftpd.beasts.org/.

Setting up a Print Server

If you want to share a single printer (or group of printers) among a number of users, then what you need is a **print server**. The print server manages the print requests and puts them into a queue for processing. It can manage:

❑ Sharing of printers between many users

❑ Authentication, so that only permitted users can print to a given printer

❑ Print queues

❑ Configuration of many printers in a single location

In this section we will examine how to configure our Linux machine as a print server for managing print jobs.

Print Servers on Redhat Linux 9

Red Hat Linux 9 provides two different print server software packages: cups and LPRng. The **LPRng** package relates the old line printer daemon, and while popular for many years is now being superseded by the more recent **Common UNIX Printing System** (**CUPS**). CUPS is a printing service for Unix-based platforms, capable of managing printer jobs and queues and supporting network printer browsing.

The Red Hat Linux 9 installation process should install the cups package by default. To check, launch the RPM (for example, using Main Menu | System Settings | Add/Remove Applications), locate the Printing Support package group, which is under the System category, click its Details button, and ensure that the checkbox (next to the cups option) is checked:

Click Close to exit this dialog, and Update to update the installed packages. If necessary, you'll be prompted to insert Red Hat Linux distribution CDs to complete the installation.

Installing a Printer

When you first install CUPS, you get a default set of sample configuration files at /etc/cups. However, it's easier to manage your printers using Printer Configuration tool that is provided by Red Hat. Each printer has its own **print queue**, so we configure the print server by using the Printer Configuration tool to add a print queue for each printer.

1. To start the Printer Configuration tool, select Main Menu | System Settings | Printing or type the following command at the command line:

```
$ redhat-config-printer
```

It will ask for the root password, unless you were already logged in with administrative privileges. The Printer Configuration window will appear:

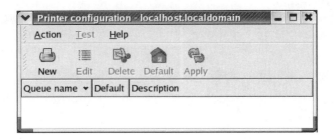

2. To add a print queue for a new printer, click on **New** button. This will open the **Add a new print queue** wizard. Click **Forward** to get past the splash screen.

3. The first thing you're prompted for is the name of the print queue you want to add. Type a unique name for the printer (for example, something like **prntr_queue-1**). If you want, you can also type a description, which will help you to identify the printer. Click **Forward**.

4. The next screen allows you to choose the queue type from the following options:

Label	Type	Description
Locally-connected	LOCAL	For a printer attached directly to your computer through a parallel or USB port
Networked CUPS	IPP	For a printer attached to a different CUPS system and accessible through TCP/IP
Networked Unix	LPD	For a printer attached to a remote Unix system and accessible through TCP/IP

Label	Type	Description
Networked Windows	SMB	For a printer attached to a remote Windows system and accessible through a Samba share
Networked Novell	NCP	For a printer attached to a remote Novell Netware system
Networked JetDirect	JETDIRECT	For a printer connected directly to the network with its own IP address

In this demonstration, we'll demonstrate the LOCAL queue type. If you have a locally-connected printer, select Locally-connected, and select a device from the list (such as /dev/lp0). Then click Forward.

If you have a networked computer, select one of the other options and follow the wizard to complete the configuration.

5. Next, you'll be prompted to select the make and model of your printer. When you've done that, click Forward, and the wizard will confirm the details you've selected.

6. The new printer will now appear in the printer list in the main window. You'll also see the following dialog:

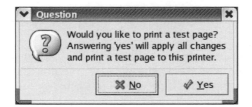

Clicking Yes will save the configuration changes to the /etc/printcap configuration file, restart the lpd printer daemon, and print a test page:

Configuring Printers

The Printer Configuration provides a number of options for managing printers. For example, you can edit or remove the properties of a printer queue by selecting the queue and clicking Edit or Delete. You can also configure a particular printer to be the default by clicking on the Default button. Whenever you make any changes, you must save them by clicking on the Apply button (which also restarts the cupsd printer daemon to take account of your changes).

You can also test a printer from the Printer Configuration tool, by choosing a printer and selecting any of the test configurations from the Test menu.

Starting (and Stopping) the Printer Daemon

To control the cupsd printer daemon, we can once again use the Service Configuration GUI. However, you may never need to do this manually – the service is configured to start automatically on system start-up by default, and restarts automatically if you change its configuration via the Printer Configuration tool.

If you do need to control the service manually, you can do it using the Service Configuration GUI (as we've described in other sections of this chapter – the service in question is called cups), or by using the service command at the command line to control the cups script:

```
# service cups
Usage: cupsd {start|stop|restart|condrestart|reload|status}
# service cups restart
Stopping cups:                                      [OK]
Starting cups:                                      [OK]
```

Printing from Applications

By default, all applications send printing requests to the default printer configured on the system; but of course, if there are more printers available then the application's Print dialog allows you to choose which print queue to send the job to.

For example, if you're printing a word-processed document from OpenOffice's OpenWriter application, then you'd do so by selecting its File | Print option from the menu bar. When you do that, you get a Print dialog like this:

As you can see, the application offers you a list of printers to choose from – the list shown above includes an entry for the prntr_queue-1 printer that we configured earlier. It also includes a **Generic Printer** entry – if you choose this, then the application will send the print job to your "default" printer (the one that your machine is configured to use automatically).

You'll need to configure the "default" printer before you use if for the first time; you can do this through the Openoffice Printer Setup tool. Select
Main Menu | Office | Openoffice.org Printer Setup, select the **Generic Printer** entry in that dialog, and click the **Properties** button:

In the resulting **Properties of Generic Printer** dialog, the default command in the **Select Command** section is lpr – this will send printer jobs via the `lpr` command to `/dev/lp0` as the default print queue. Change the command to lpr -P *printername*, where *printername* is the name you gave to your printer. Then click **OK** to save these settings.

Now you can return to your OpenWriter application, select **File | Print**, and select the **Generic Printer** option in the Print dialog to send the job to that printer.

Creating Print Jobs at the Command Line

The `lpr` utility that we've just seen can also be used to create print requests from command line. For example, if you want to print a text document called `addreses.txt`, contained in the present working directory, you can do so by typing the following at the command line:

```
$ lpr addreses.txt
```

We can also examine and control existing print jobs via the `lpq` and `lprm` command line utilities of the CUPS software suite. The `lpq` command allows us to view the contents of the print queue, and can be used as follows:

```
$ lpq
ptntr_queue-1 is ready and printing
Rank       Owner     Job     File(s)              Total Size
active     root       1      testprint.ps         15630 bytes
1st        kapils     2      (stdid)              5761024 bytes
2nd        eziodm     3      (stdid)              193536 bytes
3rd        eziodm     3      addresses.txt        1024 bytes
```

If we want to cancel a print job, we can use the `lprm` command. For example, to remove the job with ID `838` from the print queue, we can issue the following command:

```
# lprm 838
```

Of course, if you try to cancel another user's print job, and you don't have permission to do so, then CUPS will prevent you from canceling it. For example, suppose the user `eziodm` tried to cancel job 2 in the list above:

```
# lprm 2
lprm: You don't own job ID 2!
```

You can learn more about the CUPS printing system at http://www.cups.org/.

Setting up a File Server

A **file server** is essentially a shared storage space. File servers are generally accessed across a network, and provide its users with a central location for file storage. File systems are also helpful when you need to share files with other users: you can simply place your file in a public directory on the file server, where other users can access it.

Like FTP servers, there are essentially two fundamental components to a file server – the *storage* space itself and the mechanism for *accessing* it. Whether you're working on a single machine at home, or as part of a large network in a major organization, you'll be using a file system to *store* your files; what a file server adds to this is the notion that the file system is a shared one, accessible by (possibly) many users.

There are a number of benefits to be gained by implementing a file server:

❑ It reduces administration cost. Instead of having important data stored on many individual PCs (all of which would require backing up), you can store *all* your important data in one place (on the file server). Then, only the file server needs regular backing up.

❑ It provides the opportunity to enforce a more controlled and focused security policy, because the security policy needs only to be applied to the file server.

❑ It enables you to provide a more stable and reliable storage solution. It enables you to implement your storage solution on high-spec machines that provide high levels of uptime. Moreover, implementation of RAID or of mirrored SCSI disks (which help ensure data reliability) is more feasible on a central file server than on many PCs.

❑ There's also something to be gained in terms of cost of file storage (although this is less pertinent in these days of cheap storage). First, it makes best use of the available storage capacity by making it accessible to all users. Second, it provides a central repository from which common resources can be made available to all (eliminating the need for each user to store their own copy).

Once you've got a file system, what makes it a file server is the mechanism that enables the file system to be shared. There is plenty of software around for this purpose – Samba, the Network File System (NFS), the Andrew file system (AFS), and Coda are all examples. Some of these are shipped as part of the Red Hat Linux 9 distribution, and we're going to focus on one in particular – Samba.

For more information on the others, see http://www.nfsv4.org, http://www.transarc.com/Product/EFS/AFS/index.html, and http://www.coda.cs.cmu.edu.

An Overview of Samba

Samba is an implementation of the Windows SMB and CIFS protocols on Unix. The Samba project was started by Andrew Tridgell, who wanted to mount his Unix server disk space onto a DOS PC. When he'd solved the problem, Tridgell discovered that what he'd built was an implementation of the SMB (server message block) protocol – a protocol for sharing files and other resources. Tridgell named his implementation Samba, and published version 1.0 in early 1992. Since that time, the Samba project has grown tremendously, and today there is still Samba development going on in the open source community.

So, Samba is a collection of programs that make it possible to share files and printers between computers equipped to use the SMB protocol – Windows by default, Linux/Unix with Samba, and (more recently) Mac OS X. Samba is freely available under GNU General Public License, and is included as part of the Red Hat Linux 9 distribution.

In this section we'll take a look at how to install Samba, perform some basic configuration, and set up a shared file server on a Linux machine. We'll also see how to use Samba to access a Linux-hosted file server from a Linux or Windows machine, and how to access a Windows-hosted file server from a Linux machine.

There should be enough in this section to get you started working with file servers in Linux. If you want to explore further with SMB and Samba, try http://www.samba.org (and specifically http://www.samba.org/cifs/docs/what-is-smb.html).

Installing SAMBA

Again, perhaps the easiest way to install the Samba software suite is via the RPM GUI tool. Once you've started the RPM (for example, by selecting Main Menu | System Settings | Add/Remove Applications), use the Package Management dialog to locate the Windows File Server package group (which you will find under the Servers category). Ensure its checkbox is checked. If you like, click on its Details button to see the package details:

As you can see, there are two standard packages: samba and samba-client. Click on Close, and then click on Update to start the installation. You'll need the disk from your Red Hat Linux 9 distribution to complete the installation.

Starting and Stopping the Samba Service

As with other services we've seen, there are a number of ways to start and stop the Samba service. Once again, we can do so via the Service Configuration GUI tool. To launch the tool, select Main Menu | System Settings | Server Settings | Services or type the following command at the command line:

```
$ redhat-config-services
```

368

Then locate the **smb** service, as shown here:

If the service is stopped (as shown here), then start it by clicking the Start button. It's also a good idea to check the checkbox, to configure the samba service to start automatically whenever you boot up the system. For example, if you ever have to perform an emergency reboot on your file server, then the "automatic start" configuration means that the file server is immediately available to users after the reboot. When you've done this, select File |Save Changes to save your new setting.

Alternatively, you can also stop and start **smb** service at the command line, using the `service` command to run the /etc/rc.d/init.d/smb script we mentioned earlier. Typing the script name at the command line like this reveals the possible usages:

```
# service smb
Usage: /etc/rc.d/smb {start|stop|restart|reload|status|condrestart}
```

As you can see, it works in much the same way as the `httpd` and `vsftpd` scripts we've seen in earlier sections of this chapter. So, to start the service we'd type this:

```
# service smb start
Starting SMB services:                                      [  OK  ]
Starting NMB services:                                      [  OK  ]
```

This command starts both SMB and NMB (NetBIOS name server), which are both services related to Samba. To stop the service, we'd type this:

```
# service smb stop
Shutting down SMB services:                                 [  OK  ]
Shutting down NMB services:                                 [  OK  ]
```

You get the idea. Note, however, that this script only allows you to control the service manually. It doesn't allow you to configure the service to start automatically on boot-up – for that, you need the Service Configuration GUI that we described above.

Samba Configuration Files and Utilities

We won't take a look at every single item that is installed during the process described above, but it is worth pointing out some of the most important files, both to get an idea of Samba's capabilities and because we'll be using some of these files and programs later in this section. Specifically of interest to us here are Samba's configuration files and programs.

Samba's **configuration files** are contained in the directory /etc/samba. Here's a brief description of the the Samba configuration files that you'll find there:

Configuration File	Description
smb.conf	This is the main configuration file for Samba.
lmhosts	This contains Samba's NetBIOS-to-IP address mappings.
secrets.tdb	This is the Samba secrets database. It stores private information such as the local SID and machine trust password. It is generated by machine and cannot be read in a text editor.
smbusers	This is a text file that maps your Linux system's users to various SMB-specific usernames.
smbpasswd	This is an encrypted password file. The format of this file is very similar to that of the passwd file we met in Chapter 8. This file doesn't exist when you first install Samba, but is created when you add Samba users.

In order to work with file servers through Samba, we can use its many **programs**. Here's a list of some of the most important utilities provided by Samba. They're all contained in the directory /usr/bin, and we'll be using some of them later in this section:

Program	Purpose
smbclient	This is an FTP-like client, used to access SMB/CIFS resources on a file server.
smbadduser	This is a script, used for adding Samba users. It updates the smbusers and smbpasswd files.
smbpasswd	This changes a Samba user's SMB password. It is similar to the Unix passwd command that we met in Chapter 8.

Program	Purpose
smbmount	This is used to mount an SMB filesystem.
smbumount	This is used to unmount an SMB file system.
smbstatus	This lists the current Samba connections.
testparm	This checks the smb.conf configuration file for correctness.
nmblookup	This is used to query NetBIOS names and map them to IP addresses in a network using NetBIOS over TCP/IP.

In addition, we'll also make use of the script /etc/rc.d/init.d/smb, which we use to start and stop the Samba file service.

Samba Configuration with SWAT

If you open the Samba configuration files using gedit (or any text editor), you'll see that the information and syntax used is rather complex. It is possible to configure Samba by editing these files in a text editor, but if you're not familiar with it then it can be quite difficult and prone to error.

Samba provides a number of command-line utilities for configuration too (some of which we mentioned above), but perhaps the easiest way to configure Samba is by using the **Samba Web Administration Tool** (**SWAT**). SWAT is a web-based interface, which means that you can use it to configure and manage your Samba server through a web browser – if you want, you can even do it remotely across a network or even across the Internet.

> *If you are thinking of using SWAT for remote Samba management, you should note that SWAT will transmit your username and password in clear text when you log in. Across and insecure connection, this presents the risk that an unwelcome visitor could sniff out your login credentials and use them to ill effect. To avoid this, you should only use SWAT from within a secure network. In fact, as we'll see shortly, SWAT's default configuration makes it available only at http://localhost:901.*

Let's see how to install SWAT and start the SWAT service. When we've done that, we'll be ready to use SWAT to configure Samba and set up our file server for use.

Installing SWAT

Red Hat Linux 9's **Package Management** GUI tool doesn't provide an option for installing the SWAT package. Instead, we must install this package via the RPM's command line utility. the SWAT utility is made available through the samba-swat package. Here's how to install the samba-swat package at the command line:

371

1. Launch a terminal window, and switch to the root user account by using this command:

    ```
    $ su -
    ```

2. Insert Red Hat Linux 9 distribution Disk 2. Change to the directory on the CD that contains the RPM package files:

    ```
    # cd /mnt/cdrom/RedHat/RPMS
    ```

    If you get a No such file or directory message, it's probably because the CD wasn't mounted automatically when you inserted it. In this case, mount the CD manually:

    ```
    # mount /dev/cdrom
    ```

    Then try the above cd command again.

3. Use the ls command to find out the exact version of samba-swat contained on the disk. For example:

    ```
    # ls samba-swat*.rpm
    samba-swat-2.2.7a-6.i386.rpm
    ```

    If this command doesn't find any matches, then remove the disk, replace it with Disk 1 or Disk 2, and return to Step 2.

4. Install the samba-swat package you've just found, by using the rpm command:

    ```
    # rpm -ivh samba-swat-2.2.7a-6.i386.rpm
    Preparing...              ###########################################
    [100%]
          1:samba-swat        ###########################################
    [100%]
    ```

    Alternatively, view the available package files on your disk by using the Nautilus file manager GUI to navigate to /mnt/cdrom/Redhat/RPMS. Locate the file matching the name samba-swat-*.rpm. Double-click on this file – this action will open RPM GUI tool, from which you can install the package.

Starting the SWAT Service

Starting the SWAT service is a two step process:

1. Launch gedit or your favorite text editor, and open the file /etc/xinetd.d/swat. This is the configuration file for the SWAT service, and it looks like this:

```
# default: off
# description: SWAT is the Samba Web Admin Tool. Use swat \
#              to configure your Samba server. To use SWAT, \
#              connect to port 901 with your favorite web browser.
service swat
{
        port            = 901
        socket_type     = stream
        wait            = no
        only_from       = 127.0.0.1
        user            = root
        server          = /usr/sbin/swat
        log_on_failure  += USERID
        disable         = yes
}
```

Change `disable` value, like this:

```
        disable         = no
```

Save the file, and close your text editor.

As an aside, note that this default configuration ensures that the SWAT service will only be accessible through the IP address 127.0.0.1, and on port 901. The IP address 127.0.0.1 is a special address known as the loopback address, because requests to http://127.0.0.1 are sent to the web server on the same *machine as the browser from which the request is made. Hence, by default, SWAT is only available from the file server machine itself – via http://127.0.0.1:901 or http://localhost:901 (as we mentioned earlier in the chapter).*

2. Restart the xinetd service. (We must do this because SWAT runs as an xinetd service. The xinetd service is out of scope of this book, but it is enough to know that its purpose is to support Internet services such as SWAT). To do this, first launch the **Service Configuration** GUI tool by selecting **Main Menu | System Settings | Server Settings | Services**:

Then locate and select the service called **xinetd**, and click **Restart**. You'll get a dialog to confirm that the restart was successful; then you can exit the tool by clicking on **Quit**.

Using SWAT for the First Time

Now we can test SWAT. Open a browser on the Linux server and type in the URL http://localhost:901. You'll be prompted for a username and password – use the system's root username and password. Then you should see the SWAT **HOME** page:

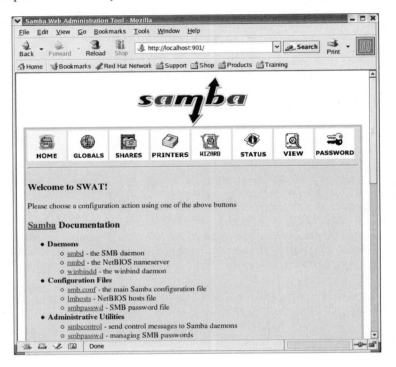

Note that this page contains the index of Samba's very comprehensive online documentation (as shown above), where you can find out much more about Samba and SWAT. There are also eight buttons listed across the top of this page, which provide access to SWAT's various utilities:

- ❏ **HOME** – the home page of SWAT, and the first page that you see when you fire up the SWAT interface.

- ❏ **GLOBALS** – for setting the global variable values of the /etc/samba/smb.conf configuration file

- ❏ **SHARES** – for creating and deleting Samba shares, and setting Samba parameters

- ❏ **PRINTERS** – for creating and deleting Samba printer shares and setting printer parameters

- ❑ **WIZARD** – like **GLOBALS**, this is also for setting various values in `/etc/samba/smb.conf`
- ❑ **STATUS** – for viewing the Samba server's status, and starting and stopping Samba-related services
- ❑ **VIEW** – for viewing the content of the `/etc/samba/smb.conf` configuration file
- ❑ **PASSWORD** – for adding, removing, enabling, and disabling Samba users, and for setting Samba users' passwords

Our SWAT is up and running, and ready to use; our next task is to use it to configure the Linux machine as a file server. To do that, we'll make use of some of the features listed above. Then, when we've set up the file server, we'll examine it from the client's perspective, by looking at how different clients use Samba to access the file server we've created.

Adding a Samba User

To grant a system account access to the Samba services, you can use SWAT's **PASSWORD** feature. Once you've logged into SWAT using the root username and password, click the **PASSWORD** button, and you'll see the following screen:

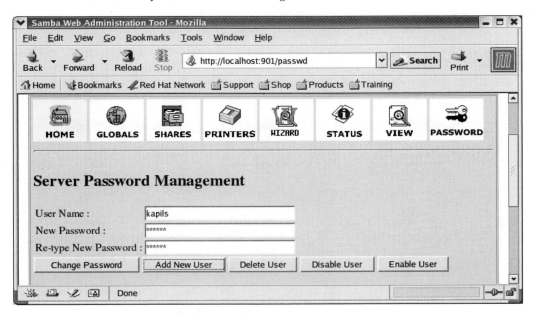

In the **Server Password Management** section, enter the name of an *existing account* on the system, and supply a password (we've already done this in the screenshot above, where we're creating Samba access for the user kapils). Then click the **Add New User** button. This will add an entry to Samba's `smbpasswd` configuration file, to indicate that this user has access to Samba's services.

Note that normal accounts that have access to the Samba services also *have access to SWAT. However, only root users have access to the full range of SWAT's utilities; normal users are only allowed to use limited features contained in the* HOME, STATUS, VIEW, *and* PASSWORD *screens.*

Creating and Configuring a Samba Share

Now we're ready to configure our Linux server as a file server, by creating a **share** (a dedicated directory on the server that will be accessible to other users). We can do all this using SWAT:

1. Create a directory, which we'll call /share, to be used for the file server. With root permission, you can do this at the command line using this command:

```
# mkdir /share
```

2. If you haven't done so already, use the Mozilla browser (or your favorite web browser) to browse to the SWAT home page at http://localhost:901, and log in using the root user account.

3. Click on the GLOBALS toolbar icon. In the Base Options section, use the Workgroup field to enter the name of the workgroup that you want your server to appear in when clients use it. (If you haven't set up a workgroup, then this is probably the default value, WORKGROUP). You should also name the service, by entering a value in the server string field – it can be any string that you want your Samba clients to see. We'll stick with the default, Samba Server:

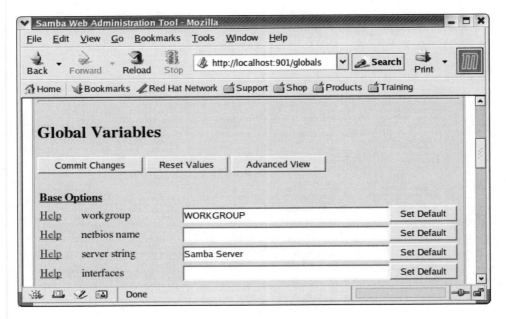

Click on **Commit Changes** to save your changes to the configuration files.

4. Now click on SHARES toolbar button at the top of the screen. We'll share our /share directory by giving it a **share name**; let's call it linuxbox-share. You should first check the entries in the drop-down list on this page, to ensure that your chosen share name hasn't already been used for a different share; then, enter the share name in the **Create Share** field:

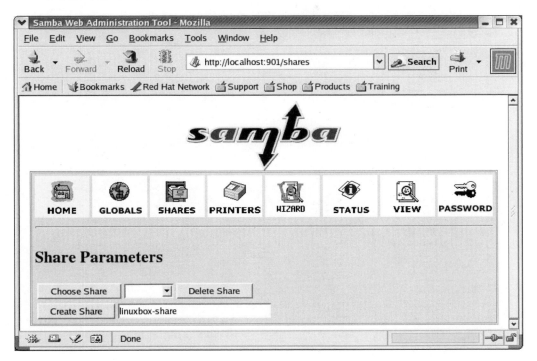

Now click on **Create Share** button to create the share. This will present you with another screen in which you can specify the properties of your share. You will certainly need to set the **path** field to the path of your share directory (in this example, it's /share). In the screenshot below, we've also specifically set a number of other fields:

Here, we've set the read only field to No to make it a writeable share; the browseable field to Yes, to allow the contents of the /share directory to be visible; and the available field to Yes, to "enable" the share (that is, make it available to users). We've also added a comment to remind us what the share is for.

When you're done, click on the Commit Changes button to commit these settings to the Samba configuration file.

If you like, you can click on the Advanced View button in the SHARES screen to set further settings (for example, you can insert a space-delimited list of users into the valid users or invalid users textboxes, to control which users are allowed or denied access to the Samba share). You can also click the VIEW button to view the complete contents of the /etc/samba/smb.conf configuration file.

5. Restart the Samba service, so that the configuration changes can take effect. To do this, click on STATUS button and then click on the Restart smbd button to restart the service. Wait for the page to reload, and then click on the Restart nmbd button to restart that service too.

Accessing the Share from a Windows NT/2000/XP Machine

Now we have a Samba share configured on our Linux server, we can access it from a range of other machines on the network. To access the share from a Windows system, you can browse to it using Windows' Network Neighborhood, and even map it to a network drive using Tools | Map Network Drive.

Accessing the Share from Another Linux Machine

You can also access your Linux file system share from any SMB-equipped client machine – for example, from another Linux machine. To do this, the client machine can use functionality that is contained within the Samba client package. In fact, there are two different applications that you can use to access your Linux file share across the network from an SMB-equipped client machine:

❑ You can use the smbclient command, which provides an FTP-like interface to perform the same functionalities like FTP

❑ If you're client machine is a Linux machine, you can use the smbmount command to mount the remote smb share as a local directory

To access an smb share via a remote machine, you will need to know the username and password of a samba user account on the remote samba server machine (like the kapils account we created earlier). Let's see how we can use this account, with smbclient or smbmount, to access the remote Samba share.

The smbclient Utility

If you're using a client Linux machine to access your Samba share, you can do so using the smbclient utility. To do this for the share we've created here, we'd run the following command at the command line:

```
$ smbclient //linuxserver/linuxbox-share -U kapils
added interface ip=192.168.0.114 bcast=192.168.0.255 nmask=255.255.255.0
Password:
Domain[WORKGROUP] OS=[Unix] Server=[Samba2.2.7a]
smb: />
```

In the smbclient command, we needed to specify two things:

❑ The name of the file server and the name of the share

❑ The name of the user we're using to access the share (that is, a user that we created using the SWAT facility's PASSWORD screen earlier in the section)

Note that you're prompted for a password. When the password authentication with samba server is successful, you will get an smbclient session, which looks rather similar to an FTP session. You can see above that the prompt for the session is smb: />. Now you can use all the available commands to work with the files in the remote file system:

```
smb: \>ls
temp1.txt       temp2.txt       temp3.txt
```

To get a list of all the commands you can use through the smbclient session, type `help` at the prompt:

```
smb: \>help
?       altname   archive    blocksize    cancel
cd      chmod     chown      del          dir
du      exit      get        help         directory
...
```

For more on using Samba shares via an smbclient session, see the documentation at http://us3.samba.org/samba/ftp/docs/htmldocs/smbclient.1.html. To exit the smbclient session, type `exit` at the `smb: \>` prompt.

The smbmount Utility (Mounting an SMB Share Locally)

The `smbmount` utility allows you to mount a (possibly) remote smb share on a client Linux computer. You can try this out if you have two Linux machines networked together – use the one with the Samba share as the server and the other one as the client. Alternatively, you can also try this out if you've only got single Linux machine – in this case the machine acts as both file server and as client of its own service.

The `smbmount` application uses a helper application called `smbmnt`, and the first thing to do is change the permissions on `smbmnt` so that your `smbmount` command can use it. By default, `smbmnt`'s permissions allow it to be used only by the root user of the machine on which it is running. Assuming you're using the client machine as a normal user, you'll need to use the root account to adjust these permissions, like this:

```
$ su -
Password:
# chmod s+u /usr/bin/smbmnt
```

You can check the new permissions, like this:

```
# ls -l /usr/bin/smbmnt
-rwsr-xr-x    1 root    root     491096    Jan 10   00.05    /usr/bin/smbmnt
```

Now you're ready to test smbmount. Change back to your normal user account, and create the directory onto which you want to mount the Samba share:

```
# exit
$ mkdir /home/kapils/mnt
$ mkdir /home/kapils/mnt/remote
```

Here, we're using the local `kapils` account on the client machine, and we've created a directory called `mnt/remote` underneath this user's home directory `/home/kapils`.

Now, run the `smbmount` command to mount the remote Samba share on the local directory:

```
$ smbmount //linuxserver/linuxbox-share /home/kapils/mnt/remote -o username=kapils
Password:
```

Here, `linuxserver` is the name of the Linux server that is hosting the Samba share, and `linuxbox-share` is the name of the share; `/home/kapils/mnt/remote` is the mount point we've chosen; and `kapils` is the name of the Samba user on the Linux server. You're prompted for the password of the Samba user.

When you've done this, and assuming the connection is good, you can navigate the contents of the Samba share as if they were contents of the mount point. For example:

```
$ ls /home/kapils/mnt/remote
temp1.txt        temp2.txt        temp3.txt
```

To unmount, you can use the `smbumount` command. However, like `smbmnt`, you may first need to use the client machine's root account to change the permissions on `smbumount`:

```
# chmod s+u /usr/bin/smbumount
```

Now you can safely unmount the share from your mount point, using your normal user account:

```
$ smbmount /home/kapils/mnt/remote
```

Accessing NT Shares from a Linux Machine

We've talked about how to set up and access a Linux-hosted Samba share, but what about if we want to use a Linux client machine to access a file system hosted by a Windows server? In fact, we can access Windows NT shares in the same way that we access Linux shares.

For example, suppose we have a Windows NT machine called `winserver`, which acts as a file server by hosting a share called `salesarchive`. We can treat the contents of this share as if it were part of the client machine's file system, by mounting it just as we've done before.

First, we'll need a directory that will act as out mount point. For example, let's create a local directory called `sales`, under our user's home directory:

```
$ mkdir /home/kapils/mnt/sales
```

Next, we use `smbmount` to mount the file system onto the mount point:

```
% su -
Password:
# smbmount //winserver/salesarchive /home/kapils/mnt/sales -o username=kapils
Password:
```

There are two points to note here. First, the normal user does not have permission to mount a filesystem, so we must change to root user before using smbmount. Second, the smbmount command itself requires that you specify a username and password. This username corresponds not necessarily to a user on the Linux machine, but to a network user that has permission to access the share.

Having achieved a connection, you can work with the files on the remote file server as if they were part of the local directory:

```
$ cd /home/kapils/mnt/sales
$ ls
sales2002Q2      sales2002Q3      sales2002Q4
sales2003Q1      salesnotes.txt
```

Your permissions on the contents of this folder will depend on the permissions assigned to the network user whose account you specified in the smbmount command. To unmount the share, use smbumount again:

```
# smbumount /home/kapils/mnt/sales
```

Accessing SMB/CIFS Shares Using Nautilus

We can even use Nautilus file manager to access SMB/CIFS resources such as like Windows and Linux Samba shares. To access Samba shares using Nautilus, first launch a Nautilus window (for example, by selecting Main Menu | Run Program and typing nautilus).

Then type smb: in the Location bar. This will cause Nautilus to show you a list of all local domains and workgroups. From here, double-click on the workgroup of your Windows machine, and then on name of the Windows machine itself, to view all directory shares on that machine.

If you are connecting to smb shares that require a username and password, you can specify the username and password within Nautilus's Location bar. In this example, the Location bar with username and password should look like this:

smb://kapil:*password*@winserver/salesarchive/

After successful authentication, Nautilus will show you all the files under that share:

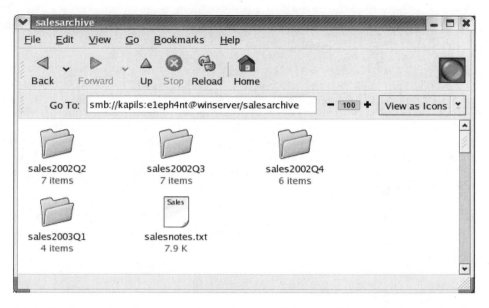

There's a lot to Samba, and we've covered only a little of the detail here. For more depth, take a look at Samba's software suite manual pages (using the man command), the SWAT documentation (on the HOME page of your SWAT tool), and the Samba official web site (http://www.samba.org). You must always check your firewall settings for SWAT port. Firewall must be configured to open port 901 for SWAT.

Setting up a Mail Server

For many of us, e-mail has become an essential part of life. When you send an e-mail, it is a **mail server** that is responsible for dispatching that mail to its intended destination; and at the other end, another mail server receives that message and passes it on to the appropriate mailbox.

A mail server can be configured to handle small home network e-mails, or large complex networks with hundreds of users. Many home users tend to use the mail server provided by their ISP. Many medium-to-large organizations host their own mail servers.

It's unlikely that you'll need to set up your own mail server, but in some situations there are good reasons for doing so. For example:

❏ Your mail server will be on the same network as your client machine, and so connection between your client machine and mail server will be much faster.

❏ If you have a dial-up connection (rather than a dedicated Internet connection), then having your own mail server allow you to work on your e-mail without ever having to connect manually to the Internet. You can configure our email server to send and receive mail in batches, by connecting to Internet at specified times.

❑ You can customize a mail server's security and monitoring rules, so that it alerts you if it receives a message that contains certain blocked words or if it detects unusual activity.

Hosting your own mail server comes with its burdens, too. There's the increased cost of support and maintenance, and the additional chance of being compromised (you're protected from this if you use an ISP's mail server). It's also more important to ensure that you keep your antivirus software up to date, and that it scans each e-mail. And there is a risk that your mail server will become an open relay SMTP server (this is where another user uses your mail server as a gateway for sending mail).

So, there's much to consider, and debate of these issues is outside the scope of this book. However, if you do decide to host your own mail server, then you won't be surprised to learn that the Red Hat Linux 9 operating system comes with a default mail server. It's called **Sendmail**, and we'll examine it briefly here.

What Is a Mail Server?

A **mail server** is a collection of applications that provide the functionality to manage the tasks of sending and receiving of e-mail, and delivering e-mail to user's mailboxes. A mail server uses a number of different protocols to transfer e-mail from one system to other. Here's a brief description of these protocols:

❑ The **Internet Message Access Protocol** (**IMAP**) is a protocol used by an e-mail client application to access the remote e-mail mailbox. The main advantage of IMAP is that users can manage the e-mail messages on remote mailboxes instead of downloading the messages on to local machine. For more information about IMAP, take a look at http://www.imap.org/.

❑ The **Post Office Protocol** (**POP**) is used by e-mail clients to download e-mail messages from a remote server and save it on their local machine. For more information about POP, please refer to RFC 1939 at http://www.rfc-editor.org/in-notes/rfc1939.txt.

❑ The **Simple Mail Transfer Protocol** (**SMTP**) is used to send e-mails (this is in contrast with IMAP and POP, which are used to *receive* e-mails). Each e-mail message is transferred between remote e-mail servers using SMTP. Red Hat Linux 9 uses sendmail as its default SMTP software.

E-mail Application Types

E-mail applications fall into the following three class:

❑ **Mail User Agents** (**MUAs**). An MUA is an e-mail client – a program that is used to retrieve and manage e-mail messages via POP or IMAP protocols. Examples of MUAs on Linux systems include **pine**, **mutt**, Ximian's **Evolution**, and **Mozilla Mail**. Microsoft's Outlook is also an MUA.

❑ **Mail Transfer Agents** (**MTAs**). An MTA transfers e-mail messages between different machines using SMTP. During the course of its journey from source to destination, an e-mail message may transfer between several MTAs, hosted on different platforms. On Linux systems, **sendmail**, **postfix**, **exim**, and **qmail** are four different MTA applications. Red Hat Linux 9 uses `sendmail` as its default MTA.

❑ **Mail Delivery Agents** (**MDAs**). An MDA is used to deliver email messages to users' mailboxes. An MTA delivers messages to an MDA, which is then responsible for delivering it to the specified mailbox. Some MTAs (such as `sendmail`) can also act as MDA. On Linux systems, example MDAs include **sendmail**, **procmail**, and **/bin/mail**. MDAs are sometimes also known as **LDAs** (**local delivery agents**).

On Red Hat Linux 9, Sendmail is both the MTA and MDA by default.

Why Sendmail?

In this section, we will look at how to use and configure the Sendmail mail server. Sendmail is a widely used mail server, which (as we've said) can act both as MTA and MDA, and is capable of serving the needs of home users as well as larger networks. It can be used to send email via the Internet as well as locally (and hence can be used as a local intranet mail server), and the latest version provides many security features. Sendmail also comes with good documentation.

Installing Sendmail

As you'd expect, installing Sendmail is straightforward when you do it through the RPM GUI tool. Once you've started the tool (for example, by selecting Main Menu | System Settings | Add/Remove Applications), you need to select the Mail Server package group (which you'll find under the Servers category). If you click the Details button you'll see the package details:

The sendmail package is selected by default as a standard package. Under the **Extra Packages**, you should also select the **imap** and **sendmail-cf** packages. The sendmail package will install the `sendmail` MTA (the SMTP server), while the imap package installs the POP and IMAP services, and **sendmail-cf** provides the facilities for reconfiguring sendmail. You can deselect all other packages. Click on **Close**, and then on **Update** to start the installation. As usual, you'll need the Red Hat Linux 9 distribution CDs handy in order to complete the installation.

Configuring Sendmail

Sendmail is very flexible and provides a lot of options for handling e-mail. While this abundance of features brings a lot of advantages and flexibility, it also brings complexity. Some aspects of Sendmail's configuration are difficult to understand, and even experienced system administrators make mistakes. We will go through a simple configuration that should get Sendmail up and running and to be able to send emails. We assume you have already configured your Linux machine to connect to the Internet connection, as described in Chapter 4.

The default installation of sendmail places the `sendmail` executable in the `/usr/sbin` (that is, `/usr/sbin/sendmail`). It also creates a symbolic link, `/usr/lib/sendmail`, which points to `/usr/sbin/sendmail`.

Sendmail's configuration files are contained within the `/etc/mail` directory. There are five configuration files of particular interest:

Configuration File	Purpose
`sendmail.cf`	This lengthy and complex file is the default main file used by Sendmail. Although you can read this document, you're not supposed to edit it;

	rather, you edit the source `sendmail.mc` file found in the same directory and then compile using the `m4` utility (see below).
`access`	This file specifies which systems can use Sendmail for relaying email. It allows us to restrict the access to the mail server by individual domains
`local-host-names`	This file specifies all aliases for your machine
`domaintable`	This file specifies domain name mappings
`virtusertable`	This file allows a domain-specific form of aliasing. It allows multiple virtual domains to be hosted on one machine.

If you look in the `/etc/mail` directory, you'll see that some of these files are stored in two formats:

❑ The `access`, `domaintable`, and `virtusertable` files are text files; they contain the configuration data that we specify in order to control how sendmail works for us, and we can configure these files using a text editor such as **gedit**.

❑ The `access.db`, `domaintable.db`, and `virtusertable.db` files are database files. These contain the same data, in a database form that the `sendmail` application can use.

Thus, whenever we adjust the configuration contained in the text files mentioned above, we must subsequently compile them into database format so that `sendmail` can use the new configuration.

Here's a brief example. If we want to allow all the systems in `linux4biz.net` domain to use our email server for relaying email, then we would add the following line in the `access` file:

```
# by default we allow relaying from localhost...
neptune.home        RELAY
localhost           RELAY
127.0.0.1           RELAY
linux4biz.net       RELAY
```

Then, we must convert the `access` text files to generate the `access.db` database file. To do this, we use the `makemap` command:

```
# makemap hash /etc/mail/access.db < /etc/mail/access
```

This will create the `access.db` file (which is not human readable and can be used only by the `sendmail` application).

Sendmail offers many configuration options, to allow you to control almost every aspect of its behavior. We can't possibly cover them all here, but there are good resources on the Internet that will help you to set your Sendmail installation up the way you want it. A good place to start is http://www.sendmail.org.

A Simple Example Using Sendmail

To prove that Sendmail works, we'll step through a little example. We'll demonstrate a little configuration of the Sendmail mail server. Then we'll see it in action, showing how it can act as an MTA – collecting incoming e-mails and filtering them into different mailboxes (according to the identity of the mail message's intended recipient).

We'll need to check the configuration of Sendmail, and then make sure all the necessary services are open. Then, to demonstrate, we'll masquerade as two different users, sending e-mails to each other across the system; and we'll see Sendmail in action, making sure that the messages get forwarded to the correct users' mailboxes.

Configuring Sendmail

By default, Sendmail listens for incoming mails only on the loopback IP address, 127.0.0.1 – and this only allows SMTP connections between the Sendmail server and the *local* machine. In fact, this is sufficient for this example, because it involves only senders and recipients whose accounts are on the local machine.

However, while we're considering this, I'll show you the part of the sendmail.mc configuration file that you'd need to change if you wanted to open up your Sendmail server to listen for incoming mails on other addresses. The line in question, in sendmail.mc, is this:

```
dnl # The following causes sendmail to only listen on the IPv4 loopback
address
dnl # 127.0.0.1 and not on any other network devices. Remove the loopback
dnl # address restriction to accept email from the internet or intranet.
dnl #
DAEMON_OPTIONS('Port=smtp,Addr=127.0.0.1, Name=MTA')dnl
```

Here, the Port parameter specifies the port on which the Sendmail server, acting as MTA, is to listen for messages (the default is smtp, which is port 25). If you wanted to make Sendmail listen for messages coming in from the Internet or across an intranet, then you remove the Addr restriction:

```
DAEMON_OPTIONS('Port=smtp, Name=MTA')dnl
```

Alternatively, you can specify a specific IP address on which Sendmail should listen. For example:

```
DAEMON_OPTIONS('Port=smtp,Addr=192.168.0.99, Name=MTA')dnl
```

If you make changes to sendmail.mc, you must then compile them into the sendmail.cf file that Sendmail uses. To do this, you simply employ the m4 utility like this:

```
# m4 /etc/mail/sendmail.mc > /etc/mail/sendmail.cf
```

As I've said, if you're stepping through this example for yourself, you can leave the DAEMON_OPTIONS directive as the default, so that Sendmail is listening only at 127.0.0.1.

Starting the SendMail Service

In fact, you shouldn't need to start the Sendmail service, because it is configured to start up automatically on system startup. You can check the service's status in much the same way as the other services we've mentioned in this chapter, via the Service Configuration GUI (Main Menu | System Settings | Server Settings | Services), where it is listed under the name sendmail:

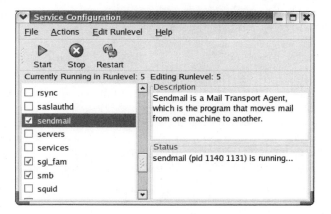

You can also start and stop the service manually at the command line by using the service command in the usual way, this time to control the /etc/init.d/sendmail script. For example:

```
# service sendmail
Usage: /etc/init.d/sendmail {start|stop|restart|condrestart|status}
# service sendmail restart
Shutting down sendmail:                                          [  OK  ]
Shutting down sm-client:                                         [  OK  ]
Starting sendmail:                                              [  OK  ]
Starting sm-client:                                            [  OK  ]
```

Testing the Configuration

If you change the Sendmail configuration, you can test the Sendmail connection by attempting to connect from a Windows machine on the same network. To do this, you could use the telnet command at the command prompt:

```
> telnet 192.168.0.99 25
220 linuxbox ESMTP Sendmail 8.12.5/8.12.5; Thu, 6 Mar 2003 13:53:33 GMT
```

A response like the one shown above proves that Sendmail is listening on IP address 192.168.0.99, port 25. In this response, linuxbox refers to the hostname of the server on which Sendmail is running. Sendmail automatically detects the hostname of the machine (this could be an FQDN or the IP address of the machine). To disconnect from this port, type quit.

Setting up Some E-mail Clients

To demonstrate this in action; we'll need two or three different user accounts. You could create some fictional user accounts using the **User Manager** tool (**Main Menu | System Settings | Users & Groups**) or the useradd and passwd command line utilities (both of which we met in Chapter 8). Here's a reminder of the useradd and passwd utilities in action, creating and activating an account for one of the authors of this book:

```
# useradd -c 'Mark Mamone' -s /bin/bash markm
# passwd markm
...
```

In this example we'll use accounts markm and kapils; you can use different accounts if you like.

We'll also need to configure them with e-mail accounts on the system. The easiest way to do this is to log on as each of these users, one at a time (and "pretend" to be that user); and then use Ximian's Evolution e-mail client application to set that user up with an e-mail account. We mentioned Evolution back in Chapter 5; we'll quickly run through the settings here to show you what to do.

If you're starting Evolution up for the *first* time, you get first screen of the **Setup Assistant**, and you should click **Next** to create an account. In the **Identity** screen, enter your full name and email address (Evolution will accept only proper e-mail addresses here). In the first of two **Receiving Email** screens, select **POP** from the options in **Server Type** field, and enter the IP address of your machine in the **Host** field (this is the IP address of the POP3 server). Enter the username, and set the **Authentication Type** to **Password**:

In the second Receiving Email screen, select Automatically check for new mail and specify the time interval between checks. Select Leave messages on server if you don't want messages deleted from the server after they've been downloaded to the mailbox. In the next screen, Sending Email, change the Server Type to Sendmail (this selection if for delivery of mail messages by passing it to the Sendmail program on the local machine; the other option, SMTP, should be should be used for delivery of e-mails through a connection to a remote mail hub):

In the next screen, Account Management, enter the name of the account (it can be any name, but we'll just use the email address here). Enable Make this my default account. In the final screen, select a time zone. Then click on Next, and later on Finish, to complete the setup.

If you *don't* get the Setup Assistant when you launch Evolution, you can enter all this information via the tabs in the Tools | Settings | Mail Accounts dialog instead.

Demonstrating the Sendmail MDA

To summarize, so far we've done two things:

❑ We've set up the Sendmail application as a mail server, capable of listening for incoming mail messages on 127.0.0.1, and filtering those messages into the correct mailbox so that the intended recipient can read them

❑ We've created some users, configure their mailboxes, and set up each user so that it can use the Evolution application as a mail client (to enable them to send messages and view the messages they've received

In a moment, we can begin to test all this – for example, by logging in as `kapils`, sending a message to `markm`, and then logging in as `markm`to check that the mail message safely arrived.

Starting the POP3 Service

There's one thing we must do before we can use Evolution to send a message: we must start the POP3 service. You can do this from the **Service Configuration GUI** (**Main Menu | System Settings | Server Settings | Services**). First, check the checkbox next to the **ipop3** entry in the list, and then check that the **xinetd** service is running.

*The **ipop3** service runs under the **xinetd** service, so if **xinetd** service is running and the **ipop3** service is enabled then the **ipop3** service will run too.*

Sending Mails

You've done the hard work; this last part is easy! Log onto one of your accounts (say, `kapils`), and launch the Evolution application by selecting **Main Menu | Internet | Evolution Email**. Then select **File | New | Mail Message**, and write a mail message to another account on the system:

Click the **Send** button to send the message. You may be asked to provide your POP password; use the account's system password.

Receiving Mails

Now log out, and log in again as the user to whom you've just send the message (markm in this example). Launch the Evolution application again for this user, and click the **Send/Receive** button at the top of the Evolution window. This button launches a process that contacts the mail server and does two things:

- ❏ It queries the mail server for any new email messages that have been sent to this account

- ❏ It passes any newly composed mail messages to the mail server, so they can be sent on to the intended recipients

You'll be asked to provide your POP password; use the account's system password. (If you have problems here, go back and check that the **ipop3** service is enabled.) Then you'll see a **Send & Receive Mail** dialog:

Allow the sendmail process to complete (as shown by the progress bar above), and then click **Cancel All** to cancel the remaining jobs. In the **Inbox** section of your Evolution window, you should now see the test message that was sent here from the first account:

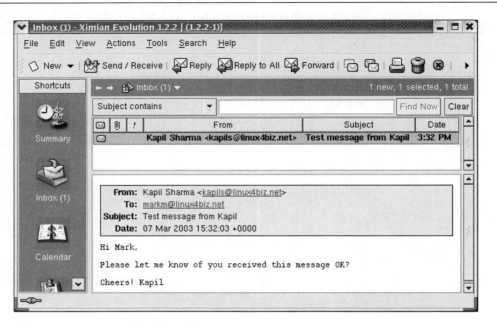

Feel free to experiment further with this – adding more mailbox addresses and hooking it up to the Internet. You can also send and receive mail from Windows machines, using Microsoft Outlook. The same configuration settings should also suffice for Outlook: you'll need set the server type to SMTP, which is the only option in Outlook for sending e-mails.

Setting up a DHCP Server

We've already come across DHCP, during the installation process back in Chapter 1 – specifically, in the step where the installation tool invites us to specify our machine's network configuration. You may remember that, in that step, we are asked to choose between two options:

❑   We can specify the TCP/IP settings (IP address, netmask, default gateway, and DNS servers) explicitly

❑   We can allow a DHCP server to dictate those settings

This is what the **Dynamic Host Configuration Protocol** (**DHCP**) is all about. DHCP is a network protocol, whose purpose is to assign TCP/IP settings to client machines. By configuring a client machine to use DHCP, we're telling it that it must contact a **DHCP server** (on the network), and get its TCP/IP settings (IP address, netmask, default gateway, DNS servers) from there.

How Does DHCP Work?

The concept of DCHP is actually quite simple. Suppose we have a client machine that is configured to get its TCP/IP settings a DHCP server – we'll call it a *DHCP client*. At the time when the DHCP client requires a TCP/IP configuration (which we'll discuss more in moment), it sends a broadcast message across the network, to request TCP/IP address information.

Elsewhere on the network, the DHCP *server* receives this request. It examines its IP pool (a pool of IP addresses that it is allowed to lend out to clients), and assigns one of these IP addresses to the client for a defined **lease** period. It sends this IP address, and other network configuration information, to the client.

The DHCP *client* then acknowledges the receipt of the network configuration information, and sets up its network configuration. Meantime, the DHCP server will not allocate the same IP address to other clients within the lease period.

So, when does a DCHP client need to request a TCP/IP configuration? The most obvious scenario is when the client is booting up and joining the network; it might also do so when its lease on the existing IP address expires, and it needs to ask for a new one.

The Benefits of DHCP

If you're a system administrator responsible for a network containing hundreds of computers, then manual TCP/IP management quickly becomes a nightmare. Each machine on the network must be configured manually, and differently from all the others – which means that you need to keep a careful note of the TCP/IP configuration of each machine. The potential for error and time-consuming manual configuration tasks is great.

Implementing a DHCP server provides relief from this burden. It allows to configure all client machines in exactly the same way – you just tell them all to use the DHCP server. It's also much more reliable than manual TCP/IP management, because the DHCP server is designed to manage its IP pool and the lease periods so that you never get two machines using the same IP address at the same time.

In addition, a DHCP server provides a single central control for all TCP/IP resources. It allows IP addresses to be tracked and reserved. Critically, it makes it very easy to perform cross-network changes – for example, if you need to change your gateway, or the range of allowed IP addresses, you can handle this smoothly and easily by updating *just* the DHCP central server configuration.

DHCP also provides the flexibility for mobile users with laptops, who need to work in different offices. If each office's TCP/IP allocations are controlled by a DHCP server, then all you need to do is configure the laptop to request its TCP/IP settings from a DHCP server. Then, whenever you plug into any office network, your laptop will automatically ask the local DHCP server to serve up the appropriate network settings to allow you to get working.

In this section we'll take a look at how to set up a Linux machine as a DHCP server.

Installing the DHCP Server Packages

As you've probably already gathered, you only need one DHCP server per network. If you decide that you need a DHCP server, then a Red Hat Linux 9 machine will suit your purposes. To configure your machine as a DHCP server, you need to install the appropriate package, and (you've guessed it) we can do that via the RPM GUI.

To do this, launch the RPM GUI (via Main Menu | System Settings | Add/Remove Applications, for example); when the dialog appears, select the Network Servers package group (which you'll find under the Servers category). Click on the Details button to view the package details:

The package we need here is the one called dhcp – the others are not important for the purposes on installing a DHCP server (though you won't want to deselect them unless you're sure you're not using them for something else!).

When you've selected dhcp, click on Close and then on Update to start the installation. As usual, you'll need the distribution CDs in order to complete the installation.

Configuring the DHCP Server

We will setup a simple DHCP configuration to provide clients with network information. The DHCP server can be configured using the default configuration file /etc/dhcpd.conf.

The DHCP server package comes with a sample dhcpd configuration file, called dhcpd.conf.sample. We will use this file as a starting point to configure DHCP configuration, take a backup of your existing dhcpd.conf file and then copy the sample file in its place:

```
# cp /etc/dhcpd.conf /etc/dhcpd.conf.backup
# cp /usr/share/doc/dhcp-3.0pl1/dhcpd.conf.sample /etc/dhcpd.conf
```

Now open the /etc/dhcpd.conf file, using gedit or another text editor, and we'll edit it so it contains all the required options. A simple dhcp configuration file looks like this:

```
ddns-update-style interim;
ignore client-updates;
subnet 192.168.0.0 netmask 255.255.255.0 {
        option routers                  192.168.0.1;
        option subnet-mask              255.255.255.0;
        option domain-name              "linux4biz.net";
        option domain-name-servers      192.168.0.1;
        range dynamic-bootp             192.168.0.128 192.168.0.254;
        default-lease-time              21600;
        max-lease-time                  43200;
}
```

You can use # characters to comment out the lines you don't need, or simply delete them to keep the file tidy. Let's have a look at the settings in this example:

❏ The first two lines of the configuration file instruct the DHCP server not to accept dynamic DNS-updates.

❏ The next line defines a subnet and netmask that will is used to supply the DHCP information. After that we defined all the options:

Option	Description
routers	Specifies the default gateway
subnet-mask	Specifies the default netmask
domain-name	Specifies the default domain-name
domain-name-servers	Specifies the name-servers for our network

397

Option	Description
range dynamic-bootp	Specifies the range of IP addresses that the DHCP server is allowed to allocate to clients. In our example, all allocated IP addresses will lie in the range 192.168.0.128–192.168.0.254.
default-lease-time	Defines the default lease time, after which the client's DHCP configuration will expire, and the client must request a new DHCP configuration from the DHCP server. In this example, the DHCP lease will expire after 6 hours, unless the client asks for a specific time frame.
max-lease-time	Defines the *maximum* lease allowed to the client.

There are other options in the sample configuration file, /usr/share/doc/dhcp-3.0p11/dhcpd.conf.sample, that we won't discuss here. There's more about these options at the dhcpd.conf man page.

The DHCP Lease Database

How does the DHCP server keep track of the IP addresses it has leased out? In Red Hat Linux 9 systems, this information is stored in the database file /var/lib/dhcp/dhcpd.leases. The data stored here includes a client identifier used by the client that requested the lease, the time and date of both the start and end of the lease, and the address of the Ethernet network interface card that was used to retrieve the lease.

*DHCP can recognize a server by the address of its Ethernet network interface card, which is unique. This address is also known as the **MAC address**.*

DHCP server stores lease information for each recently assigned IP address automatically in the lease database, and you should not modify it by hand.

Starting the dhcpd Service

You can start the dhcpd service in the usual ways – using Service Configuration GUI tool, or the /etc/rc.d/init.d/dhcpd command line script.

In the Service Control GUI tool (Main Menu | System Settings | Server Settings | Services), the service we're interested in is called dhcpd:

It's typical to check the checkbox so that the service starts automatically on startup. Don't forget to save your new settings using File | Save Changes.

Alternatively, you can use the `service` command to control the `dhcpd` script:

```
# service dhcpd
Usage: /etc/init.d/dhcpd {start|stop|restart|condrestart|status}
# service dhcpd start
Starting dhcpd:                                              [OK]
```

Assign Static IP Address Using DHCP

It's not always the best thing to have DHCP assign IP addresses dynamically. If your had a production server like a web server or e-mail server whose IP address changed every time its lease expired, then it would be impossible for other machines on the network to find them. So, for servers and other machines like this, there are two alternatives:

❑ We can either configure the machine with its own static IP address and TCP/IP information

❑ Alternatively, we can configure the DHCP server to reserve fixed IP addresses for specific servers.

The second of these options is generally preferable because it means it's still easy to make global network configurations (like changing the DNS server) in a single location (the DHCP server configuration).

To allocate a static IP address a production server, we can add a `host` clause to the `/etc/dhcpd.conf` as shown below:

399

```
host emailserver {
        option host-name "test.linux4biz.net";
        hardware ethernet 00-20-18-8B-3F-9E;
        fixed-address 192.168.0.10;
}
```

Here, the first line defines the declaration for a single computer: host is a configuration option, and emailserver is a reference name for the computer that will be allocated a static IP address. You can use any reference name here, and we usually use a name that reflects the purpose of the machine in question.

The second line specifies the hostname of the machine (test.linux4biz.net), and the third line defines the Ethernet hardware address.

You can find the Ethernet hardware address of a Linux machine by executing the following command on that machine:

```
$ /sbin/ifconfig
```

Check the first line of output, it should look something like this:

```
eth0      Link encap:Ethernet  HWaddr 00:D0:B7:0A:E7:41
```

You can find the Ethernet hardware address on a Windows machine by executing this command at the on command prompt:

```
> ipconfig /all
```

In this case, search for the line starts with thee string Physical Address, *under your Ethernet card description:*

```
Physical Address. . . . . . . . : 00-20-18-8B-3F-9E
```

The fourth line defines the static IP address to be assigned to the server whose hardware Ethernet address matches the one given.

It is recommended that you back up the /etc/dhcpd.conf file when you've finished your initial configuration, and keep it safe – just in case it gets corrupted or changed accidentally.

Installing and Configuring a DHCP Client

We've talked about how to configure the DHCP server, but what about the DHCP client? In fact, there is a default DHCP client software installed on all on Red Hat Linux 9 installations, and if you've configured your Linux machine to be a DHCP client, then it's using that DHCP client program now.

If you want to configure a Linux machine to be a DHCP client, then you can set this configuration either at installation or subsequently via the Network Configuration tool. To launch the Network Configuration tool, select Main Menu | System Settings | Network or type the following command at the command line:

```
$ redhat-config-network
```

Under the Devices tab, select the Ethernet device and click on Edit. Make sure the Activate device when computer starts option is enabled, and select the Automatically obtain IP address settings with dhcp option:

Click on OK when you're finished, then on Apply to apply the changes. The changes will take effect from the next reboot.

Configuring a Windows 2000 Machine to Use a DHCP Server

If you've got a Windows 2000 machine (for example, a Win2K laptop that you use both at home and at work), here's how to configure it to get its network settings from a DHCP server:

1. Click on Start | Settings | Control Panel to open the Control Panel window.

2. Double click on Network and Dial-up Connections and then on Local Area Connection.

401

3. Click the Properties button. In the resulting Local Area Connection Properties dialog, highlight Internet Protocol (TCP/IP) and click on Properties.

4. In the resulting Internet Protocol (TCP/IP) Properties dialog, select Obtain an IP Address automatically and Obtain DNS server address automatically.

5. Click on OK to confirm the changes, and then on OK again to implement the changes. At this point, the DHCP client program will try to get address information from DHCP server.

If you like, you can check the new IP address allocated by the DHCP server by executing the `ipconfig /all` command on the command prompt:

```
C:\>ipconfig /all
Windows 2000 IP Configuration
   Host Name . . . . . . . . . : my-win2k-laptop
   Primary DNS Suffix  . . . . :
   Node Type . . . . . . . . . : Hybrid
   IP Routing Enabled. . . . . : No
   WINS Proxy Enabled. . . . . : No
   DNS Suffix Search List. . . : linux4biz.net
Ethernet adapter Local Area Connection:
   Connection-specific DNS Suffix: linux4biz.net
   Description . . . . . . . . : Xircom CreditCard Ethernet 10/100 + Modem
56
   Physical Address. . . . . . : 00-80-C7-8B-C2-E3
   DHCP Enabled. . . . . . . . : Yes
   Autoconfiguration Enabled . . : Yes
   IP Address. . . . . . . . . : 192.168.0.129
   Subnet Mask . . . . . . . . : 255.255.255.0
   Default Gateway . . . . . . : 192.168.0.1
   DHCP Server . . . . . . . . : 192.168.0.99
   DNS Servers . . . . . . . . : 192.168.0.1
   Lease Obtained. . . . . . . : 19 February 2003 09:01:21
   Lease Expires . . . . . . . : 22 February 2003 09:01:21
```

This allows you to see the TCP/IP information that the Windows DHCP client has acquired from the DHCP server. In the above output, the DHCP Enabled property is set to Yes, indicating that the Windows client machine is configured to get IP information from a DHCP server. The physical address of this machine (its MAC address, taken from its Ethernet card) is 00-80-C7-8B-C2-E3; the DHCP server has leased the IP address 192.168.0.129 to the machine, and the lease will expire three days from when it was obtained.

Summary

We've covered six common services in this chapter. It's unlikely that you'll need them all in a home environment, and it's certainly unlikely that you'll ever install all of these services onto a single machine, except to experiment with them! Most medium-size office environments will have at least some of these services, and in a production situation you would often assign at least one dedicated machine to any of these services.

There are so many configuration options for all these services that we can't possible cover them all here. There is a mass on useful information on the web, both in formal documentation and on newsgroups, and you have the man pages too. Here are just a few sites that provide more documentation and developments on some of the services here:

- ❏ www.sendmail.org – the official sendmail web site
- ❏ www.redhat.com – the official site for Red Hat Linux
- ❏ www.samba.org – the official web site for SAMBA
- ❏ http://www.rfc-editor.org a searchable Collection of all RFCs
- ❏ http://www.isc.org/products/DHCP/ – the official site for DHCP
- ❏ http://www.tldp.org/ – the Linux documentation Project site
- ❏ http://www.linux4biz.net/writing.htm – contains useful articles on Linux
- ❏ http://www.linuxsecurity.com/ – a security news site for Linux

In the next chapter we will delve further into the realms of systems administration, by looking at system configuration, logs, backups and archives, and a closer look at the Linux kernel.

10

Advanced System Administration

We have dealt exclusively with the Personal Desktop version of RedHat Linux in this book, but we still need to perform a number of administrative tasks to keep our system running well; system administration is not limited to full multi-user servers. We have already discussed how to install the operating system and how to use it for day-to-day operations. So, our next goal is to discuss some of the more advanced administrative aspects of managing a Linux system. More specifically, we will focus on the following tasks in this chapter:

- ❏ Examining important configuration files and the information they contain
- ❏ Analyzing system log files to track problems
- ❏ Backing up and archiving
- ❏ Installing new applications from source code
- ❏ Building and customizing the Linux kernel

By understanding the rationale for performing these tasks, as well as how to actually implement them, we will get a better feel for how the operating system works and how to manage it properly. As you will see, Linux provides us with the ability to control and administer nearly all aspects of its operation, including the core part of the system, the kernel.

We will start by looking at the system configuration, including how to find the information we need and then to modify it to suit our requirements.

System Configuration

What do you think of when you hear the term system configuration? If you were to pose that exact same question to a group of people, you would, most likely, get entirely different responses. System configuration encompasses such a broad area of system administration that it is very difficult to cover all aspects. And so, we will concentrate on configuration related to users and login, hardware, booting up and startup services, networking, and security. Even though there are numerous applications that will allow you to manipulate system configuration through a graphical interface, you will have better control of the system if you know where the configuration information is stored and how to modify it manually when necessary.

Depending on the operating system, the configuration information is stored in different locations. For example, Microsoft Windows stores most configuration data in the Registry, while the Mac OS stores it in separate binary files in a special Preferences folder. How about Linux? Where does it store the configuration details? For the most part, Linux, by which I mean the core components as well as individual applications, stores the information in *plain text* files in the /etc directory or in one of its subdirectories. This gives us a number of advantages over the other operating systems, namely:

❑   We can read and edit the information easily with an text editor.

❑   We can back up the files consistently.

❑   We can maintain version control, thereby keeping track of all changes.

Unfortunately, since each component or application stores its configuration information individually in a separate file, there are bound to be differences in syntax between them. However, a majority of the files have a syntax that is easy to understand, as you will see in a moment.

Example: Finding the DNS Server

For example, perhaps you entered a DNS server address when you were installing the operating system back in Chapter 1. That DNS server address forms part of the system's configuration, and its value is stored in the appropriate configuration file under the /etc directory hierarchy.

If you take a look at the /etc directory, you'll see that there are quite a lot of configuration files there. Which one contains DNS server configuration? If you know the DNS server address, then one way to find out is to use the grep command to search for the file that contains that address. For example, if you used the primary nameserver address 192.168.1.1, then you can find the correct configuration file via the following command:

```
# grep -ri 192.168.1.1 /etc
/etc/resolv.conf:nameserver 192.168.1.1
```

The output from this command points us in the direction of the file /etc/resolv.conf – in fact, it is this file that holds all the DNS server information. You can take a look at this file, using a text editor such as gedit:

```
# gedit /etc/resolv.conf
```

You'll see that it is simply a text file with the following format:

```
nameserver 192.168.1.1    ## primary
nameserver 192.168.1.2    ## secondary, etc.
```

Let's take a look at some more configuration files.

Configuration Files

We mentioned that there are a large number of configuration files contained in the /etc directory hierarchy. They're stored in a tree structure; the diagram below gives you an idea of the common ones you might find:

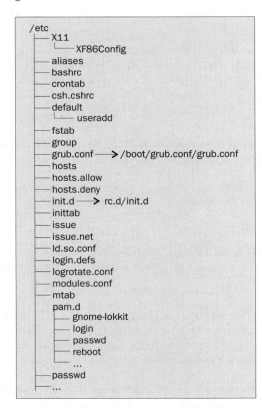

We can't possibly mention them all here, but over the next few pages we will discuss some of the configuration files that you're most likely to find important. You should take some time to explore these files to see what information they contain, either using the cat, more or less commands, or an editor of some sort; just be careful not to accidentally modify or delete any information.

/etc/XF86Config

The XF86Config configuration file controls specific aspects of the X Window System (X11) server, from keyboard and mouse to monitor. This file is essential if X11 is to work properly on your system.

> *While it is generally possible to modify configuration files by hand, we recommend that you don't try it with this one, because its configuration is quite difficult. It is best to use the following Red Hat GUI applications to manipulate the information in this file:*

- ❏   redhat-config-xfree86 (Applications | System Settings | Display)
- ❏   redhat-config-keyboard (Applications | System Settings | Keyboard)
- ❏   redhat-config-mouse (Applications | System Settings | Mouse).

/etc/aliases

The aliases configuration file contains aliases for mail users and is used by the sendmail application that we met in Chapter 9. For example, you can set up an alias such that all mail sent to the alias mickeymouse is forwarded to the system administrator:

```
mickeymouse: root
```

Whenever you modify this file manually, you must also run the newaliases application (located in /usr/bin) for the changes to take effect.

> *The postfix mail transport application, an alternative to sendmail, has a similar configuration file which is located at /etc/postfix/aliases.*

/etc/bashrc and /etc/csh.cshrc

These two configuration files set the defaults (file creation masks/permissions, shell prompts, and so on) that are used by all bash and csh shell users upon starting a new shell.

/etc/crontab

This file is a configuration file for the **cron daemon**, crond, which allows us to execute **automated tasks** – tasks that run unattended at specified times. Once a minute, the cron daemon checks for changes in the crontab file (and also in the /etc/cron.d directory, and the /var/spool/cron directory), and reloads them into memory as necessary.

Here is an example. The following is a crontab entry that records the system load averages into a file every hour from 8:00 pm until 11:00 pm on Mondays:

```
min hour  day  mon  weekday   command
00  20-23  *    *    01        /usr/bin/uptime >> /data/load.txt
```

You don't need root privileges to set up automated tasks using the `crontab` application. Any user can edit their own `crontab` entries, via the command `crontab -e`. There's more about the `cron` daemon in Chapter 6.

/etc/default/useradd

This file sets the default parameters that are used whenever a new user is created. For example, if you want all new users to have the C shell by default, then you would change the SHELL directive in the `useradd` configuration file, so that it reads thus:

```
SHELL=/bin/csh
```

/etc/fstab

The `fstab` file contains the **file system table**, which is a table of all disk partitions, and their mount points and default mount options. You can use this file to tell Linux about any and all file systems to which the machine has access.

/etc/group

This configuration file lists the group names and group IDs (GIDs) of all the groups of users known to the system. Groups are important in Red Hat Linux 9 – indeed, every user must be associated with at least one group. We discussed the subject of users and groups in Chapter 8.

If you don't want to deal with this file directly, you can use the `redhat-config-users` GUI application (Applications | System Settings | Users and Groups).

/etc/grub.conf

The `grub.conf` configuration file is used at the time you start your system (unless you specified LILO) – when you start your system, the first program that runs is the **grand unified bootloader (GRUB)**. The GRUB is responsible for transferring control to the Linux kernel. The `grub.conf` file found in the `/etc` directory is, in fact, a symbolic link to the file `/boot/grub/grub.conf` – which in turn specifies the path to the kernel and the root partition.

Here is an example of what you might find in a `grub.conf` file:

```
title Red Hat Linux (2.4.20-2.48)
    root (hd0,0)
    kernel /boot/vmlinuz-2.4.20-2.48 ro root=/dev/hda1
    initrd /boot/initrd-2.4.20-2.48.img
```

Later in this chapter, when we build our own custom kernel, we will modify the `grub.conf` file to point to our new kernel.

/etc/hosts

The hosts file allows us to set up aliases for local and remote hosts. This is a very powerful feature that can simplify host name lookups. For example, if you wanted to force all of your users to go to www.google.com when they enter google, simply add this record to the hosts file:

```
216.239.57.101 google
```

The IP address 216.239.57.101 is one of many IP addresses assigned to www.google.com. We can use the ping command to verify that the alias has taken effect:

```
$ ping google
PING www.google.com (216.239.57.101) from 192.168.254.2: 56(84) bytes of data.
64 bytes from www.google.com (216.239.57.101): icmp_seq=1 ttl=45 time=72.5 ms
...
```

Note that this will not work properly with network applications that perform their own DNS lookups, such as the Lynx text browser.

/etc/hosts.allow and /etc/hosts.deny

The hosts.allow file specifies (by name or IP address) the hosts that are allowed access to local TCP/IP services. By default, all other hosts are denied access. Or, we can specifically list the hosts for which we want to deny access in the hosts.deny file.

Suppose you want to control access to your server through the telnet protocol. Specifically, suppose you wanted to allow access only to remote users from the host www.wrox.com and to local users. To achieve this, you would specify this line in hosts.allow:

```
telnetd: LOCAL, 192.168.1., www.wrox.com
```

and this line in hosts.deny:

```
telnetd: ALL
```

All entries listed in hosts.allow take precedence over any entries in hosts.deny.

Note that you can use this access control mechanism only if tcp_wrappers (the /usr/sbin/tcpd server) is enabled for that specific service. See the xinetd.d entry, later in this section, for more information.

/etc/init.d

This is a symbolic link to a directory that contains a number of **startup scripts**. The startup scripts perform a number of functions, including initialization of network connections and startup of server daemon processes. For example, the file /etc/init.d/crond implements functionality to start, stop, restart, and reload (the configuration information) the cron daemon.

Not all of the scripts in this directory are executed when you start the system. Rather, execution is governed by the system's **run level**. We discussed run levels back in Chapter 2 – as you'll recall, the runlevels (0–6) are represented by the directories /etc/rc.d/rcX.d. Each of these directories contains symbolic links to the chosen scripts in the init.d directory. If you want a particular application or process to run within a particular run level, you can simply add a symbolic link to that application to the corresponding run level directory.

/etc/inittab

The inittab configuration file is probably the single most important file in the system – it controls the initialization process that occurs when you start the system. It is responsible for starting the init process; it contains a line to set the default run level to be used:

```
id:3:initdefault:
```

This line will set the run level to 3; see Chapter 2 for more information on the different runlevels. If you want to start your system with an X Window System interface, you can simply change this to run level 5:

```
id:5:initdefault:
```

/etc/issue and /etc/issue.net

The issue and issue.net configuration files contain the text that is displayed when you start a terminal session. Typically, this message contains the Red Hat version number and the kernel identification. The only difference between these two files is that issue.net is displayed only to remote users who log in to the system, while the contents of issue are displayed to local users only.

/etc/ld.so.conf

This file contains a list of directories in which shared libraries (*.so) can be found. The information in this file is used by the ldconfig application to create the necessary links and cache to these libraries, so that development tools (such as the dynamic linker) can find them. You need to run ldconfig whenever you add, remove, or change the entries in this file.

/etc/logrotate.conf

This file contains information that controls the rotation of log files and is used in conjunction with the logrotate application.

The main reasons for rotating log files are to keep them organized and to limit their size. If you don't control the size of your log files, then your backups take longer – and you also run the risk of your disk space filling up unexpectedly.

Moreover, when something goes wrong with the system, examination of the log files often helps us to trace the cause of the problem. But if the log files get too large, then this examination process becomes more difficult – and finding the problem is like searching for a needle in a haystack.

So the idea is that we rotate our log files periodically, or when a log file reaches a specified size. The `logrotate` application (located in `/usr/sbin`) does the work, and to do so it uses the rotation time interval or file-size limits specified in `logrotate.conf`.

In fact, the `/etc/cron.daily` directory contains a simple script called `logrotate`, which invokes the following command to rotate the logs:

```
/usr/sbin/logrotate /etc/logrotate.conf
```

If you look at the `crontab` file, you will see that all the scripts in `cron.daily` are configured to run at 4:02 am every day:

```
02 4   *   *   *   root   run-parts /etc/cron.daily
```

/etc/modules.conf

The `modules.conf` configuration file tells the kernel (or more specifically, the `modprobe` and `depmod` applications) which modules to load on demand.

For example, if you want to use the tulip driver to handle your Ethernet/network card, you would add the following line to the `modules.conf` file:

```
eth0 tulip
```

Of course, this assumes that the tulip driver (`tulip.o`) exists in the `/lib/modules/2.4.20-2.48` directory; this directory contains the modules for the Linux kernel 2.4.18-4. You can use the following command to check that the driver exists:

```
# find /lib/modules/ -name 'tulip.o'
```

We will discuss the modular nature of the Linux kernel, and the Linux Loadable Kernel Modules (LKM), later in the chapter.

/etc/passwd

The `passwd` configuration file stores the account information (including the user name, full name, and path to the home directory and default shell) for every user on the system. You can use the `redhat-config-users` application (**Applications | System Settings | Users and Groups**) if you do not feel comfortable modifying the contents of this file. See Chapter 8 for more information on adding users and groups.

/etc/rc

The `rc` file and the files in the `rc.d` directory control what applications and services run at specific run levels. The `rc.d` directory contains a number of subdirectories – each subdirectory represents a run level from 0–6. These subdirectories, in turn, contain symbolic links to startup scripts in the `init.d` directory (see the entry for `init.d` above).

The `rc` file itself is responsible for starting and stopping services when a run level changes.

/etc/resolv.conf

We discussed the `resolv.conf` file at the beginning of this chapter.

/etc/security

The `security` directory contains a list of configuration files that impose restrictions on various resources. This includes information about who can log in and from which location(s) they can log in, and the privileges that console users are given and resource limits for all users.

For example, if you want to increase the hard limit for resources allocation (that is, the number of file descriptors) to all users from 1024 to 8192, you could add the following lines to `limits.conf`:

```
*         soft      nofile  1024
*         hard      nofile  8192
```

This change, along with the following change to `/etc/pam.d/login`, will allow users to increase their file descriptor limits:

```
session      required       /lib/security/pam_limits.so
```

up until their hard limit by using the following command:

```
$ ulimit -n unlimited
```

Typically, you would increase resource limits for users and processes that are under a heavy and constant load, such as the Web server process.

/etc/shadow

If shadow passwords are enabled, the `shadow` configuration file contains encrypted passwords for all users listed in the `passwd` file. This is a more secure approach, since the `shadow` file is readable only by root. See Chapter 8 for more information on users and passwords.

/etc/shells

This file can be used to list all the valid shells on the system. The `chsh` command, which allows users to change their default shell, makes use of this list. Historically it has been used to restrict access: network services like FTP daemons have required users logging in to have a valid shell – with no valid shell, access is denied.

/etc/skel

The `skel` directory contains a list of files, which will be copied to a user's directory when the user is first created. This allows us to provide each user with a set of default resources, such as scripts, configuration, and data files.

/etc/sysconfig

The `sysconfig` directory is highly critical. It consists of important configuration files used by various applications, including hardware and network configuration.

For example, consider the information stored within the `/etc/sysconfig/network` file and the files in the `/etc/sysconfig/network-scripts` directory. This information specifies how the system is connected to an external network. Alternatively, take a look at the `iptables` configuration file, which lists the firewall rules.

/etc/sysctl.conf

This is a highly powerful configuration file that allows us to configure kernel parameters at runtime. For example, to increase the number of file descriptors system-wide from 8,192 to 32,768, you would insert the following entry into this file:

```
fs.file-max=32768
```

Some of these kernel parameters can also be changed by modifying the relevant files in the `/proc` directory.

/etc/syslog.conf

The `syslog.conf` configuration file is the main driver for the `syslogd` daemon, which is responsible for logging information. For example, take a look at the following entry in the configuration file:

```
*.info;mail.none;authpriv.none;cron.none          /var/log/messages
```

This directive instructs the `syslogd` daemon to log all messages that have a severity level greater than that of an "information-only" message (with the exception of `mail-`, `authentication-`, and `cron-`related messages) to `/var/log/messages`.

Later in the chapter, we'll look at various administrative log files, including the `/var/log/messages` log file mentioned above.

/etc/xinetd.conf

Finally, the `xinetd.conf` configuration file configures the services provided by the `xinetd` daemon, which include FTP and telnet. In fact, the `xinetd.d` directory contains a configuration file for each service. Each of these configuration files looks something like this:

```
service telnet
{
    flags             = REUSE NAMEINARGS
    protocol          = tcp
    socket_type       = stream
    wait              = no
    user              = root
```

```
server          = /usr/sbin/tcpd
server_args     = /usr/sbin/in.telnetd
log_on_failure += USERID
}
```

We had discussed the `tcp_wrappers` application as a means to implement access control when we discussed the `hosts.allow` and `hosts.deny` files earlier in this section. Incidentally, the configuration file illustrated above uses tcp_wrappers, as signified by the `/usr/sbin/tcpd server` setting. This server provides the access control for each incoming request and if the request is successful invokes the application specified by the `server_args` argument – telnet daemon in this case.

In the next section, we'll take a look at the various administrative log files to better understand what is happening with our system.

Logging

One of the best features of Unix-based operating systems is their extensive support for logging, and in Red Hat Linux 9 the same is true. Most of the core components of the system, including the kernel as well as other services and applications, such as telnet and ftp, write the status of their significant actions to specific text files. We can use this information to get a snapshot of the system to see what is going on at any given time. Viewing the contents of these log files allows us to find, among other information:

- ❑ what is happening as the system boots
- ❑ if a device failed to initialize at boot time
- ❑ when a user logged in and from what address
- ❑ any suspicious security alerts, such as failed logins
- ❑ if a user tried to send e-mail to a particular address
- ❑ all e-mail received, from whom and at what time
- ❑ status of all cron jobs

Our role as the system administrator is to use this information to properly maintain our system and take any corrective actions if necessary. There is no point in having all of this valuable information at our fingertips if we do not make good use of it. For example, if we notice from the log files that a particular user is repeatedly trying to telnet in from a specific unknown location and is unsuccessful, we can most likely assume that a hacker is trying to gain entrance to our system. At this point, we can take some decisive actions. We can use the `hosts.deny` file that we discussed in the previous section to deny complete access to that particular service for the specific host or address, and also try to inform the hacker's Internet service provider of the malicious activities.

Are you ready to look at some log files? Continue on to the next section.

Viewing Logs

Log files are plain text files, much like the configuration files that we have seen earlier in this chapter. You can find most of the system log files in one directory, /var/log, so keeping track of them is rather easy. Here are some of the more important files that you will find in this directory:

File	Description
boot.log	Boot messages
cron	crond messages
maillog	All email-related messages
messages	All informational messages except for cron, mail and secure
secure	Secure, authentication messages

We can use either the cat, more, or less utilities from the command line or the **System Logs** GUI application (by selecting **Main menu | System Tools | System Logs**) to view the contents of these plain text log files. Here is an example:

```
# more /var/log/messages
Feb 18 19:25:15 localhost syslogd 1.4.1: restart.
Feb 18 19:25:15 localhost syslog: syslogd startup succeeded
Feb 18 19:25:15 localhost syslog: klogd startup succeeded
Feb 18 19:25:15 localhost kernel: klogd 1.4.1, log source = /proc/kmsg started.
Feb 18 19:25:15 localhost kernel: Linux version 2.4.20-2.48
(bhcompile@stripples.devel.redhat.com) (gcc version 3.2 20020903 (Red Hat Linux
8.1 3.2-7)) #1 Wed Sep 4 13:35:50 EDT 2002
Feb 18 19:25:15 localhost kernel: BIOS-provided physical RAM map:
Feb 18 19:25:15 localhost kernel:  BIOS-e820: 0000000000000000 - 000000000009f800
(usable)
Feb 18 19:25:15 localhost kernel:  BIOS-e820: 000000000009f800 - 00000000000a0000
(reserved)
Feb 18 19:25:15 localhost kernel:  BIOS-e820: 00000000000e7400 - 0000000000100000
(reserved)
Feb 18 19:25:15 localhost kernel:  BIOS-e820: 0000000000100000 - 0000000007ef0000
(usable)
Feb 18 19:25:15 localhost kernel:  BIOS-e820: 0000000007ef0000 - 0000000007effc00
(ACPI data)
Feb 18 19:25:15 localhost kernel:  BIOS-e820: 0000000007effc00 - 0000000007f00000
(ACPI NVS)
Feb 18 19:25:15 localhost kernel:  BIOS-e820: 0000000007f00000 - 0000000008000000
(reserved)
. . .
```

We can also view the `messages` log file using the **System Logs** GUI application (under **System Tools**); it shows a list of log files on the left hand side, and the contents of the selected log file on the right hand side:

Go ahead and experiment with the other log files to see what type of information is logged. Simply select a log file from the left hand side, and its contents will be shown in the right frame. Unfortunately, this application does not allow us to add other log files to the menu; we are limited to the ones listed.

Application-specific Log Files

We have found a number of system log files in `/var/log`? However, a number of applications, such as Web servers and database servers, store their log files in other locations. How do we go about finding them? First, you should read the individual application's documentation, or its manual pages, for more details. Usually, the manual page will have a FILES section that will list all files used by the application, including configuration and log files. If you cannot locate the files in this manner, you should look for any application-specific subdirectories in `/var/log` or even in the `/etc` directory. If that too proves unsuccessful, the best bet then is to proceed to the application installation directory and try to find any files or subdirectories that contain the word `log` in their file name, like so:

```
# find /usr/local/thttpd -name '*log*' -print
```

Here, we are looking for any possible log files or directories in the `/usr/local/thttpd` directory; this is the installation directory for the `thttpd` Web server.

Searching Log Files

As you look through the various log files, you may soon realize that it is very difficult to keep track of failures and other alerts because of the large amount of information that is logged. For example, you may want to keep track of all login failures or certain hardware problems. How would you go about doing it? You can certainly schedule some time every day to wade through the entire content manually. However, this is far from efficient, and you could instead use your precious time for other system administration–related tasks. Or, you could use simple search tools to find specific information in the log files quickly and easily.

Searching Log Files Using the System Logs Application

The System Logs application also provides a filtering option (you can see it at the bottom of the window in the screenshot below) – this allows you to search for specific words or phrases within a log file. For example, try selecting the System Log, typing the word fail into the Filter for textbox, and clicking the Filter button to execute the search. I found a few error messages:

```
System Logs                                                    _  □  ✕

 File   Edit   Help

 Boot Log              System Log
 Cron Log
 Kernel Startup Log          📖        This is the system log file.
 Mail Log
 News Log                Feb 24 11:16:48 localhost gdm(pam_unix)[1974]: authentication failure; logi ▲
 RPM Packages            Feb 24 11:16:54 localhost gdm(pam_unix)[1974]: authentication failure; logi
                       ❶ Feb 24 11:57:03 localhost kernel: cdrom: open failed.
 Security Log            Feb 24 12:57:50 localhost gdm(pam_unix)[8959]: authentication failure; logi
 System Log            ❶ Feb 25 10:35:02 localhost kernel: smb_open: Figures/.vfs-write.tmp open fa
 XFree86 Log          ❶ Feb 25 10:59:21 localhost insmod: /lib/modules/2.4.20-2.48/kernel/drivers/r
                       ❶ Feb 25 10:59:21 localhost insmod: /lib/modules/2.4.20-2.48/kernel/drivers/r
                       ❶ Feb 25 11:00:26 localhost insmod: /lib/modules/2.4.20-2.48/kernel/drivers/r
                       ❶ Feb 25 11:00:26 localhost insmod: /lib/modules/2.4.20-2.48/kernel/drivers/r
                       ❶ Feb 25 11:01:18 localhost insmod: /lib/modules/2.4.20-2.48/kernel/drivers/r
                       ❶ Feb 25 11:01:18 localhost insmod: /lib/modules/2.4.20-2.48/kernel/drivers/r
                         Feb 26 09:49:09 localhost gdm(pam_unix)[1937]: authentication failure; logi
                       ❶ Feb 26 10:11:07 localhost irda: irattach shutdown failed         ▼
                       ◄         ///                                              ►

              Filter for:   fail                          🔍 Filter      🔄 Reset

 Search results for fail displayed.
```

The application found seven entries from the System Log file that contained the word fail. In addition, it also highlighted entries where it found the word failed; you can configure what words trigger this effect by using the application's Edit | Preferences | Alerts option.

Searching Log Files Directly

Of course, we don't have to use the System Logs application to analyze or search a log file. We can also examine a log file directly by viewing it in a text editor (such as gedit), and using its search capability to find particular keywords, such as fail, error, denied, or unable. Or, we can use the grep command from the command line to perform the search. Here is an example that you can use to search the messages log file for all occurrences of the string fail:

```
# grep -i fail /var/log/messages
Feb 18 20:01:36 localhost kernel: ohci1394: pci_module_init failed
Feb 18 20:04:21 localhost login(pam_unix)[879]: authentication failure;
logname=LOGIN uid=0 euid=0 tty=tty1 ruser= rhost=
Feb 18 20:04:23 localhost login[879]: FAILED LOGIN 1 FROM (null) FOR id,
Authentication failure
Feb 18 20:06:53 localhost xinetd[491]: pmap_set failed. service=sgi_fam
program=391002 version=2
Feb 18 20:18:00 localhost login(pam_unix)[827]: authentication failure;
logname=LOGIN uid=0 euid=0 tty=tty1 ruser= rhost=  user=johnson
Feb 18 20:18:03 localhost login[827]: FAILED LOGIN 1 FROM (null) FOR johnson,
Authentication failure
Feb 21 12:21:25 localhost xinetd[492]: pmap_set failed. service=sgi_fam
program=391002 version=2
```

As you can see, these results are identical to the output produced by the System Logs application; in both cases, we found seven entries that contained the word fail. However, having the capability to search for particular log entries from the command line affords us great flexibility and convenience. For example, we could:

❑ Write a simple shell script to periodically check for certain keywords in the log files, and send a report of this search to the administrator. In fact, there are already a number of applications that do this, including Todd Atkins' swatch, which is available from http://swatch.sourceforge.net.

❑ Build a Web interface to these log files, which allows us to view warnings and suspicious activity from other computers on a local network. In fact, we will build our own such application in Chapter 12.

Understanding the Logging Process

This is all great, but how do all of these messages get in the various log files – especially when these messages are all being generated by different applications? In fact, we discussed this briefly in the first section of this chapter, when we looked at the syslog.conf configuration file. Let's look more closely at this subject now.

The magic behind the entire logging process is the **syslogd daemon**. The syslogd daemon acts as a switchboard for messages of all types, produced by various services, daemons, and system software processes. More specifically, the daemon process listens for messages on a Unix domain socket, /dev/log, and routes them according to the rules specified in the syslog.conf configuration file.

*There is one interesting detail to note. The kernel does not communicate with the syslogd daemon directly. Instead, the kernel injects messages into another daemon, **klogd**, which is designed specifically to handle messages from the kernel. Eventually, however, the klogd daemon communicates with syslogd, and the messages get routed to the intended destination.*

Let's take a look at a few sample entries that you might find in a typical `syslog.conf` configuration file:

```
kern.*                                     /dev/console      ## tty
kern.crit                                  @dev2             ## dev2 host
*.info;mail.none;authpriv.none;cron.none   /var/log/messages ## file
authpriv.*                                 | /usr/local/bin/audit ## app.
mail.*                                     /var/log/maillog  ## file
cron.*                                     /var/log/cron     ## file
*.emerg                                    *                 ## all users
*.alert                                    root,johnson      ## users
```

We can break each entry in `syslog.conf` into three parts:

❑   The first part of each entry is the type of message to be considered. For each type of message to log, there are two components: the **facility** and the **level**. In the examples shown above, `kern`, `mail`, `authpriv`, and `cron` are facilities, and `crit`, `info`, `emerg`, and `alert` represent the different logging levels.

❑   The second part is the destination to which the message should be sent. Valid destinations include files, terminals, logged-in users, applications (via pipes), and even remote `syslogd` servers.

❑   The third column simply represents user defined comments and are optional.

As you can see, the `syslogd` application is a very powerful and flexible logging mechanism. Most of the types of messages that you would ever want to see are already configured by default when you install the operating system. However, you should monitor the logs on a regular basis for any possible problems, either using the search techniques discussed in the previous section or by using other specialized applications, such as `swatch`. That way, you can keep your system running safely and efficiently, and intervene only when necessary.

Of course, it is very important to back up and archive log files, since they represent a snapshot in time of the system's activity and status. Therefore, in the next section, we will look at several tools and applications that allow us to archive our data safely.

Backing Up and Archiving

How many times have you accidentally deleted a file, only to think, "Oops! I should have backed it up..."? This happens all too often, and it is usually because most of us don't pay as much attention as we should to creating **backups** and **archives**. In this section, we will first discuss backup strategy (when, how, and where to create backups); then we will proceed to look at the various tools and applications that we can use to implement our strategy.

There are an infinite number of different ways for us to lose our precious data. First, we could accidentally delete a file or set of files. This is one of the many reasons why you should not work as the root user on a regular basis; you will have the privileges to remove almost any file or directory at will. Imagine what would happen if you accidentally deleted the /etc directory.

Second, even if we were to be extra careful about saving files and not indiscriminately using the rm command as the root user, a bug in the editor that you regularly use, for example, could corrupt your data. Or even worse, a disk or hardware failure could wipe out all of our data in one swoop.

Luckily, there is a safeguard against these problems. And that is to back up or archive your data on a regular basis.

Backup Strategy

Before we start to look at the actual backup applications and how to use them, we need to understand a few basic principles and determine the answers to the following questions:

- ❏ What data needs to be archived?
- ❏ How often do we need to archive our data?
- ❏ Where do we archive the data to?

What Data Do We Need to Archive?

In an ideal situation, we might be tempted to back up everything: the operating system, configuration files, applications and tools, and (of course) all personal data. However, in most cases, this approach is not recommended. For example, if you can reinstall the operating system from the original source media, then there is no need to archive it.

However, when it comes to configuration files, the considerations are different. Sure, it would be possible to rebuild your configuration manually after a disaster of some sort, but building it from an archived backup of configuration files is much less hassle.

What about applications and tools? You probably don't need to back up your applications, since you can reinstall them from your purchased media or from an online repository. The key here, however, is that you need to keep track of what applications you installed in this manner. The best way to do this is to install them initially into an isolated directory, such as `/usr/local/apps`, and keep the configurations for those applications in `/usr/local/apps/etc`. That way, you can archive each application's configuration and data files separately.

Finally, what about personal data? Well, that's simple – we really should archive personal data, because it is likely to be very difficult (if not almost impossible) to re-create that data if we were to lose it.

Frequency of Backups

Having considered *what* to archive, you now need to think about *how often* you need to perform backups. The answer to this question depends on how dynamic your data is. If your data changes frequently, then you need to archive it on a regular basis to ensure that you can recover the latest versions of the data if something does go wrong.

Don't worry: frequent backups don't necessarily have to consume a lot of space, since most backup applications support **incremental backups**. An incremental backup is different to a full or complete backup, in that it archives only those files that have been added or modified since the last full backup.

Location of Archives

In addition to considering the optimum frequency of backups, you also need to consider how frequently you anticipate having to *restore* files from backup archives. This issue has a big impact on where you decide to archive your data – that is, the media you choose for storing your backups.

For example, do you find that you need older versions of your files on a regular basis? If so, you need to make sure that you back up your data onto a medium that supports fast random access, such as hard disks or network attached storage (NAS).

There are various types of media available for storing archived data, everything from floppy disks and magnetic tapes to CD-ROM, DVD, and hard disks. Here is a table that illustrates some of the advantages and disadvantages of each type of media:

Media	Advantage	Disadvantage
Floppy disk	Convenient, Inexpensive, Supported by all operating systems, Suitable for storing configuration files	Limited size: 1.44MB, Slow, Unreliable; prone to damage

Media	Advantage	Disadvantage
Removable disks (Zip, USB Flash)	Convenient	Low capacity, Not supported on all operating systems, More expensive than floppy disks, Somewhat reliable
Magnetic tapes	Inexpensive, High capacity; ideal for unattended backups	Sensitive to heat and electromagnetic fields, Relatively slow
CD-ROM, DVD	Inexpensive DVD has high capacity Reasonably fast	CD-ROM has low capacity
Hard Disk	Very fast No media to load Relatively inexpensive	Stored in the same system, which can be a liability

Keeping all of these ideas in mind, you need to decide how you will proceed to implement an efficient backup and archival strategy.

Applications and Tools for Archiving

We will now look at several applications and tools, each of which is suited for a different purpose. Let's start with the most basic application, one that is available on almost all Unix platforms, and that is tar.

Tape Archive (tar)

Tape Archive, or **tar**, is a traditional Unix tool for archiving and distributing files. It is best suited to single-user systems and systems with small amounts of data, since it lacks the sophisticated features of more complex backup applications. For example, it has very primitive support for the notion of incremental backups, since it was not designed for that purpose.

tar works by taking a specified set of files and serializing them into one big stream that consists of the **file headers** (name, owner, file creation date) and **contents**. We can store this data stream in a file on a filesystem or store it directly on a magnetic tape.

Creating a tar Archive

Let's start with a simple example:

```
$ tar -cf etc-20020110.tar /etc
```

423

This will recursively iterate through all the files and subdirectories within /etc and create a tar archive named etc-20020110.tar in the /data/backup directory. The -c option asks tar to create an archive, while the -f option specifies the file to archive to.

What if you want to see the files that tar is archiving? Simple, add a -v (verbose) switch to the command above, like so:

```
$ tar -cvf etc-20020110.tar /etc
tar: Removing leading `/' from member names
etc/
etc/sysconfig/
etc/sysconfig/network-scripts/
etc/sysconfig/network-scripts/ifup-aliases
etc/sysconfig/network-scripts/ifcfg-lo
...
```

As tar archives each file, you will see it listed on your screen. You can use the -v switch with any other option to see verbose output.

Restoring from a tar Archive

Now, how do we restore files from a tar archive? You can simply do the following (we looked at this in Chapter 3, as well, you may remember):

```
$ tar -zvf etc-20020110.tar
etc/
etc/sysconfig/
etc/sysconfig/network-scripts/
etc/sysconfig/network-scripts/ifup-aliases
etc/sysconfig/network-scripts/ifcfg-lo
...
```

tar will create a directory called etc in your current working directory, along with all the files and subdirectories that were archived. If you don't want to extract all the files, or are not sure what files are contained in an archive, use the -tf switches first to look at the files in the archive:

```
$ tar -tvf etc-20020110.tar
```

Then, you can extract a particular file, like so:

```
$ tar -f etc-20020110.tar -x etc/sysconfig/network-scripts/ifcfg-lo
```

Other tar Facilities

tar has other options, such as the ability to **compress** archives, to **include** files from multiple directories, and to **exclude** certain files. Here is another example:

```
$ tar -czvf config-20020110.tar.gz /etc /usr/local/apps/etc
```

Here, `tar` will include files from both `/etc` and `/usr/local/apps/etc` into a `gzip` compressed archive, `config-20020110.tar.gz`. You can restore this by using the `-z` switch again:

```
$ tar -zxvf config-20020110.tar.gz
```

Archiving onto Tape

Now, how do we archive files onto tape? On Linux, the expression `/dev/[n]st(n)x` points to the tape device, where the first n specifies 'no rewind', the second n indicates the device number, and x specifies the tape density:

L	low density
M	medium density
a	autoselect density
None	default density

Let's look at an example where we archive to tape:

```
$ tar -cvf /dev/nst0 /etc
```

Typically, a symbolic link `/dev/tape` points to the default tape device.

Incremental tar Archives

And finally, how do we create incremental tar archives that contain files that have been added or modified only since a specific date? Lucky for us, the newer versions of tar have an `-N` option which allows us to do this:

```
$ tar -cvf etc-20020112.tar /etc -N 01/12/03
```

This will archive files that have been added or modified after 01/12/03.

As you can see, `tar` is a very flexible and powerful archival tool, but one that is not designed to archive arbitrary files located in various directories throughout the system. For that purpose, we use the `cpio` application.

Archiving with cpio

Early versions of `tar` had its share of limitations. For example:

❑   It could not create archives that spanned multiple (tape) volumes.

425

❑ It could not handle all types of files.

❑ It could not compress the archives on-the-fly.

❑ It could not handle bad areas on a tape.

Over time, `tar` has improved greatly – to a point where these issues are no longer relevant. However, the limitations of early versions of `tar` were also the motivation behind the development of the **cpio** archiving tool.

Creating a cpio Archive

Let's look at an example of `cpio` in action:

```
$ find /etc -print | cpio -vo > etc-20020110.cpio
cpio: /etc: truncating inode number
/etc
cpio: /etc/sysconfig: truncating inode number
/etc/sysconfig
cpio: /etc/sysconfig/network-scripts: truncating inode number
/etc/sysconfig/network-scripts
cpio: /etc/sysconfig/network-scripts/ifup-aliases: truncating inode number
/etc/sysconfig/network-scripts/ifup-aliases
cpio: /etc/sysconfig/network-scripts/ifcfg-lo: truncating inode number
/etc/sysconfig/network-scripts/ifcfg-lo
. . .
```

We use the `find` command to get a list of all the files and subdirectories in `/etc`, and we pass them to the `cpio` command, which creates the archive on our file system. The `-o` switch asks `cpio` to create the archive, while the `-v` (verbose) switch gives us verbose output (just as it did for the `tar` command).

Creating a cpio Archive on Tape

If you want to create the archive on tape, you would simply redirect the output from `cpio` directly to the tape device, like so:

```
$ find /etc -print | cpio -vo > /dev/nst0
```

Selective Archiving

As you can see, passing filenames in this manner to `cpio` allows us great flexibility in selecting what files to archive and what not to archive. For example, take a look at this:

```
$ find /home/joe -name '*.p[lm]' -print | cpio -vo > pl.cpio
/home/joe/bin/ckmail.pl
cpio: /home/joe/lib/CGI/Lite.pm: truncating inode number
/home/joe/lib/CGI/Lite.pm
cpio: /home/joe/lib/Tie/Handle.pm: truncating inode number
/home/joe/lib/Tie/Handle.pm
. . .
```

Here, we ask find to locate all Perl application files that end with either a .pl or .pm extension, and send that list to cpio.

The find command is an incredibly powerful tool, and one that is particularly useful in the context of using cpio. Here's another example:

```
$ find /etc -type f -user root -mtime -5 -print | cpio -vo > latest.cpio
```

This locates all text files (-type f) owned by root (-user root), and modified within the last five days (-mtime 5).

It's worth taking a little time to learn to use the find command well. With mastery of the find command's options, you can develop a very powerful and effective backup and archival strategy.

Restoring from a cpio Archive

We've learned how to create cpio archives but have not discussed how to restore them. In fact, it is rather trivial. Here's an example that restores from a cpio file:

```
$ cpio -vi < pl.cpio
cpio: /home/joe/bin/ckmail.pl not created: newer or same age version exists
cpio: /home/joe/lib/CGI/Lite.pm not created: newer or same age version exists
cpio: /home/joe/lib/Tie/Handle.pm not created: newer or same age version
exists
11 blocks
```

In the next example, we're restoring from the tape drive /dev/nst0:

```
$ cpio -vi < /dev/nst0
```

As you can see, by default cpio will not create the files if the destination file is newer than the archived file or has not been modified. If an older version of the file exists, cpio will overwrite that file with the archived version. You can change this behavior with the --unconditional switch:

```
cpio -vi --unconditional < pl.cpio
```

Or better yet, if you want to simply restore the archive to another location, use the following syntax:

```
cpio -vi -d --no-absolute-filenames --unconditional --force-local < pl.cpio
```

What if you don't want to extract all of the files, but only a single file? First, you can use the --list option to get a list of all the files in the archive:

```
cpio -vi --list < pl.cpio
-rwx------   1 joe   eng        5112 Jan 12 03:35 /home/joe/bin/ckmail.pl
-rw-rw-r--   1 joe   eng           0 Jan 14 03:07 /home/joe/lib/CGI/Lite.pm
-rw-rw-r--   1 joe   eng           0 Jan 14 03:07 /home/joe/lib/Tie/Handle.pm
11 blocks
```

Then you can use the -E switch to extract a specific file:

```
cpio -vi -E /home/joe/bin/ckmail.pl < pl.cpio
```

Hopefully, this brief introduction to cpio has provided you with a chance to learn more about this powerful archival solution. In summary, both tar and cpio have similar functionality, though the manner in which we specify the files to archive is different. An interesting aspect to note is that since both of these applications overlap in functionality to some degree, there was an attempt to merge the two, which was named pax. We won't discuss pax here, but if you are curious, you can install it from the Red Hat distribution and try it out.

The final backup application that we will discuss is dump, which is quite different than either tar or cpio. It is more sophisticated in its approach, as we will see next.

Archiving with dump

What if you want to back up an entire partition, or filesystem, incrementally, complete with the correct ownership, permissions, and creation and modification dates? We could certainly use the tar and cpio tools, but they would be far from efficient, since we need to determine what has been modified and when. dump, however, understands the layout of the filesystem; it reads the inode tables to determine what files to back up. In addition, dump is designed to perform incremental backups, recognizing up to ten backup levels.

When you use dump, you need to assign a backup level from 0–9. The strategy is to perform a full, or complete, backup first – this is referred to as a level 0 backup. Then, periodically, you could perform incremental backups at different levels. If you are curious as to how dump keeps track of modified files, take a look at the /etc/dumpdates configuration file, which looks like the following:

```
/dev/hda2 0 Thu Jan 10 13:30:00 2003
/dev/hda2 9 Thu Jan 11 13:30:00 2003
```

For example, if you later back up at level 9, dump will archive files that have been modified only since the last backup at level 8 or lower. With this type of strategy in place, you can simply recover the entire system from several sets of backups: the full backup plus a series of incremental backups.

Creating a dump Archive

Let's look at an example:

```
$ dump -0 /dev/hda2 -u -f /data/backup/hda2-20020110-0.dmp
  DUMP: Date of this level 0 dump: Fri Jan 10 14:30:00 2003
  DUMP: Dumping /dev/hda2 (/home) to /data/backup/hda2-20020110-0.dmp
  DUMP: Added inode 8 to exclude list (journal inode)
  DUMP: Added inode 7 to exclude list (resize inode)
  DUMP: Label: /home
  DUMP: mapping (Pass I) [regular files]
  DUMP: mapping (Pass II) [directories]
  DUMP: estimated 40720 tape blocks.
  DUMP: Volume 1 started with block 1 at: Fri Jan 10 14:30:03 2003
  DUMP: dumping (Pass III) [directories]
  DUMP: dumping (Pass IV) [regular files]
  DUMP: Closing /data/backup/hda2-20020110-0.dmp
  DUMP: Volume 1 completed at: Fri Jan 10 14:30:36 2003
  DUMP: Volume 1 43190 tape blocks (42.18MB)
  DUMP: Volume 1 took 0:00:30
  DUMP: Volume 1 transfer rate: 1439 kB/s
  DUMP: 43190 tape blocks (42.18MB) on 1 volume(s)
  DUMP: finished in 30 seconds, throughput 1439 kBytes/sec
  DUMP: Date of this level 0 dump: Fri Jan 10 14:30:00 2003
  DUMP: Date this dump completed:  Fri Jan 10 14:30:36 2003
  DUMP: Average transfer rate: 1439 kB/s
  DUMP: DUMP IS DONE
```

This performs a level 0 backup of the /dev/hda2 partition to the specified file. The -u option is very important, since it asks dump to update the /etc/dumpdates file. An important task to remember is to label your backups properly, whether you are archiving your data onto hard disk or onto other media. This allows you to find your backups quickly if disaster ever strikes.

Dumping a Filesystem to Tape

If you want to dump a filesystem to tape, simply do the following:

```
$ dump -0 /dev/hda2 -u -f /dev/nst0
```

Compressed Archives

In addition, dump also supports compression on the fly. By specifying either the -j (bzlib) switch or the -z (zlib) switch, followed by a compression level from 1–9, you can enable compression. Here is an example:

```
$ dump -0 /dev/hda2 -u -z9 -f /data/backup/hda2-20020111-0.dmp
  DUMP: Date of this level 0 dump: Sat Jan 11 14:30:00 2003
  DUMP: Dumping /dev/hda2 (/home) to /data/backup/hda2-20020111-0.dmp
  DUMP: Added inode 8 to exclude list (journal inode)
  DUMP: Added inode 7 to exclude list (resize inode)
  DUMP: Compressing output at compression level 9 (zlib)
```

429

```
. . .
DUMP: Wrote 44940kB uncompressed, 29710kB compressed, 1.513:1
DUMP: DUMP IS DONE
```

Incremental Backups

After a full backup, you should typically perform a series of incremental backups, like so:

```
$ dump -9 /dev/hda2 -u -z9 -f /data/backup/hda2-20020112-9.dmp
DUMP: Date of this level 9 dump: Sun Jan 12 14:30:00 2003
DUMP: Date of last level 0 dump: Sat Jan 11 14:30:00 2003
DUMP: Dumping /dev/hda2 (/home) to /data/backup/hda2-20020112-9.dmp
. . .
```

Here are a few examples of sequences of dump levels that you may choose to follow:

```
[0]    9    8    7    6    [5]
[0]    9    9    9    9    [9]
[0]    3   [2]   5   [4]   [5]
```

You would need to restore only the incremental backups represented by the brackets. Why, you ask? Let's examine the third sequence:

Level	Date	Files
0	1/1/02	All files
3	1/2/02	Only files modified since 1/1/02
2	1/3/02	Only files modified since 1/1/02
5	1/4/02	Only files modified since 1/3/02
4	1/5/02	Only files modified since 1/3/02
5	1/6/02	Only files modified since 1/5/02

If you look at this chart, you should realize that in order to restore your system to a previous state, you would need to recover only backups done on 1/1/02, 1/3/02, 1/5/02, and 1/6/02. This is due to the redundancy present in the other backup levels. This brings us to the next topic, namely how do we actually restore these backups?

Restoring from a dump Archive

You can decide to do a partial restore, selecting a set of specific files, or a full restore. In order to do a full restore, however, you need to create and mount the target filesystem, like so:

```
$ mke2fs /dev/hda2
$ mount /dev/hda2 /home
$ cd /home
$ restore -rvf /data/backup/hda2-20020110-0.dmp
Verify tape and initialize maps
Input is from file/pipe
Input block size is 32
Dump    date: Fri Jan 10 14:30:00 2003
Dumped from: the epoch
Level 0 dump of /home on localhost.localdomain:/dev/hda2
Label: /home
Begin level 0 restore
Initialize symbol table.
Extract directories from tape
Calculate extraction list.
Make node ./lost+found
Make node ./joe
Make node ./joe/.gnome2
Make node ./joe/.gnome2/accels
Make node ./joe/.gnome2/share
...
```

This will restore the dumped archive; the -r asks restore to rebuild the filesystem, the -v switch turns on verbose messages, and the -f option specifies the dump file. If you were using a tape drive, you would do the following:

```
$ restore -rvf /dev/nst0
```

dump will request you to mount additional tapes, if they exist.

In turn, you could restore the incremental backups in much the same manner. You need to make sure that you restore the dumps in the order they were created, starting with the lowest-level dump – typically level 0.

Before we finish this section, let's look at interactive restoration of dump archives. From the dump shown above, say you want to extract the file ./joe/.gnome2/accels. You would do the following:

```
$ restore -ivf /data/backup/hda2-20020110-0.dmp
Verify tape and initialize maps
Input is from file/pipe
Input block size is 32
Dump    date: Fri Jan 10 14:30:00 2003
Dumped from: the epoch
Level 0 dump of /home on localhost.localdomain:/dev/hda2
Label: /home
Extract directories from tape
Initialize symbol table.
```

```
restore > ls
.:
    2 ./                  11 lost+found/  32001 joe/
    2 ../            256009 postgres/

restore > add joe/.gnome2/accels
Make node ./joe
Make node ./joe/.gnome2
Make node ./joe/.gnome2/accels
restore > ls
.:
    2 ./                  11 lost+found/  32001 *joe/
    2 ../            256009 postgres/

restore > extract
Extract requested files
You have not read any volumes yet.
Unless you know which volume your file(s) are on you should start
with the last volume and work towards the first.
Specify next volume # (none if no more volumes): 1
Add links
Set directory mode, owner, and times.
set owner/mode for '.'? [yn] y
restore > quit
```

You might agree with me that dump is a very powerful tool for quickly and easily backing up entire filesystems. It serves a purpose that is not filled with either `tar` or `cpio`.

In summary, backing up and archiving files is very important. Linux comes with a vast assortment of applications and tools to make archiving a convenient process. There are tools available for mirroring partitions and files, performing network backups, such as Amanda, as well as backups to CD-ROM, `cdrecord`. Once you decide on a backup strategy, you should investigate these tools to determine the application that is most suited for your purpose.

Next, we will shift gears a bit and talk about building applications from source code. Say, for example, you find a really powerful archival application. After looking at its documentation, you realize, to your disappointment, that it does not come with a pre-built binary for Linux, but only source code. How do you go about building it? Proceed to the next section to find out more.

Building from Source

So far in this book, the applications we've been using have all been installed from pre-compiled binary RedHat Packet Manager (RPM) packages. We've seen how quick and easy it is to install, modify, and uninstall programs from pre-compiled binaries. However, there are also many applications available as (uncompiled) source code, typically in a compressed archive of some sort (i.e. `.tar.gz` or `.tar.bz2`).

Many applications are made available in both formats (RPM and uncompiled source), and if we want to install such an application then we have a choice about which format to use – building applications via source code or installing pre-built binary RPM packages. In this situation, it's not clear which method is preferable; it comes down to personal preference. The following table summarizes the levels of difficulty and control involved:

Action	Binary RPM	Source Code
Ease of installation	High	Low to High; dependent on environment
Ease of un-installation	High	Low to High
Control of build process and installation	Low	Medium to High

The RPM keeps track of dependencies, and hence gives us the ability to upgrade or uninstall a package quite easily. While an RPM package tends to install the files contained in the package in disparate locations throughout the system, it is possible to use the `--prefix` and `--relocate` options to force RPM to install the files in specific directories. But, if you want even more control over the installation process, you should build the application from source code.

Of course, there are also many applications for which there is no RPM package – only the uncompiled source code is made available. If you want to install an application of this type, you have no choice but to produce the application yourself, by building and compiling the source code on your system.

In the next section, we'll download, build, and install version 2.0.14 of the gFTP application, an FTP client application with a graphic user interface – from its source code. Red Hat 9 comes pre-built with version 2.0.14 of the gFTP application, so you don't have to worry about upgrading the application. However, by learning how to build the application from its source code now, you can update to the latest version when it becomes available.

Installing Development Tools and Libraries

Before we start to build our first application from source code, we will need to install the appropriate development tools and code libraries. First, we need to have certain development tools installed, including `make` and `gcc` for initiating the build process and to compile the C source code, respectively. And second, we need to install the X Window System and GNOME software development libraries. The gFTP application uses these libraries to create a rich GNOME compliant user interface. We'll use the RPM applet to install these required packages.

1. Launch the RPM applet (either from the Applications | System Settings | Packages menu, or by executing the `redhat-config-packages` application from the command line).

2. As you peruse the list of package categories, you will see the Development package category toward the end. Click on Development Tools, which bundles the `make` and `gcc` packages, as well as the X Software Development and GNOME Software Development package groups, and press the Update button:

The installation process will take some time, but once it's finished, we can start our application building process.

Building the Application

As a good exercise, we will build the gFTP application. As you will soon see, the entire process of building and installing the application is limited to three simple steps. You can apply these same techniques when building other applications from source code as well.

Try It Out Compiling the gFTP Application

1. First, you must determine the root source directory where we will be building *any* and *all* applications. A good directory to choose is /usr/local/src, since it is separate from the standard operating system installation directories. Remember, you need to be logged on as the root user to have the necessary privileges to create and modify files in this directory.

2. Once you have decided on the root source directory, you should create a subdirectory where you will unpack the source code for the application. Some source code packages when unpacked will create a directory to hold all of their files, while others will irresponsibly dump the files into the current directory. We take this step to ensure that we do not end up with source code files cluttered all over the /usr/local/src root directory.

```
# mkdir /usr/local/src/gftp
```

3. Now, you can go ahead and obtain the source code for gFTP from the following URL:

    http://www.gftp.org/gftp-2.0.14.tar.gz

Notice that the source code is distributed as a compressed tar archive. You can download it using a Web browser, or by using the wget program, like so:

```
# cd /usr/local/src/gftp
# wget http://www.gftp.org/gftp-2.0.14.tar.gz
--19:07:51--  http://www.gftp.org/gftp-2.0.14.tar.gz
          => 'gftp-2.0.14.tar.gz'
Resolving www.gftp.org... done.
Connecting to www.gftp.org[18.244.0.188]:80... connected.
HTTP request sent, awaiting response... 200 OK
Length: 1,136,930 [application/x-tar]

100%[====================================>] 1,136,930 28.47K/s   ETA 00:00

19:08:30 (28.47 KB/s) - 'gftp-2.0.14.tar.gz' saved [1136930/1136930]
```

4. The next step is to uncompress and untar the archive:

```
# tar -zkxvf gftp-2.0.14.tar.gz
gftp-2.0.14/
gftp-2.0.14/config.h.in
gftp-2.0.14/COPYING
gftp-2.0.14/Makefile.am
...
gftp-2.0.14/README
gftp-2.0.14/gftp.spec
```

435

```
gftp-2.0.14/install-sh
gftp-2.0.14/NEWS
```

The -k switch forces tar to keep any existing files; it will not overwrite existing files with files from the archive. This is for our own safety and ensures that we will not lose any important files in case we are exposed to a rogue package that was designed to destroy existing files.

5. We now have a directory called gftp-2.0.14, which contains all of the source code for the gFTP application. Let's get into that directory and run the configure program, which configures the source code for building on our system.

```
# cd gftp-2.0.14
# ./configure --prefix=/usr/local
creating cache ./config.cache
checking for non-GNU ld... /usr/bin/ld
checking if the linker (/usr/bin/ld) is GNU ld... yes
checking for a BSD compatible install... /usr/bin/install -c
checking whether build environment is sane... yes
checking whether make sets ${MAKE}... yes
checking for working aclocal-1.4... found
checking for working autoconf... found
checking for working automake-1.4... found
checking for working autoheader... found
checking for working makeinfo... found
checking host system type... i686-pc-linux-gnu
checking for gcc... gcc
...
creating config.h
creating po/POTFILES
creating po/Makefile
```

As you can see, the configure command does a lot of work, trying to determine what type of system we have and what tools are available. We have asked the configure application to use the /usr/local prefix when it comes time to install the application. In other words, all of the files that we need to install will be installed in various subdirectories under /usr/local. This allows us to control where we store all of our custom built application's data and files.

6. Now, we are ready to compile. All we have to do is invoke the make command:

```
# make
make  all-recursive
make[1]: Entering directory `/usr/local/src/gftp/gftp-2.0.14'
Making all in intl
make[2]: Entering directory `/usr/local/src/gftp/gftp-2.0.14/intl'
make[2]: Nothing to be done for `all'.
make[2]: Leaving directory `/usr/local/src/gftp/gftp-2.0.14/intl'
```

```
Making all in docs
make[2]: Entering directory `/usr/local/src/gftp/gftp-2.0.14/docs'
Making all in sample.gftp
make[3]: Entering directory `/usr/local/src/gftp/gftp-
    2.0.14/docs/sample.gftp'
make[3]: Nothing to be done for `all'.
make[3]: Leaving directory `/usr/local/src/gftp/gftp-
    2.0.14/docs/sample.gftp'
make[3]: Entering directory `/usr/local/src/gftp/gftp-2.0.14/docs'
make[3]: Nothing to be done for `all-am'.
make[3]: Leaving directory `/usr/local/src/gftp/gftp-2.0.14/docs'
make[2]: Leaving directory `/usr/local/src/gftp/gftp-2.0.14/docs'
Making all in lib
make[2]: Entering directory `/usr/local/src/gftp/gftp-2.0.14/lib'
gcc -DHAVE_CONFIG_H -I. -I. -I.. -I/usr/include/glib-2.0 \
    -I/usr/lib/glib-2.0/include   -D_REENTRANT -I.\
    ./intl -DSHARE_DIR=\"/usr/local/share/gftp\"      -g -O2 -c bookmark.c
...
make[2]: Nothing to be done for `all-am'.
make[2]: Leaving directory `/usr/local/src/gftp/gftp-2.0.14'
make[1]: Leaving directory `/usr/local/src/gftp/gftp-2.0.14'
```

The make command follows the instructions specified in Makefile (which was customized to our system by the configure program) to build the application. In this case, there are only a small number of C source files that need to be compiled. So after a few minutes, make finishes and we have our application!

7. The next step is to install the compiled application into /usr/local:

```
# make install
Making install in intl
make[1]: Entering directory `/usr/local/src/gftp/gftp-2.0.14/intl'
if test "gftp" = "gettext" \
    && test '' = 'intl-compat.o'; then \
    /bin/sh `case "./mkinstalldirs" in /*) echo "./mkinstalldirs" ;; *) \
    echo "../../mkinstalldirs" ;; esac` /usr/local/lib /usr/local/include; \
    /usr/bin/install -c -m 644 libintl.h /usr/local/include/libintl.h; \
    @LIBTOOL@ --mode=install \
    /usr/bin/install -c -m 644 libintl.a /usr/local/lib/libintl.a; \
else \
  : ; \
fi
...
make[2]: Nothing to be done for `install-exec-am'.
make[2]: Nothing to be done for `install-data-am'.
make[2]: Leaving directory `/usr/local/src/gftp/gftp-2.0.14'
make[1]: Leaving directory `/usr/local/src/gftp/gftp-2.0.14'
```

8. Let's check to see that the new version of the gFTP application has been built and installed properly. Since you had asked the `make` program to install the application and its related files in `/usr/local`, you will find the gFTP binary executable in `/usr/local/bin`. You can execute the application with the `--version` switch to verify that it is indeed version 2.0.14, like so:

```
$ /usr/local/bin/gftp --version
gFTP 2.0.14
```

The existing version will continue to exist on your system in its original location, `/usr/bin`, which you can see for yourself:

```
$ /usr/bin/gftp --version
gFTP 2.0.14
```

It is up to you to decide whether you want to keep both versions around. Typically, when you install a new version of a software application, you should keep the older version around until you have had the chance to test the new version for some period of time. That way, you can always revert back to the original version if the newer version of the application is problematic.

Before you build any application from its source code, you should spend some time reading through the README and INSTALL files, as well as looking at some of the source code. That way, you can get a better handle for the application's features and limitations.

How It Works

We have done it! We have compiled and built our very first application, straight from source code; the process was quite straightforward for this application, though it will vary somewhat from application to application:

```
# ./configure --prefix=/some/dir
# make
# make install
```

By building applications in this manner, we have more control over the entire process and can decide how to modify or optimize the code and select where and how to install its components. For the most part, the building process is not too difficult. But, sometimes, however, you may run into difficulties getting the code to compile. It is beyond the scope of this book to discuss these various situations, so please refer to *Professional Linux Programming* for more details.

Now that we have learned how to compile source code, we will modify and build the ultimate application, the Linux kernel, in the next section.

Rebuilding the Linux Kernel

The Linux **kernel**, as you know, is at the core of the Linux operating system. One of the main responsibilities of the kernel is to provide an interface to the underlying hardware; the kernel handles all communications between applications and hardware. In addition, the kernel implements and oversees a variety of tasks, including:

- ❑ Process creation, scheduling, and termination
- ❑ Interprocess communication
- ❑ Memory management (paging, swapping, and mapping)
- ❑ Access and security control

You can loosely categorize the kernel into two main components – **device drivers** and **device independent subsystems**:

- ❑ The device drivers implement the actual communications with the physical hardware.
- ❑ The subsystems mediate access to hardware resources by providing each and every process with fair access (otherwise known as **scheduling**).

Most of these device drivers are actually separate executable objects, or kernel modules, that can be loaded and unloaded as needed. In summary, the Linux kernel is **modular** in nature, and is not one large **monolithic** entity.

Why Rebuild the Kernel?

So, if the Linux kernel is modular, why would we ever need to rebuild or configure it? After all, the fact that it is modular means that modules that are not required will not be loaded. Well, there are three reasons that stand out:

- ❑ First, the kernel provided by the standard distribution is generic in nature – it is capable of running on most Intel x86 hardware but not optimized for any particular configuration. You want to optimize the kernel for your *particular* hardware.
- ❑ Second, there are certain other drivers that are built into the kernel itself, and you may want to remove these drivers for reasons of security and performance.
- ❑ Third, you may also want to add support for your particular hardware devices directly into the kernel.

In this section, we will learn more about the Linux kernel, and we'll produce a small, lean, monolithic kernel that is perfect for use in routers and firewalls. You probably don't want to keep this kernel for the desktop or laptop machine you use on a day-to-day basis. However, you might like to try this out now (to see how easy it is) and then reinstate the default kernel afterward. Then, if you ever need to build a dedicated router or firewall machine, you'll know how it's done!

Initializing the Kernel

Before we start to work with the kernel, we need to perform two important tasks. First, we need to install the necessary kernel source packages; and second, we need to back up the current kernel and related files.

Let's install the necessary kernel headers and sources.

Try It Out   Initializing the Kernel

1. Open the RPM applet (either from the Applications | System Settings | Packages menu, or by executing the redhat-config-packages application from the command line).

2. Select the Kernel Development package group from the Development category, and press the Update button to install the necessary packages; see screenshot below. If you have installed the necessary development tools and libraries to build gFTP in the previous section, then Development Tools, X Software Development, and GNOME Software Development package groups will be checked. However, if you did not build gFTP, you would need to select the Development Tools package group, in addition to Kernel Development, to build the kernel.

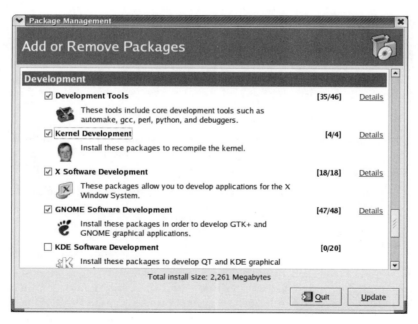

The Kernel Development package group will install the kernel source code in the /usr/src/linux-2.4.20-2.48 directory.

3. There are two more tasks to perform before we can start to configure the kernel, and that is to back up the existing kernel and make a boot disk. That way, if something goes wrong, we can always revert back to the original kernel.

    First, here is how you would back up the /boot partition:

    ```
    # tar -zcvf /root/boot-2.4.20-2.48.20020112.tar.gz /boot
    ```

    We use a combination of the kernel version along with the current date to name the compressed tar archive; this provides us a unique identifier. If you get in the habit of compiling kernels on a regular basis, this naming convention will allow you to quickly identify which archive to use for recovery if necessary.

    Second, let's make a system boot disk. Insert a clean floppy disk into the drive and enter the following command:

    ```
    # /sbin/mkbootdisk --verbose  --device /dev/fd0 `uname -r`
    grubby: bad argument --info: missing argument
    Insert a disk in /dev/fd0. Any information on the disk will be lost.
    Press <Enter> to continue or ^C to abort:
    Formatting /dev/fd0... done.
    Copying /boot/vmlinuz-2.4.20-2.48... done.
    Creating initrd image... done.
    Configuring bootloader... done.
    ```

    This essentially copies the kernel and other required files to the floppy disk, so we can use this disk to boot our system at any time.

How It Works

The /boot directory holds the kernel and related files. If you look around at the contents of this directory, you will see a file called vmlinuz-2.4.20-2.48 (or similar). This is the kernel!

> *A note about versions: if you are using Red Hat Linux 9, then your kernel is probably v2.4.20-2.48. In the Linux kernel's versioning scheme, the first digit (2 in this case) represents the major version and the second digit (4 in this case) represents the minor version. If the minor version number is odd, then the kernel is a beta version; otherwise, it is from a release/production branch. The third number (20 in this case) is the kernel patch number and the final number is the package number.*

By contrast, the Linux loadable kernel modules (LKMs) are stored in the directory /lib/modules/2.4.20-2.48. If you take a look at the contents of this directory, you'll see that there are a large number of modules available. If you are curious to know the exact number of modules here, you can execute the following statement:

```
# find /lib/modules/`uname -r` -name '*.o' -print | wc -l
898
```

We use the `find` command to locate all the modules (that is, files with a `.o` extension) in the `/lib/modules` directory associated with the system kernel. Instead of hardcoding the kernel version, we use the `uname` command with the `-r` switch, which returns the system's kernel version.

We are now finally ready to work with the kernel!

A Small, Lean Kernel

We will build a small, lean monolithic kernel that is ideal for use in routers and firewalls. Unlike the "regular" kernel that you would typically use in a desktop computer or laptop, a kernel designed for a router or firewall has to have very specific characteristics:

❑ It has to be lean so we don't use up a lot of resources.

❑ It has to be monolithic; it should not have the ability to load or unload modules.

❑ It should disable support for any hot-pluggable devices, floppy drives, and multimedia components.

❑ Advanced networking features should be enabled.

Looking at these characteristics, you might wonder why we would want to disable support for the floppy drive, for example. We certainly do not want any intruders who have potential physical access to this router or firewall server to introduce any files or executables into our server. By disabling the floppy drive altogether, we don't have to worry about this prospect.

By keeping these characteristics in mind, we will end up with a kernel that is lean, secure, and optimized for network performance. Let's build this kernel!

Try It Out   **Building a Kernel**

1. First, we need to change our current directory to `/usr/src/linux-2.4.20-2.48`:

```
# cd /usr/src/linux-2.4.20-2.48
```

2. From there, we can use the following commands to run the X Window–based kernel configuration editor:

```
# make xconfig
rm -f include/asm
( cd include ; ln -sf asm-i386 asm)
```

```
make -C scripts kconfig.tk
...
cat tail.tk >> kconfig.tk
chmod 755 kconfig.tk
make[1]: Leaving directory `/usr/src/linux-2.4.20-2.48/scripts'
wish -f scripts/kconfig.tk
```

After a short time, you'll see the configuration editor appear:

Linux Kernel Configuration		
Code maturity level options	Fusion MPT device support	Sound
Loadable module support	IEEE 1394 (FireWire) support (EXPERIMENTAL)	USB support
Processor type and features	I2O device support	Additional device driver support
General setup	Network device support	Bluetooth support
Memory Technology Devices (MTD)	Amateur Radio support	Profiling support
Parallel port support	IrDA (infrared) support	Kernel hacking
Plug and Play configuration	ISDN subsystem	Library routines
Block devices	Old CD-ROM drivers (not SCSI, not IDE)	
Multi-device support (RAID and LVM)	Input core support	
Cryptography support (CryptoAPI)	Character devices	
Networking options	Multimedia devices	Save and Exit
Telephony Support	Crypto Hardware support	Quit Without Saving
ATA/IDE/MFM/RLL support	File systems	Load Configuration from File
SCSI support	Console drivers	Store Configuration to File

If you don't have X Window installed, you can use a text-based editor by executing the following command:

```
# make menuconfig
```

As you can see from the figure below, the text-based editor looks a bit different, but supports all of the same configuration options:

File   Edit   View   Terminal   Go   Help

Linux Kernel v2.4.20-2.48custom Configuration

```
                         ── Main Menu ──
   Arrow keys navigate the menu. <Enter> selects submenus --->.
   Highlighted letters are hotkeys.  Pressing <Y> includes, <N> excludes,
   <M> modularizes features.  Press <Esc><Esc> to exit, <?> for Help.
   Legend: [*] built-in  [ ] excluded  <M> module  < > module capable

      ┌─────────────────────────────────────────────────────────┐
      │  Code maturity level options  --->                       │
      │  Loadable module support  --->                           │
      │  Processor type and features  --->                       │
      │  General setup  --->                                     │
      │  Memory Technology Devices (MTD)  --->                   │
      │  Parallel port support  --->                             │
      │  Plug and Play configuration  --->                       │
      │  Block devices  --->                                     │
      │  Multi-device support (RAID and LVM)  --->              │
      │  Cryptography support (CryptoAPI)  --->                  │
      │  (+)                                                     │
      └─────────────────────────────────────────────────────────┘

             <Select>     < Exit >     < Help >
```

For the rest of this configuration section, we will use the X Window configuration editor.

3. From the configuration editor, you can enable or disable a multitude of options and kernel modules. In this example, we plan to build a monolithic kernel; therefore, we need to disable loadable module support. To do this, click on the Loadable module support button – this brings up a dialog of the same name. Then, in the dialog, change the Enable loadable module support setting from y to n:

```
                 ┌───────────────────────────────┐
                 │   Loadable module support     │
                 └───────────────────────────────┘

   ◇ y   ◇ -   ◆ n   Enable loadable module support            Help

   ◇ y   ◇ -   ◇ n   Set version information on all module symbols   Help

   ◇ y   ◇ -   ◇ n   Kernel module loader                     Help


       Main Menu              Next               Prev
```

*If you look through some of the other options, you'll notice the presence of **three** choices before each functional description: y, m, and n. Clicking on the y enables that specific functionality, and selecting n disables it. Clicking on the m option builds that functionality as a loadable module.*

4. That's just the first setting. Now, go through the rest of the configuration – you can step from one configuration dialog to the next by using the Next and Prev buttons. Use the following recipe, which lists settings that need to be changed only; each highlighted top level section represents a major section/button in the kernel configuration:

```
Loadable module support
    - Enable loadable module support                         N

Processor type and features
    - Processor family                           Select Processor
    - Symmetric multi-processing support                     N
```

You can determine the processor name and type for your machine by simply searching for the string "CPU:" in the startup boot messages in the /var/log/messages log file, like so:

```
# grep CPU /var/log/messages
Feb 18 19:25:15 localhost kernel: Initializing CPU#0
Feb 18 19:25:15 localhost kernel: CPU: L1 I cache: 16K, L1 D cache: 16K
Feb 18 19:25:15 localhost kernel: CPU: L2 cache: 256K
Feb 18 19:25:15 localhost kernel: Intel machine check reporting enabled on
CPU#0.
Feb 18 19:25:15 localhost kernel: CPU: Intel Pentium III (Coppermine)
stepping 0a
```

Let's continue with the recipe:

```
General Setup
    - Support for hot-pluggable devices                      N
    - Kernel support for MISC binaries                       N
    - Power Management support                               N

Plug and Play configuration
    - Plug and Play support                                  Y
    -    ISA Plug and Play support                           N

Block devices
    - Normal PC floppy disk support                          N

Networking options
    - Packet socket                                          Y
    -    Packet socket: mmapped IO                           Y
    - Network packet filtering (replaces ipchains)           Y
```

445

```
        - Socket Filtering                                      Y
      - TCP/IP networking                                       Y
      -   IP: advanced router                                   Y
      -     IP: policy routing                                  Y
      -        IP: use netfilter MARK value as routing key      Y
      -        IP: fast network address translation             Y
      -     IP: equal cost multipath                            Y
      -     IP: use TOS value as routing key                    Y
      -     IP: verbose route monitoring                        Y
      -     IP: large routing tables                            Y
      -   IP: tunneling                                         Y
      -   IP: multicast routing                                 Y
      -      IP: PIM-SM version 1 support                       Y


      IP: Netfilter Configuration
        - Connection tracking (required for masq/NAT)           Y
        -    FTP protocol support                               Y
        - IP tables support (required for filtering/masq/NAT)   Y
        -    limit match support                                Y
        -    MAC address match support                          Y
        -    netfilter MARK match support                       Y
        -    Multiple port match support                        Y
        -    TOS match support                                  Y
        -    AH/ESP match support                               Y
        -    LENGTH match support                               Y
        -    TTL match support                                  Y
        -    tcpmss match support                               Y
        -    Connection state match support                     Y
        -    Packet filtering                                   Y
        -       REJECT target support                           Y
        -    Full NAT                                           Y
        -       MASQUERADE target support                       Y
        -       REDIRECT target support                         Y
        -       NAT of local connections (READ HELP)            Y
        -    Packet mangling                                    Y
        -       TOS target support                              Y
        -       MARK target support                             Y
        -    LOG target support                                 Y
        -    ULOG target support                                Y
        -    TCPMSS target support                              Y
        - ARP tables support                                    Y
        -    ARP packet filtering                               Y


  ATA/IDE/MFM/RLL support
      - ATA/IDE/MFM/RLL support                                 Y


      IDE, ATA and ATAPI Block devices
        - CMD640 chipset bugfix/support                         N
        - RZ1000 chipset bugfix/support                         N


  SCSI support
      - SCSI support                                            N
```

```
Network device support
     Ethernet (10 or 100Mbit)
          -        DECchip Tulip (dc21x4x) PCI support              Y
```

Depending on whether your system has IDE or SCSI devices, enable or disable the functionality that is suited for your hardware. You should note that the CMD640 and the RZ1000 chipsets have design flaws that could lead to corruption on 486 and Pentium motherboards. If you have a newer machine, you can probably disable these fixes, as shown above.

Also, select your Ethernet card and enable it, or choose the defaults. And finally, enable the following options if you want to support USB devices:

```
Input core support
     - Input core support                                          Y
     -   Keyboard support                                          Y
     -   Mouse support                                             Y

Character devices
     - Maximum number of Unix98 PTYs in use (0-2048)               8
     - Direct Rendering Manager (XFree86 DRI support)              N

     Mice
          - Bus Mouse Support                                      Y

File systems
     - Kernel automounter version 4 support (also supports v3)     N
     - Ext3 journalling file system support                       Y

     Network File Systems
          - NFS file system support                               N
          - NFS server support                                    N

Sound
     - Sound card support                                          N

USB support
     - Preliminary USB device filesystem                          Y
     - USB Human Interface Device (full HID) support              Y
     -   HID input layer support                                  Y
     -   /dev/hiddev raw HID device support                       Y
```

5. When you have finished going through all of these options, click on the Save and Exit button to save the configuration and exit from the editor.

6. We are almost there; you just need to make few more changes. First, we must edit the `Makefile` contained in the `/usr/src/linux-2.4.20-2.48` directory, by changing the identifier assigned to the `EXTRAVERSION` variable as follows:

447

```
EXTRAVERSION = -2.48lean
```

The –2.48 corresponds to the package number (the last part of the kernel identifier: 2.4.20-2.48) and lean is what we've added to distinguish this configuration of the kernel from other configurations. Therefore, our kernel will be installed as 2.4.20-2.48lean.

7. Next, we need to create a couple of empty files and an empty modules directory associated with our kernel, as the Makefile assumes that these files will be in place. Otherwise, we will see compile-time errors.

```
# touch drivers/pci/classlist.h drivers/pci/devlist.h
# mkdir /lib/modules/2.4.20-2.48lean
```

8. We are ready! Let's build our kernel. The first step is to create dependencies in the source code to get it ready for compiling:

```
# make dep
make[1]: Entering directory `/usr/src/linux-2.4.20-2.48/arch/i386/boot'
make[1]: Nothing to be done for `dep'.
make[1]: Leaving directory `/usr/src/linux-2.4.20-2.48/arch/i386/boot'
scripts/mkdep -- init/*.c > .depend
...
make[1]: Leaving directory `/usr/src/linux-2.4.20-2.48'
(find /usr/src/linux-2.4.20-2.48 \( -name .depend -o -name .hdepend \) \
    -print | xargs awk -f scripts/include_deps) > tmp_include_depends
sed -ne 's/^\([^ ].*\):.*/  \1 \\/p' tmp_include_depends > \
    tmp_include_depends_1(echo ""; echo "all: \\"; cat \
    tmp_include_depends_1; echo "") >> tmp_include_depends
rm tmp_include_depends_1
```

9. Next, clean up any remnants of old code, temporary object files, and other unnecessary files:

```
# make clean
make[1]: Entering directory `/usr/src/linux-2.4.20-2.48/arch/i386/boot'
rm -f tools/build
rm -f setup bootsect zImage compressed/vmlinux.out
rm -f bsetup bbootsect bzImage compressed/bvmlinux.out
...
rm -f  parport-share.png  parport-multi.png  parport-structure.png  \
    parport-share.eps  parport-multi.eps  parport-structure.eps
rm -f procfs_example.sgml
make[1]: Leaving directory `/usr/src/linux-2.4.18-
    14/Documentation/DocBook'
```

10. Now, build the kernel:

```
# make bzImage
gcc -Wall -Wstrict-prototypes -O2 -fomit-frame-pointer -o \
    scripts/split-include scripts/split-include.c \
    scripts/split-include include/linux/autoconf.h include/config
make -r -f tmp_include_depends all
make[1]: Entering directory `/usr/src/linux-2.4.20-2.48'
make[1]: Leaving directory `/usr/src/linux-2.4.20-2.48'
gcc -D__KERNEL__ -I/usr/src/linux-2.4.20-2.48/include -Wall \
    -Wstrict-prototypes -Wno-trigraphs -O2 -fno-strict-aliasing \
    -fno-common -fomit-frame-pointer -pipe -mpreferred-stack-boundary=2 \
    -march=i686   -DKBUILD_BASENAME=main -c -o init/main.o init/main.c
...
tools/build -b bbootsect bsetup compressed/bvmlinux.out CURRENT > bzImage
Root device is (3, 5)
Boot sector 512 bytes.
Setup is 2536 bytes.
System is 821 kB
make[1]: Leaving directory `/usr/src/linux-2.4.20-2.48/arch/i386/boot'
```

11. Next, install the new kernel and related files in /boot:

```
# make install
make -r -f tmp_include_depends all
make[1]: Entering directory `/usr/src/linux-2.4.20-2.48'
make[1]: Nothing to be done for `all'.
make[1]: Leaving directory `/usr/src/linux-2.4.20-2.48'
. scripts/mkversion > .tmpversion
...
sh -x ./install.sh 2.4.20-2.48lean bzImage \
    /usr/src/linux-2.4.20-2.48/System.map ""
+ `[` -x /root/bin/installkernel `]'
+ `[` -x /sbin/installkernel `]'
+ exec /sbin/installkernel 2.4.20-2.48lean bzImage \
    /usr/src/linux-2.4.20-2.48/System.map `'
make[1]: Leaving directory `/usr/src/linux-2.4.20-2.48/arch/i386/boot'
```

12. This step doesn't apply if you followed the recipe above, because we disabled loadable module support (back in Step 3). However, if you were configuring your kernel in which loadable module support was enabled, then this would be the right time to build and install the loadable modules:

```
# make modules
# make modules_install
```

13. Now, check your kernel to see how it compares in size with the original kernel. Remember, our goal was to build a small and lean kernel:

```
$ cd /boot
$ ls -s vmlinuz*
    0 vmlinuz@
  832 vmlinuz-2.4.20-2.48lean
 1104 vmlinuz-2.4.20-2.48
```

As you can see, we've reduced the size of the kernel by approximately 25%, and since it is monolithic, we don't use any loadable modules that would consume extra resources at runtime.

14. The final step in the build process is to modify the boot loader configuration, as written by the installer. First, determine the device identification for the root partition, like so:

```
$ grep ` / ` /etc/mtab
/dev/hda1 / ext3 rw 0 0
```

15. Next, edit the /etc/grub.conf file, where you will see the following:

```
title Red Hat Linux (2.4.20-2.48lean)
        root (hd0,0)
        kernel /boot/vmlinuz-2.4.20-2.48lean ro root=LABEL=/
        initrd /boot/initrd-2.4.20-2.48lean.img
```

Simply replace the root argument, like so:

```
        kernel /boot/vmlinuz-2.4.20-2.48lean ro root=/dev/hda1
```

16. Now go ahead and reboot. If the kernel was built and installed successfully, you will see two options in the GRUB bootloader screen when your system starts up: Red Hat Linux (2.4.20-2.48) and Red Hat Linux (2.4.20-2.48lean). If you choose the first option, your system will boot up using the original kernel. Otherwise, the system will boot using the lean and mean kernel that we have just built.

Reverting to the Original Kernel

Unfortunately, if we made any mistakes or if certain bugs in the source code manifested themselves during the build or compile processes, we may have a situation where the system will fail to boot. In such a case, we have three options that we can try out, starting from the easiest to the most difficult:

❑   boot from the original kernel through the GRUB bootloader screen

❑   boot from the floppy disk

❑   boot from the Red Hat 9 disk #1 in rescue mode

The first option of booting from the GRUB bootloader is by far the easiest and should allow you to boot properly into the system. Simply select the original kernel from the list and the kernel will load, assuming that this kernel was not overwritten when we built the customized kernel. This is possible only if you failed to give our lean kernel a different identifier, such as 2.4.20-2.48lean.

Once you are in the system, you can try to restore an older version of the /boot partition from the tar archive, like so:

```
# cd /
# mv boot boot.notworking
# tar -zxvf /root/boot-2.4.20-2.48.20020112.tar.gz
```

Then, try to reboot the system and see what happens!

If this option does not work, insert the floppy boot disk that we created earlier into the machine and start up your system. This is a very reliable option since the original kernel is itself stored on the floppy disk. If you can get into the system, you should again attempt to restore the /boot partition as described above and restart the system.

Finally, if both of these options fail to start up your system, you should boot your system in rescue mode using the Red Hat 9 CD-ROM #1. Once you see a splash screen, enter the following command at the prompt:

```
linux rescue
```

Eventually, you will see the following message:

```
The rescue environment will now attempt to find your Red Hat
Linux installation and mount it under the directory
/mnt/sysimage.  You can then make any changes required to your
system.  If you want to proceed with this step choose
'Continue'. You can also choose to mount your filesystem
read-only instead of read-write by choosing 'Read-only'.
If for some reason this process fails you can choose 'Skip'
and this step will be skipped and you will go directly to a
command shell.
```

Choose Continue, at which point the Red Hat installer will mount our filesystems in the /mnt/sysimage directory in read-write mode; we will be able to add and delete files. If this process is successful, we will be able to access our /boot partition via /mnt/sysimage/boot. We can do even better and make the /mnt/sysimage directory our root partition by using the chroot command:

```
# chroot /mnt/sysimage
```

Now, try to restore the original /boot partition and see if you can boot into your system.

Summary

Over the course of this chapter, we have discussed various administrative aspects of the Linux operating system, including system configuration and log files, backup and archival procedures, compiling applications from source code, and building a customized kernel.

We started out with system configuration files. Unlike other operating systems, where the system configuration is stored in some binary format or other, Linux and most other Unix derivatives store their configuration information in plain text files. This allows us to easily see and edit this configuration without much effort, and makes it easier for us to back up these files as part of our full or incremental backup procedures.

Then, we proceeded to look at log files. As you may have seen, the core Linux components, such as the kernel, as well as other services and applications, log all types of information to these text files. If we pay close attention to the content in these log files, we can find and diagnose all types of issues from hardware failures to security alerts.

System configuration and log files are very important pieces of our operating system. In order for us to maintain our Linux system running even in case of severe crashes, we need to implement a useful backup strategy. We discussed all types of backup and archival strategy, including what tools to use; how, when, and where to back up; and what types of issues we need to watch for.

We finished out the chapter by learning how to compile applications from source code. There will be many occasions where you will find an application in source code form only; no binary RPM package may be available. We can use the various development tools with the techniques discussed in the chapter to build applications. In fact, the same strategy and techniques can be used to build the most complex application of them all: the Linux kernel.

The Linux kernel is the core component that communicates with the hardware and provides an interface between applications and hardware. Since we have the entire source code available to us, we can build the kernel to suit almost need. In this chapter, we built a lean, mean, and optimized kernel suitable for use in routers and firewalls.

We have covered a lot of practical information in this chapter. It is difficult to cover all of these topics in great detail in such a short amount of space, but hopefully, you have gotten a flavor for what Linux administration entails.

11

Managing Your System with Perl

It's possible that you've already heard of the **Perl** programming language, perhaps in the context of back-end Web applications. If you've ever come across the ubiquitous term *CGI-Perl*, or references to the .pl file suffix in URLs as you surfed the Web, then you've rubbed shoulders with Perl before. Over the years, Perl's popularity has grown with the proliferation of Web applications. But what exactly is Perl for?

In a nutshell, Perl is a high-level (yet relatively easy-to-use) programming language that is particularly suited to development of various types of applications – including networking tools, database management applications, system administration utilities, and (of course) Web applications.

As you continue your journey with Linux, you will probably find that you want to take more and more control over the way that your system works. As this happens, you'll also find the features offered by Bash shell scripts increasingly limiting. The Perl programming language will help you get the flexibility you'll crave – the vast majority of professional Linux systems administrators use Perl as their preferred method for maintaining their systems. They find its power and flexibility invaluable.

Like so many things in life, the best way to do a job is often to look at how the professionals do it, and follow in their footsteps. And, of course, it's often not easy when you start out – Perl was built for power and flexibility, but not necessarily for immediate comprehensibility or beginner's ease of use (that's what the shell's for).

Nevertheless, this book would not be complete without a glimpse at the world of Perl, and so in this chapter we give you a few examples of how it can be used to make your life easier. This chapter is rather unlike the others in this book; it's not going to try and teach you key skills that you can take away and use with little or no additional guidance, because to give you that much understanding of a subject like Perl would require a 300-page chapter! Instead, we're going to condense as much information as possible into as few pages as possible. Our intention is to give you a chance to experiment with these examples, and give you a feel for the Perl technology as a whole.

If and when you begin to feel yourself constrained by the limitations of the shell, the information and examples here should enable you to make an informed decision as to whether Perl is the right choice for you.

During the course of this chapter we will look at:

❑   How to install Perl

❑   Connect to the CPAN (Comprehensive Perl Archive Network) Archive

❑   Consider a number of demonstration Perl script applications (four large examples and half a dozen smaller ones)

Finally we will touch upon a larger, more comprehensive, Perl application – a web-based systems administration assistant – which you can use to assist you in your day-to-day administrative tasks. (In fact, we will discuss this application further in Chapter 13, and you can download its code from http://www.wrox.com.)

Perl is not a simple language, but it's powerful and it's worth investigation. If you have difficulty getting started, then you can supplement the information in this chapter with a good online Perl tutorial. For example, let us recommend to you the Tutorials section of the www.perl.com website. At the time of writing this was at http://www.perl.com/cs/user/ query/q/6?id_topic=74, but if this should change, you can find it from the main menu, by selecting Resources and scrolling down to the Tutorials option.

What Is Perl?

There exist a large variety of programming languages for Linux, ranging from simple shell scripting variants like csh and bash, through high-level interpreted languages, like Perl, Tcl, and Python, to the most hardcore of them all – C and C++. Naturally, each has its own advantages and disadvantages, which you can see in more detail at The Great Computer Language Shootout:

    http://www.bagley.org/~doug/shootout/

Perl bridges the gap nicely between the two extremes, the simple and the hardcore, by supporting some of the best of both breeds features. For example, Perl allows us to write applications that interact with the shell, execute commands, and process the output with the same ease of use and rapid development that is seen with shell scripting. We can use a simple editor to write our program and then run it without worrying about linking and compiling it, which is the case with the advanced compiled languages like C and C++. On the other hand, Perl also supports advanced programming constructs, complex data structures, and a higher level of security as found in advanced high-level compiled languages, but commonly lacking in scripting languages.

Let's look at a hypothetical example that illustrates these points better. Say you decide to develop an application that needs to monitor hard disk partitions and alert an administrator if the amount of available space drops below ten percent. The application must also determine who is occupying the most space and send them an e-mail urging them to clean up by listing their fifteen largest files. What would happen if we were to try to develop this using a shell scripting language, like bash? First, we would start out using the df command, which returns a report of the disk space usage. The report could be something like the following, depending on how your machine is partitioned:

```
Filesystem            1K-blocks      Used Available Use% Mounted on
/dev/hda1              3020140    1582492   1284232  56% /
/dev/hda5              7684844    1280812   6013656  18% /data
/dev/hda2              3020172    2637411    229341  92% /home
none                    94868          0     94868   0% /dev/shm
```

We would then need to extract the percentage values from this report, which is more difficult than it seems; most shell scripting languages don't support this type of text manipulation directly. As a result, we would need to use a language such as **sed** or **awk** to get at the data that we are looking for. sed and awk are languages designed specifically for pattern matching and transformation and are used extensively in shell scripting. Once we determine that the /dev/hda2 partition (the /home filesystem) exceeds the 90 percentage usage threshold, we would need to calculate each user's individual usage and determine their largest files. How would we do that?

We would need to get a list of all the users' home directories in the filesystem, most likely using the ls command, and then iterate through each one using a loop of some sort. As we go through each directory, we would issue the du command to get a list of all the files and their sizes, like so:

```
3656      /home/postgres/base/1
3656      /home/postgres/base/16975
4         /home/postgres/base/16976/pgsql_tmp
1128708   /home/postgres/base/16976
1136024   /home/postgres/base
140       /home/postgres/global
82024     /home/postgres/pg_xlog
12        /home/postgres/pg_clog
1218232   /home/postgres
```

The most difficult part of this process is to keep track of each user's usage and their files, both the name and the size. Why is this difficult, you may ask? Shell scripting languages have very primitive support for complex logic operations and data structures. We would need to come up with an alternative mechanism to temporarily store this individual data, and then process and sort it once we finish going through all the users' directories. The final part of the application would involve sending an e-mail, both to the offending users and the administrator, using the mail or sendmail commands.

You may have noticed that we glossed over the section regarding sed and awk here. There's a reason for this – shell scripting languages allow us to develop scripts that invoke shell commands easily and without much effort. In addition, the development cycle is rather simple; we use an editor to modify and debug the script and then simply execute it from the command line. On the other hand, shell scripts fall apart when we need to implement any type of complex logical operations or store relational or structured data, since shell scripting languages were not designed for this purpose.

On the flip side, how would we fare if we developed this application using Perl? We would retain some of the advantages of shell scripting, but also have access to more advanced language features. Since Perl allows us interact with the shell, we can use the `df` command to get the disk usage report, and then use pattern matching expressions to easily parse and extract the percentage values. If we find a partition that exceeds the threshold value, we can use the internal `readdir` function, along with a `for` loop, to iterate through all of the main directories on that filesystem. Perl integrates well with the underlying operating system to abstract certain functions on all supported platforms. This allows us to use a function like `readdir` to get a list of all the files in a particular directory, whether we are using Linux or Mac OS X.

For each directory, we can use the `df` command, like we did before, to get a list of all the individual files and their sizes and then store them in a complex data structure. Once we finish iterating through all the directories, we can use Perl's `sort` function to sort and order the information in the data structure to determine the offending users and their largest files. At that point, we can send e-mail to the administrator and the necessary users, either using the external `mail` or `sendmail` commands, or a Perl extension such as `Mail::Send`. Typically, we would want to use an extension, instead of an external shell command, since it is more efficient and allows us to better implement the desired functionality. We'll actually take a look at how to write this application in Perl later in the chapter, after looking through some simpler examples first.

We won't go through the advantages or disadvantages of developing a similar application in a compiled language, like C or C++, since it is beyond the scope of this chapter. But, if you are interested in a high-level overview, a language such as C provides more control (i.e. memory management) and typically better performance, but at the expense of development time and difficulty.

Now, let's take a more in-depth look at the advantages and disadvantages of Perl. This will allow you to evaluate what Perl has to offer for yourself.

Advantages

As we discussed earlier, Perl provides a good mixture of features and performance that lies somewhere between a scripting language and a compiled language. To understand this better, here are some specific advantages of Perl:

- ❑ Perl provides us with great flexibility in developing applications. Perl does not force us to use any specific style or paradigm, but instead allows us to express our ideas and thoughts in the way that we choose. In fact, one of Perl's mottos is, *"there is more than one way to do it."*

- ❏ Perl is extensible. We can write modules or libraries in Perl to extend its functionality and make them available for reuse in other projects. The Comprehensive Perl Archive Network (CPAN) holds hundreds and thousands of freely available extensions to interface and communicate with various utilities, applications, Internet services and database engines.

- ❏ Perl is highly portable and runs on a large number of hardware and software platforms, including most known Unix/Linux platforms, Windows, Mac OS, OS/2, VMS, and even Palm. Programs that don't use platform specific functionality, such as pipes in Unix, or OLE/COM in Windows, will work unchanged across platforms.

- ❏ Perl supports powerful regular expressions for pattern matching. We can use these expressions to search for patterns or specific strings in a body of text.

- ❏ Perl has a strong developer community, which is very active in implementing extensions, fixing bugs, and providing technical support.

- ❏ Perl is free for both commercial and non-commercial use!

Disadvantages

Like any other programming language, Perl does have its share of disadvantages:

- ❏ The flexibility that Perl provides can sometimes mesmerize developers into producing hard to maintain code. Because there are so many different ways to solve the same problem, it's easy to come up with a solution that no one else can follow – especially if your documentation isn't up to scratch.

- ❏ Perl has weak exception handling abilities that make it difficult for you to handle any errors that crop up during the execution of your script – for example if a file isn't where it's supposed to be, or if write-access to one of our disks isn't permitted.

However, for the most part, Perl is perfectly capable of doing the tasks that we require of it in a sensible and organized way. We'll begin to look at some examples of this shortly, but before we can do that, we need to make sure that we've got Perl installed correctly.

Installation

Perl, along with a number of useful modules, is installed by default on your Linux system. We will use the terms extension and module interchangeably, since they have much the same meaning in Perl. If you want to check what version of Perl is installed, use the `perl` command with the `-v` option:

```
$ perl -v

This is perl, v5.8.0 built for i386-linux-thread-multi
(with 1 registered patch, see perl -V for more detail)
```

```
Copyright 1987-2002, Larry Wall

Perl may be copied only under the terms of either the Artistic License or the
GNU General Public License, which may be found in the Perl 5 source kit.

Complete documentation for Perl, including FAQ lists, should be found on
this system using `man perl' or `perldoc perl'.  If you have access to the
Internet, point your browser at http://www.perl.com/, the Perl Home Page.
```

At the time of writing this chapter, 5.8.0 is the latest version of Perl available. If, for some reason, you do not have Perl installed on your system, use the Red Hat Package Management application that we have seen in earlier chapters to install it. If you want to be on the cutting edge, you can even download the latest copy of Perl and compile it, in much the same way as we built the gFTP application in Chapter 10; *you need to install the Development Tools packages as specified in the chapter.* Simply type the following into a terminal (each line represents a different command, and you'll need root privileges for it to work):

```
# cd /usr/local/src
# wget http://www.perl.com/CPAN/src/latest.tar.gz
# tar -zxvf latest.tar.gz
# cd perl-5.8.0
# ./Configure
# make
# make test
# make install
```

Make sure to read the INSTALL file, which provides more instructions on how to compile and build Perl. While you're at it, you should also read the obligatory README file for any last minute changes, bug fixes, and so on.

Installing Extensions

Once you have installed Perl, you can use the CPAN extension to install any other extensions or modules that you may need for development. The CPAN extension automates the process of retrieving the necessary source code from The Comprehensive Perl Archive Network, uncompressing, configuring, and building it into an extension. Unfortunately, the CPAN extension is not installed by default, and is installed only when you install all of the development tools, as shown in the *Building from Source* section in Chapter 10. However, if you do not want to install all of the development tools, but simply want to play around with the CPAN extension, you can install it directly from the Red Hat 9 distribution. Place the **second** CD-ROM disk into the drive, wait a few moments for it to load, and type the following:

```
# rpm -hvi /mnt/cdrom/RedHat/RPMS/perl-CPAN-1.61-88.i386.rpm
```

But you should note that a large number of Perl extensions are written in C or C++, so they will not build properly without all of the development tools installed. Now, let's go ahead and install an extension.

Say, for example, you need an extension to send e-mail from a Perl program. Your first step should be to go to CPAN and check to see if such an extension exists. You can do this by pointing your browser to:

http://search.cpan.org

and entering **Send Mail** into the search field. You will see a number of e-mail related modules that match the criteria. Traverse down the list and you should see the Mail::Send extension that we briefly discussed earlier; the Mail::Send extension is actually part of the MailTools package as you will see in the installation example below. Now, log in as root and use the CPAN extension to install the module:

```
# perl -MCPAN -e shell

cpan shell -- CPAN exploration and modules installation (v1.61)
ReadLine support available (try 'install Bundle::CPAN')
```

The -M switch asks Perl to load the CPAN extension, which implements, among other things, a function called shell. This function is responsible for providing a user interface, or a shell, where you can search for and install modules. We can execute this function by using the -e switch. As you will see later, we can also use this switch to execute arbitrary pieces of Perl code from the command-line.

The first time you use the CPAN shell, it will ask you a number of questions, including where to store the sources and what CPAN mirror to use. You should be able to simply choose the default answer and continue. Once inside the shell, use the install command with the name of the extension to start the process of installation:

```
cpan> install Mail::Send
Running install for module Mail::Send
Running make for M/MA/MARKOV/MailTools-1.58.tar.gz
CPAN: LWP::UserAgent loaded ok
Fetching with LWP:
  http://www.perl.com/CPAN/authors/id/M/MA/MARKOV/MailTools-1.58.tar.gz
CPAN: Digest::MD5 loaded ok
Fetching with LWP:
  http://www.perl.com/CPAN/authors/id/M/MA/MARKOV/CHECKSUMS
Checksum for /root/.cpan/sources/authors/id/M/MA/MARKOV/MailTools-1.58.tar.gz
ok
Scanning cache /root/.cpan/build for sizes
MailTools-1.58/
MailTools-1.58/t/
MailTools-1.58/t/internet.t
...
```

459

```
   CPAN.pm: Going to build M/MA/MARKOV/MailTools-1.58.tar.gz

...
Checking if your kit is complete...
Looks good
Writing Makefile for Mail
cp Mail/Mailer/test.pm blib/lib/Mail/Mailer/test.pm
...
   /usr/bin/make  -- OK
Running make test
...
All tests successful.
Files=7, Tests=94,  2 wallclock secs ( 1.26 cusr +  0.13 csys =  1.39 CPU)
   /usr/bin/make test -- OK
Running make install
Installing /usr/lib/perl5/site_perl/5.8.0/Mail/Cap.pm
...
   /usr/bin/make install  -- OK

cpan> exit
Lockfile removed.
```

The entire installation process is simple and straightforward. And you can get more information on all of the commands that the CPAN shell supports by issuing the `help` command. If, however, you don't want to use the shell, you can download the source directly from CPAN and build it yourself. This will provide you with a bit more control, but you need to make sure to install any prerequisite modules that are needed by the extension that you are building before hand. But, if you do use the shell, it is intelligent enough to install these modules for you automatically, provided that the module authors followed certain conventions for specifying prerequisites.

Now that we have looked at what Perl is, how it compares to other programming languages, what its advantages and disadvantages are and how to install it, we are ready to actually learn the language. Let's start!

Learning Perl

As we have discussed earlier, learning an entire language within a span of ten to fifteen pages is rather difficult. But, we can certainly learn enough of the language to develop useful applications. We will learn by studying three example applications: one that lists the system users, another to send e-mail from the command-line and the last one to archive system load average data. These examples illustrate how to:

❑   create a Perl program

❑   store and access different types of data

    ❑   process input and output

    ❑   implement logic operations

    ❑   find patterns or strings

    ❑   interact with external applications

We will finish up the section by actually designing the disk usage application that we looked at earlier. By implementing this reasonably advanced application, you can see for yourself how well you understood some of the concepts behind Perl development. Let's start!

How to Start

We have seen examples of shell scripts throughout the book, which look something like the following:

```
#!/bin/sh

...

exit;
```

Perl programs have a similar structure:

```
#!/usr/bin/perl

##++
##   hello.pl: This is so cool, my first Perl program, can you believe it?
##--

$city    = 'Manchester';   ## Scalar variable: store Manchester in $city
$country = 'England';      ## Scalar variable: store England in $country

print "Hello, welcome to my home in $city, $country!\n";  ## Print message

exit (0);                 ## Hooray, success!
```

Once you save this code in a file – say, `hello.pl` – you can execute the program in one of two ways, either by invoking the Perl interpreter manually and passing to it the filename or asking the shell to execute it for you:

```
$ /usr/bin/perl hello.pl


$ chmod +x hello.pl
$ ./hello.pl
```

In the first case, we manually call upon the interpreter to execute the code. In the second case, however, the shell will execute the interpreter, feeding to it the program. This will work only if the program meets two specific conditions. The initial line of the program must have a line that starts with #! and specifies the path to the interpreter, in this case /usr/bin/perl. And the user executing the program must have the execute permission enabled.

Why don't you try running this program? What do you get as the output? As you look at this rather trivial program, you should be aware of a few details. First, each statement – defined as a single logical command – ends with a semicolon. This tells Perl that the statement is complete. Second, everything starting from the # character to the end of the line represents a comment. You should make it a point to add comments that describe the thoughts and logic behind your code, especially if you are implementing something that might be difficult for other people, or even yourself, to understand at a later time. And finally, Perl ignores whitespace and empty lines in and around statements, so you should use a liberal amount of whitespace to align variable declarations and indent code. This will make it easier for other developers to read and understand your code.

Now, let's look at our first main application. Each application is designed to illustrate a set of Perl's key features. Before we discuss the application, I will point out these features, explain their significance and how you can use them later to build your own programs.

Application 1: Who Can Get In?

For our first task, we'll build a simple application to open the /etc/password configuration file and display each user's login name and associated comment. If you don't remember the format of this file, which was discussed in Chapter 8, here is how it looks:

```
dcheng:x:103:200:David Cheng:/home/dcheng:/bin/bash
dzhiwei:x:104:200:David Zhiwei:/home/dzhiwei:/bin/tcsh
sliao:x:400:400:Steve Liao:/home/sliao:/bin/tcsh
```

Each record in the file consists of 7 fields, starting with the login, followed by the password, user id, group id, comment (typically the full name), home directory and the default shell. We are interested in extracting the first and fifth fields.

By understanding the code behind this application, you will learn how to open a text file, read its contents, access certain pieces of information and display the formatted results. These tasks are critical for everyday development, since most administrative applications will rely on opening, reading from and writing to one file or the other. You will be glad to know that the application we'll look at next is only nine lines long, so it should be relatively easy to comprehend:

```
#!/usr/bin/perl

##++
##   list_users.pl: display list of users and their comments
```

```
##--

use strict;                           ## "strict" mode

my (@data);                           ## Pre-declare array

open (FILE, '/etc/passwd')            ## Open the file
    || die "Cannot open file: $!\n";

while (<FILE>) {                      ## Read each record
    @data = split (/:/, $_, 7);      ## Separate the elements
    print "$data[0], $data[4]\n";    ## Print login, comments
}

close (FILE);                         ## Close file
exit  (0);                            ## Exit application
```

Perl provides us with flexibility to develop applications in the manner that we choose; it imposes very few restrictions upon us. Take, for example, the declaration of variables. By default, we don't have to pre-declare variables before using them in the program. Once you refer to a new variable, it is automatically instantiated and has an undefined value until you provide it with a set value. Unfortunately, this is not good programming practice and should be avoided, since it makes finding errors in your code very difficult if something goes wrong.

Lucky for us, Perl comes with the strict pragma, which, when enabled, requires us to pre-declare variables before using them and forces us to avoid symbolic references and bareword identifiers. We will look at the latter two requirements in other examples. But, what exactly is a pragma? A pragma is either an internal module, an outside extension, or a combination of the two that specifies the rules that Perl should follow when processing code.

Using strict

This brings us to the first line of our application. The use function imports functionality from an external module into our current application. We call on this function with the strict argument to enable the strict pragma. That is all that is needed to force us to pre-declare variables from here on. As a side note, if you look in the Perl extensions directory, typically /usr/lib/perl5/5.8.0, you will see a file titled strict.pm; this is the file that will be loaded.

Next, we use the my function to declare, or localize, the @data array. *An array is simply a data type, represented by the leading at-sign character, that we can use to store a set of scalar (single) values in one variable.* We will use this array to store all of the individual elements for each record in the file, including login and comment.

Opening the File

We proceed to open the configuration file, /etc/password, using the open function. This function takes two arguments, the first being the file handle that we want to use and the second the path to the file. Think of the handle as a communications channel through which we can read data from the file. If the open function executes successfully, which means that the file exists and we have the necessary permissions, it returns a positive (true) status. *In Perl, a status of true is represented by a defined non-zero value, and a status of false is identified with an undefined or zero value or a null string.*

If we cannot open the file, we call the die function with a specific error message to exit from the program. Notice the $! expression within the double quoted message string. *Expressions that start with the dollar sign represent scalar variables.* We can use a scalar variable to store a single value, whether it is a character, number, a text string or even a paragraph of content. However, the $! is a special Perl scalar variable that holds the latest error message, returned by either a system function call or a user-defined procedure. Typical failure messages for open include *'Permission denied'* and *'No such file or directory'*.

Look again at the entire line that is trying to open the file, and think of it as two separate statements separated by the logical OR operator, ||. The second statement will be executed only if the first statement is false; if the file cannot be opened. We are using a convenient shortcut, but you can just as easily rewrite that code as:

```
if (!open (FILE, '/etc/passwd')) {
    die "Cannot open file: $!\n";
}
```

The exclamation point in front of the open function call will negate the status returned by the function. In other words, it will convert a true value into a false, and vice versa. So, only if the entire expression within the main parentheses is true, will we end up calling the die function to terminate our program. And that will happen if the open function returns a false status.

We can also write the same statement like this:

```
if (open (FILE, '/etc/passwd')) {     ## Success
    ## Read file
    ## Parse records
    ## Print output
} else {                              ## Failure!
    die "Cannot open file: $!\n";
}
```

This should be easy enough to understand by now; if the open function returns true, we process the file or else we exit. Now, we are ready to read data from the file. But, how do we know how many records to read? Simple, we use a while loop to iterate through the file, reading one record at a time, until there are no more records to be read. And for each record retrieved from the file, Perl will execute the block of code inside the loop.

Reading Records

The expression located inside of the parenthesis after the `while` command controls when the loop will terminate; the loop will continue until this expression evaluates to a false value. The strange looking expression is the one responsible for reading a line from the `FILE` filehandle and storing it in the default Perl variable, `$_`. When there are no more lines to be read, Perl will return an undefined value, or `undef` for short. Once this happens, the expression will evaluate to a false value and the while loop will stop.

Whenever you see such an expression – an identifier of some sort enclosed between a less-than and a greater-than sign – you should know that Perl is reading data from the filehandle represented by that identifier. We can store each record read from the file in a variable other than `$_` by doing the following:

```
while ($line = <FILE>) {
    ...
}
```

Looking inside the loop, we see two statements. These are the ones that are responsible for pulling out the different elements from each record and displaying the login and comment.

Extracting the Elements

The `split` function separates a piece of text into multiple elements, based on a specified delimiter, and returns an array. It takes three arguments: the delimiter, the input string, and the maximum number of elements. Notice that the delimiter is enclosed within a set of backslash characters; this is an example of a regular expression, or commonly known as **regex**. We can use regular expressions to specify a pattern to match, as opposed to a simple one-character delimiter. We will look at regular expressions in more detail in *Application 3: What is My System Load?*

The last two arguments to the `split` function are optional. If the input string is not specified, Perl uses its default variable, `$_`. This is something you should be aware of. A large number of Perl functions operate on this default variable, so it is very convenient. We have seen two examples of it already: reading records from a filehandle and now the split function. And last, but not least, if you don't specify a maximum number of elements, you won't see a difference a majority of the time. However, there will be occasions when the last element in the text string is null, in which case, split will strip and remove this element. To be on the safe side, you should specify the number of elements that you expect to get back, so there are no surprises!

Once the `split` function returns the elements, we store them in the `@data` array. Each item in an array is associated with a specific position or index, starting at index zero. We can access a specific element in an array by specifying its associated index within brackets. We use the `print` command to display the first and sixth elements to the terminal, followed by a newline.

We repeat this process for all the records in the file. And once the `while` loop terminates, we close the file using its filehandle and exit from the application. This completes our first major Perl application!

Go ahead and run the program. What do you see? You will most likely see output like the following:

```
$ perl list_users.pl
root, root
bin, bin
...
dcheng, David Cheng
dzhiwei, David Zhiwei
sliao, Steve Liao
```

The application itself seems to work properly, but there are a few flaws that we should fix. First, there is no need to see a list of the default system users; users created by the Linux installation. And second, it would make for a good display if the two pieces of information were neatly aligned into columns.

Who Can Get In? Take II

We will change the application somewhat to implement the new features that we discussed above, namely ignoring system users and fixing the display format. Ignoring system users from the output is not difficult, but is not fully precise. How do you tell the different between a system user and a regular user? There is no one distinct flag or marker that identifies a system user. However, system users are typically, but not always, allocated a user identification number less than 100, so we will use that as the main criteria.

We also need to fix the display format. And fortunately for us, there is the pack function, which we can use to pad each data element with a certain number of spaces, thereby creating columns that are aligned. Let's look at the new version of our application:

```perl
#!/usr/bin/perl

##++
##   list_users_plus.pl: display list of users and their comments
##   in neat columns
##--

use strict;                              ## Enable "strict" pragma

my (@data);                              ## Pre-declare variables

open (FILE, '/etc/passwd')               ## Open the file
    || die "Cannot open file: $!\n";

while (<FILE>) {                         ## Read each record
    @data = split (/:/, $_, 7);          ## Separate the elements
```

```
    if ($data[2] < 100) {                    ## Ignore UID less than 100
        next;
    }

    print pack ("A16A*", $data[0], $data[4]), "\n";   ## Print
                                                       ## login, comments
}

close (FILE);                                ## Close file
exit  (0);                                   ## Exit application
```

We have changed the code very little; the changes are highlighted. If we find a user identification number less than one hundred, we use the next command to start the next iteration of the while loop. As a result, the print command never gets executed and we don't display the record.

You can also combine the next command and the conditional check into one statement, like so:

```
next if ($data[2] < 100);
```

You will most likely see this abbreviated syntax in a number of Perl programs. It is convenient and easy to use. However, you cannot use this syntax if you need to execute a block of code based on a specific condition.

Formatting the Output

Next, we use the pack command to create a string based on a specific template configuration and a set of values; these comprise the first and subsequent arguments, respectively. The A16A* template instructs pack to create a 16 character ASCII padded string using the first value from the list, followed by a string containing all other remaining values. When we execute this program, we will see the following much improved output:

```
dcheng          David Cheng
dzhiwei         David Zhiwei
sliao           Steve Liao
```

That's it for our first major application! We have learned much about Perl, including how to use its strict pragma, declare and use variables, implement while loops, read data from text files, and format output for display. In the next section, we will continue to look at more Perl syntax and constructs, including how to use the Mail::Send module to send e-mail.

467

Application 2: Send a Quick E-Mail

How many times have you wanted to send a quick e-mail, without having to use a full-fledged e-mail client? Linux provides us with a few applications that allow us to read and send e-mail from the command line, such as `mail`. But we are not interested in those at the moment. Instead, we will develop a useful Perl application that serves much the same purpose, namely the ability to send e-mail. In the process, you will learn how to check code for errors, accept input from the user, implement regular expressions, and use external modules and view their built-in documentation. Here is the application:

```perl
#!/usr/bin/perl

##++
##   send_email.pl: send e-mail messages from command-line
##--

use Mail::Send;                             ## Import/use Mail::Send
use strict;                                 ## Enable "strict" pragma

##++
##   Let's purposely inject two errors in this program so we can
##   understand the debugging process:
##      - remove semicolon at end of line
##      - spell $email as $emale
##--

my ($emale, $answer, $subject, $message)

print "*** E-Mail Sender Application ***\n\n";  ## Display header

##++
##   Prompt for recipient's e-mail address, checking for validity.
##--

while (1) {
    print "Enter recipient's e-mail address: ";
    $email = <STDIN>;                       ## Read from standard input
    chomp $email;                           ## Remove trailing newline

    next if (!$email);                      ## Repeat loop if no $email

    print "You entered $email as the recipient's address, accept [y/n]: ";
    chomp ($answer = <STDIN>);              ## Different style
    last if ($answer eq 'y');               ## Exit loop if $answer=y
}

##++
##   Prompt for subject and message body.
##--
```

```perl
print 'Subject: ';
chomp ($subject = <STDIN>);

print "Enter message, type Control-D (CTRL-D) to end:\n";

while (<STDIN>) {                        ## Read from standard input
    $message .= $_;                      ## Concatenate to $message
}

##++
##    Set defaults if empty.
##--

$subject ||= 'No Subject';
$message ||= 'No Body';

##++
##    Print summary and ask for confirmation.
##--

print "*** E-Mail Summary ***\n\n";
print "To: $email\n";
print "Subject: $subject\n";
print "Message:\n\n$message\n";

print 'Do you want to send the message [y/n]: ';
chomp ($answer = <STDIN>);

if ($answer eq 'n') {
    print "Aborting.\n";
    exit (0);
}

##++
##    Send message
##--

my ($mail, $fh);

$mail = new Mail::Send;                   ## Create new object

$mail->to ($email);                       ## Call its function/method
$mail->subject ($subject);

$fh = $mail->open();                      ## Returns filehandle
print $fh $message;                       ## Print body to filehandle
$fh->close();                             ## Close filehandle

print "Message sent.\n";

exit (0);
```

469

You can save this application in `send_email.pl` and proceed to run it, like so:

```
$ perl send_email.pl
syntax error at send_email.pl line 15, near ")

print"
Global symbol "$email" requires explicit package name at send_email.pl line 23.
Global symbol "$email" requires explicit package name at send_email.pl line 24.
Global symbol "$email" requires explicit package name at send_email.pl line 26.
Global symbol "$email" requires explicit package name at send_email.pl line 28.
Global symbol "$email" requires explicit package name at send_email.pl line 58.
Global symbol "$email" requires explicit package name at send_email.pl line 78.
Execution of send_email.pl aborted due to compilation errors.
```

Perl is telling us there are errors in our code. The first error is at or around line 15. And the second set of errors claim that we are using the $email variable without pre-declaring it first. Take a look at the code. You should see that we purposely left out the semicolon at the end of line 12 and declared a variable called $emale instead of $email. The line numbers that Perl reports in the errors may not always be exact, due to the manner in which it parses the code, so you should check the entire area around the reported error for any possible bugs.

Fixing Errors and Checking Syntax

If you are getting other errors, you may have forgotten to install the Mail::Send module properly, as shown in the *Installing Extensions* section earlier in the chapter. It is also possible that you may have made a mistake in typing the code. Why don't you fix the broken code in the application, adding the necessary semicolon and correcting the misspelled variable:

```
my ($email, $answer, $subject, $message);
```

Let's run it again, but before we do so, we will check its syntax and structure. We can use Perl's -w and -c options, which report warnings and check syntax, respectively, to check the status of our code, like so:

```
$ perl -wc send_email.pl
send_email syntax OK
```

If there are no problems with the code, Perl returns the output shown above. You should make it a point to check the syntax of your applications in this manner before running them, so that you can catch possible errors quickly. We are now ready to go through the code, after which we will look at how to actually use this application, including a screenshot of a sample session.

Loading External Modules

We looked at the use command in the first application, list_users.pl, when we talked about the strict pragma. Here, we import the Mail::Send extension, so we can use its functionality to send e-mail. You can find this module at /usr/lib/perl5/site_perl/5.8.0/Mail/Send.pm; the .pm extension stands for Perl Module. Most CPAN extensions include built-in documentation, which you can view by using the perldoc application:

```
$ perldoc Mail::Send
```

This documentation provides you more information on what the extension does and how to use it. You can also use perldoc to get information on virtually any Perl command. In this application, we use the chomp command to remove the end of line character, also referred to as the record separator. To see more information on chomp, including examples, you can type the following:

```
$ perldoc -f chomp
```

Let's go back to the code. We pre-declare the variables that we intend to use in the program and print out a header for the user. *We don't have to declare all of the variables in one place; we can declare them as we go.*

Getting Recipient's E-Mail Address

The real core of the program starts now. We wrap a block of code inside a while loop that will run until we explicitly break out. Remember our discussion from earlier in the chapter: the expression that follows the while command determines how many times the loop will execute; as long as the expression is true, the loop will continue to run. In this case, a static expression with a value of one will always evaluate to true, so the loop will never stop! Why do we want to do this, you ask?

Our job inside the loop is to ask the user for the recipient's e-mail address. If the user doesn't enter an address or accidentally makes a mistake in typing, we provide him or her the ability to enter it again. We repeat this process until the user is satisfied and affirmatively confirms the address, at which point we jump out of the loop using the last command.

Notice how we are accepting input from the user. Don't you think the syntax looks quite similar to what we used in list_users.pl to read data from a file? In fact, we can use the <filehandle> expression to read a line of data from any defined filehandle. The standard input (STDIN) filehandle is established at program startup time and allows us to read data from the user, terminal or input stream. In addition to the STDIN filehandle, we have access to STDOUT (standard output), STDERR (standard error) and DATA. We can use STDOUT to write output, STDERR to write diagnostic messages and DATA to read data stored within a Perl application. As a side note, whenever we use the print command to display a message, Perl will write it to the standard output stream.

471

Once the user enters the recipient's e-mail address and presses the Enter/Return key on his or her keyboard, the trailing newline is actually captured as part of the input. We use the chomp function to cleanly remove this end of line character from the input, as stored in the $email variable. If we don't remove it, we would have a difficult time determining if the user entered an address, since $email will still evaluate to true because it would have a length of atleast one – from the newline character.

Checking E-Mail Address

Next, we check to see if $email is false, which would occur if the user did not enter an address, and if so, we simply execute the loop again. This provides the user another chance to enter the address. However, if an address was entered, we ask the user for confirmation and exit from the loop. An advanced application might also check the validity of the e-mail address, but we are not doing it here. If you are interested in adding such functionality, you should install the Email::Valid module, as shown in the *Installing Extensions* section, and then change this application in the following manner:

```perl
#!/usr/bin/perl
    use Mail::Send;                          ## Import/use Mail::Send
    use Email::Valid;                        ## Import/use Email::Valid
    use strict;                              ## Enable "strict" pragma

    ...

    while (1) {
       ...

       next if (!$email);                    ## Repeat loop if no $email

       if (!Email::Valid->address ($email)) {  ## E-Mail address is not valid
           print "The e-mail address you entered is not in a valid format.\n";
       }

       ...
    }

    ...

    exit (0);
```

We use the address function, defined in the Email::Valid module, to check whether the specified e-mail address conforms to the RFC 822 specification, Standard for the Format of ARPA Internet Text Messages. The function simply checks the syntax; there is no way to determine whether a specific address is deliverable without actually attempting delivery.

Getting Subject and Message Body

Continuing on with the program, we ask the user to enter the subject and the body of the message. We use a while loop to allow the user to enter as much content as desired. Each time through the loop, we take the content that is entered ($_) and append it to the existing content in $message, using the concatenation .= operator. If the user types Control-D at any point, the shell ends the input stream, at which point the while loop terminates.

Then, we perform a few routine tasks. First, we assign default values to the subject and body of the message in case they were not entered. The ||= operator is very useful and is a shortcut for the following:

```
if (!$subject) {            ## or:
    $subject = 'No Subject'  ## $subject = 'No Subject' if (!$subject);
}
```

Second, we print out all of the information entered by the user and ask whether he or she wants to continue with the message. If not, we exit from the application. Otherwise, we will use the Mail::Send module to send the e-mail.

Sending the Message

If you look at the built-in documentation for the Mail::Send module, you will see several small examples on how to use the module. These examples look very similar to the code that we are about to look at. Mail::Send is a module that provides an object-oriented interface to its functionality. If you have done any C++ or Smalltalk application development, you know exactly what this means. But, if not, don't loose hope. Think of object-oriented programming (OOP) as a clean way to implement a data structure – the object – that contains not only data but also associated functions to manipulate that data.

We call the new function, typically known as the constructor, in Mail::Send to create a new instance of the object. We can use this instance to invoke defined functions (or methods) in the object. First, we call the to and subject methods to specify the recipient and subject, respectively. Then, we invoke the open method to obtain the filehandle associated with the mail transport mechanism. By default, Mail::Send uses the sendmail application to send the message. If you don't have sendmail installed on your Linux system, or need to use an external SMTP server from within a firewall environment, you can specify the server address in the open method:

```
$fh = $mail->open ('smtp', Server => 'smtp.someserver.com');
```

Unfortunately, this is not explained in the built-in documentation. If you look at the module's code, you will find that Mail::Send actually calls the Mail::Mailer module to send the e-mail. And Mail::Mailer can use sendmail, qmail or an SMTP server as the transport mechanism. Whatever arguments we pass to the open method here are simply passed on to Mail::Mailer.

The last action we have to take is to write the body content to this filehandle using the `print` command and then close the filehandle. This will send the message, at which point we display a status message and exit.

Sample User Session

Let's run through the application to see how it looks. You can see a screenshot showing the application in use below:

Developing this application was a breakthrough for us; we learned how to accept and validate user input and how to load and use external modules. There are literally hundreds of Perl extensions available through CPAN, so learning how to use them properly is extremely valuable. Whenever you need to build a new application, you should make it a habit to browse through CPAN to see if there is a module that might help you. If one exists, all you have to do is look at the built-in documentation, determine how to interface with the module and you are on your way to building an excellent application in no time!

Up till now, we have learned quite a bit about Perl and how to use it. However, we have not looked at the two features of the language that are probably the most powerful, namely regular expressions and the ability to interact with the system environment. Next, we will look at an interesting application that uses both of these features.

Application 3: What Is My System Load?

In a typical single-user environment, where the system administrator is also the only user, we don't have to pay much attention to administering, monitoring, and optimizing the operating system. However, the situation is completely different with a multi-user system; the stakes are higher as more people are dependent on the system running well. There are a number of diagnostic applications that we can use to keep tabs on the system. Take, for example, the uptime program, which returns a number of useful pieces of information, including how long the system has been up and running, the number of users currently logged on and the load averages for the past 1, 5, and 15 minutes:

```
2:06pm  up 30 days, 21:56,  7 users,  load average: 1.41, 0.93, 0.26
```

If you want to optimize the system, you should typically keep track of system activity and metrics over a certain period of time. This activity can include the number of users logged in, what applications they are running, the average system load, and how much memory is being consumed. This allows you to analyze the data and look for specific patterns. You may find, for example, that there is a large spike in the system load every Monday morning before the weekly engineering meeting. Then, you can determine how to best handle the issue: don't run other jobs on Monday mornings, add more RAM, or upgrade the processor.

In that vein, we will create an application to archive the system load averages and the number of active users. However, in order for any data analysis to be effective, we need to have enough data that captures a variety of conditions. And the best way to do that is to set up a cron job to automatically run this application every hour Monday through Friday, like so:

```
00 * * * 1-5  /home/nutt/uptime_monitor.pl /home/nutt/uptime.log
```

Even though the application is only ten lines long, you will still learn enough advanced Perl development techniques to make it worthwhile. More specifically, you will learn how to invoke an external program, retrieve its output, extract certain information from it and write the formatted output to a log file. Since there are so many useful utilities and programs that exist for Linux, the ability to interact with these tools from within Perl will empower you to develop some very interesting applications.

Now, here is the code.

```perl
#!/usr/bin/perl

##++
##   uptime_monitor.pl: archive system load averages to file
##--

use strict;                                    ## Enable "strict" pragma

my ($file, $uptime, $users, $load1, $load2, $load3);
```

```
$file   = $ARGV[0] || '/var/log/uptime.log';   ## Path to log file
$uptime = `/usr/bin/uptime`;                    ## Store output from uptime

##++
##   Parse the output of the uptime command and store the numbers of
##   users and the three system load averages into: $users, $load1,
##   $load2 and $load3.
##--

$uptime =~ /(\d+) +user.+?(\d.+?), +(.+?), +(.+)/;
$users  = $1;
$load1  = $2;
$load2  = $3;
$load3  = $4;

##++
##   We can also write the above like this:
##
##       $uptime =~ /(\d+) +user.+?(\d.+?), +(.+?), +(.+)/;
##       ($users, $load1, $load2, $load3) = ($1, $2, $3, $4);
##
##   or even:
##
##       ($users, $load1, $load2, $load3)
##           = $uptime =~ /(\d+) +user.+?(\d.+?), +(.+?), +(.+)/;
##--

##++
##   Store the data in a log file; open modes:
##
##       >> = append, > = write, < (or nothing) = read
##--

open (FILE, ">>$file") || die "Cannot append uptime data to $file: $!\n";
print FILE join (':', time, $users, $load1, $load2, $load3), "\n";
close (FILE);

exit (0);
```

One note, before we start discussing the code. Our application accepts a command line argument and uses its value to determine where to archive the load average data. This provides us with the flexibility to archive the data to different files without modifying the code at all. If you were curious as to the significance of the /home/nutt/uptime.log file in the crontab entry above, now you know; it refers to the log file.

Getting the Command Line Argument

A user can specify arguments and information to any Perl application through the command line, and Perl will make them available to us through the special @ARGV array. We don't necessarily have to use these arguments in our application, but they are there in case we need them. Here is a simple program that illustrates how command line arguments are processed:

```perl
#!/usr/bin/perl

##++
##    print_args.pl: display all command-line arguments
##--

use strict;

for (my $loop=0; $loop <= $#ARGV; $loop++) { ## $#ARGV returns the
    print "\$ARGV[$loop] = $ARGV[$loop]\n";  ## last index of the
                                             ## array
}

exit (0);
```

You are looking at the `for` loop in action. You should use this construct when you know exactly how many times you want a loop to execute. This is very different than a `while` loop, where you may not know how many times it should run; all you know is that once the loop meets some specific criteria, it should stop. We iterate through the @ARGV array, one element at a time, displaying its value. Go ahead and run the program, like so:

```
$ perl print_args.pl how are you this is a test
$ARGV[0] = how
$ARGV[1] = are
$ARGV[2] = you
$ARGV[3] = this
$ARGV[4] = is
$ARGV[5] = a
$ARGV[6] = test
```

We can treat the @ARGV array like any other array, accessing a specific element by specifying its index. Look back at our main application where we get the first command-line argument, $ARGV[0], and proceed it use it:

```perl
$file = $ARGV[0] || '/var/log/uptime.log';
```

What do you think we are trying to do? Surely, we have seen this type of construct before. If you remember, this clever one line statement is identical to the following `if-then` block:

```perl
if ($ARGV[0]) {
    $file = $ARGV[0];
```

```
    } else {
        $file = '/var/log/uptime.log';
    }
```

We use the value passed to us from the command-line as the path to our log file, storing it in $file, but only if it is defined and has a true value. Otherwise, we use the /var/log/uptime.log as our default log file. We had talked about Perl's flexibility in the beginning of this chapter. Well, this is just a simple example that illustrates it. If you don't feel comfortable using the one-line technique, you can always use the longer, but more clear, group of code shown above. And, if you are even more adventurous, you can also use the following:

```
    $file = ($ARGV[0]) ? $ARGV[0] : '/var/log/uptime.log';
```

We just saw three different techniques for performing the same exact task. Perl does not force you to use one approach over another; you are free to use whichever one you feel comfortable with.

Invoking the uptime Command

We can now invoke the uptime system command to get the load average data that we're looking for. You will be quite surprised when you see how easy it is to communicate with external applications from within Perl. Are you ready? We simply need to enclose the command to execute or the path to an application, along with any necessary command line arguments, within a set of *backticks*. Perl will then spawn a shell to execute the application and return its output back to us. In this case, we store that output in the $uptime variable. Wasn't that simple?

We are about to venture off on a long detour to better understand the intricate process of communicating with external applications. If you are not interested in learning about these techniques now, you can safely jump to the *Back to Our Program ...* section and come back to this material at a later time.

Pipes

The *backtick* approach is very easy to use and quite convenient. However, it should only be used when you know that the output generated from the invoked application is small. Imagine what would happen if an application generates megabytes and megabytes of output? Perl would then have to store this entire information in memory, which may case quite a problem. So, Perl provides us with another alternative to communicate with applications, via a pipe. For example, say you wanted to retrieve the list of currently logged-in users, here is how you would do it:

```
#!/usr/bin/perl

##++
##   current_users.pl: display list of current users
##--
```

```
use strict;

open (MYPIPE, '/usr/bin/w |') || die "Cannot create pipe: $!\n";

while (<MYPIPE>) {        ## Read one line at a time into $_
    print;               ## Equivalent to: print $_;
}

close (MYPIPE);
exit (0);
```

If you quickly glance at this program, you may think that we are simply iterating through a file and displaying each record. However, that is not the case. Instead, we are opening a pipe to the /usr/bin/w command, reading and displaying its output:

```
   5:12pm  up 15 days,  6:56,  3 users,  load average: 0.00, 0.00, 0.07
USER       TTY      FROM               LOGIN@   IDLE   JCPU   PCPU  WHAT
shishir    tty1     -                  14Jan03 15days  2.27s  0.03s startx
shishir    pts/0    :0                 4:19pm  0.00s  0.37s  0.01s perl
current_us
dzhiwei    pts/3    192.168.1.6        Fri 3pm 25:49m 17.31s  0.00s script
```

You may have seen examples of pipes throughout this book. Here is an example that finds the number of occurrences of the word **perl** in all of the files located in the /etc directory:

```
# grep -d skip perl /etc/* | wc -l
    30
```

When the shell sees this, it executes the grep command, finding all lines that contain the word **perl**, and then passes that output to the wc command as input. In other words, the output of the first command gets passed to the second as input. We are doing something very similar in our program as well. However, if you look at the line with the open command above, you will see that there is nothing specified after the "pipe" (the vertical bar) character. Where is the output going? To the MYPIPE filehandle, like this:

```
$ /usr/bin/w | MYPIPE
```

By reading data from the MYPIPE filehandle, we are in effect reading the content produced by the /usr/bin/w program. The main advantage here is that we can read the content a line at a time, which is not only more efficient, but provides us with better control. In a similar fashion, we can also use a pipe to send data to another application as input:

```
#!/usr/bin/perl

##++
```

479

```
##   sort_numbers.pl: send list of numbers to /bin/sort to get sorted list
##--

open (MYPIPE, '| /bin/sort -g') || die "Cannot create pipe: $!\n";
print MYPIPE "100\n50\n30\n70\n90\n60\n20\n80\n10\n40\n";
close (MYPIPE);

exit (0);
```

Notice the location of the pipe; it's on the left side rather than the right side. This means that we are sending our output through the MYPIPE filehandle to another application as input. More specifically, we are passing a series of unordered numbers to the sort command, which produces the following output:

```
$ perl sort_numbers.pl
10
20
30
40
50
60
70
80
90
100
```

Unfortunately, once we send information to the external application as input, we have no control over the output that it produces; the output is typically sent to the standard output stream. Before we resume looking at our main program, I will show you one more technique that you can use to communicate with other applications.

system command

What if we want to interact with a program that doesn't care about its input or output? Take, for example, a script that starts a server of some sort, or an editor, which might open an empty window. Perl provides us with the system command, which we can use to invoke an application.

Let's look back at our send_email.pl program in the previous section for a moment. Imagine how convenient it would be for the user if he or she could enter the body of the message in an editor? We can use the system command to open an editor, saving the contents in a temporary file. Then, we can read the content from the file and pass it to the Mail::Send module:

```
#!/usr/bin/perl

use Mail::Send;             ## Import/use Mail::Send
use POSIX;                  ## Import/use POSIX
use strict;                 ## Enable "strict" pragma
```

```
...

print 'Subject: ';
chomp ($subject = <STDIN>);

print "Enter the message in an editor, save and exit when you are done:";

##++
##    Call POSIX::tmpnam() to determine a name for a temporary file,
##    which we'll use to store the content of the message.
##--

my $file = POSIX::tmpnam();        ## For example: /tmp/fileTwFpXe

system ("/usr/bin/gedit $file");  ## Open the editor; Perl will wait until
                                  ## user finishes, at which point a temp.
                                  ## file is created by the editor.

{
    local $/ = undef;              ## Undefine record separator

    if (open (FILE, $file)) {
        $message = <FILE>;         ## Reads ENTIRE content from file, as
                                  ## there is no record separator

        close (FILE);
    }
}

unlink $file;                      ## Delete temp. file; ignore status

...

exit (0);
```

We won't discuss this code snippet in detail, but I hope you get the general idea. As you can see from all of these examples, communicating with external applications via backticks, pipes and the system command is reasonably straightforward, yet extremely powerful. We can interact with any application, whether it is a system program, a script of some sort or a compiled application.

Parsing Load Averages

Now comes the most difficult part of the application! We had briefly talked about regular expressions earlier in the chapter. However, we have yet to really use them in a program, with the exception of the simple regex in list_users.pl. In this application, we need to extract the number of users and the load averages from the output generated by the uptime command. Though there are many techniques we can use to accomplish this task, regular expressions are by far the best and easiest way to handle it.

Regular Expressions

What is a regular expression? Simply defined, a regular expression is a set of "normal" characters and special syntactic elements (metacharacters) used to match patterns in text. You can use regular expressions in all types of text-manipulation tasks, ranging from checking for the existence of a particular pattern to finding a specific string and replacing it.

Substitutions From the Command-Line

For example, say you have a large set of HTML files that contain, among other information, your company's physical address. Soon after you create these files, you move to a new location and now have to change the address in all of the files. How would you do it? One tedious way would be to manually go through and replace the address in each and every file. But that is simply not realistic. However, armed with Perl and its regex support, we can get this task done in absolutely no time!

Take a look at the following HTML file. I have left out everything except for the company address that we are interested in modifying:

```
<HTML>
. . .
MechanicNet Group, Inc.<br>
43801 Mission Blvd., Suite 103<br>
Fremont, CA 94539
. . .
</HTML>
```

We want to change this address to read:

```
<HTML>
. . .
MechanicNet Group, Inc.<br>
7150 Koll Center Parkway, Suite 200<br>
Pleasanton, CA 94566
. . .
</HTML>
```

There are several ways we can tackle this job. It would be beyond the scope of this chapter to discuss each approach, so we will look at one technique that is compact, versatile, and very easy to use:

```
$ perl -0777 -p -i.bak -e \
's/43801 Mission Blvd., Suite 103<br>\s*Fremont, CA 94539/7150 Koll Center
Parkway, Suite 200<br>\nPleasanton, CA 94566/gsi' *.html
```

That's it, and we didn't even have to write a full-fledged program! We are running the Perl interpreter from the command line, passing to it several arguments, including a piece of code that performs the actual substitution. We'll start with the -0 switch, which sets the record separator to the octal number 777. This has the same effect as assigning an undefined value as the separator, since the octal value 777 is not legal. By doing this, we can match strings that span multiple lines. How, you ask? Normally, the default record separator is the newline character; each time we read from a filehandle, we will get back exactly one line:

```
$record = <FILE>;    ## One line
```

However, if the record separator is undefined, one read will *slurp* the entire file into a string:

```
local $/ = undef;    ## $/ = record separator; special Perl variable
$record = <FILE>;    ## Entire file
```

This is convenient since we can search for strings or patterns without having to worry about line boundaries. However, you should be careful not to use this technique with very large files, as you might exhaust system memory. On the other hand, if you need to match only a single string or pattern, you can safely ignore this switch.

Next, we use the -p switch, which creates an internal while loop that iterates over each record from each of the specified files, storing the content in the default Perl variable, $_. If you look at the far right of the one-line statement above, you will see the list of files that Perl will process. Remember, since the record separator is undefined, $_ will contain the contents of the entire file, as opposed to just one line.

The -i switch asks Perl to modify each of these files in-place, moving the original to another file with the same name but with the .bak extension. If you don't want to create a backup copy of each file, you can simply remove the .bak after the -i switch. And finally, we use the -e switch to specify the Perl code that should be executed for each record read from a file. If you want more information on all of the command line switches accepted by the interpreter, you should look at the perlrun manpage.

Here is the code that performs the substitution:

```
s/43801 Mission Blvd., Suite 103<br>\s*Fremont, CA 94539/7150 Koll Center
Parkway, Suite 200<br>\nPleasanton, CA 94566/gsi;
```

This is equivalent to:

```
$_ =~ s/43801 Mission Blvd., Suite 103<br>\s*Fremont, CA 94539/7150 Koll
Center Parkway, Suite 200<br>\nPleasanton, CA 94566/gsi;
```

as regular expression operators work on the default Perl variable, $_, if another scalar variable is not specified. Whenever you see the =~ or !~ operators, you should automatically think of regular expressions. We can use these operators to compare a scalar value against a particular regular expression.

The s// operator replaces the left side of the expression with the value on the right side. For example, if you want to substitute the zip code 94539 with 94566, you would use the following:

```
s/94539/94566/;
```

We are simply substituting literal values here. But, in our main example, we are using regex metacharacters in the substitution pattern. These metacharacters have a special significance to the regex processing engine. Take a look at the \s token followed by the asterisk. The token matches an occurrence of a whitespace; whitespace includes a regular space character, tab, newline or carriage return. We use the asterisk as the token's multiplier, forcing the regex engine to match the token – in this case, the whitespace – zero or more times. Other than this metacharacter, the rest of the expression is simply a set of literal characters.

And finally, let's look at the expression modifiers that follow the substitution operator. Each of the three characters, g, s, and i, has a special significance. The g modifier enables global substitution, where all occurrences of the original pattern are replaced by the new string. The s modifier forces the engine to treat the string stored in the $_ variable as a single line and the i modifier enables case insensitive matching.

There are only a small subset of metacharacters supported by the Perl regex engine. We won't cover them all here, so you should take a look at the documentation provided by Perl or the Beginning Perl book by Wrox Press.

Substitutions in Many Files

What if we have many HTML files spread around in multiple directories? Can we use the one-line Perl statement discussed above to find and replace the old address with the new one? Of course! We can use the find command in conjunction with the xargs to process all the files:

```
$ find . -name '*.html' -print0 | xargs --verbose --null \
perl -0777 -p -i.bak -e \
's/43801 Mission Blvd., Suite 103<br>\s*Fremont, CA 94539/7150 Koll Center
Parkway, Suite 200<br>\n Pleasanton, CA 94566/gsi'
```

We use the find command to find all the files with an .html extension in the current directory and all underlying subdirectories. These files are sent as input, via the pipe, to the xargs command, which takes them and passes them as arguments to the ensuing perl command.

In summary, we have looked at just one regular expression metacharacter, along with a useful Perl technique for manipulating text easily and quickly from the command line. That alone should convince you of the power of regular expressions. Next, we will continue on with our main application, using the knowledge gained here to parse the relevant information from the output generated by the uptime command.

Back to Our Program...

That was a long diversion, but I hope you learned a few things about regular expressions. Are you ready to handle a much more advanced regex? Let's dissect the one that we used in our main application to extract the number of users and the load averages:

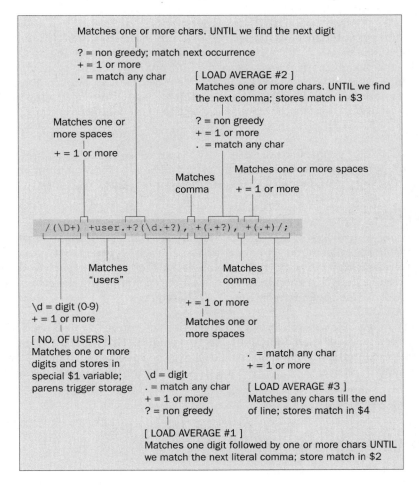

485

We can liken the process of crafting a regex to building a jigsaw puzzle: piece by piece. To jog our memory, let's once again look at the uptime output:

```
2:06pm  up 30 days, 21:56,  7 users,  load average: 1.41, 0.93, 0.26
```

The first piece involves extracting the number of users. The easiest way to do this is to find the number that precedes the literal word *user*. *We don't need to start our search from the beginning of the input string; we can create our expression to match from anywhere in the string.* And once we find the number of users, we need to store this value somewhere. We do this by enclosing the information we are interested in within a set of parentheses – see the expression above. This forces Perl to save the matched information in a special variable, $1.

Next, we need to get at the three load averages. We can use a variety of different expressions, but the simplest is to proceed through the output, starting from the string *user* and stopping when we find the next numerical digit. Once we find this number, we store all the characters from that point forward until the next comma; this is the first load average that gets stored in $2. Then, we ignore this comma as well as the following space and obtain the next load average. And finally, we extract the final load average by matching everything from the current point to the end of the line.

At first glance, regular expressions are difficult to comprehend. But, as you practice more and more, they will get much easier to handle and you will be able to implement all types of parsers, from finding errors in log files to extracting content from Web sites.

Archiving to File

Once we have the four pieces of information that we are interested in, we archive this data to a log file. We use the open command to open the file, but with a little twist. Notice the two **leading greater-than signs** in front of the file name; this tells Perl to open the file in *append* mode. Then, we use the join command to create a string containing the current timestamp and the uptime information, delimited by the colon character.

In order to accurately analyze this type of information over time, we also need to have a timestamp associated with each data point. For this purpose, we use the time command, which simply returns the number of non-leap seconds since the epoch – on Unix systems, this is 01/01/1970. Why don't you try the following to get a feel for these types of timestamps:

```
$ perl -e 'print time, "\n"'
1011168000
$ perl -e 'print scalar localtime 1011168000, "\n"'
Wed Jan 16 00:00:00 2002
```

There are a large number of Perl extensions that you can use to manipulate timestamps, in addition to the built-in `localtime` command. And last but not least, we write the delimited string to the file using the `print` command. Then, we close the file and exit.

We have looked at quite a number of new techniques in this section, ranging from accepting command-line arguments to interacting with external applications and designing regular expressions. It is not easy to understand all of this material in one sitting, so take some time to go through the material a number of times. In addition, you should refer to the built-in documentation as well as to other resources such as the Beginning Perl and Professional Perl books from Wrox Press for more detailed coverage.

In the next section, we will implement the disk usage application that we covered at the beginning of the chapter. You should use this application as a benchmark to see how well you have understood the techniques presented up to this point.

Application 4: Disk Usage Monitor

We spent a considerable amount of time and space discussing and analyzing a hypothetical disk usage monitoring application earlier in the chapter. As we have learned quite a bit of Perl since that discussion, we will actually implement the application in this section. To summarize, the application must be able to perform the following tasks:

- ❏ Monitor specified filesystems for available disk space
- ❏ Determine user directories that exceed a certain quota limit if available disk space falls below a specified threshold
- ❏ Find the fifteen largest files for each user directory that exceeds the quota limit
- ❏ Send an e-mail message to the offending user listing the largest files

In discussing this application, we will not dissect the code in extreme detail as we have done so with the three previous programs. Instead, I will show you a block of code and then briefly describe its functionality, highlighting any new constructs or syntax we see along the way. But first, here is a screenshot that illustrates an e-mail message that would typically be produced by this application if we reach the quota usage thresholds:

```
Disk Usage Alert - Message                                    _  ☐  ✕

 File   Edit   View   Actions

   Reply    Reply to All    Forward    🗐  🗗  🖨  🗑

  ┌─────────────────────────────────────────────────────────────┐
  │   From:  System Administrator <root@localhost.localdomain>   │
  │     To:  buckingham                                          │
  │ Subject: Disk Usage Alert                                    │
  │    Date: Fri, 17 Jan 2003 01:05:12 -0600                     │
  └─────────────────────────────────────────────────────────────┘

   ************************  DISK USAGE ALERT  ************************

   We are running LOW on disk space, and so we ask you to please clean up
   any unnecessary files.  For your convenience, we have attached a list
   of your 15 largest files, which you may want to look at:

   32695296          /home/buckingham/src/localapps-111220020922.tar.gz
   11068416          /home/buckingham/latest.tar.gz
   10232832          /home/buckingham/src/glibc-devel-2.2.4-13.i386.rpm
   9389056           /home/buckingham/java/test-application.exe
   9014272           /home/buckingham/roi.db
   8992768           /home/buckingham/src/glibc-common-2.2.4-13.i386.rpm
   5878784           /home/buckingham/src/glibc-2.2.4-13.i686.rpm
   5505024           /home/buckingham/mail/Inbox
   5201920           /home/buckingham/src/glibc-2.2.4-13.i386.rpm
   4784128           /home/buckingham/perl-5.8.0/Changes
   2149376           /home/buckingham/archive/reports/daily.194
   1438720           /home/buckingham/perl-5.8.0/Changes5.6
   1286144           /home/buckingham/backup/data/backup/09142000.tar.gz
   1286144           /home/buckingham/backup/data/backup/09262000.tar.gz
   1239040           /home/buckingham/html.tar.gz


   ***********************************************************************
                                                            Sincerely,
                                     Your Friendly System Administrators
```

Are you ready to look at the code? Here it is.

```perl
#!/usr/bin/perl

##++
##    disk_usage.pl: monitor disk usage and alert users via e-mail
##--

use Mail::Send;                          ## Load Mail::Send
use strict;                              ## Use strict pragma;
                                         ## must declare all vars.
```

```
##++
##    Declare constants/global variables
##--

our ($DF, $DU, %FILESYSTEMS, $QUOTA, $NO_FILES); ## Pre-declare global
                                                 ## variables

$DF          = '/bin/df';                   ## Path to df command
$DU          = '/usr/bin/du -ab';           ## Path and options to du


##++
##    The following three constants store (1) the filesystems to check and
##    their maximum allowable usage thresholds, (2) max user's disk quota,
##    50 MB and (3) the number of files to process, 15. You should change
##    these values to suit your requirements and system configuration.
##--

%FILESYSTEMS = ('/home1' => 90, '/home2' => 85);
$QUOTA       = 1_024_000 * 50;                   ## Use _ to make large
                                                 ## numbers more readable

$NO_FILES    = 15;


##++
##    Start main program
##--

print STDERR "Disk usage check in progress, please wait ...\n";

my    ($percent, $filesystem);
local *PIPE1;                                    ## Pre-declare/localize
                                                 ## filehandle

open (PIPE1, "$DF |") || die "Cannot create pipe: $!\n";

while (<PIPE1>) {                                ## Read line into $_
    if (/(\d+)%\s+(.+)\s*$/) {                   ## Match against $_ variable
        ($percent, $filesystem) = ($1, $2);     ## Store matches

        if (exists $FILESYSTEMS{$filesystem} &&      ## Does this element
                                                     ## exist in hash?
            $percent >= $FILESYSTEMS{$filesystem}) {

            print STDERR ">> $filesystem has $percent usage <<\n";
            process_filesystem ($filesystem); ## Invoke subroutine
        }                                     ## with $filesystem as arg.
    }
}

close (PIPE1);
exit  (0);
```

```
##++
##    End of main program, subroutines follow ...
##--
```

We start out by defining a set of constants – variables whose values will not change over the life of the program – using the our command. The our command allows us to define variables that have a global scope; can be accessed in subroutines. By using a constant, as opposed to a literal value, we can change its value easily without having to search and replace various instances of the actual value throughout the program.

One of the constants you should take note of is %FILESYSTEM, a data type that we have not seen so far. It is an associative array, commonly referred to as a hash, but is very different than a regular array. You can think of a hash as an array that is indexed by an alphanumeric *key*, rather than an ordered number. And each hash element has two scalar components: the key and an associated value. In this application, we are using a hash to associate filesystems with their corresponding disk usage thresholds. For example, we can access the threshold value for the /home1 filesystem by using the following syntax:

```
$home = $FILESYSTEMS{'/home1'};
```

After initialization, we proceed to use a pipe to interact with the df system command, which, in turn, produces and returns a disk usage report. Then, we iterate through each line of the report and extract the usage percentage and filesystem name with a regular expression. Based on the regex dissection that we performed in the previous section, can you understand this expression? We start our search toward the end of the input string, looking for one or more numerical digits followed by a percent sign. The numerical value will be stored in $1 and represents the usage percentage. Then, we match one or more whitespace characters and proceed to extract and save the remaining portion of the string in $2; this is the filesystem name. The trailing $ metacharacter allows us to anchor a regex to the end of the string.

Only if the line of input matches the regex do we proceed with the rest of the code. For each filesystem, we check to see if it exists in the hash and if the usage value exceeds the specified threshold. And only in that case, we print a diagnostic message and invoke the process_filesystem subroutine to process each user's individual directory.

We can use subroutines, also known as functions, methods and procedures, to make our code more modular. By placing a block of code that performs a distinct operation or set of operations in its own unique "container," we can keep the program clean, easy to understand, and possibly more efficient. Let's look at this subroutine.

```
##++
##    Subroutines
##--
```

```perl
sub process_filesystem
{
    my    $filesystem = shift;          ## Argument; read from @_ array
    my    ($dir, $path, $files);        ## Pre-declare other variables
    local *DIR;                         ## Pre-declare/localize filehandle

    opendir (DIR, $filesystem)          ## Open specified filesystem
        || die "Cannot open filesystem $filesystem: $!\n";

    while ($dir = readdir (DIR)) {      ## Get each user's directory
        next if ($dir =~ /^\./);        ## Ignore dirs. that start with .

        print STDERR "- Processing $dir directory ...\n";

        $path  = "$filesystem/$dir";    ## Add full path to user's dir
        $files = process_dir ($path);   ## Invoke subroutine

        ##++
        ##     Send e-mail to user only he/she has exceeded the quota limit.
        ##--

        send_email ($dir, $files) if (ref $files);
    }

    closedir (DIR);                     ## Close directory
}
```

The main program passes the name of the filesystem that has exceeded its specified disk usage threshold as an argument to this subroutine. Perl stores subroutine arguments in the special @_ array – analogous to the $_ default variable. We use the shift command to remove the first element from this array and store its value in $filesystem. However, if you don't feel comfortable using shift on an "unseen" array to obtain the argument, you can use either one of the following two statements:

```perl
my $filesystem = shift @_;           ## Remove first element from @_
my $filesystem = $_[0];              ## Argument; access index 0
```

Next, we call the opendir function to open the filesystem's root directory, in much the same manner as we would open a text file. We proceed to iterate through the directory, getting a subdirectory name each time we invoke the readdir command. You should be aware that each subdirectory, in turn, represent a user's home directory. Since readdir returns only the subdirectory name, we use the $filesystem value to construct the entire path to the directory and pass it to the process_dir subroutine.

The process_dir subroutine traverses through all of the user's files and returns a hash reference containing the list of the largest files, but only if the user has exceeded the quota value as defined by the $QUOTA constant. If we do end up getting back a list, then we would call the send_email subroutine to send a warning e-mail message to the user.

We have not talked about references at all in this chapter. We can use references to create complex data structures using the three basic data types that we are familiar with, namely scalars, arrays and hashes. We will look at references in more detail as we discuss this application.

```perl
sub process_dir
{
    my      $dir = shift;                    ## Argument; from @_ or $_[0]
    my      ($min, %files, $size, $file, @sorted);
    local *PIPE2;                            ## Localize filehandle

    ##++
    ##    Open a pipe to the /usr/bin/du command, with the -ab arguments;
    ##    this is defined by the $DU constant. The -a switch returns sizes
    ##    for all files, not just directories, and the -b switch returns
    ##    the sizes in bytes -- instead of the default unit blocks.
    ##
    ##    Sample output:
    ##    140      /home/postgres/global
    ##--

    open (PIPE2, "$DU $dir |") || die "Cannot create pipe: $!\n";

    $min   = 0;                              ## Keep track of smallest file
    %files = ();                             ## Initialize hash

    while (<PIPE2>) {                        ## Read record for file
        ($size, $file) = /^(\d+)\s+(.+)\s*$/;  ## Get the size and file
                                               ## from du

        last if ($file eq $dir);            ## End loop if we are finished
        next if (-d $file);                 ## Ignore if file is directory

        if ($size > $min) {
            $files{$file} = $size;          ## Store each file and size

            ##++
            ##    If we have more than 15 files in the %files hash, then
            ##    we sort the values based on the file size and delete the
            ##    file with the smallest size. At any given time, we will
            ##    only have that number of files in the hash.
            ##--

            if (scalar keys %files > $NO_FILES) {
                @sorted = sort { $files{$a} <=> $files{$b} } keys %files;
                $min    = $files{ $sorted[1] };

                delete $files{ $sorted[0] };   ## Delete smallest file
            }
        }
    }

    close (PIPE2);                          ## Close pipe
```

```
        return ($size >= $QUOTA) ? \%files : 0;    ## Return list only if user
                                                    ## exceeded quota
}
```

This is the most complicated piece of code that we have seen to date in this chapter. Our task in this subroutine is to locate and return files from a specific user's home directory that occupy the most disk space. The actual number of files to process is specified by the $NO_FILES constant defined at the beginning of the program; 15 in this case.

First, we create a pipe to the du command to get a list of each and every file and its associated size from the specified directory. We then iterate through this list one file at a time, ignoring all directories, with the exception of one. And that is the directory that has the same path as the user's home directory. This signifies the end of the output, and so we exit from the loop.

Looking inside the loop, we check to see if the size of the current file is greater than the minimum size, which is initially zero. And if so, we go ahead and store the file and its size in the hash. Then, immediately we determine the number of files currently stored in the hash, as we don't want to store more than 15 files at any given point. If the number exceeds 15, we need to remove the file with the smallest size.

The technique to remove this file from the hash is a simple one. We use the sort command to sort the hash by file size and store the sorted sizes in the @sorted array. Next, we reset the minimum file size to the second smallest size, so that from here on, we store only the files that are larger than this value. And then, we finally remove the smallest file from the hash using the delete command. We repeat this process for all of the files, at which point we will be left with the 15 largest files, unless, of course, there are less than 15 files in the directory. After the loop terminates, we return the list of these files, but only if the user's total directory size is greater than the defined quota.

There are a few things to note though. The first is the sort command and its syntax. sort expects to receive an array as input and returns the sorted array as output:

```
@array  = (100, 50, 25, 75);
@sorted = sort { $a <=> $b };   ## @sorted = (25, 50, 75, 100);
```

Our objective is to get the list of files in the %files hash ordered by their size, so we can remove the file with the smallest size. Unfortunately, sort cannot directly work with hashes, so we need to do things a bit differently. We can use the keys command to return an array of all the hash keys (file names):

```
@files = keys %files;           ## @files = ("/home/postgres/global", ...);
```

493

Then, we pass this array to the sort command, but we need to change the logic of the sort expression to make sure that we get back an array based on the file size and not the file name. The expression within the braces determines what is sorted and how it is sorted. sort takes two values from the input at a time, internally labeled $a and $b, and compares them. In our case, $a and $b represent file names, so we use these to access their respective file sizes in the hash, which are then compared. Once sort finishes its job, it returns an array of file names sorted by their size.

The next aspect we need to look at is the return command. We can use the return command to return a value or set of values back to our caller. However, the return command as seen in the subroutine is a shortcut for the following:

```
if ($size >= $QUOTA) {
    return \%files;              ## Return reference to a hash
} else {
    return 0;
}
```

Remember, an associative array and a regular array allow us to store multiple elements. If we were to return one of these data types from a subroutine, they would not be returned as one entity, but instead as multiple scalar variables. In order to avoid this, we take a reference of the hash by using the \ prefix; now it is returned as one single entity. Of course, if we return a reference to a hash in this manner, we would need to *de-reference* it outside before we can access elements in the hash. We will discuss this process in the send_email subroutine, which we will look at next:

```
sub send_email
{
    my ($user, $files) = @_;
    my ($mail, $list, $fh);

    $mail = new Mail::Send;              ## Creates new Mail::Send object
    $list = '';                          ## String to hold list of files

    $mail->to ($user);
    $mail->subject ('Disk Usage Alert');

    $fh = $mail->open();

    map { $list .= pack ("A15A*", $files->{$_}, $_) . "\n" }
                sort { $files->{$b} <=> $files->{$a} } keys %$files;

##++
##   This is a here document. It allows us to output large blocks
##   of a text at once; it prints until it finds the
##   'Message' delimiter.
##--
```

```
    print $fh <<Message;

************************  DISK USAGE ALERT  ************************

We are running LOW on disk space, and so we ask you to please clean up
any unnecessary files.  For your convenience,  we have attached a list
of your $NO_FILES largest files, which you may want to look at:


$list


***************************************************************************

                                                         Sincerely,
                                    Your Friendly System Administrators


Message

    $fh->close();
}
```

Most of the code in this subroutine should be familiar to you by now; it is nearly identical to the send_email.pl application. The process_filesystem subroutine passes the username and the hash reference to this subroutine to build and send the e-mail warning message. We are making one critical assumption here, namely that the user's e-mail address is the same as his/her home directory name. If you are adventurous, you can modify the code a bit from list_users.pl to match the home directory to the user name, and thus the e-mail address.

If you look at the code carefully, you will see one very cryptic looking statement. You should read it from right to left, instead of left to right. First, we use the sort command to sort the files in descending order; compare the position of $a and $b here to the sort expression in the process_dir subroutine. We pass the resulting array to map to build a string that lists the files and sizes in a tabular format.

To make this statement easier to understand, I will break it up into a simpler syntax:

```
@keys    = keys %$files;
@sorted = sort { $files->{$b} <=> $files->{$a} } @keys;

foreach $key (@sorted) {
    $list .= pack ("A15A*", $files->{$_}, $_) . "\n";
}
```

That's it for the application, but we are not done with Perl just yet! In the next section, we will implement a Web-based system administration application that you can use to monitor your system. But more significantly, it will illustrate how easy it is to design and develop a comprehensive application in Perl.

495

And Finally...

We'd like to give you a taste of something a little different. To begin with Perl can seem very complex – we don't dispute that; we've been through it too. And you can't really hope to understand everything from just a few pages toward the end of this book.

However, Perl is really very powerful, when used correctly, and can make your administrative life a great deal easier, especially when used in conjunction with other tools and technologies. As a demonstration of this and, we feel, an appropriate ending to our Perl chapter, we'd like to touch upon a small application we've written and included in the code download (from www.wrox.com for this book).

It's a simple systems administration assistant, with a graphical user interface, that we hope you might find a use for when you're working on your system. To install it you simply need to run the `sysadmin-install.pl` script that's in the download. It will install a `thttpd` server, and the necessary code files. Once it's up and running it looks something like this:

We'll be talking about it in more detail in Chapter 13, and there's a blow-by-blow account of how it was put together also available for download from the website.

Summary

In this chapter we've looked at how to administer and manage our Linux systems using Perl. We started by introducing the basic principals of function and syntax, before swiftly moving on to more practical topics such as interacting with your system, and using Perl to facilitate in your day-to-day administration by automating common and monotonous tasks.

We'll end our coverage of Perl here, though we'll meet it again in the coming chapters, where it is utilized to facilitate a number of our examples.

12

Security

Computer security is a vast topic, and detailed coverage is beyond the scope of this book. However, we will show you that, with a little planning and a few basic tools, it is possible to secure your Red Hat Linux system against the most likely threats. It really is worth taking the time to understand the basic principles of computer security, so you can be confident that your system is not vulnerable to accidental damage or malicious attack.

What Is Meant by Computer Security?

In a nutshell, computer security is about the protection of computing assets against threats such as theft, accidental loss, unauthorized access by a third party, and "denial of service" (whereby legitimate users of computing assets are prevented from doing so). Computing assets include things such as:

- ❏ Computer hardware
- ❏ Information stored on a computer (personal details, financial information, customer information, intellectual property, etc.)
- ❏ CPU, memory, storage, and network resources
- ❏ Computing services (Web sites, FTP, and Print servers)

The concepts involved in computer security are straightforward; we need to identify what we want to protect and the threats we want to protect them from, figure out how much effort to put into our protection schemes, and, once we've implemented them, regularly test the effectiveness of our protection. The details of how this is done can get very technical, and really serious security requirements (such as government, banks, airlines, and so on) need highly advanced skills and equipment to address them. However, where the security requirements are more modest, such as those for the normal home or business user, they are within reach of the competent beginner.

In the following sections, we'll show you how to enhance the security of your Red Hat Linux system.

Identifying What Is Valuable

The first step in planning the security of your Red Hat Linux system is to identify what you have on that system that is of value to you. You'll probably want to include the computer hardware itself (even though Red Hat Linux will happily run on machines considered by others to be nothing more than scrap), but it's a little less clear with the information stored on the system.

To help you draw up a list, consider how much effort it would take to re-create information if it was lost, and what the impact would be if the information fell into the hands of an unauthorized person – possibly with malicious intent. Think about the confidentiality of your data.

Consider also the impact of unauthorized changes to your data; if you run a business, maybe your website gets hacked and displays prices twice that of your competitors, or perhaps someone does a "search and replace" operation on your homework essay and you don't check it before sending it in. Think about the integrity of your data.

Even if your data is secure, and hasn't been modified by unauthorized people, you, and other authorized people, still need to be able to access it. One way of guaranteeing that your company's website won't get hacked is to unplug the computers on which it runs! So, availability of your data is important too.

In some environments, performance of computer systems is critical. Transaction processing systems need to meet expected response times for end users; number-crunching systems need to get their calculations done in an acceptable time; Web servers need to respond quickly to requests from Web browsers. If your system has to perform well, but is subject to – or even taking part in – a denial of service attack, then performance may be unacceptably low, so we'd better add performance to your list of things you want to protect.

Your list of valuable things that you want to protect will probably include personal information, such as your e-mail address book, financial information, and any confidential information belonging to third parties that you have an obligation to protect. In determining the value of something, it is helpful to try and work out how much time and effort would be required to re-create it. If, for example, your Red Hat Linux system was badly compromised, you might need to re-install everything from trusted CD-ROMs, then validate application data as it is restored from backups.

Potential Threats

Now we've identified what we've got that's valuable, the next step in planning our system security is to identify the potential threats.

Despite what you may read in the press about 'hackers', the most common causes of data loss are **operator error** ("finger trouble") and **hardware failure**. Nevertheless, we should still consider unauthorized access, either locally or, if the machine is connected to some sort of network (LAN or the Internet), remotely, as another potential threat.

Hacking

A hacker typically starts their activities by attempting to connect to your system using various TCP port numbers to try and find out where your system is vulnerable. This process is known as **probing**. Of course, if the hacker is somewhere out there on the Internet, they can probe your system only when you are connected, which is why people with "always on" Internet connections, such as xDSL ("broadband"), need to pay particular attention to security. A secure system will simply ignore incoming probes so the potential hacker has no indication that there is anything using the IP address they picked to probe. (Note that not all probes indicate a threat – some ISPs also probe ports on their customer's systems.)

If your system does respond to a hacker's probes, their next step will be to identify what software is listening on the ports (for example, a Web server, FTP server, Telnet, and so on) and try to exploit any security vulnerabilities in those programs. If the hacker is successful, they will be able to gain **root access** to your system, and may install modified versions of standard software that will allow them back in, or to use your system to launch attacks on other systems. Since vulnerabilities in software are found and fixed on a frequent basis, it is important to check regularly for known problems with any of the software you are running and obtain updates as soon as they become available. Fortunately, Red Hat makes this extremely easy through the Red Hat Network and the `up2date` command. We'll look at this later on in the chapter.

Denial of Service

Denial of Service attacks are designed to disrupt legitimate use of computer systems, rather than gain unauthorized access to information. These may be implemented by exploiting bugs in network services so that these services fail (for example, by sending malformed requests to a Web server, causing it to crash), or by overloading networks so that legitimate network traffic is unable to pass.

Hackers sometimes attempt Denial of Service attacks by sending the target system TCP/IP packets with the SYN flag set, as if they were starting up a TCP connection, but never completing the connection. The target system allocates some resources for each incoming connection, so if the hacker sends enough of these **SYN packets** the target system will eventually exhaust its network resources. This is sometimes called a **SYN flood**.

If your system is compromised, a hacker may use it to launch a Denial of Service attack on some other system without your knowledge. Coordinated attacks launched against a target system from a number of compromised systems are called **distributed denial of service attacks**, and these have been known to cause serious problems for the target system, no matter how large they might be.

Transferring Data

Transferring information over a network also opens up the possibility of eavesdropping – someone other than the intended recipient may intercept the information en route.

Physical Threats

Theft of computer equipment can be a big problem – especially for laptop users, and certain areas may suffer from environmental problems, such as flooding, that can damage computer equipment.

So, in summary our list of possible threats could look something like this:

- ❑ Operator error
- ❑ Hardware failure (particularly disk drives)
- ❑ Theft of equipment
- ❑ Unauthorized local access
- ❑ Unauthorized remote access
- ❑ Denial of service (DoS) attack
- ❑ Eavesdropping of network communications
- ❑ Environmental conditions damage

Countering the Threats

The list of possible threats may look a bit daunting, but each can be countered by relatively simple measures, as we'll explain below.

Hardware

Physical Security of the Hardware

Physical security is really just a matter of common sense. Keep computer equipment – especially portable equipment, such as laptops – secure. If the computer BIOS has the facility to configure a power-on password, use it. This at least will make it harder for someone to access your machine if it is stolen.

If you are unlucky enough to have your computer stolen, then you have to rely on your backups to get back the information that you lost. You do have backups, don't you? You have tested them, haven't you? Better read Chapter 10!

While we're on the subject of backups, the idea behind backing up your system is to allow you to **rebuild** it in case of some catastrophic event. This means that someone else can also build a copy of your system if they can get hold of your backups, so take care over the physical security of your backup media too.

Hardware Failure

Pay attention to the environmental conditions that your computer is working in. Computers don't like to get hot, and excessive temperature can cause premature failure of heat sensitive components, especially hard disk drives. There are ways of preventing the failure of a disk drive from causing loss of data, and these techniques rely on keeping the information on more than one physical disk.

The term **Redundant Array of Independent Disks** (or **RAID**) is widely used to describe these solutions, and the **RAID level** – a combination of digits and sometimes letters – indicates how the information is stored on multiple disks.

RAID may be implemented in hardware (typically in the hard disk adapter) or in software. If you're interested in RAID, have a look at the Linux-ATA-RAID HOWTO and the Software-RAID HOWTO on your system's documentation resources, or on-line.

Common RAID levels are:

RAID level	Data positioning
0	Data is broken up into equal size chunks (64Kbyte and 128Kbyte are common) and chunks are written to every disk in the array in turn (with four disks in the array, the 1st, 5th, 9th, ..., chunks of data are written to the first disk, the 2nd, 6th and 10th to the second disk, etc.). This pattern of data placement is called "striping", and the size of each chunk of data is called the stripe width. This gives the best performance, but worst availability, since failure of any disk will result in the loss of some data.
1	Data is copied on to pairs of disks (mirrored). Good performance and availability, but it uses twice as much disk space.
5	Data is striped across multiple disks, and protected by parity information that is also striped across the disks. Good performance for reading, but writing can be slowed by the need to update parity information. Requires extra disk capacity to store the parity information.
7	Not really RAID at all! RAID 7 is also known as JBOD (Just a **B**unch **O**f **D**isks). Here the information is not configured according to RAID, and your multiple disks are simply configured as one larger logical drive. It offers no fault tolerance advantages over simply using several disks individually.

RAID level	Data positioning
10 (or 0+1)	Data is striped across multiple pairs of disks. Combines performance of RAID 0 with availability of RAID 1.

Whether RAID is suitable for you depends on how valuable you consider your information to be – a decision that only you can make. Even if you do go for a hardware or software RAID solution for your Red Hat Linux system, please don't make the mistake of thinking that you don't need to take regular backups. Even if you set up the most extreme combination of hardware and software RAID (using software RAID to mirror data between two hardware RAID arrays, giving you effectively four copies of the data on four separate physical hard disks), the rm command can still irreversibly delete all four copies in a fraction of a second!

Local Security

So, we've sorted out the physical security of our Red Hat system. We've enabled the BIOS password so that only those who know it can start the machine up in the first place, and we've taken care with the physical location so it won't get stolen (we hope!) and the disk drives will stay nice and cool. Should we be unlucky enough to suffer a disk drive failure, we're taking – and testing – regular backups (we discussed how to do this in the previous chapter), so we're confident we can recover any lost information. What's next?

(Mis)using the root Account

You'll recall from the section on Threats that operator error was high on the list of potential threats. Computers have a nasty habit of doing exactly what we *tell* them to do, and not what we *want* them to do. So that this doesn't cause us too many problems, the trick is always to work with the lowest level of authority that we need to perform a particular task. Usually, this is **not** the root account.

Here's a little hypothetical example to demonstrate the potential pitfalls of using the root account for everyday tasks. **Don't try this at home, as it could result in serious damage to your system!**

Suppose we need to maintain the contents of a directory called /home/foo/logs by deleting files that are more than 14 days old. We could write a simple script to do this:

> **Remember, don't try this at home, folks!**

```
#!/bin/bash

LOGDIR="/home/foo/logs"
cd $LGODIR
find . -mtime +14 -exec rm \{\} \;
```

Unfortunately, we've made a typo in the script (the 4th line should say cd $LOGDIR); this means that when the cd command is run, its argument is blank (because the misspelled variable $LGODIR is not defined). This means that the cd command makes the current working directory our $HOME directory, not /home/foo/logs as we want. The find command then finds all the files below our $HOME directory (the current working directory) older than 14 days and deletes them. That's a pain if we're logged on as an ordinary user, but if we're logged on as root, this could well delete a lot of critical configuration information. (At least root's home directory on Red Hat Linux defaults to /root, which is a small mercy – on some other flavors of Unix, the default home directory for root is /, so running the above flawed script on one of those could well wipe out the entire operating system!)

Passwords

The password that we use to authenticate ourselves to the operating system when we log in is the only way we have of proving our identity, and thus keeping an intruder out. Your password is never stored on the Linux system (the operating system won't do it). Instead, a non-reversible mathematical function called a **hash** is used to combine your password with a random value (called the salt), and the hashed password is stored by the system. When you try to log in, the password you type is once again hashed with the same salt and the result compared to the one stored when the password was originally set. If the values are the same, then it's a fairly safe to assume that the password you typed is the same as the original one, and you are allowed in.

Now, you're probably thinking that someone could look at the stored hashed passwords and deduce the original passwords by reversing the hash function. However, the hash functions are chosen to make this reversal practically impossible. However, that doesn't stop someone who has access to the hashed passwords from using a program that guesses passwords to try and guess one.

Early versions of Unix stored the hashed passwords with other user information in /etc/passwd. Since the user information needs to be accessible to everyone (so, for example, user names could be shown in the output of ls -l), this also made the hashed passwords available to everyone too. Modern versions of Unix, including Red Hat Linux 9 avoid this problem by keeping hashed passwords in a separate file, called the **shadow password file**. On Red Hat, this is /etc/shadow. Since the hashed passwords need to be accessible only to authentication programs that run with root authority, the shadow password file should be accessible only to the root user.

Choosing a Strong Password

Choosing a strong password is really better phrased as avoiding weak passwords. Weak passwords are ones that can be guessed, either by humans or by password cracking programs (that will quite happily try different permutations of words from password dictionaries for days on end without getting bored).

So, avoid passwords that can be found in a dictionary (in any language), or variations of these (changing is to 1s, or os to 0s, or adding digits), passwords that someone who knows you may guess (name of family member or pet), or anything generated in a systematic way. Include punctuation and other symbols, and make use of the fact that Red Hat Linux 9 uses MD5 password hashes that allow passwords to be up to 15 characters long.

> *However, some characters shouldn't be included in passwords, because they can be misinterpreted as terminal control characters and cause problems when logging in. Avoid @, #, [backspace], and other control characters.*

For example, here are some weak passwords:

- ❑   Fred123
- ❑   Asdfghj (simple pattern on keyboard)
- ❑   B10n1c (trivial modification of dictionary word)
- ❑   Nitsob (a pet's name spelled backward)

These would have been strong passwords until they were published in this book:

- ❑   Xz%!q)_2+!
- ❑   3#&-Aa%yty?
- ❑   ap^Lj+~rZxp]

However, make sure you can **remember** your password so you don't have to write it down. As soon as you do that, you're weakening it. A slip of paper under the keyboard is a dead giveaway!

Checking passwords

The password cracking programs that are useful to hackers are just as useful to us, as we can use them to identify weak passwords on our systems. Then we can get the offending user to change them before a hacker cracks them. One of the best known of these programs is simply called **Crack**. It requires a bit of work to build and install it, so we'll go through it step-by-step here. On this occasion, we'll explain what we're doing as we go along, rather than saving it until after we're done.

> **Crack is a 2.5MB download. If you don't fancy downloading it, you can skip ahead to the Running Crack section, and we'll catch up with you in a moment.**

Try It Out   Making a Home for the Crack Program

Before we begin setting up the Crack program, we need to make a home for it. It's best to create our own directories for programs that we build and install ourselves (as opposed to installing from RPM packages) so they don't interfere with system installed packages.

Crack doesn't require root privileges to run (but we do need to be root to get at the shadow passwords to feed Crack later on), so we'll download, configure, and build it as an ordinary, unprivileged user.

1. The first thing we'll do is create a home for Crack. Open a terminal window (Main Menu | System Tools | Terminal) and type the following commands at the prompt:

```
% cd
% pwd
% mkdir crack
```

The `cd` command on its own makes the current working directory the **home directory** for the user running the command. This should be the current directory for a newly opened terminal session anyway, but we've included it here in case you're trying this out in an existing window. The `pwd` command shows us the current working directory to confirm we're where we expect to be, then the `mkdir` command creates a directory called `crack`. This is where we're going to install the Crack program.

2. The easiest way to download the Crack program is through the Mozilla Web browser. Start the browser, then point it to ftp://ftp.cert.dfn.de/pub/tools/password/Crack/, you should be presented with a list of files in a directory. Click on the file called `Crack_5.0a.tar.gz`, and when a dialog box appears asking you what you want to do, select **Save to disk** and click **OK**. Browse to the `crack` directory you've just created and click **OK**.

If you have trouble connecting to the FTP site listed above, you could try ftp://ftp.cerias.purdue.edu/pub/tools/unix/pwdutils/crack/ instead.

3. The next step is to unpack the downloaded file. The letters `.tar.gz` at the end of the file indicates that it is a **TAR** (Tape **AR**chive) format file that has been compressed with GNU Zip. (You'll sometimes see `.tgz` at the end of a file to indicate the same thing.) We therefore need to uncompress and **untar** the file.

Go back to the terminal window and type the following commands:

```
% cd crack
% tar -xzvf Crack_5.0a.tar.gz
```

The tar command extracts the files (x switch) from a compressed tar file (z switch) called `Crack_5.0a.tar.gz` (`-f Crack_5.0a.tar.gz`) and prints the filenames as they're extracted (v switch). Notice that the files go into directories under `c50a/` and that the directories are created as required:

```
ewanb@localhost:~/crack

File   Edit   View   Terminal   Go   Help

[ewanb@localhost crack]$ ls
crack5.0a.tar.gz
[ewanb@localhost crack]$ tar -xzvf crack5.0a.tar.gz
c50a/
c50a/conf/
c50a/conf/dictrun.conf
c50a/conf/rules.weird
c50a/conf/rules.suffix
c50a/conf/rules.prefix
c50a/conf/rules.perm1u
c50a/conf/globrule.conf
c50a/conf/dictgrps.conf
c50a/conf/rules.basic
c50a/conf/network.conf
c50a/conf/rules.fast
c50a/conf/rules.perm2
c50a/conf/rules.perm3
c50a/conf/rules.perm4
c50a/conf/rules.perm5
c50a/conf/rules.perm6
c50a/conf/rules.perm7
c50a/conf/rules.perm1
c50a/conf/rules.perm2u
```

4. Now there are a few configuration changes we need to make to the Crack source code before it will build and run successfully on our Red Hat Linux system. Firstly, we need to edit the **Crack script**. Change to the `c50a` directory and open `Crack` in the Gnome text editor by running these commands:

```
% cd c50a
% gedit Crack
```

5. A text editor window will pop up. Scroll through the file to the section that says:

```
#
# now pick your compiler
#
```

6. Red Hat Linux ships with the GNU C compiler called `gcc`, so the `gcc` 2.7.2 section is what we need to use (even though we've got `gcc` version 3.2). Place # characters at the start of the lines for `vanilla unix cc` to turn them into comments (a process known as **commenting out** the code), and remove the same characters from the corresponding lines in the "gcc 2.7.2" section. We also need to use the `stdlib crypt()` routine, so remove the # from the start of the `LIBS=...` line.

When you've finished, the modified Crack file should look like this:

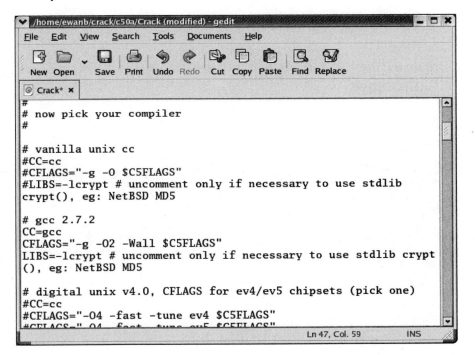

7. Save the changes and exit `gedit`.

8. Red Hat Linux 9 does not use the standard DES algorithm to encrypt passwords, but uses a stronger algorithm based on MD5 (**Message Digest 5**). Crack is set up to use DES by default, so we need to change this. The following steps are given in the Crack 5.0a README file, so type them in at the command line prompt:

```
% mv src/libdes src/libdes.orig
% cd src/util
% cp elcid.c,bsd elcid.c
```

If asked to overwrite `elcid.c`, answer y.

9. While we're here, there's one other small modification to make. The Red Hat 9 shadow password file uses salts that contain characters that the shipped version of Crack interprets as invalid (since they're not in the list of valid characters). For the purposes of this exercise, we'll modify the routine that checks for the validity of the hashed passwords to accept these characters. The routine as shipped checks that each character in the **ciphertext** (hashed password) is in a list of allowed characters. We'll switch things around so it checks that none of the characters is in a list of disallowed characters.

Edit the `elcid.c` source file by typing `gedit elcid.c`. Find the function `elcid_invalid(ciphertext)` and make the following three changes:

❏ Change the name of the variable `validchars` to `invalidchars`.

❏ Change the value of this variable to `!`.

❏ Remove the `!` in the line starting `if (!strchr...` to reverse the sense of the logic.

When you've finished, it should look like this:

10. Save the changes and exit `gedit`.

11. Now we're ready to compile the Crack program. This is done by invoking the Crack script with the switch -makeonly. So, change directory back to $HOME/crack/c50a and run the following command:

```
% ./Crack -makeonly
```

Note that we need to specify where to find the Crack program by giving the directory - ./ means the current directory. Unlike Microsoft Windows, Linux and other Unix variants do not include the current directory on the search path unless explicitly told to do so. That's never a good idea for the root account, as you really want to be sure the root user is running programs in the correct system locations and not others lying around that happen to have the same name.

12. When Crack is invoked with the -makeonly option, it makes the required program files. Make sure that it finishes with the message Crack: makeonly done:

13. Next we need to make the password dictionaries that Crack will use to try and guess the passwords on our system. Do this by running ./Crack -makedict:

14. Again, make sure that this finishes with the message Crack: makedict done.

Getting the Encrypted Passwords for Crack to Work On

Before we can try out our newly built Crack program, we need to get it some passwords to work on. The information Crack requires is held on Red Hat Linux 9 systems in /etc/passwd and /etc/shadow, and these need merging into a single file. Fortunately, there's a utility provided with Crack that will do just that for us.

Note that we need to be root to read /etc/shadow, and since the merged file contains information useful to a potential hacker (the encrypted passwords from the shadow password file), we need to make sure that it too has restricted access. The best way to do this is to create an empty file with the correct permissions (by setting our umask), then append the sensitive data to the file. (We could create the file with default permissions and then tighten them up, but there is a theoretical chance that someone could open the file before we've changed the permissions.) We'll change the ownership of the file back to the user we want to run Crack under to avoid having to do that as root.

So, run the following commands to create the merged file that is suitable for Crack to work on:

```
% su root
# umask 077
# touch passwords.dat
# scripts/shadmrg.sv > passwords.dat
# chown user1 passwords.dat
# ls -l passwords.dat
# exit
```

511

Running Crack

All we have to do now is run the following command to start Crack guessing at the passwords our users have set to see if there are any weak ones:

```
% ./Crack passwords.dat
```

When you see the word Done, it doesn't mean that Crack has finished guessing passwords. (If passwords could be guessed that quickly, we might as well not bother with them at all!) What it does mean is that Crack has started a background process running that will spend the next hours, or even days, guessing the passwords in the passwords.dat file and logging any matches that it finds. Use the following command to find the background process:

```
% ps -ef | grep crack
```

If we want to stop the background Crack process, the correct way to do this is to run $HOME/crack/c50a/scripts/plaster.

So how do we find out how Crack is doing? Simply run the Reporter script that is in the same directory as the Crack program. To find out any passwords that have been guessed, type the following command in the command line window:

```
% ./Reporter -quiet
```

If you leave off the -quiet switch, then you'll get some warning messages about locked accounts, and accounts where there is no valid password. We will expect several of these to show up, as accounts used for running system services such as printing and Web serving (such as lpd and apache) will normally be configured in this way to prevent anyone from logging in as those users.

> A final word of warning when using Crack, or any other password cracking program: Make sure that you are authorized to do this by the appropriate person, preferably in writing.

Keeping Software Up to Date

As we mentioned earlier, vulnerabilities in system software that hackers may be able to exploit to gain unauthorized access to our systems are discovered and fixed quite frequently. The Red Hat Network provides an easy way for people running Red Hat systems to be informed of important software updates and to install these updates with the minimum of hassle.

Registering for Red Hat Network

> The Red Hat Network subscription demonstrated here works only for those users who have bought a Red Hat Linux boxed set. Other users will have to buy network services from Red Hat. Details can be found on their website.

Before we can make use of the Red Hat Network, we need to register for it. Start the Red Hat Update Agent either by typing up2date at the command prompt, or choosing Main Menu | System Tools | Red Hat Network. You will be presented with the following Welcome screen:

Simply follow the simple, step-by-step, instructions that it provides you with, and you will be able to configure your system to automatically administer the latest patches to itself, while at the same time you receive email updates of the latest security vulnerabilities that affect you.

> *When choosing a user name and password, don't use the same username or password as you do on your Red Hat Linux box!*

Monitoring Security

There are several ways of monitoring the security of your Red Hat system, allowing you to spot security breaches and other potential problems.

System Logs

/var/log

The Red Hat Linux system maintains several log files that record system activity. Most of the interesting ones reside in /var/log. Here's a table describing the most important log files:

File in /var/log	Contents	View with
btmp	Record of all bad logins attempts. Updated by login program if it exists.	lastb command
cron	Messages sent to syslogd from the cron daemon (which schedules jobs on Unix systems).	Normal text viewing tools
dmesg	Kernel messages (from boot)	Normal text viewing tools
lastlog	Last login times for all users.	lastlog command
messages	Messages sent to syslogd with level of info or higher, except those from mail, cron or authentication related messages.	Normal text viewing tools
secure	Messages sent to syslogd from authpriv (i.e. authentication and security messages that should only be visible to privileged users).	Normal text viewing tools
wtmp	Record of all logins and logouts.	last command

Note that several of these files are maintained by the kernel logging daemon syslogd. The behavior of this daemon is controlled by the configuration file /etc/syslog.conf, and we can customize it if we don't like the defaults (which are pretty good). For more information on configuring syslog, check its man page.

The files /var/log/btmp and /var/log/wtmp are updated only if they exist (i.e. the programs that update these files won't create them for you). The default Red Hat Linux 9 installation has /var/log/wtmp, so all logins and logouts are logged, but not /var/log/btmp.

A diligent system administrator will regularly review the contents of these log files, either using tools such as gedit, if the file is a plain text file, or the appropriate command such as last or lastlog if the file contains formatted data. However, regularly trawling through log files for the occasional message of significance is very tedious. Fortunately, there's an automated tool called logwatch that takes away much of the tedium. Even better for us, Red Hat include a sensible default setup so it's up and running out of the box.

logwatch

Logwatch is a tool for searching through log files for interesting messages and summarizing them elsewhere. We will look at the default configuration provided with Red Hat Linux 9.

The configuration files for logwatch are in /etc/log.d. The main configuration file is called logwatch.conf, and here is the default contents (it's seems quite long, doesn't it?):

```
#######################################################
# This was written and is maintained by:
#   Kirk Bauer <kirk@kaybee.org>
#
# Please send all comments, suggestions, bug reports,
#   etc, to kirk@kaybee.org.
#
#######################################################

# NOTE:
#   All these options are the defaults if you run logwatch with no
#   command-line arguments. You can override all of these on the
#   command-line.

# You can put comments anywhere you want to. They are effective for the
# rest of the line.

# this is in the format of <name> = <value>. Whitespace at the beginning
# and end of the lines is removed. Whitespace before and after the = sign
# is removed. Everything is case *insensitive*.

# Yes = True = On = 1
# No = False = Off = 0

# Default Log Directory
# All log-files are assumed to be given relative to this directory.
# This should be /var/log on just about all systems...
LogDir = /var/log

# Default person to mail reports to. Can be a local account or a
# complete email address.
MailTo = root

# If set to 'Yes', the report will be sent to stdout instead of being
# mailed to above person.
Print = No
```

```
# if set, the results will be saved in <filename> instead of mailed
# or displayed.
#Save = /tmp/logwatch

# Use archives? If set to 'Yes', the archives of logfiles
# (i.e. /var/log/messages.1 or /var/log/messages.1.gz) will
# be searched in addition to the /var/log/messages file.
# This usually will not do much if your range is set to just
# 'Yesterday' or 'Today'... it is probably best used with
# Archives = Yes
# Range = All

# The default time range for the report...
# The current choices are All, Today, Yesterday
Range = yesterday

# The default detail level for the report.
# This can either be Low, Med, High or a number.
# Low = 0
# Med = 5
# High = 10
Detail = Low


# The 'Service' option expects either the name of a filter
# (in /etc/log.d/scripts/services/*) or 'All'.
# The default service(s) to report on. This should be left as All for
# most people.
Service = All
# If you only cared about FTP messages, you could use these 2 lines
# instead of the above:
#Service = ftpd-messages  # Processes ftpd messages in /var/log/messages
#Service = ftpd-xferlog  # Processes ftpd messages in /var/log/xferlog
# Maybe you only wanted reports on PAM messages, then you would use:
#Service = pam_pwdb   # PAM_pwdb messages - usually quite a bit
#Service = pam    # General PAM messages... usually not many

# You can also choose to use the 'LogFile' option. This will cause
# logwatch to only analyze that one logfile.. for example:
#LogFile = messages
# will process /var/log/messages. This will run all the filters that
# process that logfile. This option is probably not too useful to
# most people. Setting 'Service' to 'All' above analyizes all LogFiles
# anyways...
```

As we read through the file, we see that most of the lines are comments (since they start with the # sign, and that's a widely used way of introducing comments in most script and configuration files). So, out of all those lines, the only entries that are in effect are:

```
LogDir = /var/log
MailTo = root
Print = No
Range = yesterday
Detail = Low
```

These are highlighted in bold in the example. If we consult the man page for logwatch (run the command man logwatch), we can see that logwatch will check the log files in /var/log, looking for entries from the previous day, and e-mail a report containing a low level of detail to root.

If we've run our system for a few days and checked root mail, we'll have seen messages from logwatch, so how is this happening? Scheduling of unattended jobs on Red Hat Linux 9, and most other Unix flavors, is handled by the **cron daemon**. This daemon looks for files containing information about what to run and when to run it in the directories /var/spool/cron and /etc/cron.d, and in the file /etc/crontab. On Red Hat Linux 9, the /etc/crontab file is the one that is configured by default.

If we examine the contents of this file, we see that there are a few lines of environment information, and some other lines starting with numbers:

```
SHELL=/bin/bash
PATH=/sbin:/bin:/usr/sbin:/usr/bin
MAILTO=root
HOME=/

# run-parts
01 * * * * root run-parts /etc/cron.hourly
02 4 * * * root run-parts /etc/cron.daily
22 4 * * 0 root run-parts /etc/cron.weekly
42 4 1 * * root run-parts /etc/cron.monthly
```

The numbers specify when cron should run the command described by the rest of the line. There are five fields which are, from left to right, minute, hour, day of month, month, and day of week. Where an asterisk is used, this means "I don't care". So the four scheduled jobs in the default Red Hat Linux 9 crontab are run at the following times:

Scheduled Time	Interpretation
01 * * * *	01 minutes past each hour
02 4 * * *	04:02 every day
22 4 * * 0	04:22 every Sunday (1=Monday, 2=Tuesday, etc., Sunday=0 or 7)
42 4 1 * *	04:42 on the 1st day of every month

The jobs are essentially similar; run the `run-parts` script as `root` and pass the name of a directory (e.g. `/etc/cron.hourly` for the job run at 1 minute past each hour). The `run-parts` script simply runs every executable file it finds in the directory that it is given (except files ending in the characters ~ or ,, and a few other exceptions). If we look in the `/etc/cron.daily` directory, we'll see a file called `00-logwatch`, which is a symbolic link to the `logwatch` command.

All this means that, at 04:02 every day, the root user will be mailed a message containing summaries of important information entered into various log files in `/var/log` the previous day. This is all set up for us when Red Hat Linux is installed, but now we know how it works, we can adjust the configuration to suit. If, for example, we'd like more information in the messages, we can simply edit `/etc/log.d/logwatch.conf` and change the `Detail = Low` line to `Detail = High`. Maybe we'd like the message to be sent at a different time, say 00:15. Easy – just delete the file `00-logwatch` from `/etc/cron.daily` (so the 04:02 daily cron job no longer runs) and add the following line to `/etc/crontab`:

```
15 00 * * * root /usr/sbin/logwatch
```

It's as simple as that.

System Integrity

Once a hacker has gained access to a system, they will often want to install modified versions of system files to ensure their continued access and to gather more information that will help them achieve their objectives. If our security analysis has identified this threat as one we need to consider, we need to have some means of identifying when our system may have been compromised in this way, so we can take remedial action (restore the compromised file from a trusted backup).

But if we're checking the system for modified files, we'll not only identify files modified by intruders, we'll also identify files that may have been inadvertently modified by authorized individuals, or that have become corrupt due to hardware problems (e.g. bad blocks appearing on disk drives).

Enter tripwire...

Tripwire

Tripwire is an Open Source **system integrity checker** that is available for Red Hat Linux. It is a useful weapon in the system administrator's armory, so this section will take you through obtaining it and setting it up. Note that when Tripwire scans the system to detect changes, it's doing a lot of work and will hit the processor(s) and file I/O hard.

Try It Out   **Downloading, Configuring, and Running Tripwire**

1. Tripwire is available in RPM format for Red Hat Linux, which makes installation very straightforward. It's available on the Red Hat Linux 9 CD-ROMs, but as an interesting exercise, we'll try using the `rpm` command's built-in FTP and HTTP client. We'll use the `rpm` command to download and install the Tripwire RPM with a single command! Open a terminal window and switch to the root user and type in the following command (all on one line):

You'll need to change the httpproxy IP address and httpport port number to suit your Internet connection (omit them if you don't need to go through a proxy server to access the Internet).

```
# rpm -iv --httpproxy 10.4.65.2 --httpport 3128
http://ftp.redhat.com/pub/redhat/linux/9/en/os/i386/RedHat/RPMS/tripwire-
2.3.1-17.i386.rpm
```

The command also assumes that you're running on an Intel architecture machine. If not, replace the occurrences of *i386* with your machine's architecture.

After a few minutes (depending on the speed of your Internet connection), you should see the message **Preparing packages for installation...** followed by **tripwire-2.3.1-17**, and be returned to the command prompt.

2. You can confirm that the Tripwire package was installed by running the following command:

```
# rpm -q tripwire
```

If all is well, you'll get the package version information back; if not, you'll get a message saying that **package tripwire is not installed** (in which case, just download the RPM in the conventional way, and try again).

3. Now we've got tripwire installed, we can go on to configure its policies and complete the setup. Before diving in to the configuration, we should take time to read the README file in `/usr/share/doc/tripwire-2.3.1`, and the `twintro` and `twpolicy` man pages to familiarize ourselves with the required configuration tasks. These can be divided into three distinct steps:

❏ Setting up the policy file

❏ Initializing the Tripwire database

❏ Configuring Tripwire to run periodically and report system integrity violations

4. Let's begin with the policy file. Tripwire's policy file defines which files and directories tripwire should monitor for changes, and what sort of changes are significant. For some files, e.g. `/bin/login`, any change in file contents, modification date, or ownership is suspicious, but we'd expect them to be accessed frequently. Other files, such as log files, are expected to grow in size, but not change ownership.

The policy file that is installed with the RPM in `/etc/tripwire/twpol.txt` tells Tripwire to monitor many files that probably don't exist on our system, so we'll get lots of spurious error messages when we run an integrity check. What we really need to do is edit the policy file so that files and directories that don't exist aren't monitored, and conversely, if there are files and directories that do exist but are commented out in the policy file are reinstated. It would be tedious to do this by hand, so let's use our new-found knowledge of Perl to write a script to do it for us.

5. The algorithm we need to employ is straightforward. If we find a line that looks like an instruction to Tripwire to check a file or directory (optional whitespace, string beginning with /), then we should check that the file or directory exists. If not, we should comment out the line to prevent Tripwire from generating an error.

Similarly, if we find a line in the policy file that looks like a commented out file (optional whitespace, #, optional whitespace, string beginning with /), then we should check if the file or directory exists. If it does, then we'll remove the comment to reinstate the file.

6. We'll write the script as a filter, so it reads configuration lines from STDIN and writes to STDOUT. Any lines that don't look like either of the types of line we're interested in are passed through unmodified. It would be nice to know how much work we've saved ourselves by counting up the number of lines that the script modifies.

Here's the script (hopefully your new knowledge of Perl will give you an idea of the structure that we've employed, even if the details are still a bit beyond you – they'll come with practice):

```
#! /usr/bin/perl -w

# Filter for Tripwire policy file. Looks for lines that
# start with optional whitespace and a filename, and
# comments them out if the file does not exist. Also
# looks for commented out lines containing filename and
# removes comment if they do exist.

$Additions = 0;
$Removals = 0;
```

```
# Read each line from stdin into the $line variable
while ($line = <STDIN>) {
  # Look for lines that match a pattern (the Perl
  # pattern matching characters are enclosed in [])
  # start with optional white space [ ^\s* ]
  # then a '#' [ # ]
  # then more optional white space [ \s* ]
  # then a string starting with '/' that doesn't
  # contain white space [ \/\S+ ]
  #
  # The last part of the pattern is enclosed in ()
  # so that if the pattern matches, we can access
  # this part through the $1 variable.
  #
  # This pattern matches a commented out entry/
  if ( $line =~ /^\s*#\s*(\/\S+)/ ) {
   # Found commented out entry. If the file exists,
   # strip off the comment character.
   if ( -e $1 ) {
     $line =~ s/^\s*#//;
     $Additions++;
   }
  # Now look for a line that's like the above but
  # without the '#' comment character.
  } elsif ( $line =~ /^\s*(\/\S+)/ ) {
   # Found entry that starts with "  /". If file
   # does not exist, then comment out entry.
   if ( ! -e $1 ) {
     $line = "# " . $line;
     $Removals++;
   }
  }

  # Output the line (whether modified or not)
  print $line;
}
# Print the statistics on STDERR, so they won't get redirected by >
print STDERR "Number of additions: $Additions\n";
print STDERR "Number of removals: $Removals\n";
```

7. Create a text file containing this script and call it /usr/local/bin/cleanpol.pl, and make it executable by running the following command:

Depending on the examples you've followed earlier in the book, you may need to acquire root privileges at this point.

```
# chmod +x /usr/local/bin/cleanpol.pl
```

8. Now we can use this Perl script to produce a customized Tripwire policy file:

```
# cd /etc/tripwire
# mv twpol.txt twpol.txt.orig
# /usr/local/bin/cleanpol.pl <twpol.txt.orig \ >twpol.txt
...
Number of additions: 38
Number of removals: 125
```

This little script saved us from making 163 manual changes to the Tripwire policy file! (The number of changes made on your system will vary depending on which packages you have installed.) You can review the changes that were made with the `diff` command:

```
diff twpol.txt.orig twpol.txt
```

9. Now, use `gedit`, or your favorite text editor, to review the contents of the updated `/etc/tripwire/twpol.txt` file. In particular, there may be a problem with the line defining the policy for `/sbin/e2fsadm`. If the `cleanpol.pl` script uncommented this line, then the note `tune2fs?` at the end of the line is treated by Tripwire as a relative path to a file, and the policy file is rejected. Simply delete this note. In other words:

```
/sbin/e2fsadm      -> $(SEC_CRIT) ; tune2fs?
```

becomes:

```
/sbin/e2fsadm      -> $(SEC_CRIT) ;
```

10. Now we have set up the Tripwire policy file, the next step is to initialize the Tripwire database. This is done by running the `twinstall.sh` script in `/etc/tripwire`:

```
# ./twinstall.sh
```

This script asks us to enter site and local passphrases (a term used to describe a long "password"), generates encryption keys and cryptographically secures the configuration and policy files to prevent unauthorized changes:

```
[root@rh9 tripwire]# ./twinstall.sh

----------------------------------------------
The Tripwire site and local passphrases are used to
sign a variety of files, such as the configuration,
policy, and database files.

Passphrases should be at least 8 characters in length
and contain both letters and numbers.
```

```
See the Tripwire manual for more information.

----------------------------------------------
Creating key files...

(When selecting a passphrase, keep in mind that good passphrases typically
have upper and lower case letters, digits and punctuation marks, and are
at least 8 characters in length.)

Enter the site keyfile passphrase:
Verify the site keyfile passphrase:
Generating key (this may take several minutes)...Key generation complete.

(When selecting a passphrase, keep in mind that good passphrases typically
have upper and lower case letters, digits and punctuation marks, and are
at least 8 characters in length.)

Enter the local keyfile passphrase:
Verify the local keyfile passphrase:
Generating key (this may take several minutes)...Key generation complete.

----------------------------------------------
Signing configuration file...
Please enter your site passphrase:
Wrote configuration file: /etc/tripwire/tw.cfg

A clear-text version of the Tripwire configuration file
/etc/tripwire/twcfg.txt
has been preserved for your inspection. It is recommended
that you delete this file manually after you have examined it.


----------------------------------------------
Signing policy file...
Please enter your site passphrase:
Wrote policy file: /etc/tripwire/tw.pol

A clear-text version of the Tripwire policy file
/etc/tripwire/twpol.txt
has been preserved for your inspection. This implements
a minimal policy, intended only to test essential
Tripwire functionality. You should edit the policy file
to describe your system, and then use twadmin to generate
a new signed copy of the Tripwire policy.
```

11. The final step in initialization is to run the command `tripwire -- init`. We are prompted for the local passphrase, then Tripwire scans all the files listed in the configuration file and gathers baseline data against which all future scans are run. This may take several minutes, so be patient:

It is vital that we are confident the system is in a sound state before initializing the database, otherwise there's little point in using Tripwire. After the database is initialized, it's a good idea to put a copy on write-once media (e.g. CD-ROM) so that it cannot be altered:

```
# tripwire --init
Please enter your local passphrase:
Parsing policy file: /etc/tripwire/tw.pol
Generating the database...
*** Processing Unix File System ***
Wrote database file: /var/lib/tripwire/rh9.twd
The database was successfully generated.
```

Setting up Tripwire to Run Automatically

We've already seen how logwatch is set up to run automatically every day at 04:02. We can very easily set up Tripwire to run at the same time.

Create a two-line script called /etc/cron.daily/run-tripwire containing the following lines:

```
#!/bin/sh
/usr/sbin/tripwire --check
```

Make sure the script is owned by root and has permissions of 500 (r-x------) so it is executable only by root. This script invokes Tripwire and gets it to check the system's integrity according to the rules in the policy file, and using the database we just created as its baseline. When cron runs this script at 04:02 every day its output is sent to root (or whoever is configured in the MAILTO variable in /etc/crontab).

Updating the Tripwire Database

We'll test the script by running it now. Type /etc/cron.daily/run-tripwire on the command line as root, and check that Tripwire runs successfully. Examine the output produced carefully, and we should see that Tripwire has spotted the addition of the run-tripwire script to /etc/cron.daily and flagged it as a critical change.

To stop Tripwire from reporting this change, which we made and know is OK, as a policy violation every time it runs, we need to update Tripwire's database. We do this by running tripwire --update, specifying a Tripwire report file that we wish to use for the update. To see what files are available, run ls -ltr /var/lib/tripwire/report; choose the last report listed as this will be the most recent one.

The command to run (all on one line) is then:

```
# tripwire --update --twrfile /var/lib/tripwire/report/rh9-20030209-
040304.twr
```

replacing the report filename with the most recent `.twr` file on your system. This will produce a text file and start `vi` for us so we can edit the file. Each proposed database update is tagged with `[x]`, and if we don't want the update to be made, we simply delete the 'x'. If we don't want to use `vi`, then add `--visual gedit` to the command and Tripwire will start the graphical editor instead.

When we exit the editor, we're asked for the local passphrase, and then updates are applied to the database. Subsequent Tripwire integrity checks should no longer warn us about the change to `/etc/cron.daily`.

Network Security

Virtually all Red Hat Linux 9 systems will be connected to other computers via a network at some time. This may be a permanent connection through a network adapter to a LAN (**L**ocal **A**rea **N**etwork), an "always on" connection to the Internet, or a dial-up connection to an Internet Service Provider that is active only when required. Whatever the connection, we need to make sure that a hacker cannot use it to gain access to our system, or mount a "denial of service" attack that prevents legitimate use of our computing resources. In this section, we'll look at some of the techniques that we can use to secure our system and make life hard for the potential hacker.

Unless we are connected to an isolated network where every machine is secure and trusted, we must assume that all the information we send and receive across the network can be intercepted by a third party (i.e. someone other than us and the intended recipient of the data).

Network Services

One way a hacker may try to gain unauthorized access to our system is by exploiting weaknesses in the network services that we are running on our Red Hat Linux system. These are programs – often run in the background with no controlling terminal (called "daemons" in Unix, and "services" in Microsoft Windows) – that provide services to other computers. Examples include file transfer protocol (ftp), Web, Network File System (NFS), and print servers.

Enabling and disabling services

The first and easiest way of reducing our vulnerability is to disable all the services that we don't need. In particular, we need to be very careful about older services that send sensitive information (such as user names and passwords) across the network without any form of encryption (in **plain text**). Also, services that gratuitously hand out information about our system should be avoided where possible.

The following tables will help you to decide which services you need to run.

Service	TCP/UDP Port number	Description	Red Hat Package	Security Level	Run it?
echo	7	Sends received characters back to sender.	`xinetd`	None.	No. (Unless you really need to debug remote terminal problems)
daytime	13	Sends current date and time as ASCII string back to sender.	`xinetd`	None.	No. Use NTP for time synchronisation. It is more accurate and has better security features.
chargen	19	Generates continuous stream of ASCII characters for testing terminals.	`xinetd`	None.	No. (Unless you really need to debug remote terminal problems)
chargen	20 (data) 21 (control) Random ports >1023	File Transfer Protocol. Allows transfer of files to and from remote systems.	`vsftp or wu-ftpd`	Weak. user names and passwords sent in plain text. "Anonymous FTP" allows access with no password.	No. Use FTP instead.
ssh	22	Secure shell. Allows remote system to access command line shell on local machine.	`Openssh`	Good. Data is encrypted and connections can be authenticated to ensure remote system is the right one and not an imposter.	Only if remote access to command line required.
telnet	23	Allows remote system to access command line shell on local machine.	`telnet-server`	Weak. User names and passwords sent in plain text.	No. Use ssh instead.

Service	TCP/UDP Port number	Description	Red Hat Package	Security Level	Run it?
SMTP	25	Simple Mail Transfer Protocol. Used to transfer mail between systems.	`sendmail`	Weak. Mail tranferred in plain text.	Only if mail needs to be handled locally. Encrypt sensitive mail before sending.
time	37	Sends current time (in seconds since 00:00 1st Jan 1900) back to sender.	`xinetd`	None.	No. Use NTP for time synchronisation. It is more accurate and has better security features.
finger	79	Gives information about local system or users to remote machine.	`finger-server`	None.	No.
http	80	Web server.	`Httpd`	Depends on server configuration.	Only if Web server needs to run on system.
auth (ident)	113	Indentification protocol. Allows remote system to determine indentity of a user of a particular TCP/IP connection.	`pident`	Supports DES encryption of returned information.	Only if needed to access some public services (e.g. some ftp sites and IRC).
sftp	115	Secure File Tranfer Protocol. FTP-like data transfers over secure SSH connection.	`openssh`	Good.	Only if file transfer required.
nntp	119	Network News Transfer Protocol. Used to transfer USENET news groups.	`inn`	Depends on server configuration.	Only if newsgroup server needs to be run on system.

Table continued on following page

Service	TCP/UDP Port number	Description	Red Hat Package	Security Level	Run it?
smb	137 138 139	Server Message Block. Allows Microsoft Windows system to access Red Hat Linux filesystems as network shares.	Samba	Weak. Information passed over network without encryption. Passwords may be encrypted, but algorithm is weak.	Only use to access information that is not sensitive.
https	443	Secure Web server.	Httpd	Depends on server configuration.	Only if Web server needs to run on system.
lpd	515	Print Daemon. Allows remote machines to send print jobs to our printers.	LPRng or cups	Weak. Information passed over network without encryption.	Only run if your system has printers you want to share.
rsh/ rlogin	514	Allows remote system to access command line shell on local machine without supplying a password.	rsh-server	Weak. Relies on DNS (Domain Name Service) to identify remote system, so vulnerable if DNS compromised.	No.
nfs	2049 (requires portmapper to be listening on port 111)	Network File System. Allows other systems to access file systems remotely.	nfs-utils	Weak. Information passed over network without encryption.	Only use to access information that is not sensitive.

Having decided which services are required, we need to make sure they are started, and make sure that any of the undesirable services are stopped. This is done through the Red Hat **Service Configuration** application. As an example, we'll use the Red Hat **Service Configuration** application to turn off the lpd and portmapper services since our theoretical demonstration machine doesn't have any printers attached to it (so there's no point in running lpd), and we're not using NFS or NIS (so there's no point in running portmapper).

Try It Out   **Running the Service Configuration Application**

1. Start the Service Configuration application by choosing **Main Menu | System Settings | Server Settings | Services**, or typing `redhat-config-services` at the command prompt.

2. If you're not logged on as root (and you shouldn't be!), you'll be prompted for the root password in this dialog:

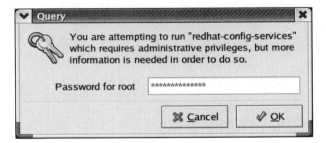

3. Now the services configuration menu appears:

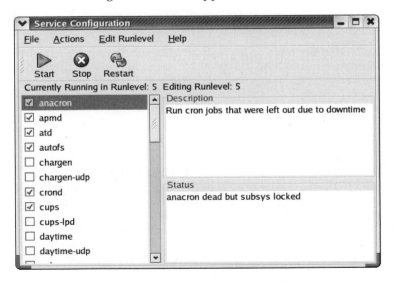

In the Service Configuration window, there are a few important things to note. First, the status line immediately below the toolbar icons shows us that the system is running in Runlevel 5, and that this is the runlevel that is being edited. (A runlevel is a particular state of the operating system, characterized by a set of processes that are started. If we haven't changed the system runlevel, then we'll be editing the default, which is just what we want. For more information on runlevels, see the man pages for inittab and telinit. Be careful if you experiment with these, as mistakes could render your system unbootable, forcing you to boot from CD-ROM to correct the problem.)

4. If you click on the name of a service, the information panels on the right of the window will show a brief description of what the service is for, together with its status.

Not all services represented here represent external services, some are internal daemons vital for the smooth running of your computer. It's a good idea to take a moment to read through all the descriptions here and start to familiarize yourself with what's available.

5. Now scroll through the list of services, and clear the check boxes next to lpd and portmapper, as these are two services that *do* allow remote connections to our system and that are enabled by default but probably aren't needed in the majority of cases.

When we make a change to any of the services, the Save button is no longer grayed out. So, when you're happy with the changes you've made, click on save to update the configuration files. Note that this does not actually start or stop any services; all it does is update configuration files so that next time the runlevel that is being edited is entered, the right services are started, and when it is being left, the right services are stopped. If you want to make the change effective immediately, highlight the service and click the Start, Stop or Restart buttons on the toolbar according to what you want to do.

xinetd

You may have noticed in the table of services and their daemons presented earlier that several services (such as echo, daytime, and chargen) appear to be provided by the same service, namely xinetd. This isn't a typo – xinetd does provide these, and it also looks after a whole lot more.

xinetd is an enhanced version of the standard Unix inetd (internet daemon) program, which manages incoming connections to many different services (hence it is sometimes called a "super server"). It is a long-running service (usually started when the system boots) that listens for incoming TCP/IP connections on ports that it has been told about in its configuration file. When a connection request arrives, xinetd checks that the connection should be allowed, then starts the appropriate server (if required) to handle the connection. In this section, we'll take a brief look at some of the configuration options xinetd has that relate to system security. xinetd's main configuration file is /etc/xinetd.conf. Let's have a look at that now:

```
ewanb@localhost:~                                              _ □ ✕
 File   Edit   View   Terminal   Go   Help
[ewanb@localhost ewanb]$ cat /etc/xinetd.conf
#
# Simple configuration file for xinetd
#
# Some defaults, and include /etc/xinetd.d/

defaults
{
        instances             = 60
        log_type              = SYSLOG authpriv
        log_on_success        = HOST PID
        log_on_failure        = HOST
        cps                   = 25 30
}

includedir /etc/xinetd.d

[ewanb@localhost ewanb]$
```

This file simply sets up some sensible default values that apply to all services managed by
xinetd (by placing them inside defaults { }), then tells **xinetd** to read configuration
information from all the files in /etc/xinetd.d. The default values have the
following meanings:

`instances = 60`	**No more than 60 instances of each sub-server will be started**
`logtype = SYSLOG authpriv`	Service log output is sent to syslogd using the authpriv facility (so that the output is logged to a file that can only be read by privileged users)
`log_on_success = HOST PID`	Logs remote host address and process id (if there is one) when a service is started or exits
`log_on_failure = HOST`	Logs remote host address when a service failed to start (with the reason for the failure)
`cps = 25 30`	Allows maximum connection rate of 25 connections per second (first number) and disable service for 30 seconds (second number) if this rate is exceeded

Monitoring Services

It is useful to be able to check what services are running on our Red Hat Linux 9 system, and especially what ports they are listening on. This is because before a remote machine can make a connection to our local machine, some process on our local machine has to be ready to receive network packets (listening) sent to its port number.

There are a couple of tools that we can use to identify what ports are listening on our machine: `netstat` and `nmap`.

netstat

Netstat is a multipurpose utility for reporting on all things relating to networks. We'll invoke it with the following flags:

Flag	Meaning
-t	TCP
-u	UDP
-l	Port sockets in state "listening"
-n	Show numeric values for hosts and ports
-p	Show process ID that owns sockets

```
# netstat -nutlp
Active Internet connections (only servers)
Proto Recv-Q Send-Q Local Address  Foreign Address State  PID/Program name
tcp     0      0 127.0.0.1:32769 0.0.0.0:*    LISTEN 718/xinetd
tcp     0      0 0.0.0.0:6000    0.0.0.0:*    LISTEN 979/X
tcp     0      0 0.0.0.0:22      0.0.0.0:*   LISTEN 704/sshd
tcp     0      0 127.0.0.1:25    0.0.0.0:*    LISTEN 832/sendmail
udp     0      0 0.0.0.0:68      0.0.0.0:*         772/dhclient
udp     0      0 10.4.65.253:123 0.0.0.0:*        803/ntpd
udp     0      0 127.0.0.1:123   0.0.0.0:*        803/ntpd
udp     0      0 0.0.0.0:123     0.0.0.0:*        803/ntpd
```

This lists the TCP and UDP sockets that are ready to receive incoming data (connections in the case of TCP and datagrams for UDP). We can see that this machine is listening on four TCP/IP ports which are the numbers after the ':' in the **Local Address** column (22 for ssh, 25 for incoming mail, 6000 for X11 and 32769 for the xinetd "super" server). It will also accept datagrams on port 68 (DHCP client) and 123 (Network Time Protocol service).

Three TCP/IP addresses appear in this local address column: 0.0.0.0 means that the server is listening on all addresses, 127.0.0.1 is the machine's loopback address, and 10.4.65.253 is the address of the machine's Ethernet card (leased from a DHCP server).

If we leave out the −l flag, netstat will show us all the active connections. If we leave out the −n flag, netstat will look up port names in /etc/services and host names using DNS, giving symbolic output. Try varying the flags to see what information is returned.

We can check the output of the netstat command to make sure that we don't have any programs listening on TCP or UDP ports that we're not expecting. The −p flag, which gets netstat to print out the PID (**Process ID**) and name of the process that opened the socket, is very useful for identifying "rogue" programs, perhaps modified by an intruder, that are listening on unexpected ports. (Of course, if we've got Tripwire set up and we're running regular scans, we'll quickly identify if an intruder has modified a program.)

nmap

Nmap takes a different approach to the problem of identifying which ports are being listened to (are "open" in nmap parlance) on a machine. It sends special packets to ports on the machine in question, and listens for the response. This enables it to deduce whether the port is open, closed, or even being blocked by a firewall (more on that later). Nmap isn't installed by default, but is on the Red Hat Linux CD-ROMs, so you may need to install it if you want to try these examples.

First, by way of example, let's get nmap to see what ports are open on our machine. We'll use the flags −sUT to tell nmap we want it to scan both TCP and UDP ports, and accept the defaults for everything else (including the port range, which is 1 to 1023, since these are the ports that privileged services use, plus others that are mentioned in /etc/services).

Here's the output from a test system:

```
# nmap -sUT localhost
Starting nmap V. 3.00 ( www.insecure.org/nmap/ )
Interesting ports on rh9 (127.0.0.1):
(The 3064 ports scanned but not shown below are in state: closed)
Port       State       Service
22/tcp     open        ssh
25/tcp     open        smtp
68/udp     open        dhcpclient
123/udp    open        ntp
6000/tcp   open        X11

Nmap run completed -- 1 IP address (1 host up) scanned in 3 seconds
```

It has identified the same ports as netstat did, with the exception of xinetd listening on tcp/32769. This is because port 32769 is not in the range 1 to 1023, nor is it listed in /etc/services, so it won't get scanned by default. If we used the −p flag to specify port numbers (e.g. added "-p 1-65535" to the command line to have all ports scanned), then the open port is found and listed with "unknown" in the service column.

Notice that nmap needs to be told which host to scan the ports on, suggesting that it can be used to scan for open ports on remote machines. Nmap is indeed capable of scanning for open ports on a range of remote machines, even choosing addresses at random. However, it is wise to get written permission from the owners of systems before scanning their ports, since this action may be seen as a prelude to illegal hacking activity. After all, it is just like walking past a row of parked cars and trying the doors on each one to see if they're locked. If a policeman caught you doing that, you'd have a hard time explaining that if you were only looking for unlocked cars so you could tell the owners to be more careful.

IP traffic

It is surprisingly easy to capture and analyze network traffic. There are many tools available that enable users with sufficient privileges to record the headers and contents of network packets into files on disk and analyze the contents later. With broadcast network media, such as Ethernet, every machine on a network segment receives all the packets, regardless of who the packet is addressed to. Normally, the receiving network card discards packets not addressed to it, but most network cards can be configured to operate in "promiscuous" mode, which allows them to receive and process packets regardless of their intended destination. (Ethernet **switches**, as opposed to **hubs**, have intelligence and effectively create a series of point-to-point Ethernet links, instead of sending all packets to all machines. This not only improves security, it can also improve performance.)

We'll use a utility called tcpdump (from the RPM package of the same name) to demonstrate just how easy it is to capture data not destined for our machine. (As with nmap above, make sure you have permission to do this if you're going to try it on a network that you don't own!)

Our theoretical test setup is this. There are three machines, all connected to a 10/100 Ethernet hub, and all on a private subnet 192.168.1/24 (that's shorthand for a subnet 192.168.1.0 with a netmask of 255.255.255.0, i.e. 24 bits). Fred (192.168.1.1) is a Windows machine that we'll use as a telnet client, Bob (192.168.1.2) is a Linux server we'll be telnetting in to, and Kate (192.168.1.3) is our Red Hat Linux 9 machine. On Kate, we su to root and type:

```
# tcpdump -i eth0 -l -q -X src or dst port 23
```

This tells tcpdump to listen to all packets on interface eth0 (-i eth0), buffer the output line-by-line (-l), don't print lots of header information (-q) but do print the packets in ASCII (-X) and show only packets where the source or destination port is 23 – the telnet port – (src or dst port 23). We'll get an acknowledgment:

```
tcpdump: listening on eth0
```

... and tcpdump will log all telnet packets it sees on the network segment.

Now we go to Fred, our Windows machine, and telnet from there to Bob, our Linux server. As soon as we do, we see the packets being logged by tcpdump, even though that's running on a machine that's not the destination for the packets!

```
# tcpdump -i eth0 -l -q -X src or dst port 23
tcpdump: listening on eth0
12:11:51.070377 fred.3335 > bob.telnet: tcp 0 (DF)
0x0000   4500 0030 317b 4000 8006 3342 0a04 4101   E..01{@...3B..A.
0x0010   0a04 4102 0d07 0017 24e6 7419 0000 0000   ..A.....$.t.....
0x0020   7002 2000 26f7 0000 0204 05b4 0101 0402   p...&..........
12:11:51.070826 bob.telnet > fred.3335: tcp 0 (DF)
0x0000   4500 0030 0000 4000 4006 a4bd 0a04 4102   E..0..@.@.....A.
0x0010   0a04 4101 0017 0d07 f267 5575 24e6 741a   ..A......gUu$.t.
0x0020   7012 16d0 e838 0000 0204 05b4 0101 0402   p....8..........
```

If we look carefully at the packet log, we can find the **Password** prompt and see what the user typed in response. The password has been highlighted to make it easier to see, but hackers don't need that much help – they'll probably use an automated password sniffer that'll decode the packets for them:

```
12:12:02.265222 bob.telnet > fred.3335: tcp 10 (DF) [tos 0x10]
0x0000   4510 0032 9d51 4000 4006 075a 0a04 4102   E..2.Q@.@..Z..A.
0x0010   0a04 4101 0017 0d07 f267 55fc 24e6 746e   ..A......gU.$.tn
0x0020   5018 16d0 2c48 0000 5061 7373 776f 7264   P...,H..Password
0x0030   3a20                                      :.
12:12:02.465557 fred.3335 > bob.telnet: tcp 0 (DF)
0x0000   4500 0028 4a7b 4000 8006 1a4a 0a04 4101   E..(J{@....J..A.
0x0010   0a04 4102 0d07 0017 24e6 746e f267 5606   ..A.....$.tn.gV.
0x0020   5010 21a8 0941 0000 2020 2020 2020        P.!..A........
12:12:03.180919 fred.3335 > bob.telnet: tcp 1 (DF)
0x0000   4500 0029 4b7b 4000 8006 1949 0a04 4101   E..)K{@....I..A.
0x0010   0a04 4102 0d07 0017 24e6 746e f267 5606   ..A.....$.tn.gV.
0x0020   5018 21a8 a337 0000 6620 2020 2020        P.!..7..f.....
12:12:03.218203 bob.telnet > fred.3335: tcp 0 (DF) [tos 0x10]
0x0000   4510 0028 9d52 4000 4006 0763 0a04 4102   E..(.R@.@..c..A.
0x0010   0a04 4101 0017 0d07 f267 5606 24e6 746f   ..A......gV.$.to
0x0020   5010 16d0 1418 0000 65fd 01ff fb05        P.......e.....
12:12:03.423073 fred.3335 > bob.telnet: tcp 1 (DF)
0x0000   4500 0029 4c7b 4000 8006 1849 0a04 4101   E..)L{@....I..A.
0x0010   0a04 4102 0d07 0017 24e6 746f f267 5606   ..A.....$.to.gV.
0x0020   5018 21a8 9736 0000 7220 2020 2020        P.!..6..r.....
12:12:03.423232 bob.telnet > fred.3335: tcp 0 (DF) [tos 0x10]
0x0000   4510 0028 9d53 4000 4006 0762 0a04 4102   E..(.S@.@..b..A.
0x0010   0a04 4101 0017 0d07 f267 5606 24e6 7470   ..A......gV.$.tp
0x0020   5010 16d0 1417 0000 6465 6420 4861        P.......ded.Ha
12:12:03.555199 fred.3335 > bob.telnet: tcp 1 (DF)
0x0000   4500 0029 4d7b 4000 8006 1749 0a04 4101   E..)M{@....I..A.
0x0010   0a04 4102 0d07 0017 24e6 7470 f267 5606   ..A.....$.tp.gV.
0x0020   5018 21a8 a435 0000 6520 2020 2020        P.!..5..e.....
12:12:03.555354 bob.telnet > fred.3335: tcp 0 (DF) [tos 0x10]
0x0000   4510 0028 9d54 4000 4006 0761 0a04 4102   E..(.T@.@..a..A.
0x0010   0a04 4101 0017 0d07 f267 5606 24e6 7471   ..A......gV.$.tq
0x0020   5010 16d0 1416 0000 0d0a 0869 6e3a        P.........in:
```

```
12:12:03.699442 fred.3335 > bob.telnet: tcp 1 (DF)
0x0000    4500 0029 4e7b 4000 8006 1649 0a04 4101    E..)N{@....I..A.
0x0010    0a04 4102 0d07 0017 24e6 7471 f267 5606    ..A.....$.tq.gV.
0x0020    5018 21a8 a534 0000 6420 2020 2020         P.!..4..d.....
```

This is what we mean when we say that the telnet protocol sends passwords in plain text across the network. If that network uses broadcast media, then every machine on the same network segment as the sender receives the unencrypted password on its network interface. Most of the time, the other machines will just ignore this data, but all it takes is one of them to be running a promiscuous mode packet logger like tcpdump and all the passwords sent by telnet can be captured. Ftp suffers from a similar vulnerability. Fortunately, there are secure alternatives to both telnet and ftp (ssh and sftp respectively) that encrypt all data they send over the network using strong encryption techniques so the eavesdropper is not able to glean any useful information from the packets.

Another packet analyzer that can be installed from the Red Hat Linux 9 CDs is called Ethereal. This has a graphical front end that makes it much easier to set up filters and interpret the contents of packets. When Ethereal is started (as root, by simply typing ethereal at the command prompt – once the Ethereal RPM has been installed, of course!), the main window opens. The Capture | Start menu option opens another window where capture options can be set:

Note the check box to put the interface (eth0) in promiscuous mode, so packets not intended for this machine can be captured. Once capturing is running, another window is updated continuously with packet counts.

```
Ethereal: Captur  _ □ ✖

Captured Frames

Total       29    (100.0%)
SCTP        0     (0.0%)
TCP         28    (96.6%)
UDP         1     (3.4%)
ICMP        0     (0.0%)
ARP         0     (0.0%)
OSPF        0     (0.0%)
GRE         0     (0.0%)
NetBIOS     0     (0.0%)
IPX         0     (0.0%)
VINES       0     (0.0%)
Other       0     (0.0%)

Running    00:00:26

            Stop
```

With the options chosen in the example capture window, the main display is also updated in real time:

```
The Ethereal Network Analyzer                                              _ □ ✖

File   Edit   Capture   Display   Tools                                     Help

No. .  Time       Source         Destination      Protocol  Info
    1  0.000000   10.4.65.1      10.4.65.2         TCP       4442 > ssh [SYN] Seq=515666144 Ack=0 Win=8192 Le
    2  0.000916   10.4.65.2      10.4.65.1         TCP       ssh > 4442 [SYN, ACK] Seq=916252342 Ack=5156661
    3  0.001612   10.4.65.1      10.4.65.2         TCP       4442 > ssh [ACK] Seq=515666145 Ack=916252343 Wir
    4  0.006747   10.4.65.2      10.4.65.1         TCP       ssh > 4442 [PSH, ACK] Seq=916252343 Ack=5156661
    5  0.012749   10.4.65.1      10.4.65.2         TCP       4442 > ssh [PSH, ACK] Seq=515666145 Ack=9162523E
    6  0.013733   10.4.65.2      10.4.65.1         TCP       ssh > 4442 [ACK] Seq=916252366 Ack=515666173 Wir
    7  0.013739   10.4.65.2      10.4.65.1         TCP       ssh > 4442 [PSH, ACK] Seq=916252366 Ack=5156661°
    8  0.035138   10.4.65.1      10.4.65.2         TCP       4442 > ssh [PSH, ACK] Seq=515666173 Ack=9162526<
    9  0.073531   10.4.65.2      10.4.65.1         TCP       ssh > 4442 [ACK] Seq=916252642 Ack=515666329 Wir
   10  0.154416   10.4.65.2      10.4.65.1         TCP       ssh > 4442 [PSH, ACK] Seq=916252642 Ack=5156663°
   11  0.349632   10.4.65.1      10.4.65.2         TCP       4442 > ssh [ACK] Seq=515666329 Ack=916252654 Wir
   12  2.923632   10.4.65.1      10.4.65.2         TCP       4442 > ssh [PSH, ACK] Seq=515666329 Ack=9162526°
   13  2.924388   10.4.65.2      10.4.65.1         TCP       ssh > 4442 [ACK] Seq=916252654 Ack=515666349 Wir
   14  3.052772   10.4.65.2      10.4.65.1         TCP       ssh > 4442 [PSH, ACK] Seq=916252654 Ack=5156663<
   15  3.249929   10.4.65.1      10.4.65.2         TCP       4442 > ssh [ACK] Seq=515666349 Ack=916252666 Wir
   16  5.902340   10.4.65.1      10.4.65.2         TCP       4442 > ssh [PSH, ACK] Seq=515666349 Ack=9162526F

⊞ Frame 1 (62 bytes on wire, 62 bytes captured)
⊞ Ethernet II, Src: 00:e0:4c:c1:36:d9, Dst: 00:e0:4c:c1:37:3d
⊞ Internet Protocol, Src Addr: 10.4.65.1 (10.4.65.1), Dst Addr: 10.4.65.2 (10.4.65.2)
⊞ Transmission Control Protocol, Src Port: 4442 (4442), Dst Port: ssh (22), Seq: 515666144, Ack: 0, Len: 0

0000  00 e0 4c c1 37 3d 00 e0  4c c1 36 d9 08 00 45 00   ..L.7=.. L.6...E.
0010  00 30 9b 12 40 00 80 06  c9 aa 0a 04 41 01 0a 04   .0..@... ....A...
0020  41 02 11 5a 00 16 1e bc  70 e0 00 00 00 00 70 02   A..Z.... p.....P.
0030  20 00 2c 08 00 00 02 04  05 b4 01 01 04 02          ..,..... ......

Filter:                                      ▼  Reset  Apply  <live capture in progress>
```

537

This example shows the start of an `ssh` session between two machines. This time, we won't be seeing any plain text passwords!

The point of showing `tcpdump` and ethereal is not to encourage you to go sniffing for packets on networks, but rather to illustrate just how easy it is to capture sensitive information such as passwords that are sent across broadcast networks, such as Ethernet. However, if you make sure that you use protocols such as `ssh` and `sftp` that encrypt sensitive data, then it won't matter if someone is capturing the packets you send.

Firewalls

Firewalls are another useful tool for improving the security of our system. They come in different flavors, but all do essentially the same thing; network traffic passing through the firewall is analyzed and the decision about what to do with the traffic (let it through, throw it away and tell the sender, throw it away and don't tell the sender, etc.) is made based on the rules configured by the firewall administrator.

Some firewalls analyze network traffic at the packet level; these are called "packet filters". They can work with any network traffic, but can implement only fairly simple rules based on the contents of the packet header (typically where the packet came from, where it's going to and what flags are set). Other firewalls understand more about the higher level protocols used for e-mail and web browsing. They can perform more complex tasks such as scanning e-mail attachments for viruses, or requiring users to authenticate themselves before allowing access to certain Web sites. In a typical corporate environment, the protection provided by simple packet filtering firewalls is enhanced with more sophisticated firewalls and proxies that can analyze the contents of the packets as well as their headers.

Since the Linux kernel has built in packet filtering capabilities, we'll look at how we can configure these to enhance the security of our Red Hat Linux system.

Network Connections

Before we get into the mechanics of configuring the Red Hat Linux built in firewall, we need to understand how network connections work. For TCP/IP connections, there are two basic protocols; TCP (**T**ransmission **C**ontrol **P**rotocol) and UDP (**U**niversal **D**atagram **P**rotocol).

TCP is a connection-oriented protocol. This means that when two machines wish to communicate via TCP, their TCP stacks negotiate a connection and the application (such as a Web browser talking to Web server using HTTP), and TCP ensures that packets are delivered to the application in the right order, with no duplicates. The mechanism for setting up a connection involves the exchange of TCP packets between the systems that have different flags set in their headers. First, the client (that's the machine that wants to establish a connection) sends the server (the machine the client wants to connect to) a TCP packet with the SYN flag set. The server replies with a packet whose header has both the SYN and ACK flags set, and when the client receives this packet, it sends one back with just the ACK bit set. From this point on, the connection is established, and the client and server can exchange packets.

When the connection is no longer required, either party can request that it is closed by sending the other end a TCP packet with the FIN flag set. The recipient replies with a packet having the ACK flag set, then performs whatever termination steps are required by the application. When this is done, a packet with the FIN flag set is sent back to the end that initially requested the connection to be closed. When this is acknowledged with a packet where the ACK bit is set, the connection is finished.

UDP is a much simpler, connection-less protocol. All that happens here is that the originator sends the UDP datagram to the recipient, and the network layer tries its best to deliver it. Unlike TCP, delivery is not guaranteed, and datagrams traveling over long distances may go by different routes and therefore arrive out of order at the other end. All the logic for synchronizing client and server, or re-trying failed packets, has to be handled by the application code.

It is important that we understand the differences between TCP and UDP when configuring firewalls. With TCP, the direction of the connection (i.e. incoming, where the client is remote and the server is on our machine, or outgoing where the client is local and the server is remote) is determined by the exchange of SYN, SYN+ACK, ACK packets at the start of the connection, but with UDP, there is no connection, so incoming and outgoing simply refer to the direction of the packet.

Configuring the Red Hat Linux Firewall

Configuring the Red Hat Linux firewall is very straightforward. Start the Security Level Configuration application by choosing Main Menu | System Settings | Security Level, or by typing `redhat-config-securitylevel` at the command prompt. If you are not logged on as root, and you haven't recently supplied the root password to enable you to update system wide settings, you'll be prompted to do that before the Security Level Configuration starts. When it does, you'll see this window.

Under the Security Level: drop-down list, the options are High, Medium, and No firewall:

❑   The High setting configures the firewall to reject all incoming TCP connections (by blocking TCP packets that have the SYN flag set, and ACK cleared), and reject all incoming UDP packets, with the exception of replies to DNS queries on port 53 that come from the name servers we told Red Hat Linux about when we configured the network settings. (If the DNS replies were blocked, then we would be unable to resolve any host names that aren't defined in the local /etc/hosts file, which would make using the Internet very tedious.)

> **Note that, since incoming connections are blocked, we can't run a Web server or any other kind of server behind such a firewall.**

❑   The Medium setting configures the firewall to reject all incoming TCP connections to ports in the range 0 to 1023, and also incoming UDP packets for these port numbers. NFS and X11 traffic are also blocked. The significance of the ports in the range 0 to 1023 is that these are "privileged" ports, and a program has to be running with root authority in order to open sockets on them. However, this does not mean that ports with numbers 1024 to 65536 can only have unprivileged programs opening sockets on them. It is quite possible to set up a Web server running with root authority listening on, say, port 8080.

❑   If we select No firewall as the security level, then the firewall is disabled.

If we find that the default firewall rules do not meet our requirements, then we can select the Customize radio button. This enables the remaining options on the window:

If we check the box against a network interface in the **Trusted devices** section, this configures the firewall to allow all traffic to and from that interface (because we trust all the machines connecting via that interface). However, can we be sure that one of these machines has not been compromised and that the packets coming from it are the work of a hacker?

The other options on the dialogue enable us to allow incoming connections on a selection of well-known ports for different services. For example, let's pretend that our example machine will be running a Web server, and we'll need remote access via ssh for administration, so the WWW and SSH boxes need to be checked. This ends up looking like this:

When we press the OK button, the firewall configuration is updated and saved so that the machine will reboot with the new configuration in place.

Lokkit

There is another tool that we can use to configure the firewall on our Red Hat Linux systems. It's called Lokkit (installed from the gnome-lokkit RPM). It is a simple to use configuration tool that asks a series of simple questions and configures the firewall according to the answers you supply. It's not as versatile or powerful as the method we've just discussed, so we'll make no more mention of it here.

> Note that Lokkit is not meant for custom firewall configuration and has fewer options than the Red Hat `redhat-config-securitylevel` tool.

There is one significant drawback with using the Security Level Configuration or Lokkit applications to configure our packet filtering firewall; both configure only rules that selectively block incoming network traffic. Outgoing traffic and traffic that is forwarded (that is received on one network interface and sent out on another) by our Red Hat system are not checked in any way. This means that, should you have a system behind your firewall that has been compromised (hacked or maybe infected by a virus), it is free to transmit whatever it likes through your firewall. It is a good idea to configure your firewall to block selected outgoing and forwarded traffic too. For example, you may want to force all Internet access for machines behind the firewall to be handled by secure proxy servers. This can be done by blocking outgoing Internet access for all machines except the proxy servers. More detailed firewall configuration like this is done with the `iptables` command, so let's look at how to do that.

iptables

> This section is a brief introduction to setting up customized security beyond what is possible with the GUI tools provided by Red Hat. It's not meant to be comprehensive, as everyone's needs are different, and it'd be impossible to cater to them all. However, hopefully it'll give you a taste of the tools available.

Blocking and allowing traffic based on direction (i.e. incoming or outgoing) and port number gives some degree of control over network traffic, but there are situations when we need finer control. For example, we may want to run a Web server that can be accessed only from machines within our department, and not from machines elsewhere. Or we may want to prevent users on certain machines from being able to FTP files from our machine while allowing others to do so. The firewalling code in Red Hat Linux 9 is perfectly able to cope with these situations, and far more complex ones, but we have to roll up our sleeves and configure it from the command line.

This is where the `iptables` command comes in. It is used to manipulate the kernel's packet filtering tables, so we can fine tune the firewall settings to our environment. Let's see how to implement a concrete example.

Imagine our Red Hat machine has two network interfaces: eth0 has the IP address 192.168.1.1 and eth1 has the IP address 192.168.10.1. Both interfaces have netmasks of 255.255.255.0. We're running a Web server listening on port 80, and an FTP server that uses ports 20 and 21. We need to allow machines with IP addresses starting with 192.168.10 access to the Web server, but nobody else. We also need to allow all machines in the 192.168.1.0 network access to the FTP server, except 192.168.1.57. How do we configure this?

The first thing to do is look at the existing firewall configuration. Log on to the machine and switch to the root user. Run the following command to get a verbose listing of the current firewall rules:

```
# iptables -L -v
```

Rules are grouped together into **chains**. There are three default chains:

- ❑ INPUT, which handles incoming network packets destined for processes on the local machine
- ❑ OUTPUT, which handles outgoing network packets produced by the local machine
- ❑ FORWARD, which handles packets that arrive on one interface and leave on another (i.e. the local machine is forwarding them).

There may be other user defined chains too.

To set up our machine to meet the above specification, we'll clear out (or **flush**) the existing rules with the following command:

```
# iptables -F
```

We can use this command to delete the named user-defined chain:

```
# iptables -X name
```

We're going to be dealing only with packets coming into our machine in this example, so we'll be configuring rules in the INPUT chain. Our first step is to configure the default behaviors – or Policy – for the INPUT chain so that if it receives a packet that doesn't match any rules, it drops (discards) it. This is the most security conscious approach, as it means that everything is blocked unless we explicitly allow it. The command to set the policy on the INPUT chain to DROP is:

```
# iptables -P INPUT DROP
```

As soon as we type that in, all incoming network packets are dropped, so before we do so, we'd better make sure that we're logged in to the machine on the console. If not, then we'll lose our connection to the machine and won't be able to get it back!

*We could also have used REJECT instead of DROP as the policy. This would result in a message being sent back to the sender of a blocked packet informing them that the port is not reachable. This is polite, and could prevent a hapless user from continually retrying a connection attempt that will never work. However, it also confirms our presence to a would-be hacker. The policy of DROP silently discards the incoming packet, so our would-be hacker won't even know there's anything listening at our IP address. Of course, this is only valid if we never respond to **any** requests – once you've responded to one, you've given the game away.*

Now, we need to allow machines with IP addresses on the `192.168.10/24` network access to the Web server. This is listening on TCP port `80`. We'll add a rule that says accept any packet arriving on interface `eth1` from a machine in the `192.168.10/24` network that is destined for port `80`. The syntax for this is:

```
# iptables -A INPUT -p tcp -s 192.168.10/24 -i eth1 --dport 80 -j ACCEPT
```

Here:

❏   `-A INPUT` means append the rule to the `INPUT` chain

❏   `-p tcp` means match packets for the TCP protocol

❏   `-s 192.168.10/24` means match packets with a source address in the `192.168.10/24` network

❏   `-i eth1` means match packets on the `eth1` interface

❏   `--dport 80` means match packets with a destination port of `80`

❏   `-j ACCEPT` means jump to the `ACCEPT` target (that is, allow the packet through)

   We don't have to specify the network interface, but doing so would prevent someone spoofing an IP address on the wrong network from gaining access.

Our second requirement is to allow ftp access to hosts in the `192.168.1/24` network attached to `eth0`, except `192.168.1.57`. We'll have to do this as a pair of rules; the first is a specific rule to block ftp access from `192.168.1.57` and the second is a more general rule that allows the others in. Since packets are passed to rules in order, we want to place our more restrictive rules first to ensure that they match. So, our two new rules are created with:

```
# iptables -A INPUT -p tcp -s 192.168.1.57 --dport 20:21 -j DROP
# iptables -A INPUT -p tcp -s 192.168.1/24 -i eth0 --dport 20:21 -j ACCEPT
```

If we view our tables with the following command, we'll see our rules... eventually:

```
# iptables -L -v
```

If DNS is configured on our machine, we'll find that all the DNS queries time out because we've blocked all the DNS traffic! So, we need to add some more rules to allow important network traffic through:

```
# iptables -A INPUT -p all -s nameserver --dport domain -j ACCEPT
```

(We need to replace *nameserver* with the TCP/IP address of our nameserver.) Now our name server queries should work again. Here's what our rules look like:

```
# iptables -L -v
Chain INPUT (policy DROP 26 packets, 2276 bytes)
 pkts bytes target    prot opt in   out   source          destination
    0    0 ACCEPT   tcp -- eth0  any   192.168.10.0/24    anywhere          tcp
dpt:http
    0    0 DROP     tcp -- any  any   192.168.1.57       anywhere          tcp
dpts:ftp-data:ftp
    0    0 ACCEPT   tcp -- any  any   192.168.1.0/24     anywhere          tcp
dpts:ftp-data:ftp
    0    0 ACCEPT   all -- any  any   nameserver         anywhere          tcp
dpts:domain


Chain FORWARD (policy ACCEPT 0 packets, 0 bytes)
 pkts bytes target    prot opt in   out   source          destination

Chain OUTPUT (policy ACCEPT 1190 packets, 430K bytes)
 pkts bytes target    prot opt in   out   source          destination
```

Once we've configured our rules, we need to make sure that they work as expected. In this example, we'd try ftp and Web server access from different hosts to see that they were allowed or blocked as required. Once we're happy with the rules, we need to save them so that they will be reactivated if the machine is rebooted. We do this with the following command:

```
# service iptables save
```

Security Awareness

The final part of this chapter deals with "softer" security concerns, such as maintaining awareness of security issues.

Security Alerts

Security problems with software are found and fixed on an almost daily basis. It is important to be aware of any security vulnerabilities that affect software you have running on your system as soon as they are discovered. Perhaps the easiest way to do this is to subscribe to a security alert service. Red Hat provide their own through the Red Hat Network, we mentioned earlier, and its is very useful because you will be notified only of problems that affect the RPMs that you have installed on your system. You'll also get notified immediately if there's an update to a Red Hat supplied RPM that you've just installed.

As well as the Red Hat Network, there are many Web sites offering useful security information. Here are just a few of them.

Red Hat Errata Web Site

Red Hat provides another Web site that you can use to check out security related fixes for the packages that you have installed. The URL for this site is http://www.redhat.com/apps/support/errata/. From this page, you can access Security Alerts, Bug Fixes and Enhancements for all currently supported releases of Red Hat Linux. There's also a link to the Red Hat Security Resource Center, where you can subscribe to a monthly security newsletter, and find links to other, security-related, resources.

Computer Emergency Response Team (CERT)

The CERT Coordination Center is run by the Software Engineering Institute of Carnegie Mellon University. Their Web site, http://www.cert.org/ provides a wealth of up-to-date information about security problems. You can also subscribe to a mailing list so that you receive security alerts by e-mail.

Bugtraq

Bugtraq is a mailing list for the detailed discussion of computer security issues. You can access the Bugtraq archives at http://www.securityfocus.com/, and find several mailing lists to which you can subscribe. Click on the Mailing Lists button on the toolbar, and then click on info against the mailing list of interest. A popup window will appear which includes instructions on how to subscribe.

Mailing lists you might want to check out include

- ❑ bugtraq
- ❑ focus-linux
- ❑ linux-secnews

Logging out

It is vital that whenever we leave a computer system that we logged in to (such as our Red Hat Linux server, or our online banking Web site), we log out again. If we do not, there is a risk that someone else can come along and take over our connection, accessing the system as ourselves without having to go to the trouble of cracking passwords or intercepting network traffic.

Checking site certificates, signatures, checksums, and so on

With increasing awareness of security issues, more and more online resources (Web sites, RPM downloads, etc.) are authenticated in some way. When we access these resources, we may have an opportunity to verify their authenticity. This may be a pop-up window from our Web browser, or a checksum for an RPM. Whatever mechanism exists, we should always use it to check that the Web page we are accessing, or the RPM package we are about to install, is the genuine article, and has not been tampered with by anyone else.

Where to find out more

The Official Red Hat Linux Security Guide can be downloaded from https://www.redhat.com/docs/manuals/linux/. This is a good read for people who need a deeper understanding of security issues surrounding their Red Hat Linux systems. There are also lots of good Linux HOWTOs that cover security related topics. Check out the `Security-HOWTO` and `Firewall-HOWTO`, for starters.

Summary

Security is largely a matter of common sense. Different people value different things, so there is no one security configuration that will be exactly suited to everyone. However, Red Hat Linux does a pretty good job "out of the box", so most security work will be in fine tuning your setup to meet particular requirements, rather than urgent actions required to fix glaring security holes.

The most important points for you to try and remember are:

❑ Choose strong passwords

❑ Avoid using insecure protocols like telnet and FTP if possible

❑ Do use secure protocols like ssh and sftp wherever possible

❑ Disable network services that are not required

❑ Configure Tripwire to monitor the integrity of your system on a regular basis

If you can do all of these things, then you can confidently use your Red Hat Linux 9 system on the Internet, knowing that you're as secure as you reasonably can be, and that all but the most determined hackers will go and find an easier target.

13

Where to Now?

Over the course of this book, we have examined the Linux operating system in detail, covering everything from its history and installation to everyday administration and even an introduction to programming in Perl. But that's not all! Linux has much more to offer; we have only scratched the surface of what is possible. There are hundreds upon hundreds of open source applications that are able to run on Linux. Whether it is exciting games, office productivity applications, or sophisticated development tools, you will be able to find software that meets your needs. Therefore, our main goal in this chapter is to get a taste of this vast frontier of the open source movement.

We will break this chapter into three sections:

❑ In the first section, we'll give a brief snapshot of where to look for resources online, what you will find, and a summary of widely used licensing schemes.

❑ In the second section, we will discuss several administration applications that we can use on a daily basis to monitor and optimize our Linux system.

❑ The third section will be of particular interest if you are interested in development. It looks at a number of programming languages, development utilities, and database engines that can be used effectively with Linux.

For each of the applications covered in this chapter, we will examine the reason for using the application, where to obtain it, and how to install it properly on your system.

Before we take a hard look at the applications themselves, we'll start with some references and background information about helpful documentation and online resources that you can use to find applications and utilities that may interest you.

Online Resources and Licensing Schemes

It seems that more than ever these days, there is a proliferation of information on Linux and open source – discussions on the open source initiative, articles on whether open source is good or bad, and references to the success of Linux. However, the best resources on Linux arguably can be found at the **Open Source Development Network (OSDN)**. OSDN is a network of a number of web sites, including the famous Slashdot.org, SourceForge.net, and Freshmeat.net.

Software Resources

Suppose you are in the mood to play a game of Battleship – the game where you try to sink your opponent's ships – but you are not sure if a version exists for Linux. How do you find out? Just head on over to Freshmeat.net and search for *Battleship*, and see what you get. Or better yet, take a look at the figure below:

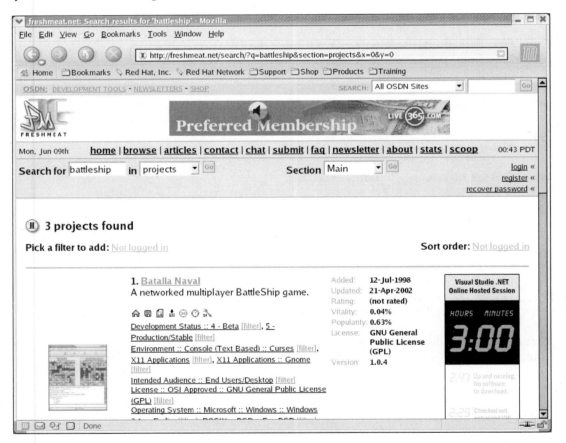

This is just an example. Go ahead and search for other software that you may be interested in; you will be pleasantly surprised at how much software you will find. In addition to Freshmeat.net, you can also search for software at its sister site, SourceForge.net, and also at the GNOME and KDE project web sites at http://www.gnome.org/softwaremap/list and http://apps.kde.com.

Documentation Resources

If you're looking information on how to perform a particular task (say, how to set up a Wireless LAN or how to implement software RAID), then you can do worse than visit the Linux Documentation Project (http://www.tldp.org). Here you will find documents referred to as **HOWTO**s – each HOWTO contains concise, to-the-point instructions on how to perform a particular task. Here are a few examples of HOWTO documents:

Document	Description
Cable-Modem	Answers basic questions on how to connect your Linux box to cable modem or cable Internet provider
Diskless	Describes how to set up a diskless Linux box
Infrared	Provides an introduction to Linux and infrared devices, and how to use the software provided by the Linux/IrDA project
KickStart	Briefly describes how to use the RedHat Linux KickStart system to rapidly install large numbers of identical Linux boxes
Software-RAID	Describes how to use Software RAID under Linux
Wireless	Explains how to setup Wireless in Linux, compatibility problems, something about geographic requirements and more

As you acquire more and more of these resources, whether software or documentation, you will find that most of them are governed by some form of license. So, let's take a look at some of the more common licenses.

Open Source Licenses

For all of the advantages of open source software – such as freely available source code and reduced cost of ownership – the licensing requirements sometimes seem to get in the way. The problem is that there are so many open source licenses out there that it is difficult to keep track of them all.

But help is at hand. You can find more information on a variety of open source licenses at Google's Web Directory:

http://directory.google.com/Top/Computers/Open_Source/Licenses/

There are dozens of licenses listed here, and we cannot possibly examine all of these licenses in this chapter. However, we will look at three that are widely used:

- ❏   The GNU General Public License (GPL)
- ❏   The GNU Lesser General Public License (LGPL)
- ❏   The original BSD License

In order to comprehend the requirements imposed by these licenses, we need to have a better understanding of what is really meant by the term *open source*. An **open source** software application or utility is one that typically provides the user complete access to its source code, and the right to produce derived works and to distribute them without restriction.

The GNU GPL and GNU LGPL Licenses

Both the GNU GPL and the GNU LGPL fall into the category of **copyleft licenses**. These licenses permit unrestricted modification and redistribution, on condition that either all or portions of derivative works retain the same terms as the original license. These licenses were created to assure developers that any software they develop and distribute would always remain "free" and open source (here, "free" refers to rights rather than to financial matters).

Let's consider the *Battleship* example for a moment. Suppose you did go looking for a *Battleship* application, and that you found an application that is licensed under the GNU GPL. Having found it, we can certainly play the game as much as we want; we can also distribute it to our friends, and even burn it on to a CD-ROM and sell it; the license entitles you to charge enough to reasonably cover your packaging and distribution costs.

Here's the crux, though. Supposing we want to *change* the application (say, by adding some interesting artificial intelligence algorithms) and distribute the new version only in compiled form, so that our algorithms remain closed, or proprietary. If we did that, we would be in violation of the GPL, since we tried to redistribute the modified application without making the source code available. Remember, we can change the application, but if we do then we must release the *entire* source code, including the code that we added or modified, under the terms of the original license. This ensures that the *Battleship* game always remains open source, even as developers add and modify its feature set.

The GNU LGPL has one exception to this. We can use any code libraries licensed under the LGPL within our own proprietary code, and we're not obliged to release our *entire* software under the original license. For example, suppose the *Battleship* game contains a set of libraries, licensed under the LGPL, that display the game board and accept input from the user. Under the LGPL, we can incorporate these into our own version of the *Battleship* game (thereby saving time and money), but we would not be required to release our *entire* application under the terms of the LGPL.

The BSD Licence

The BSD license is a lot simpler and much easier to understand. Unlike the GPL, whose main purpose is to ensure that derivative works remain free for everyone, the BSD license encourages people to use and distribute software. More specifically, the BSD license allows us to use, modify, and distribute the source code or binary form of the software without restriction, as long as the original license is included.

System Administration Applications

Now, let's move on to some real applications! In this section, we will look at a number of system administration applications, each of which implements a different set of functionality. Though there are plenty of administration, monitoring, and tracking applications that come with the standard Red Hat Linux distribution, the ones we will discuss are very powerful and a little bit different.

The SysAdmin Application

You may remember that we first mentioned this in Chapter 11. As an example of the power and flexibility of Perl, we've put together a small System Administrator Helper application, which we hope you may find a use for. It's not as complex and functional as the others we'll be introducing in this chapter, but in many ways this can be seen as a strong point – it shows you the bare-bones information about your system that you'll need to refer back to time and time again.

To install the System Administration Helper, simply download the files from the www.wrox.com website, where they form part of the book's code download. There are two .tar.gz files, and a .pl installation script. Once you've got the files on your machine (probably in /usr/local), simply run the installation script and follow the instructions provided.

> You'll be asked to specify a username and password. Make a note of these, as you'll need to supply them every time you log in to the application.

When you load the System Administration Helper in your browser, you should see something like this:

The application presents you with information about your Hardware, Software, Network, and User settings, together with a list of the latest Linux Security vulnerabilities that have been detected, and may apply to your system. Many of these headings contain sub-sections that you can use to further explore and configure your system. Try it and see!

This application uses its own thttpd web server. This is started automatically as part of the install, but for security reasons isn't configured to run all the time (it runs only until your machine is shut down). So, before browsing to the program, you'll need to start the server, by issuing the command /etc/init.d/thttpd start from the command line.

The GNOME Workstation Command Center

You may remember our Perl systems administration applications from the previous chapter. If you imagine that application with a few more features, and converted into a standalone GNOME application that can be run from the desktop, then you have a fairly good idea of the **GNOME Workstation Command Center** (or **GWCC**). Here is a screenshot that illustrates GWCC in action:

You can use GWCC to show network activity and connections, view current processes, monitor disk usage, and invoke network utilities. Because it is a standalone application (and hence does not rely on the existence of a web server running in the background), you can conveniently use this application at any time without having to worry about possible security issues.

If you want to give this application a try, go ahead and download the binary RPM package from SourceForge.net:

http://gwcc.sourceforge.net
http://sourceforge.net/projects/gwcc/

To install the package, you can use the rpm command with the -hvi switches from the command-line, like so:

```
# rpm -hvi gwcc-0.9.8-1.i386.rpm
```

Then you can execute it using the command /usr/bin/gwcc. Its convenience and small memory footprint may convince you to have it running all the time.

Webmin

GWCC and our sysadmin tool are definitely nice and useful applications. But now, we are about to look at the king of them all – **Webmin**. Before we even discuss what Webmin can do, you should take a look at this screenshot:

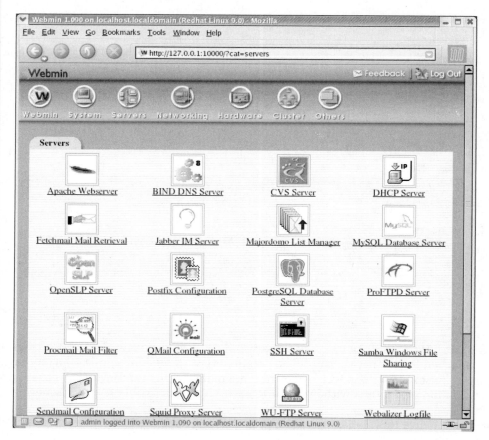

Look at all of those features! Webmin, like our sysadmin application, provides a web interface to a variety of system administration tasks. For example, we can use Webmin to:

❑ Configure the Apache Web server

❑ Manipulate MySQL databases

❑ Modify Sendmail configuration

❑ Install RPM packages

❑ Set DNS client information

❑ Edit user information

❑　　View system and network status

And that's just a small subset of Webmin's capabilities.

You might be surprised to learn that Webmin is also written in Perl! If you are interested in developing Perl applications, then a look through Webmin's source code will provide you with a good learning experience. In addition, Webmin implements its own Web server, rather than using an external one such as Apache or thttpd. This can be a double-edged sword as well. Since the server and the applications are tied together closely, there is better integration and a higher level of security. We do not have to worry about taking the time to learn how to manually install or configure any extra components. Unfortunately, this type of integration can be a security risk as well, albeit a small one. The widely used Web servers, such as Apache, are being used and abused by a large community of users, hackers, and developers on a regular basis, so any bugs or security holes found are typically fixed very quickly. On the other hand, we cannot depend on the same amount of response and support by the smaller number of Webmin developers, and rightly so. Having said that, however, there are no outstanding security issues with Webmin at the time of writing this chapter.

You can download a compressed tar archive or binary RPM package from:

http://www.webmin.com
http://www.webmin.com/download.html

Once you've downloaded it, you can install it in much the same manner as GWCC. Webmin is one application that you should thoroughly use, since it will teach you a lot about your Linux system and how to maintain it properly.

RT: The Request Tracker

Now we will shift gears a bit and cover a different type of administration application. If you are the administrator for a multi-user system, then, no doubt, you will receive all types of requests from your users, such as:

❑　　Can you give me more disk quota?

❑　　I accidentally deleted my presentation. Can I get it back?

❑　　I need to be able to log in from home. Can I?

❑　　Can I install the latest version of Java?

If you get a lot of these requests, then it soon becomes very difficult to keep track of who asked what and when. This is where the **Request Tracker** comes to our rescue. RT is a ticketing system/bug tracker that allows us to manage requests from users by storing them in a central repository, assigning priorities and keeping track of resolutions and dates.

557

If you haven't guessed it already, RT is also written in Perl. You can download the source code and documentation from:

http://www.bestpractical.com/rt/
http://www.fsck.com/rtfm/

To install, follow the instructions specified in the second URL listed above. Unfortunately, the installation process can get a bit laborious, since you need to have a web server and the MySQL database engine installed. (Web server installation is covered in Chapter 9, and MySQL is discussed at the end of this chapter.) However, once you have RT installed and are using it actively, you will wonder how you ever managed as an administrator without it.

Development Applications

If you're interested in developing your own applications, or if you simply enjoyed the material in Chapter 11, then this section is for you. In it, we will look at a number of development tools, including editors and integrated development environments (IDEs), and several programming languages.

jEdit

Before we can start to write code, we need a good and useful editor. The standard Red Hat Linux distribution comes with a whole slew of text editors, including `vi`, `gedit`, and `emacs`. However, you should also take a look at **jEdit**, which touts itself as the "open source programmer's text editor."

jEdit has a number of interesting features, including auto-indenting of code, syntax highlighting for languages, and special plug-ins that extend the core functionality of the editor. These plug-ins implement, among other features, connections to FTP servers to transfer files, access to the external shell, and support for interfacing with project management applications. You can see some of these features in the screenshot below:

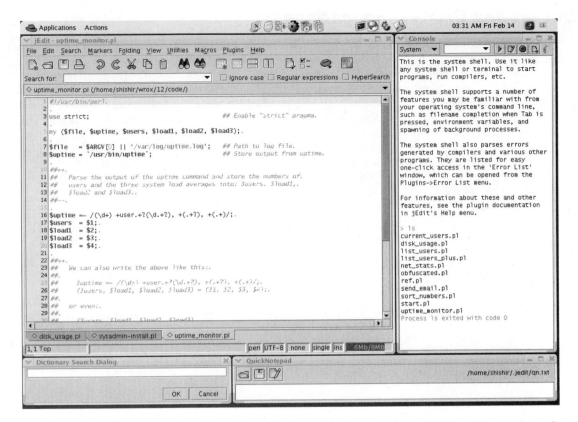

If you're ready to download and try this editor, you can download the binary RPM package from:

http://www.jedit.org
http://www.jedit.org/index.php?page=download

You can use the rpm command to install the application from the command line.

Note that before you can use the editor, you need to make sure that you have the Java language compiler installed on your system. You can do this by downloading the Java 2 Standard Edition (J2SE) Runtime Environment from either Sun Microsystems at http://sun.java.com or from IBM DeveloperWorks at http://www.ibm.com/ developerworks/java; the IBM version is more optimized for Linux.

Then, go ahead and type jedit and you are on your way to developing some cool applications!

Developing C/C++ Applications

We discussed Perl and how to develop applications with it in Chapter 11. The **C** programming language is similar, in both syntax and operation. Like Perl, it has high-level constructs, can produce efficient applications, and be compiled on a large number of hardware platforms. However, C allows the developer to program at a much lower level, interface with hardware easier, and provides greater control and the potential for better performance. There is a reason that other programming languages, such as Perl and Python, as well as the Linux kernel are written in C. Unfortunately, this also makes C a more difficult language to learn.

Most of the software applications that you will see at **Freshmeat.net** and **SourceForge.net** are written in C (or its object-oriented counterpart, C++). Here's a simple program written in C, to allow you to get a taste for it:

```
[ number.c ]

#include <stdio.h>

int main(void)
{
    int number;

    printf ("Enter a number: \n");
    scanf("%d", &number);
    printf("You entered %d, am I correct?\n", number);

    return (0);
}
```

In order for you to compile this program, you need to install various development tools, including the **gcc compiler**, which are covered in detail in the *Building from Source* section in Chapter 10. Once you have installed the necessary tools, you can enter the following commands to compile and run the example program shown above:

```
$ gcc -o number number.c
$ ./number
Enter a number: 79
You entered 79, am I correct?
```

This will create a binary executable called `number`. For example, the `*.exe` files that you see on the Windows platform are examples of binary executables that have been created by a compiled language, such as C or C++. In fact, this is one of the major differences between Perl and C; Perl is an *interpreted* language, so the interpreter has to parse the program code each time it is run. By contrast, C and C++ are *compiled* languages – we compile the code into binary some time before they are needed.

To make C and C++ development easier, you can use one of the various integrated development environment (IDE) applications in existence. These types of tools provide you with a single integrated interface from which to edit, compile, link, and debug your applications – eliminating the need to jump between your editor, your command line, and your debugger. Take a look at the **Anjuta DevStudio** in action:

```
Anjuta: /usr/local/src/apache_1.3.27/src/modules/standard/mod_rewrite.c (Saved)

File   Edit   View   Project   Format   Build   Bookmark   Debug   CVS   Settings   Help

                                                                      Tags:      CHECK_QUOTATION [3989]

mod_rewrite.c  x

182          { "RewriteLogLevel" , cmd_rewriteloglevel, NULL, RSRC_CONF,    TAKE1,
183            "the level of the rewriting logfile verbosity "
184            "(0=none, 1=std. ... 9=max)" },
185          { NULL }
186        };
187
188          /* the table of content handlers we provide */
189     static const handler_rec handler_table[] = {
190          { "redirect-handler", handler_redirect },
191          { NULL }
192        };
193
194          /* the main config structure */
195     module MODULE_VAR_EXPORT rewrite_module = {
196          STANDARD_MODULE_STUFF,
197          init_module,                /* module initializer              */
198          config_perdir_create,       /* create per-dir    config structures */
199          config_perdir_merge,        /* merge  per-dir    config structures */
200          config_server_create,       /* create per-server config structures */
201          config_server_merge,        /* merge  per-server config structures */
202          command_table,              /* table of config file commands   */
203          handler_table,              /* [#8] MIME-typed-dispatched handlers */
204          hook_uri2file,              /* [#1] URI to filename translation   */
205          NULL,                       /* [#4] validate user id from request */
206          NULL,                       /* [#5] check if the user is ok _here_ */


mod_asis.c        mod_cgi.c        mod_include.c     mod_negotiation.c  mod_userdir.c
mod_auth_anon.c   mod_digest.c     mod_info.c        mod_rewrite.c      mod_usertrack.c
mod_auth.c        mod_dir.c        mod_log_agent.c   mod_setenvif.c     mod_vhost_alias.c
mod_auth_db.c     mod_env.c        mod_log_config.c  mod_so.c
[root@localhost standard]#

Build    Debug    Find    CVS    Locals    Terminal    Stdout    Stderr

Project: None    Zoom: 0    Line: 0001    Col: 000    INS    Job: None    Mode: Unix (LF)
```

You can download this IDE in binary RPM package format from:

http://anjuta.org
http://anjuta.sourceforge.net

Then, you can install it using the rpm command. You will need to play with the IDE for a while before you start to feel comfortable with its functionality. And once you are ready to develop serious C or C++ applications, you can find a host of resources and helpful tutorials on the web, including:

http://www.cs.cf.ac.uk/Dave/C/CE.html
http://www.desy.de/gna/html/cc/Tutorial/tutorial.html

Developing Python Applications

What is it with these scripting languages anyway, with names such as Perl and Python? **Python** is an object-oriented interpreted language that shares many similarities with Perl, such as:

❑   High level syntax and constructs

❑   Complex data types, such as arrays and hashes

❑   Powerful regular expression support

❑   Large source code, module and extension repository

❑   Active community of developers

This is one of the reasons why there is a fierce rivalry between Perl and Python users, each claiming that their language is better. You might want to read the following two columns where each author tries to make a case for why one language is superior to the other:

http://www.linuxjournal.com/article.php?sid=3882
http://www.perl.com/pub/a/language/versus/python.html

In reality, these two languages support much the same functionality. The choice of language boils down to which syntax you prefer, some of which you can see in the second article listed above. In fact, the majority of the Red Hat Linux installation scripts and GUI applets are written in Python, so it is likely that the interpreter and most necessary libraries should already be installed on your system.

To find documentation, tutorials and examples of Python scripts and modules, visit the Python home page and the Vaults of Parnassus – the equivalent to Perl's CPAN:

http://www.python.org
http://www.vex.net/parnassus/

Though the development cycle for creating applications using a scripting language is often simpler than for using a compiled language, we can nonetheless still use an IDE to improve our efficiency. The Komodo IDE by ActiveState is one that you can use with both Python and Perl:

You can find Komodo at:

http://www.activestate.com/Products/Komodo/

Komodo is a commercial application that costs $29 for a single user license at the time this chapter was written. Having said that, it is well worth the cost and can save you a lot of valuable time when developing large-scale applications.

What, you want more? We have one more scripting language to look at, though this one is a bit different. Have you ever wanted to develop Web applications? Then, read on.

PHP: Hypertext Preprocessor

The **PHP Hypertext Preprocessor** (or just **PHP**) is a cross-platform scripting language. It was designed primarily for web development, though it can be used for other purposes as well.

To understand how PHP works, it might help to compare it with our Perl sysadmin application. The sysadmin application keeps all of the HTML code in separate templates and uses Perl's `HTML::Template` module to replace specially marked tokens with dynamic values on the fly. This allows us to keep the logic separate from the display semantics.

With PHP, on the other hand, we take the opposite approach. We can embed PHP code within the HTML, and the PHP processor evaluates it dynamically. Here is an example:

```
[ time.phtml ]

<html>
<head>
  <title>Simple Time Example</title>
</head>
<body bgcolor="#FFFFFF">
<?php

$hour   = date("G");
$minute = date("i");
$second = date("s");

echo "<font>$hour:$minute:$second</font>\n";

?>
</body>
</html>
```

As you can see from this example, the PHP code is enclosed within a special `<?php ... ?>` tag; within each page, we can use as many of these tags as we want. Some developers prefer this approach, since they can keep the display and logic in one place, without fear of misplacing or deleting the additional dependent files. It boils down to a matter of personal preference.

Fortunately for us, PHP comes with most of the popular Linux distributions, including Red Hat Linux, so it is just a matter of installing it. You can install PHP from the Package Management applet located at Main Menu | System Tools | Packages. If you click on the Web Server option (which is in the Servers category), and examine its Details, you will see a number of packages selected, including mod_perl, mod_python, mod_ssl, php, php-imap, php-ldap, squid, tux, and webalizer. Since we will not use most of these tools, we will install only the PHP related packages shown below:

Web Server Package Details

A package group can have both standard and extra package members. Standard packages are always available when the package group is installed.

Select the extra packages to be installed:

- ☐ mod_python - An embedded Python interpreter for the Apache Web server.
- ☐ mod_ssl - Cryptography support for the Apache Web server.
- ☑ php - The PHP HTML-embedded scripting language. (PHP: Hypertext Preprocessor
- ☑ php-imap - An Apache module for PHP applications that use IMAP.
- ☑ php-ldap - A module for PHP applications that use LDAP.
- ☑ php-mysql - A module for PHP applications that use MySQL databases.
- ☑ php-odbc - A module for PHP applications that use ODBC databases.
- ☑ php-pgsql - A PostgreSQL database module for PHP.
- ☐ squid - The Squid proxy caching server.
- ☐ tux - User-space component of TUX kernel-based threaded HTTP server.
- ☐ webalizer - A flexible Web server log file analysis program.

Package Information

Full Name: php
Size: 3,984 Kilobytes

✕ Close

Click on the **Close** button to close this dialog, and then on the **Update** button to install the packages; when it's complete, you will have a PHP-enabled Apache Web server. You can refer to Chapter 9, *Building Networks*, for more information on how to configure the Web server.

PHP supports a very large amount of functionality that allows us to build all types of web applications, from dynamically generated graphics to database manipulation. There are many resources out there to help you make the most of PHP's power. For example, you can find extensive documentation on PHP at its web site:

    http://conf.php.net
    http://www.php.net

You could also try *Beginning PHP4*.

We have discussed C, C++, Perl, Python, and PHP, but these represent only a small number of the available programming languages. There are others – like Tcl, Ruby, and Smalltalk – which are also quite popular. You can really pick and choose which one suits your needs, though there are a few things you should be aware of:

❑ If you are intent on learning a language, learn one where you have access to developers who are familiar with the language, so you can avoid some of the common programming pitfalls.

❑ Look at as many examples as possible, and search for any available modules or extensions to cut down on your development effort.

❑ PHP has a smaller learning curve than Perl. For limited Web applications, PHP is preferable, though Perl and Python are more flexible and have a much wider scope.

❑ You should typically not tackle C or C++ if you are new to development; it is better to start with Perl or Python and move up when you are ready.

We had mentioned database manipulation several paragraphs back in the context of PHP Web applications. But what database do we use? Certainly, Oracle and Sybase are not released under any of the open source licenses. But, MySQL is!

MySQL Database Engine

MySQL is probably the most widely used open source database engine. Though it does not support some of the enterprise database features found in Oracle or Sybase, like online (hot) backups, sophisticated transactions, and an internal procedural language, it has more than enough functionality and power to suit most applications. And best of all, it is released under the GPL license, which means we can use it free of charge for both commercial and non-commercial applications.

You can find the MySQL installers, as well as documentation and information on support plans, at:

http://www.mysql.com

However, MySQL also comes with the Red Hat Linux 9 distribution. To install it, launch the Package Management applet and click on the SQL Database Server option (which you'll find in the Servers category). Click on the Details tab and select the mysql-server option, as shown below, to install the application:

SQL Database Server Package Details

A package group can have both standard and extra package members. Standard packages are always available when the package group is installed.

Select the extra packages to be installed:

▽ **Standard Packages**

    perl-DBD-Pg - A PostgresSQL interface for Perl.

    perl-DB_File - DB_File module for Perl

    postgresql-server - The programs needed to create and run a PostgreSQL server.

    unixODBC - A complete ODBC driver manager for Linux.

▽ **Extra Packages**

    ☑ mysql-server - The MySQL server and related files.

Package Information

    Full Name: mysql-server
    Size: 2,716 Kilobytes

✗ <u>C</u>lose

Once you have installed MySQL, you can enter the following commands as the root user to start the server and view a list of the database users stored in the internal user table:

```
# /etc/init.d/mysqld start
# mysql mysql
mysql> select * from user;
...
mysql> \q
```

The select... query that you see above is an example of Structured Query Language, or SQL. Most of the commercial relational database systems, including Oracle, Sybase, Informix, as well as open source alternatives, MySQL and PostgreSql, allow us to use SQL to manipulate the database. You can find more information on learning SQL at:

    http://sqlzoo.net/
    http://www.w3schools.com/sql/sql_intro.asp

Alternatively, you can grab a copy of *Beginning SQL Programming* or *Beginning Databases with MySQL*.

567

If you want to avoid learning SQL, you can use one of the many database administration GUI tools that exist – such as **Aqua Data Studio**, available from:

http://www.aquafold.com

Here is a screenshot that illustrates the convenience of this application:

Finally, you should note that installing the SQL Database Server from the Package Management applet also installs the PostgreSql database server. While this database engine is not used as widely as MySQL, it is designed for the enterprise and supports many features that are found in Oracle and Sybase, but are lacking in MySQL. Feel free to investigate and learn more about this application.

Summary

We hope you enjoyed the brief tour of some of the more intriguing and useful open source applications and utilities. However, we have covered only the tip of the iceberg; there is a vast amount of software out there that you can use to your advantage. Most of this software is not only free from a financial standpoint, but comes packaged with the entire source code. We can modify this source code to fix bugs, optimize functionality, and add new features. Moreover, even if we are not in a position to make these types of changes, we will at least have some peace of mind knowing that it is possible.

Installing and configuring your Linux system is just the beginning. You should take some time to explore all of the resources presented in this chapter. Surf on over to **www.osdn.com**, search for your favorite applications, download and test them out. Eventually, you will get to a certain point where you want to implement your own open source software or modify one that exists to suit your needs. Then, you can decide on what programming language to use and how to develop an application. The bottom line is that you will be able to make your operating system run the way you want it to, instead of the other way around.

GNU General Public License

Version 2, June 1991

Copyright © 1989, 1991 Free Software Foundation, Inc.

59 Temple Place, Suite 330, Boston, MA 02111-1307, USA

Everyone is permitted to copy and distribute verbatim copies of this license document, but changing it is not allowed.

Preamble

The licenses for most software are designed to take away your freedom to share and change it. By contrast, the GNU General Public License is intended to guarantee your freedom to share and change free software — to make sure the software is free for all its users. This General Public License applies to most of the Free Software Foundation's software and to any other program whose authors commit to using it. (Some other Free Software Foundation software is covered by the GNU Library General Public License instead.) You can apply it to your programs, too.

When we speak of free software, we are referring to freedom, not price. Our General Public Licenses are designed to make sure that you have the freedom to distribute copies of free software (and charge for this service if you wish), that you receive source code or can get it if you want it, that you can change the software or use pieces of it in new free programs; and that you know you can do these things.

To protect your rights, we need to make restrictions that forbid anyone to deny you these rights or to ask you to surrender the rights. These restrictions translate to certain responsibilities for you if you distribute copies of the software, or if you modify it.

For example, if you distribute copies of such a program, whether gratis or for a fee, you must give the recipients all the rights that you have. You must make sure that they, too, receive or can get the source code. And you must show them these terms so they know their rights.

We protect your rights with two steps: (1) copyright the software, and (2) offer you this license which gives you legal permission to copy, distribute and/or modify the software.

Also, for each author's protection and ours, we want to make certain that everyone understands that there is no warranty for this free software. If the software is modified by someone else and passed on, we want its recipients to know that what they have is not the original, so that any problems introduced by others will not reflect on the original authors' reputations.

Finally, any free program is threatened constantly by software patents. We wish to avoid the danger that redistributors of a free program will individually obtain patent licenses, in effect making the program proprietary. To prevent this, we have made it clear that any patent must be licensed for everyone's free use or not licensed at all.

The precise terms and conditions for copying, distribution and modification follow.

Terms and Conditions for Copying, Distribution, and Modification

0. This License applies to any program or other work which contains a notice placed by the copyright holder saying it may be distributed under the terms of this General Public License. The "Program", below, refers to any such program or work, and a "work based on the Program" means either the Program or any derivative work under copyright law: that is to say, a work containing the Program or a portion of it, either verbatim or with modifications and/or translated into another language. (Hereinafter, translation is included without limitation in the term "modification".) Each licensee is addressed as "you".

    Activities other than copying, distribution and modification are not covered by this License; they are outside its scope. The act of running the Program is not restricted, and the output from the Program is covered only if its contents constitute a work based on the Program (independent of having been made by running the Program). Whether that is true depends on what the Program does.

1. You may copy and distribute verbatim copies of the Program's source code as you receive it, in any medium, provided that you conspicuously and appropriately publish on each copy an appropriate copyright notice and disclaimer of warranty; keep intact all the notices that refer to this License and to the absence of any warranty; and give any other recipients of the Program a copy of this License along with the Program.

    You may charge a fee for the physical act of transferring a copy, and you may at your option offer warranty protection in exchange for a fee.

2. You may modify your copy or copies of the Program or any portion of it, thus forming a work based on the Program, and copy and distribute such modifications or work under the terms of Section 1 above, provided that you also meet all of these conditions:

    a) You must cause the modified files to carry prominent notices stating that you changed the files and the date of any change.

    b) You must cause any work that you distribute or publish, that in whole or in part contains or is derived from the Program or any part thereof, to be licensed as a whole at no charge to all third parties under the terms of this License.

    c) If the modified program normally reads commands interactively when run, you must cause it, when started running for such interactive use in the most ordinary way, to print or display an announcement including an appropriate copyright notice and a notice that there is no warranty (or else, saying that you provide a warranty) and that users may redistribute the program under these conditions, and telling the user how to view a copy of this License. (Exception: if the Program itself is interactive but does not normally print such an announcement, your work based on the Program is not required to print an announcement.)

    These requirements apply to the modified work as a whole. If identifiable sections of that work are not derived from the Program, and can be reasonably considered independent and separate works in themselves, then this License, and its terms, do not apply to those sections when you distribute them as separate works. But when you distribute the same sections as part of a whole which is a work based on the Program, the distribution of the whole must be on the terms of this License, whose permissions for other licensees extend to the entire whole, and thus to each and every part regardless of who wrote it.

Thus, it is not the intent of this section to claim rights or contest your rights to work written entirely by you; rather, the intent is to exercise the right to control the distribution of derivative or collective works based on the Program.

In addition, mere aggregation of another work not based on the Program with the Program (or with a work based on the Program) on a volume of a storage or distribution medium does not bring the other work under the scope of this License.

3. You may copy and distribute the Program (or a work based on it, under Section 2) in object code or executable form under the terms of Sections 1 and 2 above provided that you also do one of the following:

a) Accompany it with the complete corresponding machine-readable source code, which must be distributed under the terms of Sections 1 and 2 above on a medium customarily used for software interchange; or,

b) Accompany it with a written offer, valid for at least three years, to give any third party, for a charge no more than your cost of physically performing source distribution, a complete machine-readable copy of the corresponding source code, to be distributed under the terms of Sections 1 and 2 above on a medium customarily used for software interchange; or,

c) Accompany it with the information you received as to the offer to distribute corresponding source code. (This alternative is allowed only for noncommercial distribution and only if you received the program in object code or executable form with such an offer, in accord with Subsection b above.)

The source code for a work means the preferred form of the work for making modifications to it. For an executable work, complete source code means all the source code for all modules it contains, plus any associated interface definition files, plus the scripts used to control compilation and installation of the executable. However, as a special exception, the source code distributed need not include anything that is normally distributed (in either source or binary form) with the major components (compiler, kernel, and so on) of the operating system on which the executable runs, unless that component itself accompanies the executable.

If distribution of executable or object code is made by offering access to copy from a designated place, then offering equivalent access to copy the source code from the same place counts as distribution of the source code, even though third parties are not compelled to copy the source along with the object code.

4. You may not copy, modify, sublicense, or distribute the Program except as expressly provided under this License. Any attempt otherwise to copy, modify, sublicense or distribute the Program is void, and will automatically terminate your rights under this License. However, parties who have received copies, or rights, from you under this License will not have their licenses terminated so long as such parties remain in full compliance.

5. You are not required to accept this License, since you have not signed it. However, nothing else grants you permission to modify or distribute the Program or its derivative works. These

actions are prohibited by law if you do not accept this License. Therefore, by modifying or distributing the Program (or any work based on the Program), you indicate your acceptance of this License to do so, and all its terms and conditions for copying, distributing or modifying the Program or works based on it.

6. Each time you redistribute the Program (or any work based on the Program), the recipient automatically receives a license from the original licensor to copy, distribute or modify the Program subject to these terms and conditions. You may not impose any further restrictions on the recipients' exercise of the rights granted herein. You are not responsible for enforcing compliance by third parties to this License.

7. If, as a consequence of a court judgment or allegation of patent infringement or for any other reason (not limited to patent issues), conditions are imposed on you (whether by court order, agreement or otherwise) that contradict the conditions of this License, they do not excuse you from the conditions of this License. If you cannot distribute so as to satisfy simultaneously your obligations under this License and any other pertinent obligations, then as a consequence you may not distribute the Program at all. For example, if a patent license would not permit royalty-free redistribution of the Program by all those who receive copies directly or indirectly through you, then the only way you could satisfy both it and this License would be to refrain entirely from distribution of the Program.

If any portion of this section is held invalid or unenforceable under any particular circumstance, the balance of the section is intended to apply and the section as a whole is intended to apply in other circumstances.

It is not the purpose of this section to induce you to infringe any patents or other property right claims or to contest validity of any such claims; this section has the sole purpose of protecting the integrity of the free software distribution system, which is implemented by public license practices. Many people have made generous contributions to the wide range of software distributed through that system in reliance on consistent application of that system; it is up to the author/donor to decide if he or she is willing to distribute software through any other system and a licensee cannot impose that choice.

This section is intended to make thoroughly clear what is believed to be a consequence of the rest of this License.

8. If the distribution and/or use of the Program is restricted in certain countries either by patents or by copyrighted interfaces, the original copyright holder who places the Program under this License may add an explicit geographical distribution limitation excluding those countries, so that distribution is permitted only in or among countries not thus excluded. In such case, this License incorporates the limitation as if written in the body of this License.

9. The Free Software Foundation may publish revised and/or new versions of the General Public License from time to time. Such new versions will be similar in spirit to the present version, but may differ in detail to address new problems or concerns.

Each version is given a distinguishing version number. If the Program specifies a version number of this License which applies to it and "any later version", you have the option of following the terms and conditions either of that version or of any later version published by the Free Software Foundation. If the Program does not specify a version number of this License, you may choose any version ever published by the Free Software Foundation.

10. If you wish to incorporate parts of the Program into other free programs whose distribution conditions are different, write to the author to ask for permission. For software which is copyrighted by the Free Software Foundation, write to the Free Software Foundation; we sometimes make exceptions for this. Our decision will be guided by the two goals of preserving the free status of all derivatives of our free software and of promoting the sharing and reuse of software generally.

No Warranty

11. BECAUSE THE PROGRAM IS LICENSED FREE OF CHARGE, THERE IS NO WARRANTY FOR THE PROGRAM, TO THE EXTENT PERMITTED BY APPLICABLE LAW. EXCEPT WHEN OTHERWISE STATED IN WRITING THE COPYRIGHT HOLDERS AND/OR OTHER PARTIES PROVIDE THE PROGRAM "AS IS" WITHOUT WARRANTY OF ANY KIND, EITHER EXPRESSED OR IMPLIED, INCLUDING, BUT NOT LIMITED TO, THE IMPLIED WARRANTIES OF MERCHANTABILITY AND FITNESS FOR A PARTICULAR PURPOSE. THE ENTIRE RISK AS TO THE QUALITY AND PERFORMANCE OF THE PROGRAM IS WITH YOU. SHOULD THE PROGRAM PROVE DEFECTIVE, YOU ASSUME THE COST OF ALL NECESSARY SERVICING, REPAIR OR CORRECTION.

12. IN NO EVENT UNLESS REQUIRED BY APPLICABLE LAW OR AGREED TO IN WRITING WILL ANY COPYRIGHT HOLDER, OR ANY OTHER PARTY WHO MAY MODIFY AND/OR REDISTRIBUTE THE PROGRAM AS PERMITTED ABOVE, BE LIABLE TO YOU FOR DAMAGES, INCLUDING ANY GENERAL, SPECIAL, INCIDENTAL OR CONSEQUENTIAL DAMAGES ARISING OUT OF THE USE OR INABILITY TO USE THE PROGRAM (INCLUDING BUT NOT LIMITED TO LOSS OF DATA OR DATA BEING RENDERED INACCURATE OR LOSSES SUSTAINED BY YOU OR THIRD PARTIES OR A FAILURE OF THE PROGRAM TO OPERATE WITH ANY OTHER PROGRAMS), EVEN IF SUCH HOLDER OR OTHER PARTY HAS BEEN ADVISED OF THE POSSIBILITY OF SUCH DAMAGES.

End Of Terms And Conditions

This book includes a copy of the Publisher's Edition of Red Hat Linux from Red Hat, Inc., which you may use in accordance with the license agreements accompanying the software. The Official Red Hat Linux, which you may purchase from Red Hat, includes the complete Official Red Hat Linux distribution, Red Hat's documentation, and may include technical support for Official Red Hat Linux. You may also purchase technical support from Red Hat. You may purchase Official Red Hat Linux and technical support from Red Hat through the company's web site (www.redhat.com) or its toll-free number, 1.888.REDHAT1.